THE INFINITE RESOURCE

University Press of New England | Hanover and London

the infinite resource

the power of ideas on a finite planet

RAMEZ NAAM

University Press of New England
www.upne.com
© 2013 Ramez Naam
All rights reserved
Manufactured in the United States of America
Designed by Mindy Basinger Hill
Typeset in Minion Pro

University Press of New England is a member
of the Green Press Initiative. The paper used in
this book meets their minimum requirement
for recycled paper.

For permission to reproduce any of the material
in this book, contact Permissions, University Press
of New England, One Court Street, Suite 250,
Lebanon NH 03766; or visit www.upne.com

Library of Congress Cataloging-in-Publication Data

Naam, Ramez.
The infinite resource : the power of ideas on
a finite planet / Ramez Naam.
        p.   cm.
Includes bibliographical references and index.
ISBN 978–1–61168–255–7 (cloth : alk. paper) —
ISBN 978–1–61168–376–9 (ebook)
1. Renewable natural resources.
2. Natural resources. 3. Sustainable development.
4. Conservation of natural resources. I. Title.
HC85. N32 2013
333.7—dc23   2012026803

5   4   3

contents

preface a tale of two planets

"It was the best of times, it was the worst of times." The opening line of Charles Dickens's 1859 masterpiece, *A Tale of Two Cities* applies equally well to our present era. We live in unprecedented wealth and comfort, with capabilities undreamt of in previous ages. We live in a world facing unprecedented global risks—risks to our continued prosperity, to our survival, and to the health of our planet itself. We might think of our current situation as *A Tale of Two Earths*.

This is a story about these two conflicting realities of our present day. The core argument of this book is that the force that's propelled us to our present well-being is also the most powerful resource we have to tackle our future challenges: innovation. If we tap into and direct that force correctly, we have the very real potential to lift global wealth and well-being while reducing our impact on the planet and even reversing the damage we've done. If we fail to tap into that force, we flirt with the very real prospect of disaster.

Exceptional claims demand exceptional evidence. I'm claiming in this book that it's possible for humanity to live in higher numbers than today, in far greater wealth, comfort, and prosperity, with far *less* destructive impact on the planet than we have today. I'm claiming that raw energy, materials, and the other resources we need to survive are plentiful on Earth and limited primarily by our understanding of how to collect, harness, and efficiently use them. I'm claiming that in the midst of this abundance of matter and energy the most valuable resource we have and that we have ever had is the sum of our human knowledge—our comprehension of how the universe around us functions and how to manipulate it to our ends. I'm claiming that if we act quickly enough and decisively enough, we can have our cake and eat it too—a healthy thriving planet, and a human civilization of ever-growing wealth. These propositions are at odds with the prevailing wisdom that energy or land or oil or fresh water are our most precious resources, that their finite nature and growing scarcity place fairly imminent caps on the size, wealth, and sophistication of human society, and that living sustainably on this planet necessarily means living more modestly and accepting slower or even halted economic growth.

To back those claims up, I'll show how new ideas have overcome physical resource limitations again and again in the past. I'll show how our progress in science and technology have the potential to leapfrog us past our current challenges of energy, climate, water, food, minerals, and other resources. And I'll show how high the true limits on this planet are.

Just because something is possible doesn't mean that it will come to be. While it's possible for us to grow our numbers and our wealth while preserving and repairing our planet, there's no guarantee that we'll do so. The problems we face are very real. In the face of similar challenges, some societies in the past have crumbled. Others have prevailed. I'll show in this book that what separates the cultures that have thrived from those that have stagnated or declined is the choices they made. Those choices guided different cultures' rates of innovation, guided their usage of resources around them, and ultimately determined their fates. If we want to overcome the looming challenges that face us, we need to make the right choices ourselves. We need to innovate not only in science and technology, but also in the economic system that governs resource usage and motivates innovation. I'll show what those needed changes are and how to make them in ways that enrich us and enrich our planet.

We stand poised between an unimaginably better world and an unimaginably worse one. Which world the future holds is largely up to us.

In that spirit, I'll close this preface with a few more words from Dickens that I think aptly capture our current situation.

> It was the best of times, it was the worst of times,
> it was the age of wisdom, it was the age of foolishness,
> it was the epoch of belief, it was the epoch of incredulity,
> it was the season of Light, it was the season of Darkness,
> it was the spring of hope, it was the winter of despair,
> we had everything before us, we had nothing before us,
> we were all going direct to heaven, we were all going direct the other way
> —in short, the period was so far like the present period, that some of its
> noisiest authorities insisted on its being received, for good or for evil, in the
> superlative degree of comparison only.

R.N.

part one
the best of times

one the rise of innovation

In the fall of 2008, three friends and I traveled with our bicycles to Vietnam. We planned to bike down a few hundred miles of the country's scenic coast. We'd heard that Vietnam was a beautiful place, remarkably friendly to Americans, considering the history between the two countries. The image in our minds was of rice paddies, dirt roads, and of local Vietnamese riding bicycles to get from one place to another. The vacation was lovely, but things weren't quite as we expected. The coastal road wasn't dirt any more—it was a modern highway, flush with traffic of all sorts, and entirely paved except for one short stretch under construction. And while we thoroughly enjoyed bicycling in Vietnam, we didn't see many others doing the same. In fact, the only other people on bicycles we encountered were young school children, who consistently said "hello!" and practiced their English on us, and a lone Japanese tourist riding his bike in the other direction. The roads were full of Vietnamese on scooters and in cars and trucks. Everywhere we went, from the biggest cities to the smallest towns, the streets were full of people with cell phones. Every town had its share of buildings under construction. Our vision of Vietnam as a quaint place full of poor farmers was out of date. The world had moved on. The Vietnamese were growing richer.

I was born in Egypt, in 1973. In 1976, in one of the most important events of my life, I came with my parents to the United States. The trip was originally intended to last just a few years, long enough for my mother to complete her studies for a PhD in physiology, and then we would return to Egypt, where she was to teach. Instead, my parents recognized the obvious—that the United States was a far superior place to live, work, and raise a child—and they embarked on a ten-year process of seeking permanent immigration to the United States. Ultimately they succeeded. We would stay here. I would become a U.S. citizen rather than returning to live in Egypt.

Growing up an immigrant made me acutely aware of just how lucky I was to live in the United States. Life in Egypt was clearly harder. I learned from my parents that people there lived in small, cramped apartments. Cars and televisions were luxury items, afforded by the few. Freedom of speech and political participation were nonexistent. Polio still paralyzed thousands of children each year. Five of my mother's siblings died in infancy from preventable diseases. Three of my father's siblings died the same way. It's telling that infant deaths were so common that my dad wasn't even the first child of his parents to bear his name. He was named after the boy before him, who was born and died before my father was conceived.

Over the years, I came to realize that what I was getting wasn't just a look at another country, but a look back in time. Polio was common in Egypt in the 1970s, but that wasn't far different from what it had been in the United States just two decades earlier. In 1952, nearly 60,000 cases of polio were recorded in the United States, with 3,000 deaths.[1] Infant mortality in Egypt was 14.7 percent in the year I was born. I had better than a one-in-seven chance of dying in my first few years. I was lucky not only in coming to the United States, but also in living long enough to do so. Yet had I been born in the United States in the early decades of the twentieth century, my chances of infant death would have been just as great as they were in the Egypt of 1973. Indeed, the CDC reports that in some U.S. cities in 1900, infant mortality was 30 percent. Nearly one in three children would die in infancy.[2] Today polio is gone from the United States, gone from Egypt, and on its last legs around the world. Infant mortality is around 0.7 percent in the United States, and 2 percent in Egypt. It's fallen by a factor of 7 in Egypt since I was born, and by a factor of 40 in the United States since the beginning of the twentieth century. The change is stunning.

Looking at the progress we've made, in the United States, in Egypt, in Vietnam, and across the world as a whole, it's difficult not to be impressed. We live in a period of health, wealth, and freedom never seen before.

The Great Divergence

The source of all this improvement in our lives has been the continual accumulation of new ideas, new inventions, and new knowledge about the world. We've learned to grow more food, reducing malnourishment. We've learned the value of sanitation and how to cure diseases through modern medicine. We've learned to harness energy to build buildings and move people and supplies from one place to another. We've learned to harness electricity to light and power our homes and offices, and to use the electromagnetic spectrum to communicate our thoughts, words, images, and information of all sorts from one corner of the globe to another. And along the way, radical new ideas have established the rights of the governed to choose who governs them, have reduced our propensity for warfare, and have lifted the well-being and freedom of women and minorities of all sorts.

For most of history, innovation has kept pace with population. New technologies made it possible to support more people, but didn't raise the wealth of the average person. Royalty and a few rich aristocrats and merchants saw their well-being rise, but for most of humanity, things were little better than they had been for tens of thousands of years.

The Renaissance that swept through Europe from the fourteenth through seventeenth centuries changed all that. The world went through the most spectacular explosion of innovation it had ever seen. The inventions, discoveries, and political and philosophical writings of that era gave birth to the Scientific Revolution, the Industrial Revolution, and the Enlightenment. The use of electricity, the germ theory of disease, the discovery of the laws of chemistry and physics, the development of the steam engine, and thousands of other innovations that touch our lives every day all owe their existence to discoveries and thinking from this period. The Renaissance began a long and continuous surge of wealth unlike any seen before, and extending up until this day.

But why did it happen in Europe? What conditions led to rapid innovation there, and not in the rest of the world?

If you'd toured the planet in the early thirteenth century, China might have seemed the civilization most likely to drive technological progress for the next several hundred years. Late Song Dynasty China was a wealthy, sophisticated place. The Chinese had invented paper, wood block printing, and gunpowder. They were the first to use paper currency. They were hundreds of years ahead of Europeans in the working of iron. China had a population of more than 100 million, compared to Europe's 50 or 60 million.[3] The two largest cities in China, Kaifeng and Hangzhou, were both teeming metropolises with populations in excess of a million people.[4] They were cities the likes of which had not been seen in Europe since the fall of Rome. The Chinese empire as a whole was administered by 20,000 scholar-officials who served beneath the emperor, selected from a pool of as many as 400,000 educated applicants who completed a multiday written exam to vie for roles in the administration of the country.[5]

Meanwhile, the Europe of this time was a collection of thirty or more small warring kingdoms, ruled by hereditary rulers and warlords. The bulk of the European economy, such as it was, rested on the backs of serf farmers tied to manorial lands. While coin existed, most transactions were built on barter. Europe's largest city, Paris, at 200,000 people was smaller than a single suburb of Kaifeng.

Yet from that point onward, Europe steadily gained, while China fell behind. Chinese economic development and technological innovation continued, but at a pace little different from the previous thousand years. In Europe, by contrast, the rate of progress dramatically increased, going ever faster each passing century. When the two cultures would clash during the Opium Wars of the 1800s, the much more numerous Chinese forces fighting on their home soil would find themselves routinely routed by smaller but better-armed European forces fielding fearsome steamships that could sail against the wind and tides, and advanced muskets that could shoot farther and faster than those the defenders used. The Chinese, who used coal to forge steel centuries before the Europeans, who'd invented gunpowder itself, who'd been the technological superiors of Europeans for nearly a thousand years, found themselves on the losing side of a technological battle.

How did this come to be? The answer lies in the relative rates of technological innovation in the two cultures. European culture, unwittingly, accelerated the evolution of ideas. Chinese culture suppressed it. We can, it turns out, make choices about the structure of our societies that affect the pace of innovation. And the choices that Europe and China made from the thirteenth century onward did just that.

Darwin among the Memes

To understand why Europe prospered while China fell behind, we need to view innovation through the lens of one of the greatest thinkers of the last thousand years—Charles Darwin.

Darwin didn't invent the notion that species evolve. While it was anathema to the church, the idea had already taken hold by the time Darwin voyaged around the world on the *HMS Beagle*, taking notes on the ecologies of places he visited that would eventually lead him to write *On the Origin of Species*. What Darwin brought to the table was not the idea of evolution per se, but a specific idea of how evolution works.

Plants and animals reproduce, Darwin noted. When they reproduce, their offspring carry forward traits of the parents. Parents that have traits that assist in their survival and reproduction—that help the parents live longer and have more children—tend to pass those traits on to their offspring. And because their offspring are more numerous than those of creatures with less beneficial traits, the beneficial traits tend to spread. Plants and animals are in constant competition with one another. Those that are most successful see their traits flourish. Darwin talked of these phenomena in terms of reproduction, inheritance, and natural selection.

Yet most offspring aren't carbon copies of their parents. They inherit a unique mix of the traits of each parent. What's more, new traits can also arise through random mutation. This generation of new variety, through both sex and mutation, creates more candidates for natural selection to work on. The most helpful of these new traits—the ones that most increase the odds of a plant or animal surviving and reproducing—tend to become the most common. Variety is fed into natural selection.

Yet the mechanism that Darwin observed isn't limited to biological creatures. Evolution through natural selection should work on any sort of entity that can reproduce, that passes on traits to its offspring, that can generate new variety, and in which natural selection and competition between different entities exists.

In 1976, Richard Dawkins, in his classic *The Selfish Gene*, proposed the notion of memes. A meme is any bit of information that can spread from one human mind to another. Memes, Dawkins pointed out, share many of the traits of genes. They can reproduce by copying themselves from one mind to another. As you read this book, memes that have entered my brain are being copied into your brain. They undergo a form of natural selection, with some memes dying out and some flourishing. If I tell you a thoroughly entertaining story, for example, or use a brilliant analogy to describe something, it will stick longer in your memory than if I give you some dry recitation of facts. If it's interesting enough, you may even pass it on to someone else. (Please do!)

And memes, like genes, can be mutated or combine with others to produce new variety. Science writer Matt Ridley talks about the combination of ideas into new forms as "idea sex." Just as sex in biological organisms has (along with mutation) led to the generation of all sorts of new traits and trait combinations, some of which have been selected by natural selection, so the intersection of ideas with other ideas has led to new variety.

This, then, is the core of a Darwinian evolutionary view of innovation. Ideas are copied from person to person and place to place. New variety is generated when humans accidentally mutate ideas, when they intentionally experiment with changes to those ideas, and when ideas meet ideas and give birth to new generations through idea sex. And then, ultimately, natural selection comes into play, weeding out ideas that are utterly forgettable, and selecting for those ideas that lodge in the mind and that tend to spread from person to person.

Ideas stick and spread for all sorts of reasons. A catchy bit of song may lodge in the mind for no apparent reason. A folk tale or a comforting lie may take hold and spread more easily than a useful but complex scientific truth.

Yet not all drivers of the retention and spread of new ideas are mysterious or counterproductive. One of the most reliable factors of evolutionary fitness of ideas throughout history has been the raw value that an idea offered to those who adopted it. The wheel spread from Sumer to Egypt and then to the rest of the world not because of any top-down plan, not because it was fashionable or catchy, but because it offered an advantage to anyone who used it. It spread because of the practical self-interest of people everywhere, who saw that they'd benefit from using it. The same is true of the plow, of three-field crop rotation, of eyeglasses, of antibiotics, and of tens of thousands of inventions and ideas throughout history. Practical self-interest isn't the *only* evolutionary fitness factor for ideas—far from it—but it's a consistent one.

We can see the effects of more minds, more connections, and natural selection based on self-interest throughout history. When humans went from hunting and gathering to farming the land around 10,000 years ago, populations increased, as did population densities. That increased the number of minds. It also increased the connectivity of minds, as agricultural villages tended to be larger, denser, more closely spaced to one another, and more likely to trade with one another than hunter-gatherer tribes. Now more people could create or improve on ideas. And ideas could more easily spread from mind to mind until they encountered someone who would further improve upon them, or encountered another idea with which to mate.

The result was a dramatic acceleration of innovation. It took 90,000 years from the dawn of humanity to the invention of agriculture. From there it was less than 5,000 years until the vastly increased brainpower of humanity produced the inventions of the wheel and sail, and not much farther to the inventions of writing, arithmetic, bronze, steel, watermills, wind mills, saddles, and far more. Each of those innovations stuck in human culture and then spread from place to place because they offered real value. And when they ceased offering value they died out. Cultures that encountered iron working quickly adopted it and abandoned the construction of inferior bronze tools. Cultures that encountered the Egyptian spoked wheel (lighter and thus faster) quickly abandoned the old solid-disk wheel of the Sumerians. Natural selection guided the explosion of new-idea diversity. Boosting our brainpower and the connectivity between our brains supercharged the Darwinian evolution of ideas.

Thousands of years later, the difference in rates of Darwinian innovation would determine the outcome of another natural experiment—the relative rates of progress in Europe, Asia, and the Islamic world across the thirteenth to nineteenth centuries.

The Connector

The invention most symbolic of the Renaissance, Johannes Gutenberg's moveable type printing press, captured no additional energy, grew no additional crops, and cured no diseases. But it did something more important—it accelerated the spread of ideas. It intensified the web of connections between minds. In so doing, it amped up the Darwinian process of idea evolution, accelerated the process of innovation, and thus, indirectly, it increased our access to energy, increased our ability to grow food, and accelerated the development of medicine, science, and all the other domains of human knowledge that have enhanced our lives.

The printing press boosted the power of ideas to copy themselves. Prior to low-cost printing, ideas could and did spread by word of mouth. While this was tremendously powerful, it limited the complexity of the ideas that could be propagated to those that a single person could remember. It also added a certain amount of guaranteed error. The spread of ideas by word of mouth was equivalent to a game of telephone on a global scale. The advent of literacy and the creation of handwritten scrolls and, eventually, handwritten books strengthened the ability of large and complex ideas to spread with high fidelity. But the incredible amount of time required to copy a scroll or book by hand limited the speed with which information could spread this way. A well-trained monk could transcribe around four pages of text per day.

A printing press could copy information thousands of times faster, allowing knowledge to spread far more quickly, with full fidelity, than ever before.[6]

Gutenberg's printing press itself is an example of the intersection of and recombination of ideas—Ridley's "idea sex." Woodblock printing, first developed in China, had been imported into Europe to print patterns onto fabric. Woodblock printing had been tried for text, but was painfully labor intensive. Every page required its own block of wood, which would be hand carved with all the words to be printed. The wood blocks, being softer than metal, wore out quickly. Rag paper was invented by the Chinese sometime around the seventh century. In the eighth century, a large Arab army from the Abbasid Caliphate (the major Islamic empire of the time) defeated a major Chinese force in the battle of Talas, in modern-day Kyrgyzstan. The battle gave the Arabs a foothold in central Asia. Perhaps more importantly, the prisoners the Arabs took included several Chinese craftsmen skilled in the creation of rag paper. From the battleground in Talas, the creation of rag paper spread south and west into the middle east, then west across North Africa, north into Moorish Spain, and finally into Europe in the 1200s. Meanwhile, Italian painters of the very early Renaissance had developed oil-based paints for use in creating canvases.

Gutenberg combined these ideas and brought his own knowledge base as a goldsmith to bear. Why not make printing blocks out of something more durable than wood, he wondered? And, since every page was really just a different combination of the same letters, why recarve (or remold) the printing block each time? If the unit of printing could be an individual *letter* rather than a page, then those letters could be recombined in a nearly infinite number of ways to make new pages, without the hugely labor-intensive process of casting new blocks. Voila.

The printing press, itself a product of idea sex and Darwinian evolution of ideas, was so obviously useful that it spread rapidly through Europe. And the press, itself, would accelerate the ability of all ideas to spread, meet, and recombine into new forms. Humanity had invented a turbocharger for innovation.

The Catalysts

While the printing press accelerated the rate at which ideas could spread, meet, and recombine, Europeans also produced two cultural innovations—two new *institutions*—that would further fuel innovation.

The first of these was the beginning of market economics, which would reward the producers of new ideas, thus encouraging more ideas to be created. The other was the invention of the scientific method, which would more rigorously test ideas to determine which were true and which were not.

The wave of market-based economics that eventually conquered the world started in the aftermath of disaster. In England, the Great Famine of 1315 and the Black Death of the mid-1300s had decimated the population, leading to social upheaval. Prior to this point, agriculture had been dominated by the manorial system. Manor lords held land. Serfs were bound to that land, cultivating small plots for themselves, communal land for the population of the village, and the manor lord's own land for the lord's benefit. They owed their lord crops and labor, and in return, they received protection from bandits and other lords, some food, and little else. The fourteenth century turned this system on its ear. With fewer people to work the fields, the use of technology became ever more important. Serfs, in greater demand due to their shortage, began to bargain for and demand better terms. Lords and royalty responded by passing the Statute of Laborers, which placed a *maximum* on the wages of serfs and further limited their mobility.

In 1381, English serfs rose up in revolt. Fifty thousand of them marched on London, destroyed the Savoy Palace of the king's uncle, stormed the Tower of London, and beheaded the lord treasurer and the lord chancellor. While the revolt was put down soon after, it marked a sea change in the relationship between lords and commoners. Commoners would no longer be serfs, bound to the land. They would have the rights to negotiate their wages, to buy or rent land, and to settle where they chose. By the end of the century, serfs had become tenant-farmers, leasing or buying their land with currency rather than labor, and selling the food they grew at market for a profit. Where manorial serfs saw little incentive to growing more food, as most of it went to the manorial lord, this new breed of tenant-farmer could earn money in direct proportion to the amount and quality of food they brought to market. For the first time, working hard and innovating served the interests of most European farmers directly. And as a result, agricultural output soared, as did the output of other farm goods like wool.

The rising agricultural output, meanwhile, freed more people from working the land. With fewer people tied up in agriculture, the fraction of Europe that could work in crafts, in industry, and in producing new innovations rose.

More human brainpower became available for the task of creating new and useful ideas.

The brilliance of the market is that it rewards workers for producing things that others value. That was soon extended to reward innovators for producing *ideas* that others value. In 1449, the world's first patent was issued to John Utyman, a Venetian glassmaker, for his process of creating colored glass. Utyman was granted a twenty-year monopoly on the technique in England, in exchange for which he was required to teach his technique to apprentices, guaranteeing that the knowledge would spread. From there, patents took hold. With patent laws in place, an inventor had a greater chance of making a fortune from a new invention. With more profits to be made, more of the educated class turned their efforts to innovation. The inventors of the first several steam engines, the incandescent light bulb, the mechanical loom, the cotton gin, and the automobile were all motivated, at least in part, by the availability of patents. Patents are far from perfect. Rewarding innovators increases innovation. But doing so by giving them a monopoly on the man-ufacture of their new invention slows the spread of that invention. Rewards that avoided that monopoly could, in principle, work even better. Even so, patents are temporary, while the knowledge produced through new innova-tion lasts forever. And the patent system of rewards to inventors accelerated the creation of new ideas.

The other brilliant new cultural innovation was that of the scientific method. Francis Bacon, in 1620, proposed the idea that any scientific theory must be testable by experiments, that those experiments should be reproduc-ible by other scientists, and that experiments could *disprove* theories. Today that idea is so basic to our understanding of science that it's hard to imagine a time before it. Yet Bacon's notion was revolutionary at the time. It ushered in an age of empirical science. It provided another effective selection method for Darwinian evolution of ideas.

Higher food production, markets for products of all sorts, incentives for inventors, greater ability to communicate ideas, and the scientific method all combined to fuel more and more rapid innovation. Ideas built on ideas, often in surprising ways. Lens making for eye glasses let craftsman work decades longer, even after their eyesight faltered. It also gave birth to telescopes when early inventors discovered that lenses could be placed in front of other lenses to make distant objects appear near. The telescope then gave birth to the microscope. The microscope uncovered the world of micro-organisms too small for the eye to see. The discovery of micro-organisms, and the ability to look for them on food, in water, and in samples taken from the body, led to the germ theory of disease. That in turn led to modern medicine and longer lives.

Everywhere, ideas competed against other ideas and inventors competed against other inventors to bring new ideas to fruition as quickly as possible. Everywhere, the profits to be made drew people and resources to innovation. Edison methodically tested 3,000 different materials as possible filaments for his light bulb before finding one that worked reliably. His research was spurred by a race against dozens of others working to perfect and patent the light bulb as well. It was funded by investors who knew that if Edison could perfect a practical light, they stood to profit.

Even as inventors competed, they built upon the knowledge created by their rivals and predecessors. James Watt produced and sold the world's first *practical* steam engine in 1776. But to do so, he built upon the patents that described Thomas Newcomb's less efficient 1712 engine and the published scientific papers of Joseph Black on the concept of "latent heat." And Watt spent nearly twelve years perfecting his steam engine, years where his research was funded by venture capitalists who stood to benefit from the invention only because the patents on it would protect Watt's ability to make money selling the engine or licensing it to others.

The Renaissance and the Industrial Revolution were made possible by the increased ability for ideas to spread, the more vigorous competition between them that the market and science brought, and the new rewards for innovation that attracted bright minds to the task.

Standstill

While Europe soared through the Renaissance, the Enlightenment, and the Industrial Revolution, the pace of change elsewhere was far less impressive. China, the world's largest and wealthiest empire as of the year 1200 AD, made gains over the centuries that followed, but none as explosive or rapid as the changes that swept through Europe. Japan, far smaller but also culturally and technologically advanced, fell behind as well. The Ottoman Empire, Western Europe's closest neighbor and heir to the Eastern Roman Empire's territory and wealth, also failed to keep pace with the advances happening just to its west.

Of all of these, China is the most puzzling. Between the fall of Rome and the early stirrings of the Renaissance, China was undoubtedly the richest and most populous empire on Earth. It was clearly technologically superior to Europe.[7]

Why then didn't the Renaissance, the Scientific Revolution, and the Industrial Revolution happen in China? Why didn't the printing press, an invention first created in Germany, accelerate innovation in China the way it eventually did in, say, England or Spain? Given the higher level of affluence and literacy China enjoyed, the head start it had in knowledge base over Europe, surely the odds were in favor of China maintaining that momentum or even pulling ahead. Instead, Chinese technology and the Chinese knowledge base changed at a far slower pace than Europe's between 1000 and 1800 AD.

Understanding this is important. Our future depends on maintaining and increasing our rates of innovation.

Among those historians who don't chalk up the different rates of scientific and technological knowledge development in China and Europe to simple historical accident, there are two primary answers given. The first is that the success of China's large empires actually hindered the development of new ideas. Medieval Chinese culture was top heavy compared to medieval Europe's. While the Chinese enjoyed greater riches, greater population, greater literacy, and more advanced technology, they also lived in a system of more stringent central control. As opposed to medieval Europe, where local manorial lords made many decisions, and where the highest authority was divided over as many as forty kingdoms, China maintained a strong imperial bureaucracy and strong imperial control over aspects of life throughout the Middle Ages and the European Renaissance and Industrial Revolution.

Europe's fragmented nature meant that the continent was a hotbed of competition. Nations and city-states competed incessantly for dominance. They fielded armies against one another, raced to discover and claim more distant lands first, and sponsored inventors and explorers to attempt to create an advantage over their rivals. That competition further sharpened the process of Darwinian natural selection among ideas, driving an ever-accelerating pace of innovation that led through the Renaissance to the Scientific Revolution and ultimately the Industrial Revolution. China, with its strong central control, lacked this robust internal competition.[8]

Second, the emperor and the bureaucracy around him were able to heavily influence public thought and stifle dissent in a way that no single European monarch could. A seemingly crazy idea in Europe might find patronage from one monarch or aristocrat even if all the rest rejected it.

Columbus, for example, failed to convince the royalty of his native Genoa to fund his expedition to find a western sea route to Asia. He tried twice to convince John II, the king of Portugal, and was denied each time, on the counsel of John's advisors. He returned closer to home, hoping to convince the rulers of Venice to fund his expedition, and was denied again. Through his brother Bartholomew he attempted to gain the financial backing of Henry VII of England, and was denied there. In 1486 he was finally granted an audience before the Spanish king and queen, Ferdinand and Isabella. The advisors to the Spanish crown advised that his request be turned down. It was not until 1492, after six more years of continued persuasion and negotiation, and at least one outright rejection from Isabella, that Ferdinand granted Columbus his financial backing. Even then, the Spanish may not have expected Columbus to return. It was a high-risk, high-reward investment.[9]

Similar stories abound throughout the history of Europe. With more than forty monarchs, hundreds of great lords, and thousands of wealthy investors, the continent had a wide diversity of ideas, ventures, thinkers, and artists gaining patronage. An entrepreneur or budding scientist denied support from one royal court or from one potential investor often found it from another.

In Imperial China, however, this was impossible. The emperor had near absolute power to deny or approve a venture, to sanction a new line of philosophic or scientific enquiry, or to censure it. As a result, the intellectual landscape was far more homogeneous.

The emperor and his mandarins effected a homogeneity of thought in other ways. Consider the Imperial Exams undertaken to enter the employment of the empire as a member of the civil service. The exams were brutal in length, lasting from twenty-four hours to seventy-two hours, usually spent in an isolated cell, with the desk doubling as a bed for short periods of sleep. The applicants to the civil service were tested on their knowledge of music; arithmetic; writing; knowledge of important ceremonies to be performed in public and private life; civil law; tax law and tax collecting; agriculture; geography; and, perhaps most importantly, knowledge of Confucianism. The exams had a tremendous effect on Chinese society. In the thirteenth century as many as 400,000 Chinese would sit for the exams every three years. At most, 20,000 or so would score well enough to join the civil service. Many of the rest, however, became teachers, scholars, local merchants, or state employees in other ways.[10]

The Imperial Examinations were quite remarkable in providing a nominally level playing field to enter the powerful civil service. Any male who scored well enough, regardless of how low his origin, could find himself in an important role. At the same time, they served to homogenize Chinese thinking. The path to a better life was to be able to recite rote answers to a massive standardized test. The effect was that almost all of China's literate population studied for and took the exam. Even for the large majority who didn't pass it, the exam had a powerful impact on mind-set. It set the tone and expectations of the empire. Studies for it squeezed out time for thought on other subjects.

In Europe, by contrast, the path to prosperity, for those not born to it, was often success as a merchant or trader. That success didn't require an education in history, geography, religion, or law. It did often require innovation in the products provided, in the ways of doing business, in the choice of suppliers, and more. Europe's decentralized system, with competition of ideas at the local, national, and international levels, encouraged innovation. China's highly centralized model encouraged homogeneity.

Chinese state control went far further. The state had monopolies on all sorts of staples: salt, iron, tea, and alcohol, among them. There was no viable way for a private individual to launch a venture in any of those or many other areas and hope for profit. If, indeed, a new business was formed that proved profitable, the state would often nationalize it. For much of the Song and Ming dynasties the state had a monopoly on education. It had a monopoly on the press. China scholar Étienne Balázs has written that in ancient China, there was "no private initiative, no expression of public life that can escape official control. . . . [T]he providential State watches minutely over every step of its subjects, from cradle to grave."[11]

Chinese Imperial monopolies were so stringent that when Song Yingxing, one of the greatest scholars of China in the 1600s, produced his encyclopedia *The Exploitation of the Works of Nature*, almost all copies of it were burned. Why? Because the encyclopedia gave detailed drawings and explanations of metalwork, salt-making, and coin-casting, all of which were monopolies the empire kept for itself.[12]

Ancient China was, in other words, a tremendously top-down culture. No government has absolute control. The emperor didn't dictate every aspect of life in China. Innovation did occur. But that rate of innovation was suppressed by the centralization of control and power that China's culture and empire created. While Europe, bereft of Imperial control from Rome, at times seemed anarchic and constantly at war with itself, its lack of a center nevertheless brought with it incredible competition and diversity of ideas and approaches. Its invention of a market that rewarded productivity and innovation further fueled competition. China, at every level, had far less competition and diversity of ideas than Europe.

China not only dampened internal generation of and natural competition between ideas. It also hindered the importation of ideas from elsewhere. In 1405, the Yongle Emperor, third emperor of the Ming Dynasty, sent a huge fleet to explore the region, headed by an admiral named Zheng He. Launched nearly ninety years before Columbus's voyage of 3 small boats and 90 men, Zheng He's fleet of more than 300 ships and more than 25,000 sailors traveled as far west as present day Iraq, Saudi Arabia, and the eastern coast of Africa. They made numerous stops in India. They explored Vietnam, Thailand, Cambodia, Malaysia, and modern-day Indonesia. Had the voyages continued, they very likely would have discovered New Zealand and Australia to the south, and run into European Crusaders in the Middle East. With time they might have discovered the Americas, decades ahead of Columbus. The world would have been a very different place.

Instead, in 1424 the ships were burned. The great voyages had been a brief departure from the philosophies of the Ming dynasty. Hong Wu, the founder of the Ming dynasty, had held the opinion that China, in its great resources, needed nothing from the outside "barbarian" world. He put in place the policy of *haijin*, or "sea ban." Haijin prohibited most trade and restricted foreigners from entering the country, on fear of beheading. Under Yongle, Haijin was briefly lifted, but eventually the xenophobia returned.

Zheng He, the great admiral who'd sailed his fleet across half of the world, had no alternate monarch, prince, or bank to appeal to for support. He could not, like Columbus, travel from court to court and city to city, hoping to find a wealthy ruler or merchant prince who would back further expeditions.* In Chinese society, the word of the emperor was absolute. The homogeneity and centralization of Chinese society stifled any further exploration.

Over the next few hundred years, restrictions on trade would come and go.

*Arguably, Zheng He could have gone elsewhere, such as to Japan, seeking support. However, given that Haijin meant that he would be beheaded if caught, and that there were simply far fewer independent governments in Asia than in Europe, his choices were both fewer and much higher risk.

Some trade and some importation of ideas from the outside world occurred, but far less than occurred between the highly porous, richly intertwined countries of Europe.

China's relative isolation and centralization proved to be disastrous. In the 1840s, Britain was able to defeat and humiliate China in the Opium Wars through its superior technology. That technology also afforded Europeans and Americans greater health and well-being. In 1900, life expectancy at birth in China was roughly thirty years, while in the United States it stood at forty-seven. The knowledge revolution that had occurred while China's borders had been closed had brought wealth, health, and prosperity to the outside world, but not to China.

18 THE BEST OF TIMES

China wasn't the only nation to adopt a highly isolated attitude in the late Middle Ages. In the 1630s, the Tokugawa shogun Iemitsu created the policy of *sakoku*, prohibiting Japanese to leave their nation and foreigners to enter it, under pain of death. Decades later, all Western books were burned. The isolation of Japan would last, with brief respites, until 1854.

The Ottoman Empire, Europe's closest neighbor and the heart of Islamic society, made its own isolationist and innovation-suppressing mistakes. For hundreds of years, Islamic society had been the keeper and propagator of science. Many of the advances in medicine and astronomy over the second millennium were made by Muslims. And the writings of Aristotle, Plato, and others, lost to Western Europe after the fall of Rome, were preserved in Arab nations and reintroduced to Europe after contact with Islam during the Crusades. Yet the Sultans of the Ottoman Empire feared the explosive and decentralizing power of the printing press. Thus, while they allowed Greeks and Jews to set up printing presses to produce works in other languages, starting in 1483, the Ottomans prohibited printing in Arabic (the alphabet that Turkish was written in at the time), on pain of death.

The results for both societies were as disastrous as for China. While well-being, education, and military might all soared in Western Europe, the Ottomans and Japanese were left behind. It wasn't until the nineteenth century that both cultures—along with the Chinese, would scramble to attempt to modernize. In the case of the Ottomans, that scramble came far too late to halt a decline that culminated in their defeat and dissolution at the end of World War I.

The point of this analysis isn't to disparage the Chinese, Japanese, or Ottoman people of that time or of the present day. Indeed, in many ways, all three nations were far more advanced culturally and technologically than Europe from around the fall of Rome until the Renaissance. The lesson here is that the choices societies make affect their rates of innovation.

Fortunately, Europe, by happenstance, did fall into the kind of decentralized, highly connected, and highly competitive structure that encouraged innovation. And as we're about to see, the whole world today is reaping the benefits.

two the incredible present

The explosion of new ideas in Europe, and later in North America, led to the incredible prosperity of our current age. For centuries, Europe and North America raced ahead of the rest of the world in innovation, and thus in wealth, health, and well-being. That created much of the rift between the countries we now think of as "developed" and those we think of as "developing." The opening of China, Japan, and much of the rest of the world in the nineteenth century started the process of erasing those differences and allowing the developing world to catch up with the rich nations. The market reforms of China, India, and Central America in the 1970s, '80s, and '90s accelerated that—bringing the benefit of open competition and powerful incentives to most of the rest of the world. The process isn't complete, but it's moving at an incredible pace. Today, most countries in the world are seeing their highest ever levels of wealth and human well-being. Those are rising everywhere. And the developing countries are rising faster than the already rich countries.

By the Numbers: Living Longer, Living Healthier

But don't take my word for it. Let's look at the numbers. To begin with, let's look at life expectancy—the average age that someone born in a given year can expect to live. Life expectancy is perhaps the best overall measure of human physical well-being, since it correlates with so many other things we care about. High life expectancy depends on good nutrition, access to health care, lower infectious disease rates, clean water, sanitation, and security from war and other types of violence. It correlates with educational levels, with living space per person, with access to electricity, and with living in a democracy. When we see life expectancy rise, almost invariably those other measures are headed in the right direction also.

Since 1950, life expectancy around the world has risen by more than twenty years. An average child born into the world in 1950 could expect to live forty-seven years. A child born today, averaged across all the regions of the world, can expect to live sixty-eight years, and a child born in the developed world can expect to live nearly eighty years.[1]

While life expectancy in the United States has risen substantially—around twelve years since 1950—it's risen roughly twice as fast in still-developing nations. In 1950, the life expectancy gap between developed and still-developing countries was twenty-five years. Today it's down to thirteen years, and still shrinking.[2] Even in the former Soviet Union and in sub-Saharan Africa, two regions that saw life expectancy drop in the 1990s due to the effects of the breakup of the USSR and the scourge of HIV, respectively, longevity is rising again.[3]

The rise in life expectancy around the world reflects progress against death and disease of all sorts. Perhaps most significantly, worldwide infant mortality around the world has plummeted. For most of history, childhood was filled with dangers. Poor nutrition, poor sanitation, poor conditions, and lack of effective medical care meant that children died early and in great numbers. They died of measles, mumps, diarrhea, pneumonia, typhoid, typhus, influ-

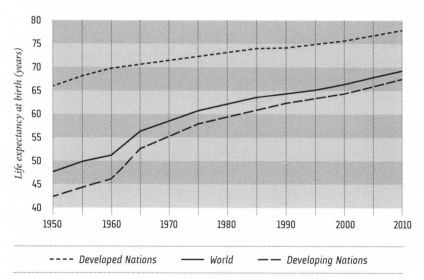

Figure 2.1. Life expectancy rising worldwide. Life expectancy is rising around the world, and fastest in the developing nations. Data from World Health Organization.

enza, cholera, and malaria. They died of congenital defects and malnutrition. They died of exposure to the bitter cold of winter and the unrelenting heat of summer. In 1850, around 30 percent of all children born around the world died by their fifth birthday. In 1950, the worldwide rate was down to less than 14 percent (though still over 20 percent in my native Egypt). And by 2010, the worldwide rate had fallen by a further factor of 3, to around 4 percent.[4]

Reductions of death rates aren't limited to infants. In fact, across all causes combined, the odds of a person around the world dying in a given year have dropped by more than half since 1950. That broad drop reflects massive progress against disease, improvements in nutrition, reduction of war, and improvement in medical care. Infectious disease, once responsible for two thirds of deaths everywhere in the world, today accounts for just 18 percent of deaths in rich countries, and around half in developing nations.[5] Cancer death rates in the United States have dropped around 20 percent in the last twenty years.[6] Death rates for stroke have dropped nearly a third in that time, while death rates for cardiovascular diseases have dropped by a whopping 64 percent since 1963.[7] Other rich nations have seen similar results.[8]

Not only are we living longer, we're doing so in better health. The disability rate for men and women over age sixty-five in the United States dropped from 26.2 percent in 1980 to 19.7 percent in 2000, and continues to drop.[9] Debilitating diseases are not only rarer and less lethal, they strike later in life. Nobel Prize winner Robert Fogel has found that over the course of the twentieth century, the average age of a person's first incidence of heart disease was delayed by nine years, cancers by eight years, and respiratory diseases by eleven years.[10] For example, among men born in the 1830s, the average first age of heart disease was fifty-six. Among men born in the 1920s, heart disease first appeared, on average, nine years later, at age sixty-five. In the 1830s group, arthritis and respiratory diseases first appeared at an average age of fifty-four, and cancer at an average age of fifty-nine. In the group born in the 1920s, they first appeared at age sixty-five and sixty-seven, respectively, a postponement of eight to nine years.

Much of this is a result of improved nutrition. That improved nutrition has also changed human height in rich countries and now appears to be doing so worldwide. The average adult man in the United States in 1850 stood five foot seven inches tall. The average thirty-year-old American man in 1980 stood five foot ten inches tall. Data from France and Norway show the same trends. Fogel writes that, "similar changes have occurred in every other country of the developed world and are now occurring in almost every country in the world as a whole."[11] We not only live longer, we live longer in better health, in bodies that are working better.

Less Poverty, Less Hunger

As the people of the world live longer, fewer of them are doing so in poverty. In 1970, more than a third of the developing world lived on less than $1 per day. Today, adjusting for inflation, that number has shrunk by a factor of 7, down to 5 percent.[12]

In fact, no matter what measure of poverty we look at around the world, the incidence of it has shrunk over the past few decades. In 1970 almost half of the planet lived on less than $1,000 a year. Today that's down to less than one-fifth.[13]

That reduction in poverty has brought with it a reduction in hunger and malnourishment. The combination of better seeds and farm technology with free-market systems of agriculture that gave farmers incentives to grow more food have led to dramatically higher farm yields. At the same time, the rising wages of people in the countries that have adopted free markets has given them more buying power with which to buy more food. More food

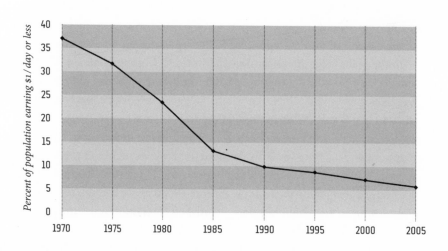

Figure 2.2. Percent of developing world in extreme poverty. Worldwide extreme poverty has plunged from more than 35 percent of the world population to around 5 percent. Data from Xavier Sala-i-Martin, Columbia University.

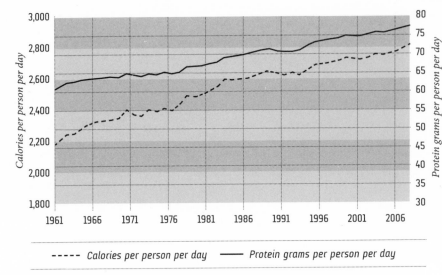

Figure 2.3. Calories and protein available per person rising worldwide. Around the world, the number of calories and protein grams available per person in the food supply have risen, outpacing population. Data from Food and Agriculture Organization of the United Nations.

plus greater buying power for people everywhere has meant less hunger. In 1970, roughly a quarter of the world and more than a third of the people living in developing nations were malnourished. By 2007, that percentage had dropped by half, to around 13 percent of the world, and just over 15 percent of the citizens of the developing world.[14]

In the 1960s a common fear was that world food production wouldn't be able to keep up with soaring population. Best sellers warned that we were headed for massive famines. But what's happened is the opposite. Food production has risen *faster* than population. In 1960, there were roughly 2,200 calories available per person per day on Earth in our food supply. By 2010, that number had risen to 2,800. In 1960, there were roughly sixty grams of protein available per person per day in the world's food supply. Today there are nearly eighty grams available per person. As fast as population has risen—from just over three billion in 1960 to around seven billion in 2010—food production has outpaced it.[15]

There is still far to go. Nearly a billion people in the world don't have enough to eat. We've made real progress. If we had the hunger rates of the 1970s, there would be *two billion* hungry people alive today. But one billion

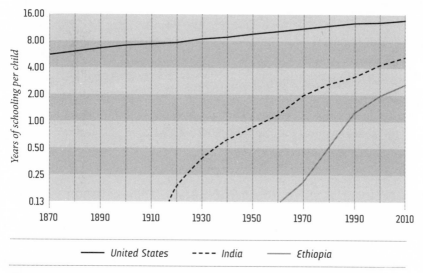

Figure 2.4. Average years of schooling per child, 1870–2010. Average years of schooling is rising in every region of the world. The United States, India, and Ethiopia displayed as examples. Data from Daniel Cohen and Marcelo Soto.

remains too high. As a global society, we're moving forward. Our challenge is to continue that progress.

As poverty drops, people around the world gain access to more and more of the conveniences, luxuries, and life-saving benefits of modern life. In 1970, 77 percent of the world had access to clean water. In 2010 that number reached 87 percent. In 1970, only an appallingly low one in four residents of the developing world had access to electricity. Today that number is 70 percent.

Higher Literacy and Education

Perhaps the greatest enabler of human potential in the world is education, and within that, literacy. Around the world, both are increasing. In 1970, only 63 percent of the adults in the world could read and write at a basic level. By 2010, that number had risen by a third to 84 percent, and is still rising. It's risen fastest among women (from around 50 percent in 1970 to today's 79 percent) and in the poorest part of the world, sub-Saharan Africa, where literacy has more than doubled since 1970, rising from around 30 percent of adults to today's level of 70 percent of adults.

Schooling has gone hand in hand with this. In 1950, the average child in sub-Saharan Africa received less than one year of formal education. By 1980, that had more than doubled, to two years of formal education. Today the average amount of schooling in that poorest part of the world has doubled again, to four years. Asia and Latin America have progressed as well, going from around five years of schooling for the average child in 1980 to eight years today. As with hunger, we still have far to go in global education, but we're headed in the right direction.[16]

Greater Access to Information and Communication

As education, wealth, and electrification increase, so does access to information and communication. My first international trip as an adult (after receiving my U.S. citizenship) was with a friend to China in 2000. That trip ranged from the metropolis of Beijing to remote Yunnan province, just one mountain range away from Tibet. Everywhere we went we saw signs of China's growth. But mobile phones, which by 2000 nearly everyone I knew in the United States had, were largely absent. There were a few high-end shops with cell phones in the windows, but I never saw a Chinese man or woman use

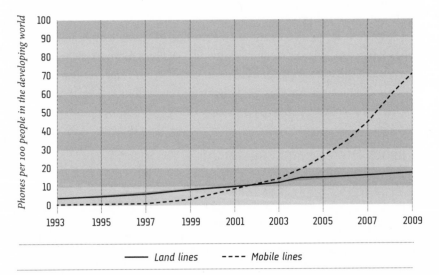

Figure 2.5. Phones per one hundred people, developing world. Mobile phones have saturated the developed world, and now reach three quarters of the developing world as well. Data from International Telecommunications Union.

one. When I returned in 2007 on business, things were completely changed. Shopkeepers, school children, passengers on the bus, taxi drivers, street-side food vendors—all of them were wired. Everywhere I went, mobile phones were ubiquitous. I found the same in Vietnam in 2008. When my traveling companions and I found our poor mastery of Vietnamese insufficient to conclude a tricky negotiation with a hotel employee, the young man pulled out his phone, called a friend who spoke English, and used him as a remote translator.

In the last twenty years, mobile phones have gone from a niche technology for the wealthy to a mass technology across the developed world and, increasingly, across the developing world. In 1997, only 18 percent of people in the developed world had a mobile phone, and less than 10 percent of people in the developing world had a phone of any sort, mobile or land line. By 2009, mobile phones had surged past their older, established landline phone cousins to reach more than 70 percent of people in the developing world, and nearly everyone in the developed nations.[17]

The rise of the Internet is the other great improvement in access to information and communication. Internet use, something barely heard of as recently as 1994, is now all-pervasive in the developed world. And, while less pervasive in the still developing world, it's rising there rapidly. Worldwide, more than two billion people now have access to the internet, a full 30 percent of humanity. With Internet access come opportunities to learn, to gain useful information relevant to one's life, to communicate with others anywhere in the world, and to make one's voice heard. Neither Internet nor cell phone access is a panacea, but both give people new options in life.[18]

And just as the printing press accelerated the evolution of ideas, so too are today's communication technologies. If the past is any lesson, we're equipped today to innovate at rates never before seen.

Shrinking Costs, Larger Lives

In 1980, economist Julian Simon challenged biologist Paul Ehrlich to a bet. Pick any five commodities, he told Ehrlich, and Simon would put money down that they would cost *less* in 1990 than they did in 1980. The bet summarized their respective views on the world. Ehrlich, author of the 1968 best seller *The Population Bomb*, held the view that rising population would make everything in the world more scarce, and thus more expensive. Simon, the author of *The Ultimate Resource* (a book with more than a passing relation to this one), held the view that human innovation would increase access to and efficiency of use of resources faster than a growing population could consume them. Thus, he expected prices to decline.

Ehrlich accepted the bet, and with the help of two Stanford colleagues picked five metals (chromium, tin, copper, nickel, and tungsten) as his commodities of choice. Between 1980 and 1990, world population increased by 830 million people, or 28 percent. Yet Ehrlich lost the bet. In 1990, Ehrlich sent Simon a check. Of the five commodities, *all five dropped in price* over those ten years—$1,000 worth of the metals in 1980, adjusted for inflation, cost just over $600 in 1990.[19]

Simon would have lost the bet if it had been made in the 1970s or if it had run until 2007. Not every decade shows dropping prices of resources. But over the long run, the trend has been toward a massive decline in the prices of commodities. Between 1900 and 2000, the prices of metals, adjusted for inflation, fell by a factor of 4.5. The price of food fell by a factor of 3. The price of nearly everything, in fact, fell.

Even that, though, understates the extent to which things have become more affordable. Income has risen faster than inflation, even as prices of raw materials have fallen relative to inflation. The result is that, relative to average salaries in the United States, the price of food dropped by a factor of 25 and the price of metals by a factor of 35 across the twentieth century.[20] The prices of energy, clothing, furniture, appliances, and electronics have all dropped when compared to income in the last decade, and in *every decade* since World War II.[21]

And while the fraction of earnings that people in the United States spend on housing has changed only slightly over the last sixty years, Americans are getting *more* housing. The average home size has more than doubled over that time, while the average number of people per home has dropped by a quarter. Americans have almost three times as much living space per person as they did in 1950. And those homes are more likely to be filled with appliances, large color televisions, computers, and other conveniences than ever before.[22] We're spending less on the basics, with more left to buy the things we want. As innovation drops prices and raises incomes, we're living larger.

What about the Great Recession?

Will we keep getting richer? One of the most frequent objections I've heard is that the financial crisis of 2008 and the resulting recession have put an end to growing wealth. The 2008 financial crisis was indeed a major blow. But it's best to put it in context.

The Great Depression of the 1930s knocked the GDP of the United States down by 26 percent. Fifty percent of the banks in the country failed. Unemployment soared by 20 percentage points to 25 percent. By comparison, the 2008–2009 recession, GDP dropped by 3.3 percent, less than 1 percent of the banks in the country failed, and unemployment rose by 5 percentage points to 10 percent. The Great Depression was many times worse than the 2008–2009 recession.

Yet the remarkable fact about the Great Depression is that economic growth recovered from the event and continued upward. Indeed, if we look at per capita GDP in the United States from 1900 to 1928, and again from 1950 until 2010, it would be easy to miss that the Great Depression even happened. If

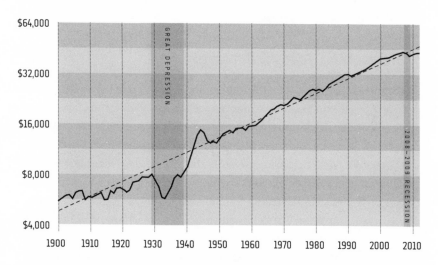

Figure 2.6. United States per capita GDP, 1900 to 2012. Per person GDP in the United States, adjusted for inflation, has grown continuously over the past century. The Great Depression of the 1930s derailed economic growth for approximately ten years but had no obvious effect on the long term trend. Data from Louis Johnston and Samuel H. Williamson.

anything, growth from 1950 to 2010 has been faster than the growth prior to the Great Depression.[23]

There is plenty to learn from the 2008 financial crisis and the euro crisis of 2011. Both events should guide changes to the world's financial system. Government policies were a key part of pulling out of the Great Depression and staying out of it, and they are again today. But over the long run, the numbers suggest that the 2008–2009 recession will have a lasting impact smaller than that of the Great Depression. And while that has been and will continue to be a very real impact, it's clear that the U.S. economy and the world economy have bounced back from far worse before.

What of rising income inequality? Some of that will need to be addressed through changes in our society and our laws. But much of it has little to do with the top 1 percent, and more to do with education. As we'll see later in the book, as humanity comes to value innovation more and more, the gap between those with advanced educations and those with less education has grown wider and wider. Improving our education system is something that's vital both for continuing and boosting our rate of innovation, and for closing that gap, and it's something that we'll look at in Part IV of this book, when we come back to solutions for the problems that face us.

Imperfect but Better All the Time

In summary, we live in a world where people live longer than ever before, with greater health, less disease, more comfort, more ability to travel, more education, more access to information and communication, more food, less hunger, less poverty, and more freedom than at any point in our history.

This is to be celebrated. We don't live in the best of all *possible* times. We can imagine far better worlds in which poverty and hunger have been eliminated, freedom is universal, and disease is nonexistent. We may never reach such a world, but we can approach it. Our current era is the closest we have come. This is, indeed, the best of times so far.

Almost all of this progress has come as a result of human innovation. We've made discoveries and created inventions that have cured diseases, allowed us to grow more food, given us access to energy that we can use to enrich our lives, and enhanced our ability to communicate. Just as importantly, we've innovated in our social, political, and economic systems as well. Democracy is a human invention. Civil rights are a human invention. Organized education is a human invention. All of those inventions that make our lives better are, at their heart, new *ideas* that we've created. They're all products of our minds.

Fueled by our ability to produce new ideas, the prosperity of the world has been on a steady rise for at least the last 150 years. At this rate, future generations will be tremendously more prosperous than we are today. Indeed, the average person alive today is far better off than many of the richest people in history.

Your Enormous Wealth: Crassus and You

Historians have debated for some time the question of "who's the wealthiest man to ever live?"* Genghis Khan once ruled all of Asia, and fully one out every ten people alive today in the areas he conquered is a direct descendent of his.[24] Mir Osman Ali Khan, the last ruler of the independent state of Hyderabad and Berar, and one of Genghis Khan's distant descendants, was called the richest man alive as recently as the 1940s. He reportedly used the 185 carat Jacob diamond, the seventh-largest diamond in the world, as a paperweight.[25] During the Renaissance, the Medici family of Italy was so rich that they were able to install four of their own as popes of the Catholic Church and another two as queens of France.

The strongest case may be for the Roman Marcus Licinius Crassus. When Spartacus led a renegade army of slaves against the might of Imperial Rome, it was Crassus who put down the rebellion and ordered the crucifixion of the rebels along the Appian Way. From 59 to 53 BC Crassus ruled all of the Roman Empire with Pompey and Julius Caesar as the First Triumvirate. Their power extended through most of Europe and the Mediterranean world.

Crassus built his wealth through property speculation. When fire struck in Rome, Crassus would rush to the site, buy up the burning home and the endangered ones surrounding it at a pittance, and then instruct his men to put out the fire by demolishing the building. After the fire was out, Crassus would rebuild and then sell or rent the property and the surrounding, often undamaged homes, at far more than he had paid. The behavior made him notorious in Rome and brought him the nickname *Dives* (roughly "Money-bags"). It also put him in ownership of a substantial amount of Rome's real

THE INCREDIBLE PRESENT

---

*The question of "who is the wealthiest woman to ever live?" is asked far less often. Perhaps in the next century the assumption that great wealth is the bailiwick of men will be overturned.

estate. At the peak of his wealth, Crassus was worth an estimated 200 million sestertii. When he met his death in an attempted parley during an ill-thought-out campaign to conquer Parthia (in modern-day Turkey), legend has it that his enemies had his head chopped from his body and poured molten gold into his open mouth to quench his unending thirst for wealth.[26]

How rich was Crassus? Two hundred million sestertii was equivalent to the annual budget of the Roman Republic at that time. By comparison, the annual budget of the United States Federal Government is close to $3 trillion. If the comparison is apt, Crassus was worth, in today's terms, thirty times as much as Bill Gates was worth at the peak of his fortune in 1999.

Yet Crassus never tasted chocolate, never saw a film, only heard music when he had minstrels on hand to play for him. When he traveled from place to place, it was on horseback or in a horse-drawn carriage for long days or weeks over painfully bumpy roads. If he became ill, he had no access to antibiotics or even a simple aspirin. He could communicate only by his voice or by the slow passage of letters over land or sea. He had access to neither air conditioning nor central heating, and so he lived in palaces that were too hot in summer and too cold in winter, buildings as impressive as any in their time but dark and drafty by today's standards. If he wished to read he had a small set of scrolls to choose from compared to the millions of books that exist today. His light was a flickering candle or lamp.

In terms of the conveniences of life, in terms of the comfort of our homes, the ease with which we travel from place to place, communicate with others near or far, find and enjoy music or books or films or any other entertainment, in terms of our health, the age we can expect to live to, and the medicine we have available to help us when we're injured or become ill—in all these ways we are tremendously more wealthy than Marcus Licinius Crassus, who may well have been the richest man ever to live.

We live lives more comfortable, more convenient, and more secure in the likelihood of health than Genghis Khan, than the Medici popes and queens, than Mir Osman Ali Khan. The source of our comfort, our convenience, our access to information and entertainment, our ability to travel and communicate across distances, and all the other ways in which we are richer than most of the richest men in history, is the result of the continual accumulation of human knowledge across the ages. The new innovations we've produced, the designs for inventions as now common as air conditioning, television, radio, the Internet, air travel, telephones, antibiotics, painkillers, and every other invention we interact with in the course of our lives—those innovations are the sources of the greater capabilities and conveniences that we enjoy.

Not only are those of us in rich nations better off than Crassus and other super-wealthy individuals of the past, but so are billions of other men and women, in both the developed and developing world. Almost every adult in the developed world, and now more than half the adults in the nations of the developing world, has a cell phone. Two-thirds of the people on Earth have access to electricity. Billions have access to antibiotics. The average resident of Shenzhen, China, or Hyderabad, India, or even Lagos, Nigeria, has access to conveniences and capabilities that Crassus or Julius Caesar or Napoleon or any of a host of emperors of the past would have killed for.

And on almost every metric, whether it be life expectancy, infant mortality, median income, access to cell phones or Internet, access to cars, living space per person, or levels of education—the rich world is continuing to make progress, and the developing world is rising even *faster*. On a global scale, the rich are getting richer, but the poor are gaining in wealth even more quickly. The global gap in wealth and well-being that the early rise of Europe in the Renaissance and Industrial Revolution opened up is shrinking as knowledge and technology transcend national borders. And as the entire world catches up to the levels of affluence seen today in the rich world, billions and billions of people on planet Earth will be living lives that the richest kings and princes and emperors of history could only dream of.

This is the best of times. And if the trends in our innovation and wealth continue, even better is yet to come, for those of us who live in nations that are already rich, and for the billions whose homelands are rising into wealth even as we speak.

I'd love to stop this book here, and tell you only the good things. Alas, there are ways in which the world is heading in the wrong direction, and there are dangers building that could wreck all we've achieved—dangers larger than just about any we've ever faced before, and dangers that will take all of our innovative power and more to overcome.

part two
the worst of times

three running out of steam

On Christmas Day of 2005 I woke before dawn, dressed quickly, then stepped out of my hut to fall in with a small group hiking through the Guatemalan jungle. Our guide led us along a dirt path cut through two miles of thick brush and densely packed trees, with only our flashlights to illuminate the way. Eventually we reached the base of an enormous stone pyramid, 212 feet tall, with sides that sloped down steeply, like a spear tip sticking up from the Earth. Wooden stairs installed in recent decades led up and out of sight. We climbed and climbed those stairs to the pyramid's apex in the predawn darkness. At the peak we were above the tree tops, looking down on the jungle canopy below us. Mist rose up from it. A howler monkey roared somewhere off to our left, perhaps half a mile away, marking its territory in a deep bass that echoed off the stone pyramid. Off to our right, another bellowed out a response. I felt like I'd been transported to the set of *Jurassic Park*.

Templo IV, the structure we were on top of, faces east, toward the other pyramids and structures of the ancient Mayan city of Tikal. As the sky lightened with the approach of the dawn, the soaring tops of those other buildings began to take shape out of the darkness, thrusting their way up above the jungle. The farthest of them, Templo I, was a full mile distant from me, on the other side of the city core of what had once been a metropolis of as many as 90,000 people, at the heart of a civilization of 10 or 20 million. My companions and I had climbed the highest skyscraper the Western Hemisphere would know until the nineteenth century, and from it we surveyed all that remained of one of the greatest cities of its time.

Tikal, like many Mayan centers, spent centuries as a proverbial "lost city in the jungle." The first pyramids and platforms were built around 400 BC, before Rome grew into its power. The first inscriptions with dates in the Mayan calendar appear around that time. By the middle of the eighth century AD,

Tikal was one of the greatest cities in the Mayan world, and Mayan civilization itself was at its peak of population, art, and architecture. Less than 100 years later, Tikal was all but abandoned, as were Copan, Calakmul, Palenque, and most of the other great cities of the Maya. The last dated inscription on any Mayan artifact, anywhere, is 909 AD. While some Maya lived on, their great cities were abandoned, and the overall population of the area was a bare one-tenth of what it had been.

Somehow, after growing steadily in numbers, in sophistication, and in the scale of their projects for well over a thousand years, Mayan civilization collapsed almost completely in a matter of decades. Their cities were eventually so thoroughly forgotten that their existence became little more than a legend. When Tikal was rediscovered in the mid-1800s, the buildings were covered in plants and trees growing in the foot of topsoil that had accumulated in the centuries since they'd been abandoned. Even today, as you walk around the periphery of any uncovered Mayan city, you'll see thousands of large green mounds, perhaps small hills, covered in trees and vegetation. Those mounds aren't hills. They're ancient Mayan buildings that have been thoroughly reclaimed and covered by the jungle.

Why am I telling you about the collapse of the Maya? Because, while innovation is the ultimate source of wealth, it wasn't enough to save them from the forces that ultimately devastated their civilization. The Maya were a large and sophisticated culture. They undoubtedly saw themselves as the masters of their domain. They had unparalleled technology and wealth. Yet all of that was yanked out from under them.

How? The Maya, it seems, exhausted their natural resources. They exhausted the primary source of energy for their society—the land beneath their feet. Archeological evidence and samples of pollen from sediments in the bottoms of lakes suggest that the Maya had almost completely deforested their region by the tenth century AD. With fewer trees, soil blew away on the wind, reducing their ability to raise food. Forests capture moisture from the air and recycle it, increasing rainfall in the region. Fewer trees meant less rain, further stressing agriculture. Simultaneously, the irrigation canals the Maya had dug to water their land began to silt up. And when a rapidly changing climate hit the region with severe droughts in the tenth century AD—droughts that might have been exacerbated by the deforestation of the area—the Maya found themselves with no buffer. Food production fell precipitously. Violence increased as city warred on city for the dwindling resources of the region. They fell victim to challenges that we're beginning to see in our civilization today.

The End of Easy Oil

The primary energy source of *our* civilization is fossil fuel. And among the fossil fuels, the most vital is oil. We consume more than 80 million barrels of it each and every day. Oil fuels our cars. Oil fuels the trucks, planes, and ships that transport food, raw materials, and goods around the world. Oil is used to make the plastics that fill our homes and offices and the synthetic fibers that we wear on our bodies. Oil fuels the farm equipment that plants and harvests the grains that feed us and that feed the livestock that we depend on. Oil fuels the mining equipment that extracts the ores containing the steel, aluminum, and other metals and minerals that our industrial society consumes.

And oil is finite. There is only so much of it that has ever been created by the slow high-pressure cooking of decaying plants.

I don't recall the very first time I heard the idea of peak oil—the notion that the amount of oil we can get out of the ground each year will soon peak and decline—but I know that I didn't take it seriously. My first more substantial encounter with the idea was in April of 2005. I was promoting my first book with a book reading and signing at the iconic Stacey's Bookstore on Market Street in San Francisco—sadly now gone. After the reading and the signing of books, a store employee approached to tell me that, as a thank you, Stacey's offered every speaker at the store a free book of his or her choice. At the time there were two prominent books on peak oil out. My agent, who'd come to hear me speak, told me which one had gotten better reviews. I chose that one and thanked the store manager.

That night, in my hotel room, I read the first few chapters of the book. What I learned was that some rogue experts outside the oil industry believed that oil reserves were much smaller than what the industry reported; that in the 1950s a geologist named M. King Hubbert had somewhat accurately predicted a peak and decline in U.S. oil production between 1965 and 1970; and that Hubbert's models predicted a peak and decline in world oil production by 2000.

I did a little bit of research online. What I found was that oil production over the previous twelve months had been at an all-time high in world history, and that experts at agencies like the U.S. Department of Energy and the International Energy Agency didn't see any peak to oil production in sight.

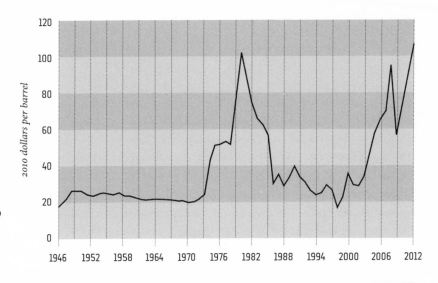

Figure 3.1. Oil prices, 1946–2012 (adjusted for inflation). Oil is once again at prices not seen this century except during the oil crisis of the 1970s. Data from Capital Professional Services.

I tossed the book aside, unfinished, and unconvinced by its proposition. Seven years later—seven years of mounting *evidence* later—I'm more convinced that peak oil is real.

Market Forces

The most palpable evidence of peak oil it is at the gas pump. Adjusted for inflation, gasoline prices in the United States have risen by a factor of 3 between 1998 and 2012. They've risen that rapidly because the price of oil has soared. In 1998, in inflation-adjusted dollars, oil cost around $16 per barrel. In 2008, just before the global recession cut demand, oil reached a high of almost $150 per barrel. Average prices across 2008, even including the period during the recession, were almost $100 per barrel. Prices soared because global demand for oil has kept rising, while production growth has stalled.[1]

In the twenty years between 1950 and 1970, worldwide oil production rose by a factor of 5–400 percent. Between 1970 and 1990, oil production rose only 40 percent. Between 1990 and 2011, oil production rose only 25 percent. The world has been unable to grow supply at the pace it once did.

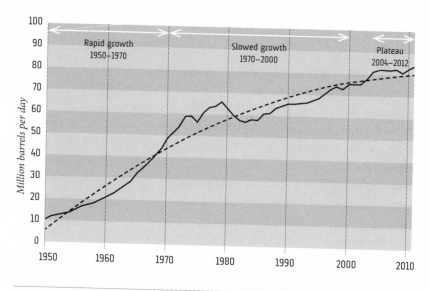

Figure 3.2. World oil production, 1950–2012. World oil production over sixty years. The rate of growth has slowed and perhaps halted. Source: BP Statistical Review of World Energy

What's worse is that, in the six years between 2005 and 2012, crude oil production was nearly flat. In those seven years it grew by just 2 percent. In the 1950s, by contrast, production rose by 70 percent in seven years, or thirty five times faster.

The most basic thing most of us know about economics is the law of supply and demand. When supply is high and demand is low, prices are low. When demand is high and supply is low, prices go up. Supply and demand explains why oil prices have hovered near $100 per barrel through 2012. There's huge demand for oil around the world, while supplies are tight.

Yet there's another law of economics that's even more telling in this situation. It's simply called the law of supply. What the law of supply says is that, unless physical constraints prevent it, demand *creates* supply. If there's more demand for restaurants in an area, restaurants will open. If there's demand for flat-screen TVs or couches or homes or cars, they'll be produced. Businesses follow the money. They produce what they know will sell.

So why then, with prices for oil above $100 per barrel, have oil producers not managed to pump substantially more oil? It's not for lack of trying. In 2011, the oil industry spent an estimated $490 billion on exploration.[2] Yet the industry still pumped more oil out of the ground than it discovered in new fields. Why haven't oil producers raised production in the face of high demand and high prices? The simple answer is that they can't.

No one disputes that there's plenty of oil in the ground. Estimates range from 900 billion barrels of recoverable oil up to trillions of barrels. Yet oil in the ground is not the same thing as oil flowing from a well. Conventional oil fields are vast pressurized reservoirs. Tap into one that has never been tapped before, and oil flows freely. Drill more wells and oil keeps flowing at a rapid rate. Total production rises, but so too does the relief of pressure from the field. Eventually, as the pressure continues to drop, oil flows less quickly. More work is required for each additional barrel. Oil producers drill yet more wells to try to increase the flow. They insert detergents to lower oil surface tension, allowing it flow more freely. They pump in high-pressure water or pressurized gas to force the oil out. They insert heated steam to reduce viscosity.[3]

These techniques work. They increase the total amount of oil recoverable from a field. But each successive effort involves more labor, more energy, and more dollars spent on pulling oil out of the field. The result is that each barrel pumped from an oil field is more expensive than the last, and that inexorably, after reaching a peak rate of flow, a field begins to drop in productivity.

Hubbert's Peak

In 1956, U.S. geologist M. King Hubbert observed that he could model the production from a single field as a bell-curve. The Hubbert Curve, as it was later called, gave good results in predicting the long-term flow from an oil field. When Hubbert applied his model to the entire continental United States, also in 1956, he found that it predicted a peak of U.S. oil production from the lower forty-eight states sometime between 1965 and 1970.

Much as Hubbert predicted, continental U.S. oil production rose to a peak in 1970, hovered within 10–20 percent of that peak until 1985, and then began to rapidly decline.[4] In 1970, the United States produced around 10 million barrels of oil per day. Even with today's record high prices—which should motivate oil companies to explore more, drill more, and find more creative ways to produce—and even with today's best-ever oil-extraction technology that can recover a higher-than-ever fraction of the oil in a well, U.S. oil production is only 5.5 million barrels per day, a little over half of what it was in 1970.

Around the world, other signs of potential peaking of oil can be seen. Some of the once largest and most productive fields in the world are in decline. The Burgan field, Kuwait's largest oil field, which once produced 2 million barrels a day, is now down to 1.7 million barrels a day.[5] The Cantarell field in Mexico which once produced 2.1 million barrels a day now produces less than 800,000. Even Ghawar in Saudi Arabia, the largest oil field in the world, now produces 5.1 million barrels a day, down from its peak of 5.7 million barrels a day.[6] The giant U.S. Prudhoe Bay field, which once produced more than 1.5 million barrels a day, now produces only 300,000.[7] Worldwide, of 50,000 total oil fields, a mere 500—1 percent of those fields—account for 60 percent of total world oil production. And out of a sample of 331 of those fields, 261 of them—79 percent—are in decline.

Scaling up from fields to nations doesn't improve the picture. As of 2008, only seven major oil-producing countries in the world are producing at their all-time highs or claim to be able to do so. Another forty are clearly off their peaks, including the United States, Russia, Venezuela, Kuwait, Iraq, Iran, Libya (before its unrest), Egypt, Syria, Brunei, Argentina, the United Kingdom (even including the North Sea), and more. All together, the countries that are growing or stable in production, or that claim to be able to reach their former heights of production, accounted for roughly 39 percent of production in 2008. The countries clearly off their peak accounted for 61 percent of production in that year.

Hubbert, in fact, predicted that the world as a whole would peak. His success predicting the peak and decline of U.S. oil production gave credence to his predictions of a peak in global oil production. In 1971, he wrote *Energy and Power* in which he predicted a peak of world oil production between 1995 and 2000 at a peak production rate of somewhere between 66 and 101 million barrels per day.[8] That is not far off from the near-plateau that oil production has been on since 2005.

Oil production hasn't peaked yet. It's still slowly rising. But the slowdown of production suggests we may be approaching the peak Hubbert predicted. And beyond the peak, Hubbert's model predicted a plateau and then eventual decline in worldwide oil production. Hubbert's model did have one large hole. It didn't take into account the huge incentive that higher prices would create for more exploration. It's possible that this incentive will eventually re-ignite oil production, and that we'll look back at the last several years as a period where new investments just hadn't paid off yet.

Faster Than We Find It

Yet that doesn't seem likely. Since the mid-1980s, world production of oil (pumping it out of the ground) has been consistently higher each year than the amount discovered in new fields. The world's stated economically feasible oil reserves have risen in that time, but not primarily because of new discoveries. New discoveries of oil have consistently been lower than production since the late 1980s. In 2009, for instance, the oil industry discovered somewhere between 12 and 18 billion barrels of oil in new fields.[9] The *New York Times* proclaimed that the oil industry was on a "hot streak" of discoveries. Yet in

the same year, the industry pumped 31 billion barrels of oil out of the ground.[10] 2010 was the best year for oil discoveries since the 1980s, but even so, the oil discoveries of 28 billion barrels were notably short of the 33.4 billion barrels the world used.[11]

Even when we hear of huge new discoveries, they're usually dwarfed by the amount of oil we use. For example, in November of 2011 the Associated Press described a "huge oil discovery" in Argentina. How large was the discovery? 927 million barrels, in a field that will require years of work to develop.[12] The world burns that much oil in twelve days. The U.S. Geological Survey estimates that the huge Bakken Shale formation under Montana and North Dakota, which has been hailed as restoring the U.S. oil industry, holds 4.3 billion barrels of recoverable oil, less than what the world burns in two months.[13] The largest oil find of 2011, in the North Sea by Norway's Statoil, is estimated at a maximum of 1.2 billion barrels, a two-week supply for the planet.[14]

Yet estimates of oil reserves have kept rising. They've risen because oil companies and oil-producing states have upped their estimates of what fraction of the fields they're already pumping they can eventually recover. Some of those estimate increases have been political. OPEC countries have their oil quotas set in part based on their published estimates of reserves. The higher a country claims its reserves are, the more it's allowed to pump.

Other estimate increases have been technological. New enhanced recovery techniques have made it conceivable to retrieve 60 percent or even 80 percent of the oil from a field, where once that number was only 40 percent. That's a mixed blessing. It's a positive example of the power of innovation to seemingly create (or make available) new resources. But it also indicates that we really are running down these fields. No recovery technique will ever take them past 100 percent. Unless the rate of discovery of new fields substantially increases in the coming years—something few expect—then the amount of conventional oil we have access to will decline.

Unconventional Sources

The world's most obvious ways to increase oil flow center around so-called "unconventional oil," and in particular oil sands. In northern Alberta, almost directly north of the rapidly melting Glacier National Park, are some of the world's largest oil sands. What's there isn't oil, exactly. It's bitumen, better known as asphalt. And Canada has more than a trillion barrels worth of it, enough to make a serious impact on the world oil market.

Naturally occurring bitumen is a black, sticky, tar-like hydrocarbon. At room temperature it's a semi-solid mass. It melts into a liquid at 977 degrees Fahrenheit.[15] Unlike a field of liquid oil, where you can pump hydrocarbons out of the ground simply by drilling a hole and letting the natural high pressure do the rest, oil sands take tremendous work to harvest. Electric shovels five stories high scoop out tons of oil sands (and tons of topsoil above them) and deposit them in chemical "upgraders" that chemically process the bitumen to the point where it can be handled by normal refineries. The combined effort of strip mining and upgrading is expensive in dollars, in water used, and in energy.

Extracting a barrel of fuel from oil sands can use a quarter to a third as much energy as is in the barrel. People in the energy field think of this in terms of EROI—the energy returned on energy invested. It takes energy to mine or pump fossil fuels. It takes energy to build nuclear reactors or hydroelectric dams or solar cells or any other energy technology we have. A key question for each is: how much energy do you get back for each unit you put in? For conventional oil, one barrel's worth of energy can produce perhaps 20 barrels from a healthy oil field. By contrast, oil sands look closer to an EROI of 3 or 4. That means that they take 5 to 7 times more energy to get oil out of than current fields, which in the end means that we'll get less out of them.

The other challenge with oil sands is that they're capital intensive. It takes a large investment in mining equipment, upgraders, and other facilities to start an oil sand field. To get one barrel of oil from an oil sand field requires moving four tons of topsoil and sand, a cost and effort that far outstrips that of drilling wells into pressurized fields. That may be why production from oil sands was just 1.35 million barrels per day in 2009, and projected to rise only to 3.1 million barrels per day by 2030.[16] By contrast, world demand is expected to rise by 2 percent per year, meaning that it will grow by nearly forty million barrels per day in the same time.

The next unconventional oil source frequently mentioned—oil shale—is an even harder option. While the world likely possesses two to three trillion barrels worth of kerogen—a waxy substance containing carbon and hydrogen that can be refined into oil—bound up in oil shale rocks, extracting and refining them is estimated to use up as much as half of their contained energy. Estimates for the EROI of gasoline from oil shale range from just over 1 (meaning it is just better than break even) to 1.7.[17] It takes thirteen to twenty times as much energy to get oil out of oil shales as conventional fields. And oil shale, like oil sands, is capital and equipment intensive to extract and process. Similar to oil sands, production of oil from shale is around 1 million barrels per day at present. The Energy Information Agency of the United States sees that increasing by less than another million barrels per day over the next twenty years.[18]

None of the options for replacing conventional oil with unconventional sources look particularly attractive from the perspective of the amount of money and energy that must be invested to retrieve them. On the other hand, neither does a long plateau or a year-over-year decline in liquid fuel availability.

Will natural gas or coal be able to make the difference? Coal can be converted into a liquid fuel. And vehicles can be converted to run on natural gas rather than gasoline. Yet neither is likely to be a full solution. The United States is currently seeing a boom in natural gas supplies, with production near an all-time high and prices near an eight-year low. But the entire amount of natural gas produced in the United States—around sixty billion cubic feet a day—contains only around half the energy of the oil burned in the United States. And that natural gas is already spoken for by home heating and electricity generation. Natural gas looks extremely attractive as an alternative right now, but if any significant switchover to it occurs, prices will rise.

What about coal? The world is currently producing a record amount of coal, as well. The total amount of energy in the roughly twenty million tons of coal mined each day is roughly the same as the energy in the oil produced each day. Coal can't directly run cars, trucks, and planes, but through a process called coal to liquids it can be turned into a gasoline-like fuel. That process is only 50 percent efficient, however, meaning that half the energy is lost.[19] That, in turn, means that all the world's coal could take the place of half the world's oil. And while the world's coal production is at an all-time high, demand is even higher. Coal prices spiked in 2008 at nearly five times their pre-2000 levels and today are at nearly three times their pre-2000 price. Even more so than natural gas, coal is spoken for already. Added to that is the capital cost of building coal-to-liquids plants. As a result, even the most optimistic estimates from the coal industry show an aggressive coal-to-liquids effort—*with* billions in government subsidies—could replace only around 10 percent of U.S. oil consumption by 2030.

The net of all of this is that oil production looks unlikely to rise substantially over the coming years. It may rise slowly as higher prices make it economical to retrieve oil deposits that are currently too expensive to turn a profit. Or it may hold flat as the new supplies and new technologies just manage to offset the decline in current fields. Or—if current fields decline faster that new supplies come online—it may drop.

Deep Impact

Even the International Energy Agency, a body that for years saw no peak of oil production in sight, now sees it arriving imminently. The IEA's 2009 report didn't mention peak oil as a top level issue at all. The *2010* report gives it a full section.[20] Fatih Birol, the chief economist of the International Energy Agency (effectively the chief energy economist in the world) told the British newspaper the *Independent* that the IEA now sees the peak of worldwide oil supplies—from all sources, including unconventional oil such as tar sands—occurring by 2020. He went on to say, "One day we will run out of oil, . . . and we have to leave oil before oil leaves us, and we have to prepare ourselves for that day. The earlier we start, the better, because all of our economic and social system is based on oil, so to change from that will take a lot of time and a lot of money and we should take this issue very seriously."[21]

In 2011 he amplified his comments, telling Australia's ABC radio that an IEA study of 800 oil fields had shown that "the decline[s] in the existing fields, are very, very deep. . . . The existing fields are declining so sharply that in order to stay where we are in terms of production levels, in the next 25 years we have to find and develop four new Saudi Arabias," and that "the age of cheap oil is over."[22]

Indeed, as demand for oil rises by an estimated 2 percent per year, if total oil production remains flat, or rises at the 0.5 percent rate the IEA predicted in 2012, prices will rise further. If oil production *declines* as the International Energy Agency and dozens of other experts now expect, the price rise will be even greater. Those price changes have a substantial effect on the global economy.

Economist James Hamilton has calculated that ten of the eleven post–World War II recessions in the United States were predicted by spikes in the price of oil.[23] The larger the oil price change, the larger the recession. In 2010, three economists at the Federal Reserve Bank of St. Louis reinforced Hamilton's point with a separate analysis that concluded that "an average sized shock to . . . oil prices increases the probability of recession in the U.S. by nearly 50 percentage points after one year and nearly 90 percentage points after two years."[24] A 2005 paper from Stanford's Energy Modeling Forum agrees: Gradual oil price rises don't predict recession, but sharp spikes, such as the one in 2008, do.[25] It's possible that we've put too much of the blame for the 2008–2009 recession on financial shenanigans, and too little on the spike of oil prices to nearly $150 per barrel that occurred in 2008.

A recession in the United States or in other developed countries such as Japan or the nations of Europe means unemployment, home foreclosures, and economic uncertainty. As it ripples out to the developing world, it means much worse: hunger, disease, death. The 2008 recession coincided with an increase in worldwide hunger of more than a 140 million people. Much of that was a consequence of rising food prices (which, as we'll see, may also be linked to oil prices), but a large fraction was the impact of stagnating or dropping wages in the developing world during the recession.

Indeed, rising oil prices mean a negative impact on the price of everything. Transportation becomes more expensive. Raw materials like iron ore and aluminum become more expensive as fuel for mining operations rises in prices. Manufactured goods get more expensive as both the raw materials they consume and the transportation of those materials and the finished goods rise in price. Food becomes more expensive as mechanized farm equipment becomes pricier to operate, and as the transportation of food from farm to table becomes more costly.

All of those price increases and economic impacts happen in a world where oil production is flat while demand rises. If oil production *drops*, the situation becomes much, much worse. As the developing world, and in particular China, grows in wealth, more diners are trying to feast on the global pie of oil. That is pressure enough. If the pie is also shrinking, price spikes will be larger, and tensions between nations vying for the same finite resources will increase.

That is not a world we want to see.

Certainty and Risk

Is peak oil a certainty? History is littered with energy predictions that have failed to come true. Some have been overly optimistic—nuclear powered cars, electricity too cheap to meter, oil at $20 per barrel in 2011. Others have been overly pessimistic—a worldwide peak of oil in the 1970s, for example. High oil prices motivate more drilling and exploration. They make resources that weren't previously economical to pump worthwhile. And they encourage research into new technologies that can lower costs and increase the amount of oil coming out of a field. It's generally a mistake to bet against human ingenuity, and throughout most of this book I'm betting heavily *on* human ingenuity. It's utterly possible that new technological breakthroughs will make it possible to find new oil fields faster than we are today, or to pump oil from places that we can't today. Twenty years from now, we might be awash in a glut of oil. Dismissing that possibility would be foolish.

The current trend is against that, though. What we're looking at now is stagnating supply, despite high prices. It's fields being depleted faster than new fields are being found. It's higher prices and lower return on energy for each additional barrel found. And so, if we were taking odds, we'd have to acknowledge that there's a significant probability that we *won't* be able to raise oil production as fast as demand, or worse, that we won't be able to maintain oil production even as high as it is today.

Certainty is hard to come by when predicting the future. The way to look at peak oil isn't in terms of what *will* happen. It's in terms of *risk*. Peak oil is a risk to our current way of life. It's a risk of recessions, of surging prices, of conflict over remaining supplies. Even a relatively small likelihood of peak oil would be enough to justify taking precautions against it. And right now, the risk of having less oil available than the world is accustomed to using doesn't look small. It looks rather high.

four peak everything?

Feeding the Planet

The notion that the prices of things other than oil could soar isn't hypothetical. It's happening as I type these words. In 2008 the world woke up to soaring food prices. For the first time since the oil crisis of the 1970s, basic food prices left their historic lows. By spring of 2008, basic food ingredients (wheat, corn, rice, milk, meat, sugar, and oil) were nearly 80 percent more expensive than in 2004. Prices dropped almost back to normal by the end of 2008, only to start rising again in 2009. By the summer of 2012, worldwide food prices were two to three times as high as they'd been in 2004.[1]

Residents of developed nations hardly noticed this in their food bills. In the United States, Europe, Australia, and Japan, raw ingredients are a small fraction of overall costs. Packaging, transportation, marketing, and convenience are all larger. In the developing world, however, the change was devastating. After forty years in decline, the fraction of people without enough to eat rose for the first time in decades, by more than 100 million people.

The rise in food prices has been attributed to everything from the shift of land to growing biofuel crops to high oil prices to bad weather. All of those played a role. But the largest ongoing cause is the imbalance between demand and supply. Over the last few years, worldwide farm production has stayed fairly level, while rising wealth in China and the rest of the developing world has sharply increased demand for food, especially for grain-intensive meat.

Even more troubling is that, in the decades ahead, we will need tremendously more food than we have available today. The Food and Agriculture Organization estimates that demand for food will rise 70 percent between today and 2050. A growing population, greater urbanization, and rising wealth in the developing world will all serve to increase demand for grains and meat. Between 2010 and 2050, grain production will need to increase by almost half, and meat production will need to more than double to meet demand.[2] If we fail to achieve that, the price shocks of 2008 will look tiny in comparison.

Finite Everything

Food isn't the only thing that got more expensive in the peak of 2008. Copper prices rose by a factor of 5.[3] Iron ore prices rose by a factor of 10.[4] Aluminum prices more than doubled. Cotton prices quadrupled. Lead prices went up by a factor of 5. Uranium prices tripled. All of these numbers are adjusted for inflation. After more than a century of everything getting cheaper, all the things I've just mentioned, from oil to food to building materials and industrial ores, are getting more expensive.

The IMF lists dozens of other commodities that have all seen their prices rise precipitously over the last decade: Lamb, ground nuts, nickel, hard logs, soft logs, olive oil, sawn wood, tin, tea, wool, zinc. From 1992 through 2003, the IMFs composite index of forty-nine world commodities averaged a price

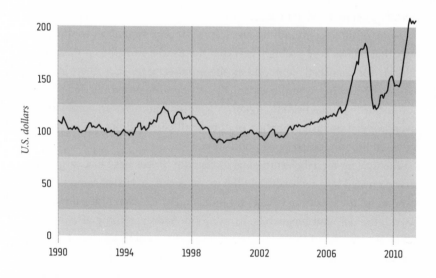

Figure 4.1. Worldwide food prices (100 = 2002–2004 average). Food prices doubled between 2002 and 2010. Source: Food and Agriculture Organization

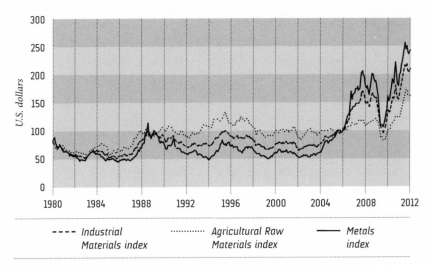

Industrial
Materials index

Agricultural Raw
Materials index

Metals
index

Figure 4.2. Prices of agriculture, industrial materials, and metals. Prices of
three broad IMF indices since 1980 show all rising significantly in 2007–2008 and
even more so in 2010–2011. Source: IMF

of 57. From the beginning of 2005 through the middle of 2011, it averaged a
price of 139.[5] The IMFs index of prices of metals, raw agricultural products,
and all industrial materials have similarly risen. If Julian Simon and Paul
Ehrlich's bet had ended in 2012, Ehrlich would have won.[6]

None of these commodities has seen a drop or stagnation of supply the
way that oil has. The problem isn't that there's less available on the market.
Indeed, for almost all commodities, the supplies on the market are at record
highs and growing by multiple percent per year. Copper production per year,
for instance, was 80 percent higher in 2010 than in 1990.[7] The problem isn't
even population, as production of almost all commodities has equaled or,
more commonly, outstripped population.

The driving force behind rising commodity prices has been surging demand created by new wealth. As the world is getting richer, as market economics lift the wealth of China and India and other parts of the developing
world, the demand for metals, wood, food, and everything else is rising.
Since the middle of the last decade, demand for commodities of all sorts
has outstripped supply. That phenomenon is just as dangerous as stagnant
or dropping supply. It drives prices up, can create shortages, and can create
conflict over resources. And as the developing world continues to grow its
wealth, billions of people there will be clamoring for—and willing to pay for—

commodities that once went primarily to the already developed countries. If demand continues to rise faster than supply, prices will rise.

Price is not the only concern. Some resources may eventually run out, or reach peaks of production similar to peak oil. Concerns have been raised about potassium (an input into synthetic fertilizer), rare earth elements such as neodymium and tantalum (used in many electronics, among other places), uranium, helium, and of course coal and natural gas. And indeed, the Earth contains finite amounts of all of these.

As just one example, consider phosphorous. Seldom thought of as a vital resource, phosphorous is critical in creating fertilizer for agriculture. Without the addition of phosphorous to soils, modern farming would produce at best half the amount of food it does today. Without added phosphorous we simply wouldn't be able to feed the world.

Yet phosphorous is finite. It's mined from phosphate rock. Between 2007 and 2008, the price of phosphate rock soared by a factor of 7, from $50/ton to $350/ton. Like oil, phosphorous is becoming harder to extract over time. The highest-quality, most phosphorous-rich phosphate rocks have been mined. Those that remain are lower quality, with less phosphorous per ton of rock. The result, according to researchers at the Global Phosphorous Research Initiative, is that we could hit peak phosphorous within the next thirty years.[8]

Similar calculations, with longer or shorter time scales, apply to almost any material resource you can name.

Disappearing Fish

Fish are an essential human food source. Worldwide, they provide 16 percent of the protein humans consume. In Africa, they provide 21 percent. In Asia, a whopping 28 percent.[9] In some individual countries, fish are even more vital. Fish provide 65 percent of the protein available in Ghana, 58 percent of the protein available in Indonesia, and 50 percent of the protein available in Bangladesh. Worldwide, a billion people rely on fish as their primary protein source.[10]

Fish are, in principle, a renewable resource. They breed to create more fish, turning nutrients in the ocean into forms that humans and other animals can readily consume.

Yet even renewable resources have their limits. When hunted too rapidly, fish populations can collapse. The number of adult breeders that remain can be too low to rebuild the population as they deal with predators, with competitor species, and with the continued pressure of human fishing. That sort of collapse has happened again and again in recent years, with disastrous impacts for both fish species and humans.

In 1971, Peru was a major source of anchovies. In 1968, a fleet of 1700 Peruvian fishing boats brought in a catch of 10.5 million tons of anchovies alone, most of them going to 150 fishmeal factories employing 25,000 local workers. By 1972, that industry was in collapse, bringing in 4.4 million tons, less than half of their previous catch.[11] In the late 1980s, the total fish catch in the Black Sea was around 800,000 tons a year. By 1991 it had plummeted to 200,000 tons a year.[12] Worldwide cod production peaked in the late 1980s at just under 14 million tons a year. Now it's below 8 million tons a year.

Total fish stocks have shrunk fast as well. In 1950, the area around Newfoundland was estimated to have 1.6 million tons of cod. Today they're nearly impossible to find, and the area has less than 100,000 tons of cod. The western Atlantic once held 50,000 tons of bluefin tuna. Now it holds less than 10,000 tons. The eastern Gulf of Mexico once held more than 100,000 tons of Red Snapper. Today less than 20,000 tons of red snapper remain.[13]

Worldwide, fisheries peaked in 1995 with a total catch around 93 million tons. The catch held steady until 2004's total catch of 92.4 million tons, then began to decline. In 2009, the catch was down to 90 million tons. We've been hovering on a plateau of fish catch for fifteen years, and may have gone past that plateau and into a zone of falling catches. The northeast Atlantic Ocean, once the second most productive area for fishing in the world, has seen its total catch drop from more than 12 million tons a year to less than 9 million. The northwest Atlantic has seen its output drop by half, from more than 4 million tons a year in 1970 to less than 2 tons a year today. The southeast Pacific has gone from 20 million tons a year to 12 million tons a year.[14]

You can see the effect of reduction of fish stocks in the increased effort needed to catch the same amount of fish. When fish are plentiful, they can be caught easily. As stocks are depleted, fishing fleets have to venture farther from home, stay out longer, and burn more fuel to catch the same amount of fish. Dozens of studies have found that the catch per unit effort (usually defined as tons of fish brought in divided by the product of fishing boat tonnage and length of trip) has steadily declined over the last century. A study of the catch per unit effort of deep trawl fishing boats in the United Kingdom, for example, found that it had dropped by a factor of 20 from 1880 to 2010. That is to say, it now takes twenty times as much effort to haul in a ton of fish as it did at the end of the nineteenth century.[15]

Today, the Food and Agriculture Organization of the UN estimates that a third of fish species have either crashed already or are overexploited and pushed to the edge. Another half of all fish species are fully exploited, with no room to grow production. If the demand for fish continues to grow at or near past rates, the FAO believes global fisheries could completely collapse by 2050.[16]

If we want to keep eating fish for the rest of this century, we need to find a better way to acquire them.

Freshwater Shortages

Beneath the American high plains of Nebraska, Kansas, northern Texas, and five other states lies the Ogallala Aquifer, a giant underground reservoir of freshwater that farms and people in the region depend on. Ogallala is full of "fossil water"—the remnants of the glaciers and ice sheets that retreated from this area more than 10,000 years ago, melting and filling underwater basins as they went. That fossil water is used to irrigate 27 percent of the farmland in the United States.

Ogallala's water level is dropping, in some places as fast as three feet per year. In two months the water we withdraw from Ogallala is enough to fill a cube a mile on a side, enough to cover every inch of the island of Manhattan in more than 200 feet of standing water.[17]

Water is abundant on our planet. Oceans cover 70 percent of the Earth's surface. Their combined volume is huge. Even freshwater is vast in quantity. It literally falls from the sky.

Yet the rate at which we consume water—particularly for agriculture—exceeds the rate at which we can capture it from rain or via sustainable withdrawals from rivers. To feed our planet, we've turned to more extreme methods, draining some rivers dry, and pumping water out of aquifers that will take thousands of years—if not longer—to refill once we're done with them.

The Indus River Valley Aquifer under India's breadbasket is being drained at a rate of twenty cubic kilometers—a cube 1.7 miles a side—every year. Water tables in Gujarat province are falling by as much as twenty feet a year.[18] The giant North China Plain Aquifer, which provides irrigation for fields that feed hundreds of millions, has been found to drop as much as ten feet in a single year. A World Bank report cautions that in some places in northern China, wells have to be drilled nearly half a mile deep to find freshwater. Hebei Province, one of five atop the aquifer, has seen more than 900 of its 1,052 lakes dry up and disappear due to dropping water tables.[19] In Mexico's agricultural state of Guanajuato, the water table is dropping by 6 feet a year. In north eastern Iran, it's dropping by as much as ten feet a year.[20]

Water is being withdrawn from rivers as well. Seasonal water levels are dropping on China's Yellow River, on the Nile in Egypt, on the Indus as far north as Pakistan, and on the Rio Grande in the United States.[21] Parts of the Colorado River are a stunning 130 feet below their historic levels.[22] The river no longer reaches the sea. Nor does the Yellow River or dozens of others around the world that have been tapped for irrigation. The rivers that flow through Central Asia have been so massively drained for agriculture that the vast Aral Sea they once fed, once the fourth-largest freshwater lake in the world, is now little more than a dry, salty lakebed, its former shore dotted with abandoned fishing villages and the bones of beached boats.[23]

Water is life. Agriculture depends upon it. Nearly 70 percent of the water humanity uses is for irrigation. Growing food for an average human diet requires an estimated 320 gallons of water a day. For an average American diet the number is closer to 900 gallons of water a day.[24] To produce that water, we're drawing down rivers, lakes, and fossil water aquifers at an unsustainable rate. On current course and speed, the Ogallala Aquifer will run dry before this century is over, and possibly much sooner. The North China Plain aquifer will run dry. The Indus River Valley aquifer will run dry. And when they do, the cost to agriculture—and thus to human life—will be enormous.

Threatened Forests

From my home in Seattle, Washington, it's less than an hour's drive to Washington's old-growth forests in the Mt. Baker—Snoqualmie National Forest. These are some of the few old-growth forests left in the United States. Colonial and American demand for fuel, for building materials, and for land on which to farm have cut down 90 percent of the forests that stood in the lower 48 states as of 1620. The same is true around the world.

New forests have been planted in many areas. Even today, after centuries of logging, chopping, and tilling, forests cover around one-quarter of the world's land surface, roughly half the area they covered in antiquity. A small fraction of that, around 20 percent, is classified as old-growth forest, meaning that it's 200 years old or older. Those old forests are concentrated in three areas: the boreal forests of northern Canada and Alaska, the related and similar forests of Siberia, and the lush tropical forest of the Amazon and its neighbors.

The UN reports that between 2000 and 2010, the world's forest cover dropped by an average of 5.2 million hectares (or 20,000 square miles) a year. That's an area almost the size of West Virginia lost each year. Across those ten years, the forest loss was 20 percent larger than the total area of the state of California.

These are the good times. In the previous decade, 1990–2000, the area of forest lost was 8.3 million hectares, or 320,000 square miles, twice the size of the state of California.[25]

The situation is especially dire in the tropics. Rich nations, most of them in temperate areas, have largely slowed or halted deforestation. Developing nations haven't. There the combination of poverty, rapidly growing populations, and in particular the need for large amounts of land for agriculture are still fueling destruction of forests. Over the last six decades, 60 percent of tropical rainforest has been destroyed.[26]

The planet's forests are, as the *Economist* magazine called them, the world's lungs. They consume carbon dioxide from the atmosphere, converting it into wood and leaf. They emit a quarter of the oxygen that feeds all animal life on Earth, including humans. They provide a safe haven for millions of species found nowhere else. The rain forests alone are estimated to contain 75 percent of the biodiversity found on land. Forests keep topsoil in place that would otherwise fly away. (Sadly, when topsoil that was once forest blows away, forests suffer even further, as subsistence farmers chop more trees down to acquire more land to make up for the drop in productivity of their current lands.) And, through a process called evapotranspiration, forests bring rain to areas downwind of them. Tropical rainforests alone produce around 20 percent of the world's oxygen and 30 percent of the world's freshwater.[27] Human activity that damages them has wide-reaching effects.

Extreme weather has also been hurting tropical forests. In 2005, the Amazon experienced its worst drought since records were kept, stretching back to at least 1902. Water levels in the Amazon River, and particularly its large tributary, the Rio Negro, dropped to their lowest recorded levels. In places where riverboats or canoes had once been the prime form of transportation, locals switched to walking and bicycling. The drought affected more than

700,000 square miles of the Amazon, an area more than two and a half times the size of Texas. And 2010 was worse. The second "once-in-a-hundred-years drought" in five years affected 1.1 million square miles, more than four times the size of Texas.

Worse yet may be in store. A majority of climate models predict increasing drought for the Amazon. Human-driven deforestation will whittle at the edges of the forest, decreasing rainfall over the forest as a whole. Drought will make trees more vulnerable. Fires will become more likely. At a certain point, the world's forests may not be circulating enough precipitation to keep the areas of the world they're in moist. If so, they'll hasten their own destruction.

A world without forests is difficult to imagine. It would be a world with less rain, with larger and more severe drought. It would be a world where agriculture was more difficult as a result of soil erosion and changes to the water cycle. It would be a world where hundreds of thousands of additional species were extinct.

Perhaps the best warning of the consequences of deforestation comes from Easter Island. When European sailors discovered the island in 1722, it was a barren place, devoid of trees, with a small population, but studded with hundreds of immense stone statues called Moai. Eight hundred eighty-seven Moai dot the island, some as large as 33 feet tall and 82 tons in weight. In a central quarry there's an unfinished behemoth 69 feet tall and weighing 270 tons. Art work on that scale clearly took substantial amounts of skilled labor to create and immense amounts of both wood and muscle to move from the quarries to the coastal areas where they were erected. That, in turn, implies a large and prosperous society that could support so much labor and expenditure of effort. Yet the Easter Islanders the first Europeans met were few, scattered, and barely able to scratch out a subsistence living on the harsh island.

Deeper investigation, using the contents of cooking pits, ancient refuse heaps, and old bones, revealed what had happened. Easter Island had once been a densely wooded place, home to a large and prosperous civilization. At the height of their prosperity, around 1200–1500 AD, the Easter Islanders used trees for fuel, to make homes, to carve dugout canoes with which to fish the waters, and to build platforms and sleds to drag their immense statues.

All that changed when the Easter Islanders, driven by the needs of a growing population, finally overharvested their trees. The native palm tree that had covered the island went extinct. Unable to create more canoes, the Easter Islanders became more dependent on food that could be grown on the island.

Without tree roots to hold the soil in place, and with less rainfall to water the ground, agriculture collapsed. Streams dried up. Fire became a luxury. The population plummeted. Strife and warfare took hold in the few remaining bands. Cannibalism emerged.

By the time Europeans reached the island in 1722, nothing remained of the once great civilization but its hundreds of immense stone statues and a few warring tribes.

Our world is an island. If we don't want that fate for ourselves or our descendants, we must take precautions.

A Very Large Footprint

Summing up all of these ways in which humans consume resources from the Earth, a number of groups have attempted to calculate a single "ecological footprint" that can be used to measure the impact of any person, country, or the human population as a whole. Simply put, how much of the planet do you consume? How much land for growing food, how much land for mining steel and copper and aluminum, how much oil, how much forest and plant territory to absorb your carbon emissions, how much freshwater, and so on.[28]

It's a tricky calculation, to say the least. Different groups have gone about estimating it different ways. Generally, they come to similar conclusions. The world has about 1.8 hectares of useful living land per person on it. Yet the average citizen of the world uses up 2.7 hectares of that land via their lifestyle. (A hectare is around 2.5 acres, so that's around 6.7 acres.) The Global Footprint Alliance sums it up as 0.6 hectares of land per person for growing crops, 0.2 hectares of land for grazing livestock, 0.3 hectares of forest land per person for wood and other resources, 0.1 hectares of fishing land, 0.1 hectares of land that has been converted from nature to homes, offices, malls, and roads, and 1.4 hectares of land needed to reabsorb the carbon dioxide and other greenhouse gasses the average person emits.[29]

At those levels of per capita consumption, the planet can't support the 7 billion people it has on it, let alone the 9 to 10 billion it will have by midcentury. It can support only about two-thirds of the current population of the planet, or around 4.7 billion people. So what becomes of the 2.3 billion people the planet can't support today? The 4 to 5 billion surplus people we'll have by midcentury?

Of course, the average resident of a rich country uses much more than the average resident of a developing country. "High-income countries" average 6.1 hectares per person in their ecological footprint. And the United States comes in at 8.0 hectares per person. If every person on the planet consumed 8.0 hectares of living land, the planet's carrying capacity would be far smaller—around 1.6 billion people. That's 5.4 billion people less than the world has on it today. It's roughly 8 billion fewer people than the planet will have on it in 2050.

To sum this up another way, the world's population right now is using up 1.5 planets' worth of natural resources. And if everyone on Earth lived like an American, we'd be using up 4.4 planets' worth of natural resources. The gap between what the planet can support and the amount we're consuming—and on path to consume—is staggering. This doesn't look like a situation that can be maintained indefinitely.

five greenhouse earth

Glacier National Park sits along the northernmost edge of Montana, pressed up against the southern borders of British Columbia and Alberta. Every year two million Americans, Canadians, and tourists from farther abroad visit the park. Soon, though, there may be no glaciers in Glacier Park. In 1850 the region that is now the park was home to 150 active glaciers. In 2004 the number was 27. In 2005 the Forest Service announced that two more ice fields had shrunk below the minimum size of twenty-five acres required to be considered a glacier. Glacier National Park is running out of glaciers.

Photos of the park show it clearly: large white expanses of ice and snow in older photos, bare rock in recent photos of the same spots. Twenty-five active glaciers remain as I write these words. By the time you read this book, the number may well be lower. By 2030, at the current rate, and perhaps much sooner, there may be no glaciers left in the park at all.[1]

Our planet is warming. The evidence is all around us. Mount Kilimanjaro, the highest peak in Africa, was covered a century ago by twenty square kilometers of glacier. Today it's covered by less than three.[2] The Arctic Sea surrounding the North Pole, as recently as 1980, was covered in September by almost 8 million square kilometers of polar ice. In September 2012, that was down to 3.4 million square kilometers, and dropping faster each year.[3] Submarine cruises under the arctic ice have found that the ice is also only half as thick as it was in the 1960s, down from around ten feet of thickness on average to around five feet thick today.[4] With dropping coverage and thinner ice, in 2008, for the first time ever, humans were able to circumnavigate the North Pole in ships.[5]

In Fairbanks, Alaska, ground that has been frozen as permafrost for more than 10,000 years is beginning to thaw, collapsing to open sinkholes and undermining the foundations of homes.[6] Similar things are happening in

Figure 5.1. Shepard Glacier in Glacier National Park. Photo on the top is 1913. Photo on the bottom is 2005. The glacier is essentially gone. Photo courtesy of USGS.

Siberia and northern Canada. The residents of the town of Newtok, Alaska, voted en mass to move to a new location rather than stay in homes that were slowly sinking into the melting land.[7]

Climate change is being felt first and hardest in the coldest parts of the world. The poles and the regions around them warm three to four times as fast as the rest of the world. They serve as canaries in the coal mine for the rest of the planet. But even in more temperate places, the impact is being felt.

In Europe, half the mountain glacier cover seen a century ago in the Alps is now gone. In Switzerland, 20 percent has disappeared in the last fifteen years.[8] In Britain, researchers looking at the flowering of plants and the migration of animals find that spring is coming eleven days earlier than it did in the middle of the twentieth century.[9] In the United States, researchers see spring plant and animal behavior creeping three days earlier each decade, around twelve days earlier since 1970.[10] Sea levels around the world have risen seven inches in the last century, and their rate of rise has doubled in the last ten years.[11]

1896

The earlier spring and opening of polar sea routes are events that would have been celebrated by the first man to predict human climate change, who saw it as a great potential benefit to mankind. That was the Swedish physicist, chemist, and eventual Nobel Prize winner Svante Arrhenius. In 1896 he predicted that human release of carbon dioxide would warm the planet, making his homeland of Sweden a gentler and more habitable place.

Arrhenius had read the work of Joseph Fourier, who had determined that atmospheres help keep planets warm. A planet with no atmosphere reflects the sun's energy back into space. A planet with an atmosphere traps some of that energy locally. Arrhenius knew that carbon dioxide, in particular, was a potent trapper of heat, as a scientist named John Tyndall had shown in 1861.[12] Molecules of carbon dioxide allow visible light to pass through them, but they absorb infrared light.

All warm objects give off infrared light. Night vision cameras work by picking up the infrared light and turning it into an image people can see. Human bodies, car exhausts, and fires glow in infrared because they're hot. Our whole planet glows infrared. As air, water, and land are warmed by the sun, they radiate some of that energy back into the world around them. Carbon dioxide, water vapor, and other substances in the atmosphere that absorb or reflect infrared light trap some of that heat near the planet, warming it. The greenhouse effect is vital to life on Earth. If there were no greenhouse gases in our atmosphere, the planet would be around 90 degrees cooler on average than it is.[13]

In the late 1800s, another Swedish scientist, Arvid Högbom, first quantified human emissions of carbon dioxide from industry, estimating that the world's factories, trains, and ships emitted around 500 million tons of it. Arrhenius reasoned that all that CO_2 should serve to capture more heat in the atmosphere, warming the planet. Over a year of arduous hand calculations, he concluded that every doubling of CO_2 levels in the atmosphere should lead to a rise in temperature of about 4 degrees Celsius (7.2 degrees Fahrenheit).

Arrhenius, a Swede, believed this would be a very good thing. Sweden is a cold place. Higher temperatures would mean a longer growing season, more energy for plants, a boon to agriculture. At late nineteenth-century rates of emissions, he calculated a doubling of carbon dioxide levels in the atmosphere would take around 3,000 years.[14] Looking forward to this time, he wrote that "our descendants, albeit after many generations, might live under a milder sky and in less barren surroundings than is our lot at present."[15]

What Arrhenius didn't expect was the incredible acceleration in carbon dioxide emissions that would occur as industry spread and intensified. The industry of Arrhenius's time released 500 million tons of carbon dioxide into the atmosphere. Today, we release more than 30 *billion* tons each year, sixty times more than at the beginning of the twentieth century. As a result, levels of CO_2 in the atmosphere have soared. Before the industrial revolution, CO_2 made up 280 parts per million in the atmosphere. In November 2011 it stood at around 390 parts per million (or ppm). And because CO_2 emissions are rising, the concentration in the atmosphere is rising faster each year. On the current course, the doubling that Arrhenius thought would occur around the year 5000 will instead be reached around 2050.

Warming, Confirmed

There are four stages of questioning climate change. The first is: "Is the planet warming?" That's followed by "Are humans causing the warming?" Then, "Does the warming really matter?" And finally, "Is there anything worth doing about it?" Let's start with the first.

There are three large and long-running sets of measurement of temperatures on land. Each is based on thousands of temperature readings from weather stations and ships, going back at least 150 years. NASA has one. The U.S. National Oceanic and Atmospheric Administration (NOAA) has one. And Britain's Met Office (the national weather service of Britain) and the University of East Anglia have one that they maintain together.

Each of those three totally independent records has found that the planet has warmed around 2.5 degrees Fahrenheit since the 1850s, and that warming has accelerated recently. Each of those records finds that about half the warming of the planet, between 1 and 1.5 degrees Fahrenheit, has happened since 1970.

Those temperature records aren't perfect, though. They contain readings from reliable weather stations and from weather stations that have been unreliable, through human or mechanical error. They contain temperature readings from stations that are near cities and may suffer from "urban heat island" effects, where cities warm more rapidly than does the countryside.

To try to pull the truth from sometimes messy data, in 2009 a team at the University of California at Berkeley embarked on a project called the Berkeley Earth Surface Temperature study, or BEST. BEST would aggregate all data from temperature studies to date and rigorously screen and filter the data to isolate urban heat islands, low-quality measurements, misbehaving stations, and other sources of error. Most of the members of the BEST team were new to climate science. The head of the team, Richard Muller, is an astrophysicist who described himself as skeptical of climate change. Muller has, in the past, criticized Al Gore's *An Inconvenient Truth* and various climate scientists for exaggerating climate data and trying to hide places where data was messy. He's described climate change science as "polluted by political and activist frenzy."[16] With a climate skeptic at the helm, the study won $150,000 in funding from the conservative Koch Foundation founded by oil billionaires David and Charles Koch.[17]

Over the course of two years, the BEST team pulled together information from more than 39,000 weather stations, comprising 1.6 *billion* total temperature readings. They used statistical methods to flag and separate heat island effects, low-quality stations, duplicate readings, and other sources of error. In March of 2011, Republicans in the House of Representatives called Muller before the Science, Space, and Technology Committee to testify about the group's findings so far.

What Muller told them in 2011 was that BEST's preliminary data showed "a warming trend . . . very similar to that found by the prior groups: a rise of about 0.7 degrees C since 1957."[18] In October of 2011, the Berkeley team released their full findings, which raised the numbers to 0.9 degrees Celsius, or 1.6 degrees Fahrenheit, since the 1950s. Their findings also confirmed that warming continued in the past decade. They write that, "Though it is sometimes argued that global warming has abated since the 1998 El Nino event . . . we find no evidence of this." Between 1998 and 2010, they found warming happening at a rate of 5.1 degrees Fahrenheit per century.[19]

In late 2011, in a piece in the *Wall Street Journal*, Muller said it plain and simply. "Global warming is real," he wrote. "When we began our study, we felt that skeptics had raised legitimate issues, and we didn't know what we'd find. Our results turned out to be close to those published by prior groups."

In other words, according to this climate skeptic, and the largest ever study of surface temperatures, the planet is warming.

We can see the temperature rise in other ways. Satellite and balloon-based measures show the planet warming at a pace of around 0.2 to 0.4 degrees Fahrenheit per decade since 1979.[20] Measurements of ocean temperatures show the world's waters warming at about half that rate.[21]*

Across the world, the twenty warmest years on record since the 1800s have all occurred since 1981. The fifteen warmest have all occurred since 1995. The ten warmest have all occurred since 2000. The single warmest year ever on record was 2010, and 2011 was the ninth warmest year on record and ranked as the warmest ever "La Nina" year.[22] In the last few years, dozens of cities in the United States have recorded their highest-ever temperatures. Low temperatures still occur, of course, but high temperatures occur more often. Across the country, in the last decade, record high temperatures occurred twice as often as record low temperatures. In the 1950s they occurred with equal frequency.

A changing climate doesn't mean that every year will be warmer than the last or that every spot on the planet will warm. There's still variability from year to year and place to place. The Berkeley study found that, of the 39,000 weather stations they took data from, one-third of them showed a cooling trend. But two-thirds showed a warming trend. Climate change is lumpy and

*Water has a higher "thermal momentum" than air. It warms more slowly, but also cools more slowly. Even if the atmosphere stopped heating up today, the oceans would continue heating for decades to come.

uneven. The temperature record, year to year, is noisy. Two steps up, one step down. Any given year or any given place may look cooler, but bit by bit, the world as a whole gets warmer.

Are Humans Responsible?

Is the warming due to human activity? Svante Arrhenius, who welcomed global warming and looked forward to its effects, would look at our current carbon dioxide levels and expect a warming world. His simple models based on CO_2 levels in the atmosphere would predict that levels similar to today's would, over time, warm the planet by 4–6 degrees Fahrenheit. Just like a greenhouse gradually warms once exposed to the sun, our planet will gradually warm to temperatures a few degrees warmer than today, even if CO_2 levels remain exactly as they are. Even if we hadn't measured temperature rises already, the basic and long-established fact that CO_2 absorbs infrared light—and thus absorbs heat radiating from the Earth and traps it in the atmosphere—would be reason to expect warming in the future.

Nor is the carbon dioxide the only greenhouse gas. Water vapor traps heat. So does methane, a molecule made of one carbon atom and four hydrogen atoms. So does nitrous oxide, a molecule made of one nitrogen atom and two oxygen atoms. And humans have raised levels of methane and nitrous oxide in the atmosphere to all-time highs as well. By raising the temperature through these means, we've also increased the amount of water vapor the atmosphere can hold, creating yet another warming force.

Could some other effect be responsible? We don't need to resort to one to explain warming, but it's good to look at other explanations. The most frequently raised one is that the sun's activity has changed, leading to an increase in the intensity of sunlight hitting the planet. And indeed, solar output rose by about 1/1000th over the last thousand years. Some of the warming up until 1960 is the result of a slightly more energetic sun. But since 1960, solar output has been *declining*, even as the planet has kept warming. Analyzing the data, more than a dozen studies conclude that changes in the sun's activity are at most a small fraction of the warming the world has seen. A study by Judith Lean and David Rind, for instance, found that, "solar forcing contributed negligible long-term warming in the past 25 years and 10 percent of the warming in the past 100 years."[23]

Volcanic activity is another topic raised as a possible explanation for apparent warming. Volcanic eruptions release sulfur-based molecules, aerosols, that linger in the upper atmosphere and reflect some of the sun's light back into space before it can warm the planet. As opposed to carbon dioxide, which can last in the atmosphere for more than a century, sulfur aerosols that reflect sunlight last for just a few years. That means that if a period has *low* volcanic activity, more of the sun's light can reach the atmosphere and warm the planet. And indeed, from about 1925 to 1960, the world had an unusually low number of volcanic eruptions. Some of the warming in that time was a result of that lower volcanic activity. But between 1960 and 2010, the period when warming has happened fastest, volcanic activity has been fairly normal. A study published in Climate Dynamics in 1999 found that low volcanic activity could account for some of the warming between 1925 and 1960, but that volcanoes "are clearly not sufficient to explain the observed 20th century warming and more specifically the warming trend which started at the beginning of the 1970s."[24]

Another criticism of carbon dioxide as the driver of climate change is that nature emits far more of it than humans do. This is absolutely true. Decaying vegetation on land and in soils emits around 440 billion tons of CO_2 each year. The oceans emit another 330 billion tons per year. Human activity produces only around 30 billion tons per year, around 4 percent of the total emissions of CO_2 on the planet. Given that, how could we blame humans for the warming?

The problem is that oceans and land vegetation only absorb so much CO_2. Before the industrial revolution, the amount that plants and oceans released into the atmosphere was roughly the same as the amount that they absorbed back from the atmosphere. The human emissions, while a small slice of the overall pie, slowly accumulate in the atmosphere. In a single year, human emissions don't raise CO_2 concentrations much. But over ten years, twenty years, thirty years, the slow buildup becomes significant. That's why CO_2 levels today are 390 parts per million, while a century ago they were around 300 parts per million. That buildup hasn't happened overnight. It's taken time.

There's one more important reason to believe that the high CO_2 levels we see today are raising temperatures. Throughout the history of the planet over the last several million years, whenever CO_2 levels have been high, temperatures have been high; whenever levels have been low, temperatures have been low. Scientists can determine this by taking samples from ice in Antarctica and Greenland and from sediments in the bottoms of lakes. Both are laid down in layers, one year at a time. Air bubbles trapped inside them can show us the level of carbon dioxide in the atmosphere when those layers were deposited and, by analyzing the ratios of other molecules present, what the temperature was.

At least four separate deep cores drilled in the ice of Antarctica and Greenland show that, for the last million years, CO_2 levels have varied from around 180 parts per million, during ice ages, to 280 parts per million, during warm periods. The different cores, drilled thousands of miles apart, show almost exactly the same changes in CO_2 and similar changes in temperatures. The swing in temperatures between those times, forced by that 100 ppm difference, was around 10 degrees Fahrenheit. Now, we're 110 parts per million higher than any point in the last million years before the industrial revolution. And we're on track to reach levels of somewhere around 1,000 ppm by the end of the century, levels that haven't been seen in *tens* of millions of years.[25]

Observant climate skeptics point out that, while carbon dioxide levels and temperatures in the past go hand in hand, the temperature tended to start rising *before* CO_2 levels did. This is also correct. The warming periods of the last million or so years have been driven primarily by changes in the Earth's orbit called Milankovitch cycles. Every 100,000 years or so, the combination of the Earth's orbit around the sun and the Earth's season-creating wobble create a period of several thousand years of peak sunlight falling on Antarctica and the Southern Hemisphere during the Southern Hemisphere Spring. That starts off a chain reaction: Glaciers melt, exposing darker land below them, which in turn captures more sunlight as heat. The warmer temperatures then trigger the release of methane (CH_4) and CO_2 from the ocean—from frozen methane under the sea floor and from organic matter that was once frozen in soil but can now decompose. That release of greenhouse gases then warms the planet further. The warming of the *Northern* Hemisphere happens not as a result of more sunlight, but because of the greenhouse gases that have been released into the atmosphere. CO_2 didn't start past warming cycles, but it accelerated them.[26]

Should that make us less concerned about the release of CO_2? Long before humans mastered fire, forest fires were triggered by lightning strikes. Yet that doesn't make us any more wary of discarding lit cigarettes or matches into dry forests. Once the fire starts, it will fuel itself by spreading to more wood. The climate system is the same. It doesn't matter what the initial source of warming is. Any way we generate more heat trapped in the atmosphere, we

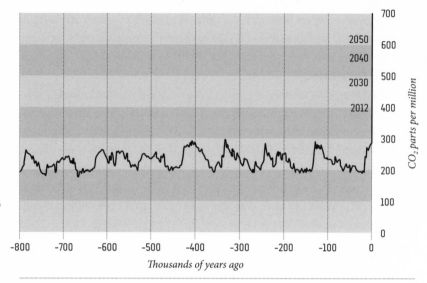

Figure 5.2. Carbon dioxide levels, history and projections. Carbon dioxide concentrations are now higher than at any point in the last million years. By 2100, they may be three times as high as any point in the last million years. Data from National Oceanic and Atmospheric Administration.

start off a cycle of planetary warming. And the amount of carbon dioxide, methane, and other greenhouse gases now in the atmosphere is trapping *more heat* than any solar cycle or past release of greenhouse gases in the last million years. Indeed, examination of bubbles trapped in sediments shows that we're most likely at the highest levels seen in the last *fifteen million years*.[27]

We can directly see the CO_2 trapping heat in the atmosphere. Carbon dioxide and methane absorb certain wavelengths of infrared light. Satellites peering down at Earth through the atmosphere show that less energy is escaping the planet in the wavelengths that carbon dioxide absorbs and in the wavelengths that methane absorbs. It's like looking through a window and finding it just a bit tinted. That tint is the result of certain wavelengths of light being absorbed. Our atmosphere is getting more tinted, in colors that are invisible to the naked eye but visible to satellite sensors. And that growing tint represents energy that isn't leaving the planet the way it once did. It represents heat that's being trapped in our atmosphere.[28]

Even if warming weren't man made, it would still be a reason for concern. Volcanic eruptions, earthquakes, and tsunamis aren't man made. That doesn't make them any less destructive. If you live near a fault line, it's best to be prepared for earthquakes, even though they're natural. And if we had evidence that the number of natural disasters were rising, we'd look for something to do about it, even if the cause of the disasters had nothing to do with humans.

That said, the warming we're seeing *is* almost entirely man made. Observation, theory, and history all agree. We see the planet is warming. We know CO_2 in the atmosphere captures enough heat to explain that. And we can see that when CO_2 levels have been high in the distant past, the planet has been much warmer than it is today.

Will Peak Oil Stop Climate Change?

I'm sometimes asked if peak oil will save the climate. Sadly, it doesn't look that way. The new sources of oil that we're pursuing are dirtier than the conventional oil pumped from the majority of wells today. Because extracting oil from tar sands or oil shales requires the input of more energy, and that energy is typically generated by burning coal and natural gas, "nonconventional" sources of oil produce more CO_2 than conventional oil. Oil from oil sands results in up to 20 percent more CO_2 emissions than conventional oil in total.[29] Carbon dioxide and other greenhouse gas emissions from oil shales are up to *75 percent* greater per barrel than for conventional oil.[30]

The other potential source of gasoline-like fossil fuels is perhaps the most abundant and the most damaging. Coal can be converted into liquid fuels that will work in conventional gasoline or diesel engines. World War II Germany, cut off from many oil sources, used the process extensively to create fuel and lubricants.[31] The process has been done at scale recently, with 30 percent of South Africa's fuel supply coming from it.[32] Like oil sands or shale oil, starting a coal-to-fuel facility is capital expensive. The larger problem is that making fuel from coal is incredibly carbon intensive. Gallon for gallon, coal-derived fuel results in twice the CO_2 emissions that oil-derived fuel does. Switching completely from oil to coal would increase world greenhouse gas emissions by more than a third, and bring the worst consequences of climate change decades closer.[33]

The result, ironically, is that the peaking of conventional oil fields may not reduce human CO_2 emissions. Instead, it may drive us to other sources that are dirtier and that drive climate change forward more quickly.

Consequences

The climate is warming. Does that matter? Warming, certainly, will have its upsides. Vast cold stretches of Canada, Siberia, Scandinavia, and Alaska will become more hospitable for human occupation, more viable for agriculture and other activities. Shipping routes between Northern Europe, Canada, Alaska, and Russia will open up in the Arctic. Oil and natural gas exploration there will turn up new oil fields, extending the lifetime of fossil fuels by perhaps a few years. Svante Arrhenius would certainly have seen these as good things for the world. Personally, I'd be delighted if Seattle were just a few degrees warmer.

Given thousands or tens of thousands of years to make the transition, a warmer planet might not be such a bad thing. More energy trapped in the biosphere means more energy for life, after all. With a warmer world, more plants could grow, providing nutrition for more animals. We could grow crops in more places. Heating bills would go down.

But the current and accelerating *rate* of change poses severe problems. Organisms adapt to the set of conditions that hold during their evolution. When those conditions change too much, too rapidly, their survival is at risk. That holds true for the wild plants and animals that make up the bulk of our biosphere. It holds true for the domesticated plants and animal species we produce in vast quantities to feed ourselves. And it holds true for humanity.

If we continue on our current rate of increased emissions each year, following the "business as usual" path, CO_2 levels in the atmosphere are expected to be around 1,000 parts per million by 2100. The last time the planet had that much CO_2 in the atmosphere, around thirty-five million years ago, temperatures in the tropics were somewhere between 9 and 18 degrees Fahrenheit warmer than they are today. Temperatures at the poles were around 30 degrees Fahrenheit warmer than today.[34]

It takes time for CO_2 to lead to a buildup of temperature, though. So projections for the temperature in 2100 are lower than this. Climate modeling isn't an exact science. The Earth's climate is a complicated system, with both positive and negative feedbacks. Some feedbacks can slow warming. For example, more CO_2 in the air can help more plants grow, which can then remove CO_2 from the atmosphere, slowing warming. In the other direction, warmer temperatures melt ice and snow, exposing darker land and water underneath that absorbs more heat, speeding up warming. Some feedbacks are even both positive and negative. Warmer air means more cloud cover. Clouds reflect sunlight back into space, slowing warming. But they also trap heat that's radiated by the ground, accelerating warming. Which of those is a bigger factor is still an open question.

An MIT study in 2009 that attempted to model all known factors found that, along the business-as-usual path, average temperatures would rise around 9 degrees Fahrenheit by 2100. But more interesting than the figure they picked is the range of confidence they had—somewhere between 6 and 13 degrees Fahrenheit by 2100.[35] They project that around a third of that temperature rise will happen by 2050.

Forecasts now show seas rising three to six feet by the end of the twenty-first century, enough to displace millions of people from coastal cities and villages. In the United States, nearly all of New Orleans, and large chunks of Miami, Tampa, Virginia Beach, and New York City are three feet above sea level or less. London, Bangkok, Tijuana, Lima, Buenos Aires, and Rio de Janeiro all have large chunks below three feet above sea level. On present course and speed, a child born this year is likely to live to see the day when some of those cities are just memories.

Here and Now: The Extremes

Yet the changes aren't just in the future. We're seeing some of them now.

As we trap more heat in the atmosphere, weather patterns become more volatile. A rise in temperature of 1 degree can translate into an increase in the most severe extremes by several degrees. And warmer air can move more moisture around more quickly. For every degree Celsius that the planet warms, the atmosphere can absorb 7 percent more moisture. That 7 percent isn't uniform, though. The greater moisture capacity of the air means that water can be sucked out of one area and deposited in another. Moisture becomes more concentrated in a few times and places, leading to droughts in one area or one season, followed by torrential rains in another. And indeed, across the United States, while precipitation is up 6 percent, droughts are also up, and the amount of rain that falls in the hardest 1 percent of rainstorms is up 20 percent.[36] There's more rain, concentrated in fewer places, with more left to dry out, and those that do get rain receive more intense rainstorms.

In August of 2003, Europe was hit with the hottest summer on record since at least 1540. More than 70,000 people died. France lost 20 percent of its wheat harvest. Fires destroyed 10 percent of the forests of Portugal. Ukraine lost a whopping 75 percent of its wheat harvest.[37]

In early 2009, the worst drought in fifty years hit northern China, wiping out nearly half of the winter wheat harvest.[38] A year later, in March of 2010, the worst drought in a century struck southwestern China, leaving twenty million people without adequate drinking water, and drying up wells in Guangxi that had provided water since 1517.

When the rains returned to China in 2010, they did so with a vengeance. In May of 2010, hard and sudden rain started the worst flooding seen there in a century. The floods killed more than 3,000 in central China, and caused the evacuation of more than 15 *million* people. More than a million homes were destroyed by the floodwaters. The total economic impact was in excess of $51 billion.[39]

In July and August of 2010, another heat wave struck Russia, setting record high temperatures of 111 degrees Fahrenheit, killing more than 55,000 people across the country, and costing Russia an estimated $15 billion.[40] In Moscow alone, 11,000 people died in July and August from effects of the heat.

While a heat wave killed tens of thousands in Russia, heavy monsoon rains inundated Pakistan, killing close to 2,000 people, and flooding an area twice the size of the state of California.[41]

In 2011, the American South went through one of the worst droughts on record, second only to the dustbowl of the 1920s. In Texas, the nine months from October 2010 through June 2011 were the driest nine-month period since record keeping began in 1895.[42] Texas lost two-thirds of its wheat crop, helping to keep wheat prices high around the world.[43] The United States as a whole had the lowest hay crop in a century, hitting cattle ranchers hard, and driving up beef prices.[44]

America is rich, though. Texans have options, ranging from pumping water from elsewhere to simply buying food grown in regions that are doing better. That isn't so elsewhere. As Texas broiled, the Horn of Africa went through its worst drought in sixty years. As crops failed, famine killed 30,000 people in Somalia in the summer of 2011 alone.[45] As always, when disaster strikes, the poor are the hardest hit.

It's impossible to attribute a single, specific extreme weather event to climate change. Even if CO_2 levels had never risen on Earth, *some* extreme weather events would occur. But while we can't say if a particular flood or hurricane or drought was a result of climate change, we can look at overall trends and see if extreme weather events are becoming more common as the planet warms.

Evidence for increasing frequency exists. The U.S. Global Change Research Program (a federal program created by President George H. W. Bush in 1989 that spans the departments of Commerce, Defense, Energy, Agriculture, and others) finds that "Many types of extreme weather events, such as heat waves and regional droughts, have become more frequent and intense during the past 40 to 50 years."[46]

Heat waves are the clearest example. Record highs are now twice as common as record lows. But *both* record highs and record lows are now more common, as a warmer, more energetic atmosphere can move masses of air around more rapidly. Looking at just one example, Stefan Rahmstorf at the Potsdam Institute for Climate Research published a study showing that, without the warming that has occurred on the planet already, the deadly 2010 Russian heat wave that killed 55,000 people would have been only one-fifth as likely to occur.[47]

Hurricanes are another source of extreme weather that may be increasing as the planet warms. Hurricanes are giant heat engines. They feed off the energy of warm water below them. The heat of the water, transferred into the air, provides the energy that powers hurricane winds. Models show that the warmer the surface of ocean waters is, the more destructive hurricanes will be.

Evidence of actual hurricanes seems to support the models. A study in August 2005 found that the total amount of energy and destructive power of hurricanes in the Atlantic had risen by about 75 percent over thirty years. Interestingly, the study found that this tracked closely to rising sea surface temperatures in the Atlantic.[48] Another study found that, while the frequency of hurricanes in general was unchanged, the frequency of Category 4 and Category 5 hurricanes, monsters with sustained wind speeds of over 130 miles per hour, had doubled over that time.[49] Both of those studies suffer from the fact that older records aren't entirely reliable. But the records that do exist support the heightened destructiveness of hurricanes over recent decades, just as models predict.

Wildfires have also markedly increased. Between 1960 and 1978, wildfires in the United States generally burned between half a million and one million acres of land a year. In 2000, five million acres burned. In 2011, nearly *nine million* acres burned.[50] Four million acres burned in Texas alone that year,[51] more than four times the historical average for the entire United States. In all, wildfires in the United States in the 1990–2009 period burned six times as much land as they did in 1970–1989, as rising temperatures and aridity have taken their toll.[52]

What will happen if the planet warms as expected on the business-as-usual path? Models show decade-long dustbowls in the United States, Africa, China, and parts of Europe, combined with torrential rains and monsoons in other areas, stronger and more frequent hurricanes in the Atlantic, and incredible periodic heat waves over much of the world.[53]

Drought in particular is incredibly worrisome. Climate models predict that, in the next thirty years, the western United States will be at risk of droughts as severe as the one that wracked Ethiopia in the 1980s. Drought severity is measured on a scale called the PDSI, the Palmer Drought Severity Index. A positive number indicates a wet period. A negative number indicates a dry period. The worst drought in the last half century was in the early 1980s in Africa's Sahel region. It scored a –3 to –4, destroyed crops in Ethiopia, and quadrupled grain prices in the area. More than a million people died of famine in 1984 alone, and eight million were affected in some way. A BBC news crew in Ethiopia, the first to report on the event, called it "a biblical famine in the 20th Century" and "the closest thing to hell on Earth."

If the planet continues to warm on its current path, then in the coming decades much of the world, including large parts of China; almost the entire Mediterranean region of southern Europe, the Middle East, and North Africa; and the American South, West, and Midwest would be at risk of decades-long droughts of severities of –6 to –10, droughts far worse and far longer than the catastrophe that hit Ethiopia in 1984.[54]

Those droughts that climate models predict would be worse than any in recorded history. No written records from the past tell us of anything this bad, ever, in thousands of years of history. No archeological evidence, ice cores, or tree rings suggest that humans have ever encountered such conditions. These would be droughts beyond anything our species has ever faced. Then again, there hasn't been this much carbon dioxide in the atmosphere for fifteen million years, far longer than our species has existed.

We've voided the warranty on our atmosphere. Its behavior may no longer conform to what we've come to expect as the norm.

Pressures on Agriculture

Changes in precipitation, rising temperature, more frequent extreme weather, and the melting of glaciers all put pressure on agriculture. No technology is more vital for our survival as a species—and for elimination of poverty and lifting human well-being—than our ability to grow food. As world population rises, and as people in developing countries start to demand higher protein and higher meat diets, food production has to increase to keep up. To do so, we need to increase the amount of food the world produces by an estimated 70 percent by 2050.[55]

How do we do that on a planet wracked by drought? A planet where heat waves, storms, or sudden floods can kill a crop across a country-sized area?

We don't need to wait for the future to see these impacts. They're happening already. Stanford University researchers who looked at farming outputs between 1980 and 2008 found that climate change reduced yields in 2008 by 3 to 4 percent relative to where they should have been. That's hardly a staggering amount, but in a world that needs to nearly double food production over the next forty years, it's movement in the wrong direction. Early experiments predicted that more carbon dioxide in the atmosphere would lead to faster crop growth. But the Stanford study, and other recent studies, dash that hope. Plants sequestered in pest-free greenhouses with added CO_2 do produce more and heavier seeds, but plants grown in more realistic situations with higher CO_2 levels and higher temperature struggle with moisture retention, with weeds (which also depend on CO_2), and with increased attraction of insect pests, wiping out any gain from higher CO_2.[56] When researchers add higher ground-level concentrations of ozone—which are also expected as the planet warms—crop yields actually decline by 20 to 30 percent.[57] And all of that is without the impact of droughts, floods, and storms.

Looking at the vast array of threats, and especially the risk of massive drought and precipitation changes, the Food and Agriculture Organization of the United Nations warned in March 2011 of "potentially catastrophic" impacts on food production in the latter half of this century, particularly in the developing world.[58] If massive droughts, super storms, floods, and other threats drive down world food production, rich countries may be able to pay more. People in poor countries won't. The gains we've made against poverty, against hunger, and in increasing human well-being across the board will be erased or reversed.

Dead Forests, Acid Seas

We share this planet with millions of other species. Climate change is, if anything, harder on the rest of the planet's inhabitants than it is on humanity. Humans have the chance to adapt, to move from place to place, to change how we grow food, to build bulwarks against rising seas. Plants and animals aren't blessed with our capabilities. The result is that, as the planet warms, many species on this planet will be wiped out.

Climate change, with its ability to create drought, puts forests at increased risk. Around half the dry weight of a tree is carbon, making living forests a powerful tool for sequestering carbon dioxide from the atmosphere. As forests dry out, they release much of that carbon dioxide, which accelerates climate change. The Amazon typically absorbs around 1.5 billion tons of carbon dioxide in a normal year. But drought kills trees. As those trees decompose, they emit some of their carbon. In the Amazon's 2005 drought, the forest, instead of capturing 1.5 billion tons, emitted an estimated 5 billion tons of carbon dioxide.[59] In its 2010 drought, the Amazon emitted 8 billion tons of CO_2, roughly the same amount that the United States emitted that year by burning fossil fuels.[60] Forests, as they suffer from climate change, accelerate their own destruction.

The oceans are even more at risk. They suffer the twin burdens of a warming planet and of the direct effect of carbon dioxide when combined with seawater. Of the CO_2 we pump into the atmosphere, roughly half is absorbed by the oceans. If that weren't the case, the planet would be warming even faster than it is today.

Carbon dioxide, dissolved in water, creates carbonic acid. You've had carbonic acid yourself. Any time you drink a carbonated soda or a glass of champagne, you're consuming a little. Carbonic acid exists in your blood, as your body works to move CO_2 out of your cells and to your lungs where it can be released. A little carbonic acid is not a problem.

A lot of carbonic acid is. Since the beginning of the industrial revolution, we've lowered the pH of the ocean's upper waters by 0.11 points. That means we've increased the amount of acid in the ocean by around 30 percent. By 2050, we will have increased the amount of acid in the oceans by 70 percent. That change in acidity poses particular problems for calcifiers, those ocean species that use dissolved calcium to make shells or other structures that they depend on. Calcifiers include bivalves (clams, oysters, mussels), crustaceans (shrimp, crabs, lobsters), gastropods (conch, abalone, sea snails) and two particularly important groups: corals and calcifying phytoplankton.

Corals and phytoplankton are so important because they're key to virtually all other sea life. Phytoplankton are at the bottom of the ocean food chain. They turn sunlight, water, and minerals into the fats, proteins, and carbohydrates that other life in the ocean depends on. Just as all the animals on land depend, ultimately, on plants to turn solar energy into nutrients that they can eat, almost all the fish in the sea depend on phytoplankton to turn solar energy into nutrients that sea life can consume.

Corals, meanwhile, are the rainforests of the sea. More than 25 percent of the biodiversity of the oceans is found around coral reefs. In tropical seas in particular, the warm temperature of the surface waters prevents minerals and other nutrients from rising up from the depths. Coral reefs host algae, which photosynthesize light, providing nutrients for the rest of the food chain. They serve as nurseries to newly hatched fish of staggering varieties, giving them someplace safe to grow before venturing into dangerous open waters. Large parts of the ocean food web depend upon them. And they are already under massive pressure. Worldwide, more than 20 percent of coral reefs are dead, and another 50 percent are in serious danger from warming seas and human activity.[61]

Ocean acidification places coral reefs under greater pressure and threatens the phytoplankton that the entire ocean's food web depends upon. Dozens of studies looking at different species of calcifiers have found thinner shells, reduced growth, smaller size, or lower survival at higher acidities that model those the oceans will reach in coming decades.[62]

A decade ago researchers believed that ocean acidification damaged all calcifiers. In the last few years new research has painted a more complex but still quite troubling picture. Some species respond poorly to even slight acidification. Others fare well until CO_2 concentrations reach their expected levels for the end of this century. Others actually calcify at a higher rate in more CO_2-infused waters, growing their shells more quickly.

For instance, in experiments where lobster, shrimp, and blue crab were exposed to more CO_2-rich water, all actually built shell material at a faster rate. On the other hand, oysters, scallops, and clams, which blue crabs eat, respond very poorly to acidification. In concentrations of CO_2 similar to those expected in 2050, soft clams build shells at half their normal rate. In concentrations of CO_2 similar to those expected in 2100, they don't calcify at all. If acidification strengthens the shell of the blue crab but wipes out its prey species, blue crab will still be in danger.[63]

Ecosystems are dynamic. If one species is removed from an ecology, others will rush in to take its place. The process makes ecosystems resilient to the loss of a single species, particularly if that species isn't at the bottom of the food chain. The ocean food chain would likely keep on functioning without some species of shellfish. Predator species that dine on them would find new sources of food through adaptation or evolution.

But every system has its tipping point. At least half the marine species studied calcify worse, grow more slowly, or are less likely to survive to adulthood in more CO_2-laden waters. Wipe out half the species in an ecosystem in a geologic blink of an eye, and that ecosystem may well collapse. Wipe out pivotal species like phytoplankton and corals, both of which respond negatively to levels of CO_2 similar to those we expect within this century, and the collapse is even more likely.

Additional evidence for the potentially cataclysmic effect of acidification on our ecosystems comes from our ancient past. Fifty-six million years ago, the planet went through an event called the Paleocene-Eocene Thermal Maximum (PETM). The PETM was a period where an estimated 2 trillion to 6.8 trillion tons of carbon entered Earth's atmosphere over a period of around 10,000 years. The carbon release warmed the planet by 9 to 16 degrees Fahrenheit (5 to 9 degrees Celsius). And it wreaked havoc on the oceans.

The calling card of the PETM can be seen in sediments from the sea floor today. Deeper than the 56-million-year mark, the old sediments are chalky white with the accumulated shells of deep calcifiers that died and drifted to the ocean bottom. Abruptly, at 55.8 million years ago, the white disappears. The sediment becomes red clay. No more shells of deep sea calcifiers were falling to the ocean bottom. Fossils of deep sea calcifiers are similarly gone from this period. The ocean changes had wiped them out.[64]

The PETM's combination of severe acidification and rising temperatures also wiped out coral reefs around the world. Sea levels were tens of meters higher at the time. The lower sea level of today means that researchers can find ancient coral reefs on dry land, and study them. What they see is that of seventeen sites around the world that had active coral reefs just before the PETM, only one (in the Pyrenees) still had a reef just after. In the other sixteen, the reefs were wiped out.[65]

The only good ocean news from the PETM is that shallow water and surface calcifying phytoplankton, as a group, survived. In response to the warming waters and markedly higher CO_2 concentrations, they went through a surge of evolution, giving birth to new species that could survive the new conditions. That's an important reminder for us that nature can adapt and evolve to cope with new conditions.[66]

Unfortunately, that rate of evolution may not be rapid enough. The carbon release during the PETM extinction that killed virtually all of Earth's coral reefs and all the deep sea calcifiers happened over 10,000 years. Yearly carbon release may have averaged somewhere between 200 million and 680 million tons of carbon. In 2011, by contrast, we released roughly 9 *billion* tons of carbon into the Earth's atmosphere in a single year. We're pumping carbon into the atmosphere and into our oceans at somewhere between ten and fifty times the rate that happened during the PETM extinction. And that rate is rising as our carbon emissions grow year over year. Even evolution may not be able to keep up with that rate of change.

The Methane Bomb

All the dangers I've just described are based on the assumptions of linear climate change. They're based on models where we keep pumping out carbon dioxide at a steadily rising rate, and that CO_2 is the major way that we have an impact on our climate. But those assumptions may not hold. They ignore the ever-growing risk of setting off chain reactions in our environment that could speed up climate change by decades, if not centuries. We're approaching a tipping point in climate.

Beneath the snows of Siberia there's a time bomb, ticking away. No one knows exactly when it will go off, but when it does, it could make our current and predicted rate of warming look gentle in comparison. That time bomb is frozen methane, buried in the tundra.

Methane is CH_4—one carbon atom and four hydrogen atoms. Pound for pound, carbon atom for carbon atom, methane is a tremendously more powerful greenhouse gas than carbon dioxide. Every ton of methane in the atmosphere traps more than 100 times the heat that a ton of carbon dioxide does. We're fortunate that methane breaks down quickly. Whereas CO_2 persists for more than a century, CH_4 lasts for an average of 8–12 years before reacting with other molecules in the atmosphere to form water and CO_2. Over a full century, a ton of methane (including the CO_2 it will degrade into) traps an estimated 25 times as much heat as a ton of carbon dioxide.

Because more than half of that heating happens in the first twenty years, methane is an explosive greenhouse gas. Release some carbon dioxide and it will have a long, steady, slowly declining impact on temperature, spread out over more than a hundred years. Release some methane and it will start to heat the planet noticeably *now*. Its biggest impact is immediate and rapid.

Trapped in the frozen tundra of Siberia, alone, is an estimated 500 billion tons of carbon in frozen plants. As the tundra warms, that plant matter decomposes. If it decomposes in the presence of oxygen, it's released as carbon dioxide. If it decomposes under the snow or in the soil, *without* oxygen, it's released as methane. We know it's decomposing now, as the planet warms. We don't know how fast it will decompose, or what fraction of it will come out as methane. But the worst case is truly staggering.

All of human activity since the start of the industrial revolution has released around 1.1 trillion tons of carbon dioxide.[67] But methane is 100 times more powerful in its immediate impact, 72 times more powerful in the first 20 years after its release, 25 times more powerful over a century. If even one-tenth of the carbon trapped in Siberian permafrost were released as methane, it would have an additional 100-year heating effect as great as all human emissions to date. And over the first 20 years it would have a heating effect more than 3 times that of all human emissions to date.[68]

If *all* of the Siberian tundra thawed, the release could have ten times the effect of all human activity to date. In the first twenty years the heating effect could be a whopping thirty times that of all human activity to date. And Siberia has only a third of the world's frozen tundra. Summing up deposits in Alaska, Canada, Siberia, and other arctic regions, researchers now estimate frozen arctic regions contain 1.5 *trillion* tons of carbon, twice as much carbon as the world's atmosphere.[69]

All the potential effects of climate change I've discussed—the droughts, the floods, the heat waves, the increased hurricane intensity, the massive impact on crops—those could arrive in a single decade rather than spread out over a century.

And the tundra is thawing. The permafrost is becoming mud. "Thaw lakes" are forming where once there was only ice. In 2006, Russian scientists reported in the journal *Nature* that they had observed plumes of methane bubbles rising up through newly thawed Siberian lakes.[70] That same year, researchers in Alaska reported that Alaskan tundra thawing was proceeding at an unprecedented rate, and accelerating, threatening to melt 10–30 percent of the Alaskan permafrost.[71]

The release from thawing permafrost is still slow. It's believed to be millions of tons a year at the moment. As a current climate input, it's a small fraction of what's happening in the world. The fear is that as humans warm the planet and cause the thaw of the arctic, the vast amount of carbon trapped there over the last ten thousand years could be released, perhaps explosively, triggering far faster climate change.

How likely is this threat? The 2007 Intergovernmental Panel on Climate Change report called it "unlikely." But since then, warming in the region has accelerated. Since 1970, the planet has warmed an average of 1 degree Fahrenheit. But warming has come most rapidly in the coldest areas, with the Arctic warming by 4–6 degrees Fahrenheit. And as the Arctic ice cap melts, the white ice that reflects heat and sunlight gives way to darker waters that absorb the sun's energy instead, accelerating local warming.[72]

If the methane trapped in the Arctic starts to vent in large quantities—hundreds of millions of tons a year, say—it may be hard to stop. The methane released will accelerate warming of the planet, particularly in the short term. That warming will lead to more permafrost thaw, leading to more carbon release, leading to more rapid warming.

That runaway warming event is what climatologists fear most. If it starts, it won't stop with permafrost. The world's forests and peat bogs contain another trillion tons of carbon that could be released as carbon dioxide.[73]

Deep under the oceans lies the biggest bomb. On the sea floor, where the temperature approaches freezing, there are slushy, semifrozen methane deposits called clathrates. They hold trillions of tons of carbon. By one estimate, clathrate deposits amount to 6.4 trillion tons of methane, several times that of tundra.[74] And they're starting to go. In 2010, a group funded by the National Science Foundation (NSF) reported finding hundreds of plumes of methane bubbles rising up from the clathrate deposits under the shallow waters of the East Siberian Arctic Shelf, with methane concentrations in the water up to 1,400 times those of the atmosphere.[75] In late 2011, a Russian survey ship found more than a hundred "fountains" of methane rising from the shallow sea floor off Siberia. Some were more than half a mile across. And the survey ship looked at less than 1 percent of the shallow waters above the East Siberian Ice Shelf. The leader of the survey, Igor Semiletov, told the UK's *Daily Mail* newspaper that "These are methane fields on a scale not seen before. . . . It's amazing. Over a wider area there should be thousands of them."[76]

Best estimates are that the total amount of methane being released from the Arctic is, as of yet, small compared to overall greenhouse gas emissions. Yet it's not clear we know exactly how much is being released. New finds such as Semiletov's are painting a picture of an Arctic that's rapidly changing, and releasing methane as it goes. At a minimum, the shrinking ice, melting tundra, and bubbling methane are a warning that we might be approaching a tipping point.

All of these stores of carbon are at risk of being released into the atmosphere—partially or completely—as the world heats up. Tundra may be currently the most vulnerable, but if they go, the risk of massive drying and burning of the world's forests and peat bogs increases, the deep oceans will warm, and methane clathrates become less stable.

Such a chain reaction is only a possibility at this time, and not a certainty. It's difficult to say exactly what level of warming would trigger it. But it's also impossible to rule out the level of warming anticipated in the next few decades. In particular, if reports that 10 to 30 percent of the tundra could thaw in the next few decades turn out to be true, that would release enough carbon to more than double the rate of global warming, putting the world at severe risk of sliding into runaway climate change.

Such events have happened before. The PETM event fifty-six million years ago warmed the planet by 9 to 16 degrees Fahrenheit. This dovetails with findings of other groups who've discovered fossils of tropical trees and bones of crocodile-like cold-blooded reptiles in Antarctica, findings that show that the continent was once tropical in climate.[77] More recently, around 11,000 years ago, the geological age called the Younger Dryas ended, giving way to our current age, the Holocene. In that transition, temperatures soared by around 18 degrees Fahrenheit over a period of several decades.[78] Around half of that temperature spike, or 9 degrees Fahrenheit, happened in a period of just 15 years.[79] Nor is the Younger Dryas unusual. Ice core data from Greenland and Antarctica show evidence of another ten rapid warming events over the last million years. In each case, a little bit of initial warming seems to have led to the release of large quantities of methane and eventually carbon dioxide, sending the world into a rapid cascade of further warming that resulted in a temperature rise of several degrees or more, all within a span of years to decades.[80]

A change as fast or even close to as fast as the end of the Younger Dryas—9 degrees Fahrenheit in fifteen years—would be disastrous. Crops would fail around the world. Extreme weather events would dwarf the worst we've seen thus far. Corals, which are extremely sensitive to rates of temperature change, would die off in large numbers. Oceans would acidify at a dramatic rate. Perversely, northern Europe could find itself suddenly far colder in such a transition, as ocean currents that pull warm water from the tropics up to Europe faltered in response to a flood of freshwater from melting glaciers and ice caps.

This would be a nightmare world. Hurricanes and floods drowning cities and countrysides. Massive droughts killing off harvests. Sea levels rising at unprecedented rates, inundating coastal areas and displacing millions. Heat waves igniting wildfires larger than any we've seen. Plummeting food supplies sending the world plunging into hunger. Famine and disease killing hundreds of millions, if not billions. Superpowers warring over the food supplies and productive agricultural lands that remain. Massive extinctions of sea life, plants, and animals that aren't able to adapt to new temperatures and ocean acidities quickly enough.

We don't know how to handicap the odds of an event like the end of the Younger Dryas happening again. We know global climate is capable of strong and rapid change. We know that we're sitting on a time bomb made of enough frozen, buried, or trapped carbon to dramatically accelerate global warming. We know that every bit of warming increases the odds of release of some of that carbon, and that every bit of additional carbon released increases the odds of the rest of it going up. We know that, on our current course and speed, eventually we will set off those climate feedback loops. We know that if the resulting runaway climate change starts, stopping it will be nearly impossible. The feedback loops in the system will be working against us as high temperatures put ever more carbon at risk of release into the atmosphere.

Critics point to the complexity of climate models and future predictions as a reason not to worry about climate change. And climate models are indeed complex. Predicting the future is difficult, and it's not exact. Even if we could know exactly how much CO_2 will have been released by a given date, we still couldn't say exactly what the temperature that day would be, or even what the average temperature that year could be. That's why it's important to look at the range of possibilities. There's always a chance that we'll come in at the bottom end of the range. But there's also a chance that we'll come in at the upper end of the range. The bottom end is bad enough. The upper end is far worse.

And past climate projections, in general, have *underestimated* future changes. The IPCC—the Intergovernmental Panel on Climate Change, which is the world's main body for assessing climate changes—has made mistakes in both directions. But the more serious ones have been in understating future changes. Carbon dioxide emissions in 2010 and 2011 were higher than the IPCC's *worst case* estimates in 2007. The IPCC predicted that CO_2 concentrations in the atmosphere would rise by at most 2 ppm per year. Now they're rising at 2.5 ppm per year. The IPCC failed to anticipate the rate at which the Arctic ice cap is melting. It didn't anticipate melting that we see now in the Greenland ice cap. It didn't anticipate the melting we see now in the tundra of Alaska, Canada, and Siberia. It didn't take the emissions of carbon dioxide and methane from that melting tundra into account. Its models didn't anticipate the increase in wildfires we've seen, or take into account the CO_2 those fires release. It didn't anticipate the drying out of the Amazon, or the CO_2 resulting from it. It didn't anticipate the bubbles of methane rising from clathrate deposits on the warming sea floor, or the potentially vast impact of clathrate release.[81]

The IPCC has predicted simple, linear warming, not the positive feedback loops that we're looking at now. Not the tipping points that we may be approaching.

In short, as a planet, we're sitting on a keg of gunpowder, and we're enjoying a smoke. Maybe we'll finish this cigarette, put it out, and nothing will happen. People get away with foolish risks all the time. Or perhaps a bit of falling ash will ignite the explosive mass below us. We don't even know how to assess those odds properly. Maybe the odds of runaway global warming in this century are 30 percent. Some scientists would say they're far higher and that an explosive global climate catastrophe is virtually assured to happen this century if we continue on our current course. Perhaps the odds are only 10 percent—closer to the range the IPCC's 2007 assessment places them. Maybe they're just a tiny 1 percent.

No matter which of those numbers you choose, the risk is too high. When the lives of billions of humans and the survival of millions of species are at stake, when the collapse of our entire civilization is not an implausible outcome, then it's worth driving the odds as close to zero as possible. Until we step well away from the explosives and put out our cigarette, we—the whole human race—won't be truly out of the danger zone.

There's a mechanism we've invented to deal with risks that are low probability but high cost. It's called insurance. More than 6 percent of the world's GDP gets spent on insurance today, across health insurance, home insurance, car insurance, life insurance, and all the other types. We've learned through history that guarding against catastrophes and wild cards is worth doing. It's time to invest in some insurance against the worst possibilities of climate change.

Safe Levels

How much carbon dioxide, methane, and other greenhouse gasses can we safely pump into the atmosphere? No one knows for sure. The system is not one we can predict the behavior of with complete accuracy. It's a matter of relative risk.

Historically, CO_2 levels have stayed under 280 ppm. Today we're at 390. Climate models suggest that at a level of 450 ppm, there's 50 percent chance of keeping average worldwide temperature increases under 2 degrees Celsius, or 3.8 degrees Fahrenheit this century. Because the oceans warm more slowly, and the poles warm more quickly, that would translate into a 7 to 8 degree Fahrenheit increase this century in inland areas like the U.S. Midwest, and near-Arctic areas such as Alaska, parts of Canada, and Siberia. So 450 ppm is now the mainstream target for stabilizing the climate. To get there, we would need to cut CO_2 emissions by a factor of 4 to 5 by 2050.

Unfortunately, 450 ppm may not be such a safe goal. With tundra already changing from permafrost to mud, and with methane bubbles starting to rise from clathrate deposits under the sea floor, it's not clear that we can tolerate an 8 degree temperature rise in the Arctic. Increasingly, climatologists have been calling for reducing CO_2 levels down to 350 ppm. That is still higher than the 280 ppm that we've lived with as the maximum level for the last million years. But it's close enough that climatologists think the risk of runaway warming would be low. To get to 350 ppm, we need to cut CO_2 emissions by a factor of 4 to 5 by *2030*, and then drive net CO_2 emissions close to zero by 2050.

That is a very tall order. Between today and 2050, as billions of people rise out of poverty in China, India, and the rest of the developing world, the demand for cars, manufactured goods, larger homes, televisions, computers, and energy of all sorts is going to rise. We aren't going to shut down our factories, stop driving cars, or turn out the lights. Not willingly, at any rate. Most likely, we're going to be using *more* energy decades from now than we do now. Along those lines, the International Energy Agency expects world-wide energy demand to double by 2050. Meeting that demand is already a substantial challenge. Doing it while dramatically reducing our emissions of carbon dioxide and other greenhouse gasses is even more daunting.

This may well be the largest challenge humanity has ever faced.

six end of the party?

From Such Great Heights

We live in the most perilous of times. We have unprecedented wealth, prosperity, and global well-being. Yet we have made unprecedented withdrawals from our planet to get there. Our civilization is under pressure from the threat of running out of easy oil, of running out of the metals and minerals that go into the things we build, of running short of food in the face of a growing population, of running short of water to grow that food. And at the same time our hunt for more resources is placing our forests under threat, is killing off the fish we feed on, and is trapping an ever greater amount of heat in our atmosphere.

We're on a precipice. We've ascended to these great heights, but one false step, one unexpected burst of wind could send us tumbling down. Worse, it now appears that just continuing to climb in the way we have will eventually take us over the edge and into a long, long fall.

We wouldn't be the first culture to fail. The Roman Empire, overstretched, focused on the wrong priorities, with an economy that encouraged plunder rather than creation, declined for two centuries before finally collapsing under the combined weight of the pressures upon it. The Maya went from the height of their wealth to near-complete ruin in a matter of years. The Easter Islanders were at their very peak, building their most impressive statues yet, when they finally collapsed.

Those past civilizational crashes killed millions. This time, if our civilization falls, the death toll will be in the billions. And unlike the fall of Rome or collapse of the Maya, there won't be other pockets of civilization on the planet, continuing progress. In this interconnected age, our eggs are truly all in one basket. Our wealth has reached heights never seen before. Our civilization and its capabilities are unprecedented in their global scope. And at the same time our problems are unprecedented in their size, their impact on the planet as a whole, and the speed at which they're rushing toward us.

The End of Growth?

So is the party over? Must our ascent stop here? Must we, indeed, back away from this precipice and descend our mountain of prosperity to some lower, safer point, where we can sustainably linger?

That is the argument one hears increasingly from smart, well respected, and influential environmentalists. Bill McKibben, author of half a dozen environmental books and a leading activist for a low-carbon world, calls economic growth "the one big habit we finally must break."[1] McKibben refers frequently to the Club of Rome's 1972 book *The Limits to Growth*, the best-selling environmental book of all time, which argued that we cannot continue the rate at which we consume resources on this planet.

Paul Gilding, former head of Greenpeace International, titled his most recent book *The Great Disruption*. He writes, "The earth is full. In fact our human society and economy is now so large that we have passed the limits of our planet's capacity to support us and it is overflowing. Our current model of economic growth is driving this system, the one we rely upon for our present and future prosperity, over the cliff."[2]

Richard Heinberg of the Post-Carbon Institute, author of *Peak Everything*, named his latest book *The End of Growth*. He opens his book with his thesis: "Economic growth as we have known it is over and done with. The 'growth' that we are talking about consists of the overall size of the economy and of the quantities of energy and material goods flowing through it. . . . The general trend-line of the economy (measured in terms of production and consumption of real goods) will be level or downward rather than upward from now on."[3]

In the 1970s, Paul Ehrlich and others introduced the concept of IPAT, or $I = P \times A \times T$. The equation stands for Impact (on the environment) equals Population times Affluence times Technology. As population grows, the world has more people consuming resources. As their affluence grows, the resources used by each person increase, clearly a multiplier. And as technology develops, it enables each person to consume more. If this equation holds for our current world, it bodes ill for us. We are already at an ecological footprint (our impact) of 1.5 planet Earths. Yet our population, already at an all-time high, is set to rise by at least another 2 billion people in the next few decades. The average affluence of people around the world is at an all-time high, and looks set to soar as billions in China, India, and the rest of the developing world surge toward Western levels of prosperity. Our technology is more powerful than ever, and if anything, appears to be advancing more quickly than ever. All of these, when applied to Ehrlich's IPAT equation, suggest that our impact on the planet will keep rising, quite possibly faster than ever before, that our ecological footprint will keep rising at the same pace, until we find ways to lower the Population, Affluence, and Technology.

To put it another way, we've already exceeded Earth's carrying capacity by 50 percent. If Ehrlich's IPAT equation is correct, then the changes in population, affluence, and technology that appear to be on their way will propel us to a point where we're exceeding the carrying capacity of the Earth by 100 percent, 200 percent, 300 percent, or more.

We must hope that Bill McKibben, Paul Gilding, Richard Heinberg, and Paul Ehrlich's IPAT equation are *not* right, because if they are, the world is in for a dark and bleak era of poverty, strife, and destruction.

Indeed, the challenge before us isn't just one of halting growth—it's one of reducing the harm that we're doing. It's not enough to freeze the rate at which we're pumping CO_2 into the atmosphere. We need to reduce it by a factor of 4 or 5. It's not enough to freeze the rate at which we're withdrawing water from rivers and fossil water aquifers. We need to cut freshwater withdrawals in half. It's not enough to freeze the rate at which we're hunting fish to extinction. We need to turn that around.

Voluntary Measures

Can living more simply get us there? It can help, but it's unlikely to be more than a small part of the pie. Eating less red meat can reduce the amount of land and water needed to provide your food by half. Biking to work, car-pooling, or taking public transportation can reduce your carbon emissions from transportation. Living in a smaller home, with better insulation, with a thermostat that's set warmer in the summer and cooler in the winter has an even bigger impact on your carbon emissions, as the average American uses more energy on heating and cooling their home than on driving their car, much of it produced by coal plants.

If you cut the size of your home in half, drove your car half as much, lowered the thermostat 2 degrees in winter and raised it 2 degrees in summer, and ate a vegetarian or mostly vegetarian diet, you might cut your energy use, water use, land use, and carbon emissions in half. That's an excellent step. It's also not enough. You'd still need to cut your emissions by another factor of 2 to 3 in order to reach the levels that climate scientists think are safe.

And how many Americans or residents of any developed country are willing to take those steps? Three percent of Americans eat a vegetarian diet, a number virtually unchanged in the last thirty years. Meat consumption per capita has risen by a quarter since the 1960s.[4] The fraction of Americans who drive a single-occupancy vehicle hasn't dropped and may be rising.[5] The average weight of cars on the road has increased since the late 1980s by 500 pounds, and the average weight of "light trucks" such as SUVs has increased by 1,000 pounds.[6] Meanwhile, light trucks have gone from being 15 percent of all autos sold in the 1960s to being more than half in 2010.[7] The average home size has more than doubled since 1950, while the number of people living in the average home has dropped by a quarter. Americans have almost three times the living space per person they did in 1950.[8]

None of those things are inherently bad. They reflect deep, built-in human aspirations. Almost everywhere around the world, at almost every point in human history, as people have been able to afford it, they've sought larger homes, more flexibility and freedom in the ability to move from place to place, richer diets, and more comfort and convenience in all ways. These urges seem to be hardwired into us. If we're going to reduce our dangerous impact on the planet, the large bulk of that reduction is going to come through other means.

The Rising Poor

Meanwhile, six billion people in this world live in the developing world. Those people are growing richer, year by year. Their incomes, on average, are slowly closing the gap with those of people in North America, Europe, Australia, and Japan. They're hungry for more energy, more and richer food, larger homes, more manufactured goods, and better transportation.

What would an end to growth look like to them?

Paul Gilding writes that the end of growth "becomes a much larger problem when we consider that billions of people are living desperate lives in appalling poverty and need their personal 'economy' to rapidly grow to alleviate their suffering. But there is no room left."[9]

Growth is an abstract term. *Economy* is another. But these words mean something. For someone in the developing world, growth means an increased ability to buy food for one's family. It means being able to afford a better roof over one's head, better clothing and education for one's children, more ability to get from one place to another, more access to medicines when a loved one is sick, a larger buffer to get through hard times, more of the basic conveniences like refrigeration, indoor plumbing and sanitation that the rich world has known, access to heating from any source beyond a wood or peat fire, a shot at clean water that you don't need to walk a mile to reach.

We may think in the West that an end to growth means trading in SUVs for hybrids, taking the bus or train or bicycle to work from time to time, or perhaps eating less resource-intensive meat. But it's far more serious. The areas that are driving overall world growth of consumption are China, India, and the rest of Asia. The people who will suffer most in an end-to-growth scenario, let alone a shrinking-the-pie scenario, aren't the ones in already-rich countries. It will be the global poor, who've made such tremendous progress in lifting themselves up in the last few decades, who will find their path to comfort and the meeting of basic needs blocked. On a humanitarian basis alone, we have to hope that growth can continue and do our utmost to find a way make it continue, while simultaneously dropping our depletion of the world by a tremendous degree.

Even if we wanted to block the growth of affluence in the developing world, could we? There are an estimated 800 million automobiles in operation around the world today. As more Chinese and Indians enter the global middle class, that number could easily climb to 2 billion. That rise alone poses a risk to both limited oil supplies and to the global climate. The risk from new coal-burning power plants, which emit a third more CO_2 per unit of energy than gasoline engines, and which are being built in staggering numbers in China, is even greater.

But how do you tell a Chinese engineer that she can't buy an automobile? How do you tell an Indian computer programmer that he can't use so much electricity to heat or cool his home? The human drive for added comfort and convenience, added living space, richer diets, greater mobility, and greater security is fundamental. Hundreds of millions or billions of people will want to buy a first car or move into a larger home in the coming decades. How could we possibly stop them?

And if we somehow could, would it be just? Our wealth in the developed world was created in part by burning tremendous amounts of coal and oil. Can we really turn to up-and-coming countries, still quite poor on a per-person basis, and say "Sorry, there's no more room. You have to stay poor. You can't get the riches we have." Can we? When those riches are intimately tied to life expectancy, to quality of life, to medical care, to the prosperity needed to buffer against future climate changes that have been caused primarily by emissions from factories in Europe and the United States?

Zero Sum World

This brings us to the third problem, that of the dynamics of a non-growth, zero-sum world. Richard Heinberg highlights this in the beginning of *The End of Growth*. Some businesses, regions, and nations may keep on growing, he says. "In the final analysis, however, this growth will have been achieved at the expense of other regions, nations, or businesses. From now on, only *relative growth* is possible: the global economy is playing a zero-sum game, with an ever-shrinking pot to be divided among the winners."[10]

In a zero-sum game, one player's gain comes from another player's loss. Politicians, political analysts, and the press often mistake the interplay between nations, businesses, and individuals as zero-sum, but thus far they've been wrong. In general the twentieth century was one where *almost everyone got richer and better off.* They did so through far more cooperation than confrontation. Even competition—which we engage in vigorously—has mostly been about jockeying for relative advantage, when in fact both parties are climbing in absolute wealth.

Consider the United States and China. Current geopolitical doctrine is that China is the United States' most significant rival for dominance of the world in the twenty-first century. Yet China and the United States are trading partners. In 2010, $457 billion flowed between them in the trade of raw materials and goods.[11] If we could easily measure the flow of ideas and knowledge, we'd find that it was far larger. The result enriches both countries. The United States gets cheaper goods, and China gets an influx of wealth from its far wealthier partner, which leads to more jobs, growing prosperity, better health, and so on. The United States and China cooperate far more than they compete.

On the planet as a whole, a rising tide has lifted most boats. Life expectancy has grown for the countries that hold the vast majority of the world's people. The fraction of the world living in poverty has plummeted. All of this has happened because of the non-zero-sum dynamics of the global economy. One person or nation's gain has often been another person or nation's gain as well.

We can see this in the way that nations relate to each other. Worldwide military spending was an enormous $1.5 trillion in 2008.[12] But worldwide international trade was $16 *trillion*, ten times as much, in that same year.[13] And trade, inherently, happens because both parties think they'll be better off as a result. It's profoundly positive-sum, an act of win-win cooperation where the total pie is expected to grow.

A zero-sum world would be different. If there's no way to increase wealth without taking it from another, the world becomes a much darker, more violent place. Interactions become win-lose. The motivations for trade and cooperation drop. The motivations for warfare rise. If there's no way for you and your trading partner to both profit from a trade, perhaps you should just take what you want from the partner instead.

The Pentagon's 2010 Quadrennial Defense Review notes that "Climate change and energy are two key issues that will play a significant role in shaping the future security environment."[14] Oil was certainly a major factor in the first Gulf War and possibly the second, which between them accounted for the deaths of at least 100,000 Iraqis, most of them civilians. The 2007–2010 genocide in Darfur, which resulted in the deaths of an estimated 300,000 people, was brought on, in part, by drought that ruined the grazing lands of nomadic tribes, bringing them into conflict over shrinking resources with farmers.[15]

There are plenty of examples of the link between scarcity and warfare in the past. In 2007 a group of Chinese researchers studied the link between ancient climate change, crop yields, and warfare in China. They found that shrinking crop output in times of climate change was an excellent predictor of warfare there over the last 1,000 years. Almost all peaks of warfare intensity and revolution occurred during periods of drought and shrinking agricultural production.[16]

And resource scarcity is driving current tensions. Three of the world's nuclear powers, India, Pakistan, and China, share a common corner of the world. Their borders meet at the edge of Kashmir. And they all depend on water from the area's rivers for both electricity and agriculture. For India and Pakistan the need is especially pronounced. The average Indian has access to only a quarter as much freshwater as the average person around the world. The average Pakistani has access to only *one-eighth* the global average. In those straits, every bit of available water is precious and worth fighting for.

India's half-complete Baglihar Dam sits on the Indus River, upstream from regions in Pakistan that depend on water from the river for irrigation. The fear that India could shut off the flow has so incensed Pakistanis that an editorial in a Pakistani newspaper in April 2011 warned that, "Pakistan should convey to India that a war is possible on the issue of water and this time war will be a *nuclear* one."[17]

Meanwhile, Indian politicians and newspapers have angrily claimed that China, which has 20 percent of the world's people, but only 8 percent of the world's water, is planning to redirect the Tsangpo River, which currently flows into India, to use in irrigating Chinese fields. All of that is against a backdrop of increasing water demand in all three countries, from growing populations, more intensive agriculture, and increasing industrialization. The CIA warns that if another war is fought in South Asia, it may very well be over water.

The conclusion here is simple. When resources become scarce, when growing wealth in other ways becomes impossible, conflict rises. People and nations become more likely to reach out and try to take the resources they need from others when there's no other way to grow their own wealth. And in our modern world with our incredibly powerful weapons of mass destruction, that could have staggering consequences.

In sum, then, we can't separate growth from the reduction of poverty and all that entails. Nor can we separate the prospect of growth from large scale peace and prosperity. If growth is over, whether the future is one of decline or just stagnation, billions will suffer. We must hope that growth—sustainable growth—can continue.

Crisis = Danger + Opportunity

If all of these risks have scared you, good. I'm an optimist, and this, as you'll see, is a fundamentally optimistic book. Yet, as I look at the wide range of risks to our continued and growing well-being, I can't help but feel some fear as well. The problems we're facing are quite possibly the largest humanity has ever faced. Addressing them will require ingenuity, hard work, mobilization on a vast scale, and probably some degree of luck. These are tremendous challenges for us to rise up to. Optimism doesn't mean complacency.

The Chinese character for *crisis* is the fusion of the characters for *danger* and *opportunity*. I've written in the last few chapters about the dangers, but there are also opportunities. The steps we need to take to address the dangers are also the steps that can propel us to levels of wealth, comfort, and health never before seen.

There are two huge future opportunities in front of us.

Abundant Natural Resources

The first is to switch from the small pools of diminishing resources we've based the last century of growth on to dramatically larger, longer-lasting, and more evenly distributed resources. The world's energy supplies are a prime example of this. The sun strikes our planet each year with 10,000 times as much energy as humanity currently uses from all sources combined. Some of that energy heats up air, creating wind we can tap into. Some of it evaporates water, which comes down as rainfall that powers rivers that can provide useful energy. And the lion's share of it strikes us as direct sunlight, which we can capture as electricity and as fuels to power our vehicles. As incredible as it seems, the annual inflow of energy from the sun to Earth is larger than *all* known reserves of coal, oil, and natural gas.

Water is no less scarce. Less than half of 1 percent of the world's water is liquid freshwater. Another 2 percent is locked up in ice in the polar caps and the world's glaciers. The vast majority of the world's water—more than 97 percent of it—is in our oceans. If we can learn to desalinate ocean water with less energy, it can provide more than enough to meet all of our water needs, with minimal impact on the planet's water cycle.

The sunlight that strikes today's farmland could grow ten times as much food if we were clever enough to capture it. The Earth's crust contains every mineral resource our society consumes in quantities that could last us tens of thousands of years.

The natural resources of this planet are vast. What we lack is the skill to efficiently and sustainably tap into them.

Innovation: The Infinite Resource

The other key opportunity for us is to build that skill. Throughout history, the main driver of human affluence has been the creation of new ideas, new inventions, new scientific discoveries, new technologies, and new ways of organizing ourselves to make use of the abundance around us.

All of that is human knowledge. From how to grow more food to how to cure disease, from how to build new materials, to how to make machines that can move us from place to place, new knowledge has made the biggest changes in our lives. The creation of new and useful knowledge is innovation. It's a uniquely human capability. It's one that's driven history, and it's one that has the potential to overcome our current challenges and usher in new levels of prosperity.

Knowledge—the output of human innovation—is unique among all other resources. It's not a physical resource. It's an *information* resource. Where all physical resources are depleted by use, and are divided by sharing, knowledge is different. A wheel may break or wear out, but the *idea* of the wheel will keep on working. A wheel can only be used in one place and one time, but the *design* for a wheel can be shared with an infinite number of people, all of whom can benefit from it. Ideas aren't zero-sum. That means the world isn't zero-sum. One person or nation's gain doesn't have to be another's loss. By creating new ideas, we can enrich all of us on the planet, while impoverishing none. Knowledge plays by different rules than physical resources, rules that make it inherently abundant.

And so it is that our stockpile of knowledge is the one natural resource that has *grown* over time rather than depleting. We may have drained freshwater aquifers or burned the contents of oil fields, but our store of ideas has, through all that time, grown. Knowledge accumulates.

And knowledge increases our wealth. Innovation increases our wealth. Wealth is not inherently tied to physical resources. It's not inherently tied to the destruction or exhaustion of parts of the planet we care about. We can grow wealth while *reducing* our negative impacts on the planet.

Throughout the rest of this book I'll show how, through innovating, we've substituted new, more abundant resources for older, scarcer ones. We've reduced the amount of any given resource we need to use to accomplish a task, whether it be land, water, energy, or raw materials. We've learned to transmute substances that were once considered waste into new and useful resources. And we've multiplied our ability to access the incredibly vast resources the planet contains, with less waste, and less damage.

Optimism Isn't Complacency

But innovation isn't a panacea. It isn't guaranteed to come at the rates we need, in the directions we want, or in the areas where we need it most. Whether it does or not depends in large part on the choices we make as a society.

If we rise to the challenge, invest in innovation, embrace the innovations that we produce, and use a light but steady hand to steer the direction of our economy through our laws, we have every chance of solving the problems that face us, and coming out on the other side richer, with less poverty, longer lives, access to more natural resources than ever before, and a business model for our planet that can grow our wealth and prosperity as far into the future as the eye can see.

If we *don't* tap into and steer innovation, we'll find our hand forced. Depleting natural resources—if we don't invest in innovation to multiply them—will eventually shrink the pie, until we have no choice but to live more humbly, until we see poverty rise and our wealth and freedoms shrink. That's not the path we want to go down.

We find ourselves in a race. On one side is the depletion of resources that

we need. On the other side is our rate of innovation. If depletion wins, we all suffer. If innovation wins, we can both solve the problems depletion has brought and grow the size of the global pie, increasing the wealth of everyone on the planet. Which will win? Largely that depends on the actions we take and the policies we employ. The future hasn't been written yet.

I'm an optimist. I believe we'll prevail. I believe we'll surmount the problems that face us. I believe we're smart enough as a society to make the choices that make us richer in the long run rather than poorer. But that won't happen automatically. It's up to us to ensure that the right choices get made—smart choices that increase our odds of long term-prosperity by accelerating and steering innovation in the directions we need it.

In Part III of this book, I'll walk us through history and show how we've overcome apparently insurmountable problems in the past through a combination of innovation, new ways of working together, and collective action to tackle the biggest threats. Each chapter will show us a different way that knowledge has worked to grow wealth, and how it can do so within the limits of a finite planet—by transforming matter into more useful forms, by finding substitutes for resources that became scarce, by reducing the amount of any resource we need to use to accomplish a task, by recycling apparent waste back into valuable resources, and by multiplying the resources we can safely and cleanly tap into.

In Part IV of the book, I'll walk us through the changes we need to make to give ourselves the best odds of success. How do we tap into more brain power to produce more innovations in energy, food, water, and materials? How can we improve on the market system that's brought us this far so that it creates incentives to take care of our common resources—such as our oceans and our climate—rather than depleting them? What are the technologies that could aid us that we're currently rejecting out of ill-grounded fears? And finally, if we do make the right choices, what are the true limits of life, wealth, and population on this planet?

Ultimately the thesis of this book is that innovation *can* overcome all the challenges that face us and bring us enormously greater wealth, but only if we make the right choices to embrace and encourage it.

Crisis means both danger and opportunity. Turn the page into Part III and I'll show you how we've surmounted the crises of the past, and come out richer in the process. Keep reading into Part IV, and I'll show the choices we need to make to do so again.

part three
the power of ideas

seven the first energy technology

Doom Avoided

"The battle to feed humanity is over. In the 1970s the world will undergo famines—hundreds of millions of people are going to starve to death in spite of any crash programs embarked upon now. At this late date, nothing can prevent a substantial increase in the world death rate."[1]

With those words, biologist Paul Ehrlich opened his 1968 best seller *The Population Bomb*. Alarmed by the incredible growth of human population in the twentieth century, Ehrlich predicted that food supplies could not keep up.

Others did as well. A month before *The Population Bomb* came out, the even more alarming *Famine—1975!* by agronomist William Paddock and diplomat Paul Paddock hit the shelves. Like *The Population Bomb*, the Paddocks' *Famine—1975!* forecast widespread starvation and mass death as humanity found itself unable to grow enough food to keep up with a surging population. And like *The Population Bomb*, *Famine—1975!* became a best seller.

Four years later, the Club of Rome published *The Limits to Growth* which even more broadly forecast that a massively expanding population was on the brink of exceeding the amount of food that could be grown, the amount of oil that could be extracted, the amount of metals that could be mined, the amount of wood that could be harvested from forests, and the amount of pollution that the environment could absorb. The computer models the book was based on forecast widespread collapse—fueled by surging population, overconsumption, and over-pollution—early in the twenty first century.

The authors of these books had reasons to be concerned. In 1800 there were 1 billion people on Earth. In 1900, that number had expanded to 1.6 billion. By 1965, there were 3.3 billion people on the planet. Population was rising, and the rise was accelerating.[2]

In 1965, agriculture already covered one-third of the Earth's land surface. Much of the rest was covered with cities or precious and vital forests, or it was desert, mountain, marsh, or otherwise not useful for agriculture. There was very little land left to expand into. In comparison, population was set to soar over the century by 300 percent. In the absence of rapid and strict population control, humanity was poised to far outstrip its ability to generate its most essential resource, food. The logic was difficult to argue with.

It was also wrong. The famines that Ehrlich and the Paddocks projected didn't occur. The massive collapse of the ecology and human industrial civilization that *The Limits to Growth* predicted isn't on schedule. In the 1970s, the fraction of the world suffering malnutrition and starvation dropped.[3] The number of calories in the world food supply rose faster than the population did. The world didn't run out of oil, or steel, or other essential resources. Industrial society didn't collapse.

Perhaps the best known of all "limits to growth" predictions are those of Thomas Malthus. In his 1798 book, *An Essay on the Principles of Population*, he reasoned that populations grow exponentially, increasing by a certain percentage each year, while food production grows only arithmetically, growing by a fixed amount. Each year, the population would grow by a larger absolute number than the year before, while the food supply would increase by a fixed and ever-more-insufficient amount. Thus, he reasoned, population growth would outstrip our ability to grow food. Massive famines and death would result in the early 1800s.

Malthus proved to be wrong. Quite wrong, in fact. Since the publication of his book, worldwide life expectancy has gone from just over thirty years to today's sixty-nine years. Life expectancy in England, where he wrote, is approaching eighty years. Food production hasn't grown arithmetically after all—it's grown exponentially, staying consistently ahead of population growth, which has in turn slowed down.

I highlight these past incorrect predictions of doom not because I want to instill any complacency in you. Just because we've heard false cries of "wolf!" in the past doesn't assure us that there aren't wolves at the door today. The threats to our civilization and our planet are real. We have to address them. We need not fall into despair at their size, but we can't afford to ignore them, either.

I highlight these past incorrect predictions for a slightly different reason. It's not that they were all wrong. It's that they were all wrong in the *same way*, and for the *same reason*. They all ignored or underestimated the most critical human faculty that exists, and the most important source of our prosperity.

Innovation.

Malthus, Ehrlich, and the Club of Rome all dramatically underestimated the extent to which human ingenuity could lift the production of food. They made the mistake of looking at the physical resource—land—as the most important determiner of future output. They assumed that the invisible resource—our knowledge of how to maximize yields from that land—would have only a small effect on overall productivity. The Club of Rome's predictions about energy and natural resources in *The Limits to Growth* made a similar mistake.

What we've seen is that the opposite is true. The physical resources matter. But the change in our knowledge resources—our science, our technology, our continual generation of new useful ideas—has made far more impact over the course of history. Knowledge acts as a multiplier of physical resources, allowing us to extract more value (whether it be food, steel, living space, health, longevity, or something else) from the same physical resource (land, energy, materials, etc.).

That's what has driven human history. And the continuation, willful direction, and acceleration of global innovation is our best hope of overcoming peak oil, climate change, and the whole panoply of resource limitations and environmental risks that we face.

Sibudu Cave

On the eastern coast of South Africa, in the province of KwaZulu-Natal, home of the Zulu Kingdom, twenty-five miles north of Durban and nine miles in from the coast, lies Sibudu Cave, one of the richest archeological sites in the world for early human tools. Sibudu is nearly 200 feet long and 60 feet wide, a natural cavity set in one of the steep limestone cliffs that dot the area. Today from the cliff face you can look west and south over the vast sugarcane plantation that stretches around it. Tens of thousands of years ago, the area was likely jungle. At least six times over the past 70,000 years, bands of humans made this cave their home, sometimes passing it on from generation to generation for hundreds of years at a time. In doing so, they left us ample evidence as to who they were and the lives they lived.[4]

Although Sibudu was first discovered in 1929, archeologists didn't explore it until 1983. The cave was then virtually ignored until 1998, when researchers from the University of Witwatersrand in Johannesburg returned and began regular excavations. In 2010 a team from the university found stone points dating back to 64,000 years ago. The points are smaller than spearheads, small enough and light enough to have been propelled long distances at lethal velocities. Their forward edges have microscopic deposits of bone and blood. Their sides and back edges bear deposits of a crude glue made by combining plant gum and red ochre. These stone points are arrowheads, the oldest ever found.

We are the invention species. Our ancient ancestors learned to use and create fire. They learned to create choppers and axes. They learned to fashion spears and bows. And in all of those ways, they increased the value of inert matter by infusing it with their ideas.

The bow and arrow, for example, allowed humans to do more with less. By killing from a distance, hunters could kill game that might otherwise be beyond their abilities to bring down safely. The speed of an arrow allowed hunters to kill from a stationary position rather than chasing or charging animals with spears. The bow brought in more meat with less risk, more calories with fewer expended. It increased the efficiency with which humans could gather the energy most vital to their survival.

A bow and arrow is a powerful tool made from crude, abundant, mundane materials. The parts are small rocks, red ochre, plant gum, green wood (for the bow staff and the arrow shafts), and rawhide or sinew (for the bowstring). All of those were plentiful for our Stone Age ancestors. In economic terms the individual pieces were cheap. Even the labor to make the bow and arrows was relatively short, comprising perhaps several hours of work over the course of a few days.

The real value in the bow and arrow is in its design. Its utility comes not primarily from its parts (which are abundant), not primarily from the labor to construct it (which is minor compared to a bow's benefits), but from the precise way in which those pieces fit together and work together to create something greater than the sum of their parts. The key ingredient that adds the value to the pieces and the labor is the human knowledge. That knowledge transforms the inert matter into a powerful tool.

And that knowledge spreads. The first bow was copied millions of times, and improved upon along the way. The value of a single bow is significant. The value of the *idea* of the bow is tremendously greater.

Knowledge, in the language of economists, is non-rival. Rival goods can only be used by one person, or a set number of people, at a given time. A non-rival good is something of value that any number of people can enjoy the benefits of. It is, in another way of thinking, non-zero-sum. In a zero-sum system, one person's gain is another's loss. In a non-zero-sum system, both parties can benefit. The possibility of sharing ideas makes human interactions non-zero. It allows the total size of the pie to grow.

Only information works this way. Everything else in nature is diluted or depleted by increased use. A piece of food does not become more valuable if shared by a hundred people—it just gets divided among them. A bow itself can only be used by one hunter at a time, and eventually it will break. But the *design* for a bow can be used again and again. It's software, not hardware.

Knowledge, information, is fundamentally different from physical resources. The more people who make use of a piece of knowledge, the more total impact it has on the world. It not only adds more value to everything it touches, it does so a potentially infinite number of times.

The key turning point in human evolution was our ability to tap into this non-rival, non-zero-sum resource. The day we achieved the ability to create sophisticated ideas, and to communicate them clearly to one another, our universe changed. We were no longer bound by the same constraints of population, food, and scarce resources that we and all other creatures on Earth always had been. We had tapped into a new and potentially infinite resource. Nothing has been the same since. Nothing ever will be again.

The First Energy Technology: Agriculture

The innovations of early humans centered on the acquisition of the energy source that all human life depends on: food. Without adequate food, human civilizations can't survive. They can't maintain their populations. Hunger and then starvation set in. Famine kills off surplus population. Warfare may arise as people turn violent to fight over the last scraps. Order and structure in society break down.

Over the last 12,000 years, human population has increased from roughly five million men and women to seven billion, a factor of more than 1,000. At every step of the way, that's only been possible because we've found ways to acquire more food.

Most of that gain has had little to do with increasing the amount of land we acquire the food from. By 10,000 BC, humans had already spread to most of the habitable corners of the planet and were ranging over most of that territory hunting, fishing, and foraging. The more than 1,000-fold increase in human population and human food supply hasn't come from more land. It's come from increasing the efficiency with which we acquire food from the land.

Food, in essence, is concentrated solar energy. Plants turn the energy of the sun, plus generally abundant water, carbon dioxide, and nitrogen, into carbohydrates, fats, and proteins. Animals consume that energy, and use some of it to build muscle and fat. When you bite into an apple, a piece of bread, or a steak, what you're consuming is stored-up solar energy.

The story of humanity is one of becoming more and more adept at harvesting that solar energy—turning more of the energy that hits the ground into food. As hunter gatherers, it took an average of almost three thousand acres to feed one person. Today it takes around a third of an acre.[5]

That roughly 10,000-fold increase in the amount of solar energy we capture per acre has come from a steady stream of innovations. First, agriculture itself—the idea that we could intentionally plant seeds of plants that were good to eat, and harvest them later. Almost overnight, that increased the amount of food our ancestors could grow by at least a factor of 10, and in some cases a factor of 100. Following the basic idea of agriculture came a host of improvements. Irrigation, hoes and digging sticks, harnessing oxen to pull plows.

Even in the periods of history we consider the darkest and most devoid of progress, agricultural innovation continued. The Western Roman Empire fell apart in the fifth century AD. Yet in the sixth century agricultural productivity in Europe improved as farmers learned to use the breast strap to harness horses, which can plow more land per day than oxen. The ninth century saw more improvements as the horse collar was introduced, letting horses put their full strength into plowing. The tenth century, still firmly in the so called "Dark Ages," saw the introduction of the medieval moldboard plow, which turned over the earth to aerate it, creating furrows alternated with rows of tall soil, leaving natural channels for water to flow through, and further boosting yields.

The eleventh and twelfth centuries saw the advent of three-field crop rotation, where farmers learned to plant legumes such as peas and beans to simultaneously grow food and inject much-needed nitrogen (which legumes can absorb from the air, but grains cannot) back into the soil.

Other agricultural innovations followed—the seed drill, four-field crop rotation, horse shoes, improvements to plows and scythes, and more. In parallel, farmers continued to pick seeds from the best crops to plant for the next year, and to domesticate more plants and animals for human use. In all, those agricultural innovations boosted yield by a factor of 10 between the first generation of farming and the dawn of the Renaissance. At the end of the so-called dark ages, farms produced twice as much food per acre as they had at the height of the Roman Empire.

There's a saying that "you can't eat information." That may be so, but the food we eat today is the fruit of thousands of years of increasingly high-quality information—the knowledge of how to farm—what seeds, what tools and how to use them, what times of year, what irrigation, what sequence of one crop after another on the same land. What we eat is solar energy, filtered, concentrated, and distilled through the lens of human knowledge. The energy the Earth receives from the sun each year has remained more or less constant through all of human civilization. What's allowed us to flourish is our increasingly sophisticated knowledge of how to capture an ever-growing but still tiny fraction of that energy in a form that can fuel our bodies. Every step in the advancement of our knowledge has brought with it an increase in the amount of energy we can tap into.

The Population Bomb and the Green Revolution

Greater food production allowed larger populations with higher population densities. Greater productivity of fields meant that not every person needed to be a farmer, freeing up some of the population to specialize in other tasks. Larger populations, packed more densely, with more minds freed from the burden of growing food led to faster rates of innovation. Among those innovations were sanitation, vaccination, and penicillin. Those in turn dramatically reduced the impact of disease that had kept populations down. And so, in the nineteenth and twentieth centuries, the world's population boomed. And in 1968 Paul Ehrlich wrote *The Population Bomb*, arguing that the explosion of mouths to feed would imminently surpass the ability of mankind to grow more food.

While Ehrlich was writing that the battle to feed humanity had already been lost, it was in fact being vigorously fought. In Mexico, a young plant scientist named Norman Borlaug led an effort, funded by the Mexican government and the Rockefeller Foundation, to develop new strains of wheat that could be planted more often, that would produce more and bigger seeds, and that could resist common wheat diseases.

The results in Mexico were astounding. On similar-sized plots of land, Borlaug's wheat varieties produced three times as much grain as conventional breeds, and they could be planted twice a year. By 1963, more than 90 percent of Mexico's wheat crop was planted using Borlaug's seeds. The total wheat harvest that year was an astounding six times what it had been in 1944, the year Borlaug started his work. Mexico was more than self-sufficient in wheat. It had become a wheat exporter. By 1967, Borlaug's new wheat varieties were being planted around the world and had helped stave off forecasted famines in India, Pakistan, and Turkey.[6] Three years later, the Nobel Committee awarded the unassuming, pickup-driving, one-room-schooled Borlaug the Nobel Peace Prize for his efforts, which had saved the lives of billions.

Borlaug wasn't the only one working on higher-yield crops in the 1960s. Inspired in part by his success and his methods, researchers in other parts of the world created disease-resistant, high-yield varieties of rice, corn, and other crops. Crop yields in the developing world more than tripled overall.

Of this remarkable progress William Gaud, director of USAID, noted, "These and other developments in the field of agriculture contain the makings of a new revolution. It is not a violent Red Revolution like that of the Soviets, nor is it a White Revolution like that of the Shah of Iran. I call it the Green Revolution."[7]

Largely because of the Green Revolution, the massive famines predicted in the late 1960s never happened. Decade over decade, the fraction of humanity that is hungry has dropped since Ehrlich wrote *The Population Bomb*. In late 2011, world population crossed the seven billion mark, twice the number of people who were alive when *The Population Bomb* was written. Population has indeed exploded. And yet, around the world the amount of food available, per person, is at an all-time high. Population has increased by a factor of 2. Food supplies have increased faster, by a factor of almost 2.5.

Farming the Seas

The next frontier for farming is the world's oceans. Today the majority of the fish humanity consumes isn't farmed. It's caught. That is to say, it's hunted.

Hunting and farming have crucial differences. Where farmers focus on raising animals, ensuring their health, and the health of their herds, hunters focus on finding, catching, and bringing in animals. Both hunters and farmers care about how much food they can produce, of course, but how they go about it is different. A farmer who wants to produce more food works to grow his herd, increasing the population of the animals most consumed for food. A hunter who wants to produce more food works to increase the speed and efficiency with which he can take animals *out* of the world's population.

Today, the species we hunt most aren't deer or bears or wolves—they're the fish in our oceans, rivers, and lakes. Tuna, snapper, cod, sole, bass, halibut, orange roughy, perch, and so many more. And it's no coincidence that those species are all under pressure, with most of them at all-time low populations, and that yearly fishing catches have stalled even as an ever-larger fleet of ever-larger fishing boats make ever-longer trips to try to haul them in.

By comparison, the world's population of cows, sheep, pigs, and chickens has never been higher.

The key to saving the fish in our oceans will be to transition from a culture of hunting fish to one of farming fish. That transition is underway now. Since 1990, the worldwide wild fish catch has been more or less flat at around ninety million tons of seafood per year. In that time, fish farms have grown from providing just over ten million tons per year to providing more than sixty million tons per year. For some species, like sea bass and salmon, fish farms now provide more food each year than wild-caught fish.[8]

Fish farms have come under attack for being environmentally unfriendly in other ways. In traditional open-cage fish farms, fish kept in high densities produce waste that washes out into the water and can potentially become a breeding ground for diseases and parasites that can spread to wild populations. In addition, farmed fish still need to eat, and much of what they consume is in the form of other, smaller fish. Fish farms consume those in vast quantities. Those are all legitimate criticisms.

Those problems are surmountable, though. New fish farming techniques use separated pools, where fish can be grown away from wild populations. The water in these pools is gradually recycled, allowing waste products and parasites to be caught and filtered out. And fish farms around the world are now experimenting with soy-based fish feeds and other types of feeds that reduce the need to consume large amounts of smaller fish. New ideas are addressing the environmental problems that fish farms create, while leaving in place their main advantage: a potential conservation of wild fish populations.

New ideas and new technologies are employed in wild fish hunting as well, of course. Bigger boats, larger nets, new ways of locating fish. But the main effect of these is opposite to the effect of new technology in fish farms. New developments in ocean fishing *accelerate* the rate at which fisheries harm the environment. New developments in fish farming *reduce* the harms.

Fish farms could be good for more than the health of our oceans. They're also a more efficient way to turn vegetables into meat. It takes ten to twenty pounds of feed to create a pound of beef. By contrast, it takes just around two pounds of feed to create a pound of salmon. As we bring the agricultural revolution to fishing, we have the potential to both shrink our impact on wild fish *and* increase the efficiency with which we turn land into protein.

The Ever-Shrinking Footprint

Before agriculture, a square mile (2.6 square kilometers) could feed roughly a quarter of a person. Today a square mile of cropland producing average yields feeds almost 1,300 people. The productivity of farms in the developed world is roughly twice that of the world average, feeding a stunning 2,600 people. Our innovation in farming technology has multiplied the value of a plot of land by nearly 10,000.[9]

The converse of this is that by increasing the amount of food that a plot of land produces, we've reduced the amount of agricultural land needed. We've shrunk the "land for food" footprint of a single person by a factor of nearly 10,000 over the course of human history.

And here we diverge from the expectations of the IPAT equation. Because if Impact (the amount of land we use, for instance) = Population × Affluence × Technology, then we should expect to see far more land used for agriculture now, given that our population, affluence, and technology are all at all-time highs. Yet, on a global basis, the amount of land we use to grow food is only slightly higher than it was a thousand years ago. And on a per person basis, it's dramatically less.

Our population is higher. Our affluence is higher. Our technology is higher. And that is the key. The "technology" term in the IPAT equation is working in a direction *opposite* the one expected by Ehrlich and others. Better agricultural technology is working to *reduce* the land-use impact of each person. Innovation and the accumulation of knowledge are substituting for land, a physical resource.

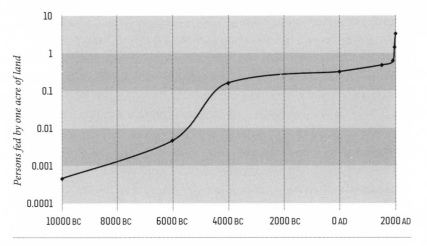

Figure 7.1. Persons fed by one acre of land. Agricultural innovations have increased the number of people fed by the same amount of land drastically and continually through human history. Data compiled from Marcus J. Hamilton, Bruce T. Milne, Robert S. Walker, and James H. Brown; B. H. Slicher Van Bath; and Food and Agriculture Organization.

Our Planet's Rising Carrying Capacity

That also means that the carrying capacity of the planet has been increased. The carrying capacity of the planet using the farming techniques of 1900 was perhaps two billion people: five billion people fewer than it is today. The carrying capacity of the planet when we were hunter gatherers was around a thousand times less than it is today—in single-digit millions. There was simply no way, in those times, to produce enough food to feed the number of people who are alive today. Yet now there is. Carrying capacity isn't fixed, it seems. The answer to the question "How many people can the planet support?" isn't a constant. It depends on both their behavior (how much those people consume) and on the effectiveness and efficiency of the technology they use to tap into the resources they need—an effectiveness and efficiency that's risen continually with time and innovation. Our technology is a physical manifestation of our knowledge base. As we've innovated and improved on that knowledge base, our technology has reduced the amount of land we need to feed a person, and thus increased the carrying capacity of the planet.

Reducing the land needed to grow food has other positive impacts. Agriculture is the number one cause of deforestation, accounting for about half of all tropical forest acreage cut down.[10] To feed the number of mouths on the planet today at the yields we knew in the 1960s, we would have had to cut down roughly half the remaining forests of the world, with disastrous impacts for climate, the water cycle, and biodiversity. The green revolution, with its pesticides, its chemical fertilizer, its massive irrigation, and its mechanization has been the greatest savior of the world's forests. Growing more food per acre leaves more land for nature.

The trend, then, is toward increasing the amount of food we can grow per acre, increasing the amount of food we can grow per gallon of water, increasing the amount of food we can grow per watt of power. We're far from done with the Green Revolution. Even now, innovations in labs point the way to potential grain yields that are double today's yields, to crops that can survive droughts or floods, to crops that are more efficient in their use of fertilizer and water, and more. Ten thousand years of innovating in agriculture suggest that at least some of these new ideas will bear proverbial—and actual—fruit, boosting the amount of food we can grow further.

How far could these trends go? There's no practical limit in sight. Today the average yields in rich countries like the United States, Canada, Europe, Japan, and Australia are around twice the overall average of the world. Lifting yields in the rest of the world to developed-world levels would, by itself, double the amount of food production, meeting or exceeding the demand expected in 2050. The additional energy required to do so, in fertilizer, fuel, equipment, and so on, would be around 3 percent of the world's total. If we can address energy concerns, we can lift yields.

Even that is far short of what's allowed by the laws of physics, chemistry, and biology. The majority of the energy in food, even in the heavily mechanized agriculture of developed nations, is that provided by the sun. Yet an acre of corn or wheat in the United States, where yields are high, captures only around a tenth of a percent of the solar energy that strikes it. Photosynthesis, in principle, can capture as much as 13 percent of the energy that strikes a plant. That means that, in theory, on the same land we could be growing a hundred times as much food as we are today.

We already know how to achieve some of that gain. For example, plant scientists at the University of Florida's Protected Agriculture Project have already shown that they can boost crop yields of many vegetables by a factor of 10 by growing them in low-cost plastic greenhouses.[11] Purdue University scientists have shown that they can double the yield of corn by growing it in passive greenhouses, and nearly triple yields by growing corn underground with artificial lights. Even in traditional open fields above ground, the farmers who win the Iowa Master Farming contest each year typically get twice the average yields of the United States as a whole.[12] There's plenty of headroom to boost food production further.

Solutions, Problems, Solutions

This is not to say that modern agriculture has no negative impacts. Cows excrete methane that warms the planet. The energy used to run farm equipment and to manufacture fertilizer produces carbon dioxide that further warms the planet. Together the two produce around 18 percent of the warming effect created by humans. Nitrogen fertilizer runs off of soil and creates ocean dead zones where fish don't live. Modern farming uses water drawn from aquifers and rivers. Pesticides used to protect crops from disease, weeds, and insects kill other plants and animals and spread into water supplies.

As is often the case, the solutions to one problem have created new problems of their own. To be sure, the new problems are smaller than the old. Had we not boosted yields through the Green Revolution, we would either have had billions starving or would have been forced to chop down the world's remaining forests to feed the world. Either of those would be a worse result than the side effects we face now. That doesn't mean that the problems of agriculture aren't real, though. All things being equal, we'd like to feed the world *and* eliminate the problems of ocean dead zones, freshwater depletion, and CO_2 emissions from the energy that agriculture uses.

There are certainly signs that this is possible. While the total input of water and of energy into agriculture have increased, they've increased *less* than the amount of food we've produced has. According to the USDA, over the last several decades, advances in farming technology have cut the amount of energy used per calorie of farm output in the United Sates roughly in half.[13] A bushel of wheat or corn or tomatoes grown today takes *half* the energy of a bushel grown in the 1950s. That energy figure includes the energy used to create nitrogen fertilizer, to create pesticides, to pump water for irrigation, and to operate mechanical farm equipment.

The Green Revolution didn't result in the use of more energy for farming. The sharp rise in population increased the amount of energy needed (by in-

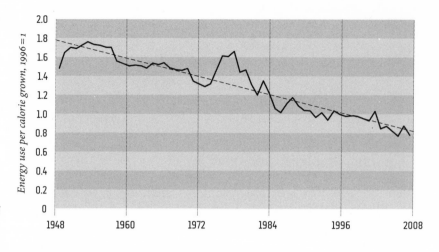

Figure 7.2. Energy use per unit of farm output. Farms in the United States use half the energy (in fertilizer, pesticides, farm equipment, and other inputs) as they did in 1948, per unit of food produced. Data from United States Department of Agriculture.

creasing the amount of food needed). The Green Revolution advances in crop breeds, pesticides, fertilizer, irrigation, and farming techniques *reduced* the amount of water, energy, and land needed for every calorie of food we grow.

Most of this is a result of better crop yields from more advanced strains. Part of this, though, is the result of more efficient ways of creating nitrogen fertilizer. Creating fertilizer today takes roughly an eighth of the energy required when the first chemical fertilizer process was created in the early 1900s, and roughly a third less energy than the processes used in the 1960s.[14]

We've also become more efficient in our use of water to grow food. While the amount of water we use in farming has risen over the course of the last half-century, it's risen slower than population and slower than farm output. In 2003, the Food and Agriculture Organization of the UN estimated that agricultural water use per capita shrank by roughly half in the forty years between 1961 and 2001.[15] Water productivity, as it's called, has continued to rise since then. In the twenty years between 1988 and 2008, for example, average irrigation per acre of U.S. cornfields dropped by 23 percent, while the amount of corn raised per acre increased by around 50 percent. The amount of corn raised in the United States per unit of water used nearly doubled in

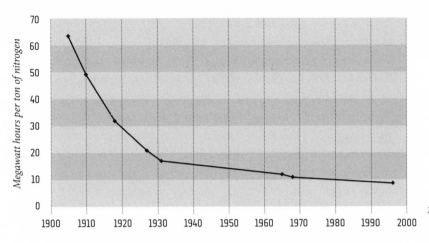

Figure 7.3. Energy needed to produce nitrogen fertilizer. Synthesizing
nitrogen fertilizer takes one-eighth the energy it did in 1900.
Data from Jeremy Woods et al.

those twenty years alone.[16] In the sixteen years between 1985 and 2001, the
water efficiency of growing rice in Australia improved just as much. Australian
farmers in the Murrumbidgee Valley used just over 2 million liters (around
530,000 gallons) to grow a ton of rice in 1985. By 2001, rising rice yields and
more efficient irrigation had reduced that to just over 1 million liters (around
265,000 gallons) per ton of rice.[17]

Similarly, the total amount of insecticide used in the United States has
dropped by a factor of 3 over the past few decades. And while herbicide use
has remained roughly flat, use of the herbicides the EPA classifies as most
toxic has dropped by a factor of 10, and concentrations of those herbicides
in rivers in the U.S. Midwest have dropped by a factor of 30.[18]

None of this is to say that agriculture's problems have been completely
solved. They haven't. But over the last few decades, innovation has reduced
the amount of energy, water, insecticide, and most dangerous herbicides
necessary to feed one person. With the right incentives, right rules, and right
innovation in new technologies, there's no reason to believe that we can't fix
those problems. They won't fix themselves. They'll require, at minimum, that
we give farmers a reason to reduce greenhouse gas emissions and runoffs of

pesticides and nitrogen. But if we decide, collectively, to do that, then the technology can be developed to make it happen.

More than 10,000 years ago, we started the transition from hunting wild animals and foraging for wild vegetables to intentionally growing and raising the food we want. Now we're on the verge of transforming seafood to that model. And at the same time, further innovation in farming on land can increase food yields further, while reducing the environmental damage of farms.

Agriculture is an amazing example of the power of ideas to multiply our resources. In the span of 10,000 years we've multiplied the amount of food energy we can extract from an acre of land by a factor of 10,000. Our continual process of innovation, of devising new ways to put matter and energy together—has multiplied the value of the finite amount of land we have again and again and again. It continues to today. And, as we're about to see, the right knowledge has multiplied the value of nearly every other resource we've ever encountered. The most valuable resource we have isn't energy or minerals or land. It's our ever-increasing store of ways to put those physical things together in new and more inventive forms that give us greater and greater value.

eight the transformer

A Scrambled Breakfast

Imagine you wake one morning, refreshed from sleep, hungry for a simple but delicious meal of scrambled eggs, toast, and orange juice. But inexplicably, instead of scrambling the eggs, toasting the bread, and juicing the oranges, you find yourself forcing the eggs into the toaster, mashing the bread against the juicer, and attempting to crack oranges into the frying pan. How enjoyable will your breakfast be?

This thought experiment is (like many thought experiments) absurd, but it also illustrates the importance of recipes (the way we manipulate and combine resources) vs. ingredients (the raw materials we begin with). The scrambled orange, toasted eggs, juiced bread breakfast starts with the same raw materials as the more conventional scrambled eggs, toasted bread, and juiced oranges breakfast. It adds the same amount of energy (supplied in the toaster, the range heating up the frying pan, and the muscle power in moving and mashing the ingredients). Yet somehow, with the same ingredients, the two recipes don't produce equivalent results. The way the ingredients are put together matters.

The recipes-and-ingredients metaphor comes from economist Paul Romer, one of the originators of modern economic growth theory. In a seminal 1990 paper with the humble title *Endogenous Technological Change*, Romer was the first economist to produce a model of economic growth that featured technological change as a key variable within the model, subject to change based on other variables.[1]

Romer coined the recipes metaphor to explain the distinction between designs (which are a kind of knowledge) and ingredients (physical resources) to non-economists. In *The Concise Encyclopedia of Economics* he writes:

Economic growth occurs whenever people take resources and rearrange them in ways that are more valuable. A useful metaphor for production in an economy comes from the kitchen. To create valuable final products, we mix inexpensive ingredients together according to a recipe. The cooking one can do is limited by the supply of ingredients, and most cooking in the economy produces undesirable side effects. If economic growth could be achieved only by doing more and more of the same kind of cooking, we would eventually run out of raw materials and suffer from unacceptable levels of pollution and nuisance. Human history teaches us, however, that economic growth springs from better recipes, not just from more cooking. New recipes generally produce fewer unpleasant side effects and generate more economic value per unit of raw material.[2]

Romer's assertion is a central one to this book. "Recipes" here are synonymous with "designs" or "processes." They're the ways we put things together, a core type of knowledge. Early human history is full of examples of new designs for tools and new processes for creating things of importance to us that produced more value out of the same resources. The design for a bow and arrow transforms sticks, stones, and rawhide into tools that can bring home more meat with less effort and less risk. Farming, compared to hunting and gathering, was a process that transformed the same amount of land, with less labor, into dramatically more food. Almost every example of progress in growing more food per acre is an example of a new recipe—a new design for a device, a new way of putting existing ingredients together. That creation of new ways of putting ingredients together to get new value out of them continues to this day.

Melt Down Your iPhone

As a thought experiment to illustrate the relative importance of recipes vs. ingredients, of designs vs. materials, consider your cell phone. Perhaps you have a smart phone such as an iPhone or an Android phone. What's the value of the raw materials in your phone? How does it compare to the overall value of the phone?

As I write this, I have an Apple iPhone in my pocket. It weighs 137 grams, or just under 5 ounces. Among its many material components are an estimated

27 grams of plastic, 20 grams of glass, 14 grams of aluminum, perhaps 30 grams of lithium-ion battery, and so on.[3]

What are these materials worth? If we melted down this iPhone (not something to try at home), separated its component materials, and sold them on the open market, the raw materials would be worth at most a few cents.* The value isn't in the raw materials then.

The value is in the design, in the recipe, in the knowledge that transforms incredibly tiny quantities of generally plentiful raw materials into a device that can connect you instantly to others nearly anywhere on the planet, that can access a sizable fraction of the world's data, that can capture, store, and replay images, sounds, and videos, and much more.

The knowledge embedded in your iPhone is a combination of multiple threads of knowledge going back at least two centuries and arguably farther. Indeed, here we must go a level deeper than Paul Romer's metaphor of "recipes." The value of the iPhone design owes much to abstract knowledge of electromagnetism, the principles of radio, materials physics, and theories of computing, which are much broader than any single design. The lineage of knowledge goes back to Benjamin Franklin's first experiments showing that lightning was electrical, to Ada Lovelace and Charles Babbage's work in the 1800s on the principles of computer programming (before any computers existed), to Faraday and Maxwell's work defining the laws of electromagnetism, to Marconi's assembly of the first functional radio, to Isaac Newton and Gottfried Leibniz's respective inventions of calculus in the 1600s (without which the design of an iPhone or its component chips would never have occurred), and more.

A design or recipe as rich and complex as that of an iPhone (or any similar or equivalent device) and all the components within it derives not just from one or two direct ancestors, but dozens, scores, or hundreds of ancestors. The recipe for the iPhone includes dozens of components that have their own recipes, which in turn include ingredients that have their own complex recipes, and so on. And all of those recipes draw upon our knowledge of the laws of physics and chemistry and principles of engineering that we've accumulated over time.

---

*Actually, we would find that no one would be willing to buy such tiny quantities of these commodities from us.

The accumulated knowledge of materials, computing, electromagnetism, product design, and all the rest that we've learned over the last several centuries converts a few ounces of raw materials worth mere pennies into a device with more computing power than the entire planet possessed fifty years ago. Twenty years ago, if you had $200, you wouldn't have been able to purchase a mobile phone, let alone one that played music, took pictures, stored your contacts, surfed the web, showed your position on a map of the world, accessed your e-mail, and could double as a flashlight, a medical encyclopedia, or any of thousands of other functions brought to it by add-on applications.

In fact, *no matter how much money you had*, it would have been impossible to have the iPhone's capabilities with you in your pocket twenty years ago. The closest you could have come would have been a luggable computer with a portable power supply, an incredibly expensive and bulky portable phone of the early generations, a pitifully slow modem, and a personal servant to carry it all. Imagine going out to a restaurant with your personal iPhone replacement following you with a giant backpack full of gear! What's replaced all of that is accumulated knowledge. And not only has it gotten rid of bulky gear, it's also made the resulting product affordable to millions of people.

This is one of the key ways in which knowledge differs from material resources. Where material resources may be used up (or, more frequently, disposed of or converted into less useful forms), knowledge simply accumulates. And the more knowledge there is available in the world, the greater the possibility there is for new and valuable combinations of that knowledge that can be manifest in novel and useful forms. We think of our world as running out of resources, and yet we are creating more and more pieces of knowledge that can be combined with one another to create more and more astounding advances. We are growing richer in ideas, richer in designs for useful devices, richer in understanding the basic laws that govern the universe, richer in discrete pieces of knowledge that can be combined into new and more useful innovations.

As Paul Romer has written, "Every generation has underestimated the potential for finding new recipes and ideas. We consistently fail to grasp how many ideas remain to be discovered. . . . Possibilities do not merely add up; they multiply."[4]

Nylon Mania, or How to Support
an Elephant Balancing on a Pencil

Consider the invention and improvement of plastics. We often think of plastic materials as being cheap, and indeed, that is one of their virtues, along with their low weight, easy manufacturing, suitability for molding into all sorts of shapes, and high degree of durability. As I write this, I can count more than thirty objects made of or containing substantial amounts of some plastic within my sight, ranging from the laptop on which I write these words to the upright lamp that provides illumination. Plastics are lighter, cheaper, and easier to mold than metals. They're lighter and less fragile than glass. They're lighter, easier to mold, and more weather and water resistant than wood. And they are a classic case of the world moving forward through the creation of new recipes.

The first plastic was invented in 1855 when Alexander Parkes, a metallurgist and inventor from Birmingham, England, combined cellulose from wood pulp with camphor extracted from laurel trees, producing a hard, flexible, transparent material he named Parkesine. When the cellulose and camphor mixture was heated, it could be molded into virtually any shape. It could be combined with dyes to give it color, something very difficult to do with metals or wood. When cooled it would keep its shape and proved light and durable. It was a perfect material for all sorts of light-duty objects.[5]

A great material did not immediately turn into commercial success. Parkes tried and failed to market the material, twice forming companies and seeing them go under. It was a pair of American brothers, John Wesley Hyatt and Isaiah Hyatt, who, in the search for a replacement for the ivory used to make billiard balls, hit the right balance of quality and cost in manufacturing, and brought celluloid to the world.

Celluloid gave birth to polyvinyl chloride, aka PVC or vinyl, which found applications for waterproof clothing, home siding, pipes and plumbing, and casings for computers and other electronics. PVC's cousin polystyrene turned out to be an extremely light and highly insulating material that went on to be called Styrofoam. PVC, celluloid, and other early plastics inspired the creation of Bakelite, an extremely tough and temperature-resistant plastic used in radios, phones, clocks, and circuit boards. World War I created a shortage of natural rubber (extracted from rubber trees) and spurred the first large-scale production of synthetic rubber (essentially a plastic). The wide variety of different plastics that had been created by the early twentieth century inspired yet more research. In 1927, DuPont Corporation, seeing the potential of devising new plastics with marketable characteristics, set out to create a synthetic replacement for silk. The result was polyamide, better known as nylon.[6]

DuPont introduced it at the 1939 World Expo, just two years before the United States entered World War II. The first product to use the material was the nylon stocking, which went on sale on May 15, 1940. They proved incredibly popular, with 64 million pairs selling in the United States between May and December of 1940 alone. Every woman had to have them. Then in 1941 the United States entered World War II, and all of DuPont's nylon production was turned to wartime needs such as parachutes for American soldiers.[7]

Eight days after Japan surrendered in 1945, DuPont announced that nylons would be in stores again soon. In November, 30,000 women lined up in New York City and 40,000 women lined up in Pittsburgh to buy 13,000 pairs. Riots broke out. Mobs of women knocked down store shelves and displays to get to the few nylons on sale. A newspaper headline in Augusta, Georgia, proclaimed, "Women Risk Life and Limb in Bitter Battle for Nylons."[8]

Such is the magic of plastics. Such was the superiority of nylon over the cotton and woolen fabrics that had been used for stockings before it. Such is the power of a new idea.

Today there are perhaps thirty major families of plastics, each of which has many variations, ranging from the polyvinylidene chloride sold as Saran Wrap to the polypropylene in bottle caps and the bumpers of cars to the hard ABS and polycarbonate used in security windows, electronics casings, traffic lights, eye glasses, and engine moldings. Plastics form the soles of shoes, the optics in LEDs, the components of electronic displays, and an increasingly large fraction of the world's cars, airplanes, clothing, and the objects in one's home.

We've learned, incrementally, how to mold matter to our desires. Our knowledge base has grown. The number of different recipes for matter that we possess, each of them with a different set of properties, has expanded over time.

We've done the same thing in dozens of other areas. Medicines are a prime example. The drugs and vaccines that have improved our lives, from the smallpox vaccine, to antibiotics, to humble aspirin, are all examples of tiny amounts of raw materials rendered valuable by the precise way those materials are cultivated and synthesized, and the discovery of the effects those materials will have on our bodies. Drugs are almost pure distilled knowledge, barely material at all.

Are we done? Have we exhausted the set of useful new recipes for matter? That perception—that we've made all the important discoveries already—has always been with us. In 1900, Lord Kelvin, one of the most eminent physicists and mathematicians of his day pronounced that, "There is nothing new to be discovered in physics now."[9] The decades that followed introduced both relativity and quantum mechanics and overturned almost all that we understood of physics. Any prediction today that we've reached the limits of our ability to produce new designs for matter is just as wrong as Kelvin's prediction was in his day.

If anything the number of new material recipes we can conceive of now is larger than at any time in the past, and the properties of the materials we are now working with are more remarkable than those of any material—natural or artificial—that we've ever encountered. Plastics are far from the end of the road in our growing ability to craft matter to our liking. We're in the midst of a material science revolution.

Consider Boeing's next major airplane—the Boeing 787 Dreamliner. The aircraft is constructed half out of carbon fiber composites, next-generation materials made from carbon and plastics that have a better strength-to-weight ratio than steel or aluminum. There is five times as much carbon composite as steel in the airframe of a 787, two and a half times as much carbon composite as aluminum. The result is that the aircraft is lighter than any previous aircraft of its size, burning 20 percent less fuel per passenger mile than its predecessors.

Beyond composites, material scientists are currently singing the praises and potentials of carbon nanotubes and graphene sheets. Carbon nanotubes, first discovered in 1952 but brought into wide awareness within the scientific community in 1991, are hollow tubes whose walls are a lattice of carbon atoms. They have incredible properties. They have a strength-to-weight ratio 300 times that of steel. A one-millimeter-thick strand of carbon nanotube can support 14,000 pounds of weight. They conduct heat 10 times as well as copper, and conduct electricity *1,000 times as well as copper*. On top of all of this, they are slightly harder than diamonds.

Nanotubes can only be constructed in small batches of short lengths today, but every year brings innovations that bring down their cost, increase their length, and increase the amount that can be produced.

Graphene sheets, essentially unrolled carbon nanotubes, or one-layer-thick sheets of carbon atoms each bonded to their neighbors, give their nanotube cousins competition in the prize for most astounding properties. Two hundred times stronger than steel and able to be made in wide sheets, a layer of graphene a millimeter thick is so strong that it would take an elephant balancing on a pencil in order to penetrate it.[10] Graphene is a better heat conductor than any known material, and at room temperature a better electrical conductor than any known material. It has potential applications in making super-hard, electrically conducting, super-heat-resistant plastics, in making highly efficient low-cost solar cells, and in making ultra-dense electrical capacitors for energy storage. Like carbon nanotubes, graphene is currently expensive and manufactured primarily in small sizes and batches, but production is improving rapidly every year.

Both carbon nanotubes and graphene sheets are new recipes for matter with new and highly desirable qualities. They'll allow us to build planes, cars, homes, furnishings, clothes, electronics, medical devices, and a plethora of other devices that are lighter, stronger, and more efficient than the ones we have now. And the primary *physical* ingredient of both is not some rare substance found only miles below the crust of the Earth. It's carbon, the fourth most abundant element in our universe.

The thing that adds the value to turn carbon into graphene or carbon fiber or carbon nanotubes is the input of our new ideas. Our set of useful recipes for matter continues to expand. There is no clear end of that expansion in sight.

The Toilet of Alessandro de' Medici

It's difficult in this context to define just how much value has been created by new inventions and the general accumulation of knowledge over time. Paul Romer estimates that half of all historic economic growth can be attributed to innovation, specifically to the creation of new designs for products and services. But surely even that estimate undervalues the impact of new knowledge. Had the idea for agriculture never been developed or never taken hold, humanity might very well still be comprised of a few million individuals, living in bands of a hundred or fewer hunter gatherers, illiterate, lacking the wheel, living a completely Stone Age lifestyle.

Shouldn't we thus say that virtually *all* economic growth has been a result of, or at least dependent upon, the invention and subsequent improvement of agriculture? Isn't a large fraction of our economic growth similarly dependent upon the inventions of the wheel, of literacy, of arithmetic, and of the printing press? Isn't almost all of the economic growth of the last two centuries dependent upon our new innovations and discoveries?

Would we be any better off than we were 200 years ago if we hadn't produced ways of generating more food from the same land? If we hadn't discovered the laws of electromagnetism and how to use them to build telegraphs, telephones, radio, television, and the Internet? If we hadn't sorted out the principles that govern the heat engines that power our vehicles and machines? If we hadn't come to understand that germs cause disease, and used that knowledge to improve sanitation, devise vaccines, and create antibiotics?

No. We'd be just as poor as we were in 1800. The average human life would be around thirty years, instead of sixty-seven across the world and nearly eighty in developed nations. The difference has not been an influx of new resources. It's been the creation of new and useful ideas, the discovery of new pieces of knowledge about how the world works. And that process is not only far from exhausted—it's accelerating.

As economist William Nordhaus has put it, commenting on the nature of innovation, and how much we underestimate the value it provides us, "The lowly toilet is classified as furniture, but delivers a service that would delight a medieval prince."

Billions of people around the world now possess flush toilets. Alessandro de' Medici, the first Duke of Florence, scion of the mighty Medici family, relative to four popes and two queens, and himself one of the richest men in Europe, never did.

nine the substitute

More Scarce Than the Milk of Queens

In Herman Melville's classic *Moby-Dick*, Ishmael, the narrator, describes what a visitor might see if he or she descended below the deck of the whaling ship *Pequod*, to the forecastle where the off-duty crew were sleeping.

"For one single moment you would have almost thought you were standing in some illuminated shrine of canonized kings and counsellors. There they lay in their triangular oaken vaults, each mariner a chiselled muteness; a score of lamps flashing upon his hooded eyes. . . . The whaleman, as he seeks the food of light, so he lives in light."[1]

Whale men lived in light because the holds of their ship were full of whale oil, "the food of light," a substance Melville has his narrator call "more scarce than the milk of queens."

Whale oil, in its time, was the premium source of illumination in the world. It produced a bright, clear flame, with less smoke than coal oil, less smell than lard oil, and more illumination than camphene (a mixture of camphor, turpentine, and alcohol.) While the middle class and poor burned lesser fuels, the wealthy chose whale oil for their lamps, or smokeless candles manufactured from whale oil.

The sperm whale, in particular, was the source of the highest-quality oil, which could be used for candles, lamp oil, soap, machine oil, and cosmetics. The very highest-quality oil, congealed into a waxy form called spermaceti, could only be harvested from the head of a sperm whale. Severed heads would be lashed to the sides of whaling boats to return to port. If that was not possible, a sperm whale head would be brought on deck, a hole would be cut in it, a sailor would climb in and hand out bucket after bucket of oil and spermaceti to be held in the ship's holds. It was a brutal process that nearly spelled the end of sperm whales.

In 1846, the American whaling fleet had 735 whaling boats in it. Whaling was the fifth-largest industry in the United States. In the early decades of the 1800s, American whalers killed perhaps 8,000 sperm and right whales a year and possibly as many as 15,000 a year, all in the search for whale oil. The nineteenth century saw the deaths of as many as a quarter million sperm whales in the quest to satisfy consumer appetites.[2]

Whales breed. They are, in principal, a renewable resource. Yet they breed slowly. A sperm whale gestates in its mother for 14 to 16 months, and then nurses for two to three years, during which time both mother and calf are extremely vulnerable. A female sperm whale will only give birth to a single calf every three to six years. Newly born sperm whales won't reach sexual maturity for a decade, or almost two decades in the case of males. The damage the American whaling industry did to sperm whale populations proved long lasting.[3] Across a few decades, whalers killed off an estimated one out of every three sperm whales on Earth.

The remaining sperm whales, many of them survivors of pods that had been decimated, became wary of humans and aggressive when approached. Melville's inspiration for *Moby-Dick*, indeed, was the sinking of the *Essex*, a 283-ton whaling ship that attempted to harpoon a pod of mostly female whales. As the *Essex* approached, it was rammed and sunk by a large and enraged bull sperm whale who struck the ship once, turned, dove, and came up to ram them again below the water line, caving in the hull before swimming away.[4]

The combination of fewer whales in the sea, more fear of human boats on their parts, and the occasional aggressive reply from a bull sperm whale made whaling a harder and more expensive proposition. Starting in the 1830s and 1840s, whaling boats had to sail farther and longer, with heavier armaments, to bring home their catch.*

While sperm whales (and their relatives, right whales) became more difficult and more expensive to catch, demand at home and abroad continued to grow. The result was a surge in prices. In 1820, whale oil sold for $200 a barrel (in 2003 prices). In the mid-1840s, prices rose sharply as demand increased. While production was also increasing, it could not keep pace with the amount of whale oil that consumers in the United States and abroad were interested in. At its price peak in 1855, whale oil sold for a whopping $1,500 a barrel. By

*Not unlike the fishing boats of today.

1864, not only was whale oil incredibly expensive, the amount available had begun to decline. Prices were so high that even the wealthy turned to lower-quality sources of light. Yet the high price continued to encourage whalers to put to sea in search of whales that could make them rich.[5]

The whale oil crisis (and the crisis in sperm whale populations) wasn't solved by the discovery of more whales. It was solved through innovation. The high price of whale oil and the fortune to be made by anyone who could produce a replacement sent people around the world in search of a replacement.

In 1846, a Canadian physician and geologist named Abraham Gesner, well aware of the whale oil shortage and the money to be made, wondered if a substitute could be found in other flammable substances. In an experiment later that year, he found that if he heated up dry coal in a glass vessel and then allowed the vapors that it gave off to condense in a separate vessel, he had a clear liquid that burned with a clean, bright, high-quality flame. He named this liquid kerosene and patented the process of producing it. Eight years later, in 1854, production began in the United States. Kerosene began to gradually replace both whale oil and cheaper, lower-quality fuels for lighting. In 1864, when whale catches collapsed, kerosene filled the gap.

By 1890, demand for whale oil had been almost completely replaced by demand for the now off-patent kerosene. The mighty whaling fleet of 735 ships had shrunk to 65 ships, less than a tenth of its former strength. The amount of whale oil on the market had dropped by 90 percent. The price of whale oil had dropped back to near its 1820 levels, even with diminished supplies. The price of kerosene was lower still. In 1865, whale oil sold for $1.77 per gallon (in 1865 dollars), and the newly available kerosene sold for 59 cents per gallon. By 1896, lack of demand had lowered whale oil's price to 40 cents per gallon (in 1896 dollars), but technological improvements, competition between suppliers, and *increases* in supply had lowered kerosene to 7 cents a gallon. The new technology was more economical, larger in supply, and more humane.[6]

Through innovation, by experimenting with new ways to solve a problem and finding one, Abraham Gesner lowered the price of illumination, and may just have saved the sperm whale from extinction.

Kerosene's day as the chief source of illumination wouldn't last long. In 1876, Thomas Edison demonstrated the first incandescent light bulb, and by the early 1900s, electric lighting was spreading like wildfire. But for a few decades, Gesner's discovery of a way to produce an illumination fuel from coal both lowered prices for consumers and slowed the slaughter of whales.

Peak Guano

The case of kerosene and whale oil is one of substitution. A new recipe for an illumination fuel, using coal and distillation, produced a new fuel that was more abundant and cheaper to harvest than the previous contender. Nor is that story unique. History is full of cases of new knowledge leading to resource substitutions, particularly in times of scarcity.

Fertilizer is one such story. For thousands of years, farmers have known that manure could be used to enrich the soil and grow more food. Manure adds nitrogen to the soil, though that wasn't understood until much more recently. But even without understanding *why* or *how* fertilizer worked, farmers used it.

Manure comes from more than cows. Hundreds of years ago, the Incas in Chile and Peru discovered that guano—droppings from birds and bats—was an effective fertilizer for their soils. In 1802 a Prussian named Alexander von Humboldt studied the technique and published his findings in Europe. By the mid-1800s Peru was exporting vast amounts of it to European and American farmers.

Six miles off the coast of Pisco, Peru, are the Chincha Islands, small pieces of rock less than a square mile in total that, in the mid-1800s, had the world's largest deposits of precious guano. Layers of the stuff up to eighty feet deep covered the land. For two decades, more than a hundred ships plied a continuous trade, bringing slaves to the islands to work shoveling the guano, and taking away holds full of the odorous fertilizer to destinations in Europe and the United States. The trade was so profitable, and guano so vital and plentiful, that in 1850 the Chincha Islands may have been the most valuable pieces of real estate on the planet. The sale of guano from them provided 60 percent of the Peruvian government's revenue. They were so important to agriculture in the United States that President Millard Fillmore mentioned them in his 1850 State of the Union address, declaring that it was the duty of his government to ensure that guano could be imported from the islands.

In other words, Peru was the Saudi Arabia of its time. The Chincha Islands were its Ghawar oil field.

The lightly guarded, incredibly valuable islands proved to be a tempting prize. In 1864, the Spanish fleet seized them, placing the Peruvian governor under arrest. The seizure infuriated the Peruvian government and ignited fears through South America (where many countries had recently won independence from Spain) of a Spanish re-conquest of the continent. Peru went to war with Spain. Chile, Bolivia, and Ecuador came to Peru's aid. The Spanish fleet shelled and burned to the ground the undefended Chilean port city of Valparaiso to punish Chile for its entrance into the war. The act very nearly drew the British and American fleets into the war on the side of Chile and Peru. Naval battles were fought. Dozens of ships were sunk. In the end, the Spanish Admiral committed suicide, his fleet limped home, and the Chincha Islands once again belonged to Peru.

Ten years later, the precious guano over which the war had been fought was gone. All of it that could be dug up had been. In all, 12.5 million tons of guano had been mined and shipped for use as fertilizer. "Peak guano" had arrived and passed. The islands that had sparked a war were once again worth next to nothing.

The end of the Chincha guano drove the fertilizer trade to another source— Peru's salt plains in the Tarapaca Desert. Charles Darwin, on his voyage of the *Beagle* had visited the desert and noted its rich supplies of saltpeter, which locals used for fertilizer. After a brief chaos, the supply of saltpeter from the desert replaced the now-ended guano shipments. The Tarapaca Desert was now one of the most vital pieces of real estate on earth. And like the guano islands, it proved to be a tempting target. So tempting that in 1879, Chile went to war with its neighbor and former ally to seize the desert. After a bloody two-year war, Chile proved victorious. In 1881, with control of the Tarapaca Desert, Chile was more than the world's Saudi Arabia. It had a near monopoly on nitrogen fertilizer. It was as rich in that resource as all of OPEC, the United States, and Russia combined are in oil.

That fact alone, combined with the prices the Chileans charged, set others around the world on the search for a replacement. So did the risk of eventual depletion. In 1898, Sir William Crookes, in his inaugural address as president of the British Academy of Sciences, announced what we might now call "peak saltpeter." Peru's supplies were running out, he said. The fertilizer extracted from the desert wouldn't last forever. At present rates of extraction, he predicted that it would be entirely mined within another twenty to thirty years. And when it was gone, agricultural yields would crash. "England and all civilized nations stand in deadly peril," he announced. "As mouths multiply, food sources dwindle."

Crookes challenged the world's chemists to find an alternate source of fertilizer, drawing nitrogen directly from the air. Since nitrogen makes up 78 percent of the atmosphere, a technique that could create fertilizer from that source would produce a nearly limitless supply. Two men rose to that challenge. In 1905, German chemist Fritz Haber demonstrated a way to create ammonia (which contains nitrogen and can be used as fertilizer) by directly extracting nitrogen from the atmosphere. From 1905 on, German chemical company BASF employed another scientist, Carl Bosch, to scale up the process. And in 1913 Bosch succeeded in using Haber's process at industrial scales. The Haber-Bosch process, as it's now called, produces almost all of the synthetic fertilizer used in the world today. One percent of the world's energy is devoted to it. That 1 percent roughly doubles the amount of food the world can grow. Innovation succeeded in both finding a substitute for the finite resources of guano and saltpeter and in using that substitute to dramatically increase the amount of food on the planet.

Substitution Everywhere

Everywhere we look, when resources are scarce or prices high, innovators flock to the task of finding a substitute.

The incredible utility of diamonds—the hardest natural substance on Earth, and an ideal drill bit tip—combined with their incredibly high price led General Electric to begin searching for a way to create them artificially in 1940. That, in turn, brought synthetic diamonds to market fourteen years later. Today they're widely and cheaply used in industrial drilling applications, while naturally occurring diamonds are reserved for jewelry.[7]

World War II provides other examples. In July 1941, the Nazi government of Germany forced France to sign a treaty for "Common Defense" of Indochina with Japan. This essentially gave Japan control of Vietnam, at the time the source of 50 percent of the rubber used in the United States. Five months later, Japanese forces invaded Malaysia, defeating British forces there and taking control of most of the remaining rubber plantations in the world. This left the Allies in a quandary. Without rubber, they couldn't create tires for jeeps, trucks, and planes vital for the war effort. They couldn't put soles on boots for soldiers. The Allies, deprived of a vital but overlooked natural resource, scrambled for a way to wage war. They found that in the work of American chemist Waldo Semon, the inventor of vinyl and then a scientist at B.F. Goodrich. Semon and the Allies scaled his process for a synthetic rubber he called Ameripol, replacing the missing natural resource with a new innovation, and ultimately allowing the war to be won.

Germany, on the other hand, suffered from a lack of oil with which to make fuel in the years leading up to World War II. At the same time, the country had substantial deposits of coal. To provide fuel, the Germans commercialized a process developed by chemists Franz Fischer and Hans Tropsch (the eponymously named Fischer-Tropsch process) to convert coal into a synthetic fuel similar to gasoline.[8]

It's said that necessity is the mother of invention. The opportunity for fortune is another. As resources become scarce, prices rise. And those high prices motivate investment in innovation. The high price of whale oil spurred Abraham Gesner and others to search for a replacement. The high price and finite supplies of saltpeter spurred Haber, Bosch, and Bosch's employer BASF to search for a replacement that could be produced in large volumes. The high price of natural diamonds spurred the search for a way to create synthetic diamonds.

Whenever the need has been great, or the financial rewards high, inventors have come calling. And innovation has allowed us to find substitutes for every resource that's come into short supply in the past. The combined global brain of humanity, mediated by the institutions of science and the market, and by our ever-increasing ability to communicate with one another, is *more* than just Darwinian. It doesn't just randomly combine ideas to get new ones and select for those that are useful. It *anticipates* problems and directs resources to solving them.

It's as if, in the millennia before a meteor wiped out the dinosaurs, evolution saw the coming event and began to intentionally select for small, warm-blooded mammals that could survive the massive global cooling that followed. But natural evolution doesn't work that way. It was purely luck that early mammals existed and were well positioned to take advantage of the cataclysm that ended the dinosaurs.

Not so our global brain. It isn't just reactive. It isn't random in the new ideas it creates or in those it selects for success. Our global brain can also peer into the future, see the problems and opportunities that are looming, and move to address them proactively. And our ability to do so is increasing with every passing year.

Why have we succeeded in finding substitutes for scarce resources while the Maya and the residents of Easter Island failed? We have more brainpower. We have more innovative capacity. We have more minds today than ever before. Those minds are less tied up in subsistence agriculture, and more freed to spend time creating and improving ideas. Each person, on average, is far more educated than ever before, increasing their ability to innovate. We're connected by ever better ways to communicate and collaborate—from the printing press up through Internet sharing of scientific papers and data, increasing our collective intelligence. We have better tools that we've invented, from slide rules to supercomputers, that amplify our ability to solve problems. And all of that is amplified and guided by the Darwinian institutions of science and the market, which accelerate the evolution of new ideas

Innovation is our most important capability. Tapping into it and further augmenting it is our best strategy for overcoming any potential limits to growth.

ten the reducer

Mount Rainier looms in the distance beyond Seattle. On a clear day, you can see the majestic nearly three-mile-tall volcano, taller than a sky scraper in perspective, its upper slopes clad in a permanent layer of white. With no other mountains around it, it stands proud, tall, and massive in its isolation. The Native Americans of the Northwest called it Tahoma, the mother of waters, for the Nisqually River that rises there from the annual spring melt of accumulated snow on Rainier's southern flanks.

In the summer of 1999, I joined a charity climb of the mountain, raising money for Washington State's National Parks Fund. On a beautiful day at the beginning of August, we started our ascent, climbing from the parking lot at 5,000 feet to our base camp at 10,000 feet, where the treacherous glaciers begin. On the upper slopes of a mountain like Rainier, the safest time to climb is in the wee hours of morning, when the cold of night has frozen snows to their hardest, reducing the risk of a melt-triggered avalanche, or the collapse of the feet-thick layer of snow below you that might cover a deep and deadly crack in the hard ice glacier. And so we bedded down before the sun set, and awoke at midnight to don our gear for the push to the summit at more than 14,000 feet.

Mountaineering gear is an object lesson in the progress of technology. In the lodge at the bottom of Rainier there are pictures of the early explorers who first reached the summit of this mountain. They're clad in heavy woolen clothing, prone to getting wet and soggy. They bear stout wooden staves to keep their balance. On their feet are leather shoes. Thick hemp ropes and harnesses connected them to one another. Gas-lit lamps provided their illumination. An expedition might take a week or more to reach the top.

By contrast, my team and I slid into light, waterproof Gore-Tex gear. In our hands were light, strong ice axes made of aluminum, titanium, or carbon fiber. A braided nylon rope the thickness of my finger and strong enough to bear the weight of a small car connected us. Small battery-powered headlamps were attached to our helmets, providing bright hands-free light. Our boots were hard rigid plastic, with a soft insulated inner boot that kept our feet perfectly warm and dry. To those boots we strapped steel crampons—artificial metal claws for our feet that would give us purchase on even slippery ice, devices so useful and effective that serious pre-crampon mountain climbers considered them "not sporting" due to the advantage they brought. Where early explorers had taken a week to climb the mountain, we would take less than a day from bottom to top.

By 12:30 AM we were fully geared up, our water bottles filled, a protein bar in our bellies. The dangerous part of the climb began. The moon was full. We crossed a long crevasse-broken field, occasionally stepping or jumping over cracks three or four feet wide but hundreds of feet deep. Crossing our trail ahead we could see the marks left in the snow by boulders that had fallen from the upper mountain. Some of them lay where they'd come to a stop, barely off our path. Looking downhill I could see a layer of cloud a thousand feet below us, lapping at the mountain like a sea.

Then, at 11,000 feet, something started to go wrong. The light from my headlamp dimmed slightly and started to fade. By 11,500 feet, it was gone. I'd made an amateur mistake. I hadn't put a fresh set of batteries in the lamp. And I didn't have any spares. I was lucky that the moon was full that night. It provided enough light to continue. I pressed on with the climb, saw the sunrise, reached the summit, and got back down in one piece. On a new moon night, or if there had been high clouds, my climb would have ended unsuccessfully. I would have put my team and myself at risk.

When I came back to Rainier in 2006 to climb the mountain again, I triple-checked that my headlamp had fresh batteries in it. A set of spares were in my pack. I was determined to not make the same mistake again. But something else had changed as well. The technology of my light had improved. The headlamp I used in 1999 had an incandescent bulb, not radically different from the bulb that Thomas Edison designed a century earlier. Ninety percent of the energy that bulb drew from my batteries was lost as heat. Only 10 percent emerged as light. The bulb itself had a lifetime of a few hundred hours before it was expected to burn out. In 2006 I returned with an LED-based headlamp that was nearly five times as efficient as the one I'd used seven years earlier, with no bulb that could burn out. Even if I hadn't brought fresh batteries and spares, it would have lasted through the night.

Knowledge can not only produce substitutes for scarce resources. It can *reduce* the amount of any resource we need to use to accomplish a task.

Over the past century and a half, innovation has reduced the amount of energy needed to produce light by a factor of nearly 500, from the energy efficiencies of candles and oil lamps to the energy efficiencies of today's top-end white Leds. And at the same time, the price of lighting has declined. The LED headlamp I used in 2006 cost me around $40. (It was worth it. I was determined to not run out of light on a climb again.) In early 2012, I had the opportunity to go for a late-night walk along an unlit stretch of beach and mangroves on Florida's Gulf Coast. Finding myself without a flashlight, I stopped in to a local sporting goods store, and came out with a new LED headlamp, smaller and brighter than the one I'd bought in 2006, for $9.95.

Using Less, Doing More

Everywhere we look, innovation has reduced the amount of energy, water, land, raw materials, and labor needed to accomplish a task.

It takes between 1,000 and 10,000 times less land to grow food than it did in antiquity. It takes 100 times less labor than it did a century ago. Since 1960, we've reduced the amount of land, water, and energy needed to grow a bushel of grain each by a factor of 2 to 3.

We use forty to fifty times less energy to turn a ton of iron into a ton of steel today than we needed to in the 1800s. Much of that gain has been in the last sixty years. In 1950, the North American steel industry used almost sixty million BTUs of energy to create a ton of steel. In 1980 it used roughly thirty million BTUs per ton. Today it uses twelve.[1] The advances in the last half century, and in particular in the last thirty years, reflect more new ideas and innovations in how to manufacture steel. Energy efficient electric arc furnaces have replaced most older natural gas– and coal-fired furnaces, reducing the amount of energy wasted.

We've reduced the energy required to keep food cool in a refrigerator, even as refrigerators have grown in size. In the 1970s, the average refrigerator in the United States had a capacity of twenty cubic feet and used 1,800 kilowatt hours per year. By the early 2000s, the average refrigerator had grown by 10 percent to around twenty-two cubic feet, but used only 500 kilowatt hours per year, or one-quarter the energy relative to the amount of food stored.[2] Other appliances have seen their energy use drop, with new dishwashers, freezers,

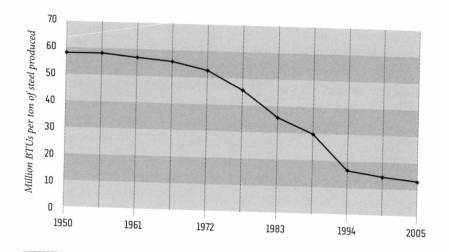

Figure 10.1. Energy needed per ton of steel produced in the United States. In the last sixty years, the amount of energy needed (in millions of BTUs) per ton of steel produced in the United States has shrunk by a factor of five. Data from Ernst Worrell, Paul Blinde, Maarten Neelis, Eliane Blomen, and Eric Masanet.

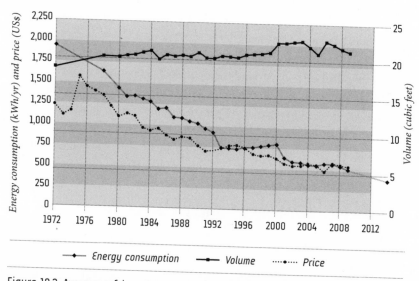

Figure 10.2. Average refrigerator energy use, columns, and price. U.S. refrigerators have dropped sharply in energy use even as they've grown in size and dropped in price. Altogether, they now use one-quarter of the energy they used in 1970 per amount of food stored. Data from Appliance Standards Awareness Project.

clothes washers, and clothes dryers in Canada, for example, using anywhere from 25 to 50 percent less energy in 2005 as in 1990.[3]

Heating has become more efficient as well. In 2011, the sixty-one-year-old boiler that pumped hot water through the radiant heating pipes of my home finally died. That boiler was a massive rounded cylinder, eight feet tall and five feet wide, made of quarter-inch-thick plate steel. I was mystified as to how the original owners could have gotten such a beast into the home, given that it was twice as wide as any doorway in the house and weighed two thousand pounds. My contractor explained to me that they hadn't. A crane had lowered the boiler onto the foundation, and then the house had been built around it. To remove the old system they brought cutting torches and took it away in pieces. The new replacement is a white box the size of a microwave oven, bolted to the wall. Where the old boiler vented half the energy it used out the exhaust of the house, the new one is more than 90 percent efficient. My heating bills have dropped by half.

My experience is far from unique. Since 1978, the amount of energy used to heat the average U.S. home has dropped by half. In 1978, for *all* purposes, including heating, cooling, and electricity, the average U.S. home used just short of 140 million BTUs of energy per year. By 1997, that energy consumption had dropped by more than a quarter to 100 million BTUs of energy per year.[4]

Air travel has become more efficient. Jet aircraft that came to market between 2000 and 2010 are around three times the efficiency of the jet aircraft of the 1960s. Through better engines and better aerodynamics, they burn around one-third as much fuel per passenger mile.[5] Those gains have shown up in cost, as well. Traveling by commercial plane, with a coach ticket, cost an average of 29 cents per mile traveled in 1979. In 2010, even with high fuel prices, the average cost was only 14 cents per mile traveled.[6]

The Learning Curve and the Accumulation

When I climbed Mount Rainier in 2006, I carried with me a small carbon-fiber knife. Weight is at a premium on a mountain climb. At 14,000 feet, the air carries only 60 percent of the oxygen it does at sea level. Your body is working almost twice as hard for every step. Every pound you carry works against you. And you're going steeply uphill, at times nearly straight up, on ice and snow, with extra food, clothing, and emergency equipment to carry, and with giant crevasses gaping wide, ready to swallow you up permanently.

Every ounce you can remove from your load is a bit more energy, endurance, and agility to get you safely to the top and back. Carbon fiber weighs one fifth what steel weighs, while providing the same strength. It won't corrode or rust. It's the perfect thing to make any metal gear you need out of.

You can buy carbon fiber gear of all sorts these days at somewhat reasonable prices. That wasn't always so. In 1970, bulk carbon fiber cost $150 a pound. Today it costs just over $5 a pound. In the 1970s and 1980s, its high price meant that it was good for the space shuttle, for multimillion-dollar fighter jets, and not much else. By the 1990s, it was a component in golf clubs, ski poles, and other outdoor and sporting gear where low weight and high strength were a priority, but where the gear itself didn't require huge quantities of it. Now it's a component in cars, in the Boeing 787 Dreamliner, in wind turbines, and in even medium-priced bicycles.

Carbon fiber isn't unique. I spent the last few pages giving you plenty of examples of areas where we've reduced the energy, raw materials, or money needed to achieve some task. But I want to use carbon fiber here to illustrate the notion of the learning curve.

The learning curve is gradual reduction in the price of any manufactured good that comes through making more of it. As more of something is created, producers learn various ways of making it more cheaply. They find ways to save steps in the manufacturing process. They find ways to use less raw material or less energy. They reduce duplication of effort. Workers get more skilled and more efficient at what they do.

We've known about the learning curve since the build-up to World War II in the 1930s, when aeronautical engineer T. P. Wright published a report showing that every time airplane manufacturing of a given model doubled, the amount of labor needed to build each plane dropped by 10–15 percent. Since then the concept has been applied to dozens of other areas—cars, solar panels, ships, machine tools, electronics, and even the extraction of raw materials. The rate of learning varies. The benefit can be anywhere from 5 percent to 30 percent reduction in effort and cost with each doubling of production, but it's almost always there.

The learning curve is the accumulation of knowledge. As carbon fiber manufacturers have produced more carbon fiber, they've learned things about how to do so more efficiently, with less labor, less time, and less energy. That new knowledge is *replacing* the use of labor, energy, and time. It's reducing the need for all of those. And over time the lessons learned in one factory, one company, one industry, or one country spread. Competitors work to bring their costs down, copying all they can from one another and accelerating the evolution of ideas. They try new approaches. Some fail, and are forgotten or left behind. Others succeed, pass the Darwinian test, and are copied and built upon.

The same is true in the incredible gains we've made in farm productivity, in the efficiency of the steam engine, of lighting, of air travel, of steel manufacturing, and hundreds of other examples. In every area, over time, new ideas are tried. Many fail. A few succeed. Those successes accumulate, and become our ever-increasing body of knowledge of how to build things and do things faster, better, more efficiently, and more cheaply than ever before.

Demand Creates Efficiency

The law of supply states that, in general, the more demand there is for a product or service, the more of it businesses will produce. The learning curve states that the more of a product or service produced, the cheaper and easier to make it will become.

Demand drives prices down. Except in cases like land, where new supply can't be created, more demand means more manufacturers enter the business. And the learning curve, the new ideas brought by each new producer, and the Darwinian competition between those ideas drive down the amount of energy, labor, time, and raw materials to produce that service.

Often that means that early adopters fund the price decreases for later adopters. Carbon fiber is as cheap as it is today because NASA and the U.S. Air Force were willing to pay $150 a pound for it. For a space shuttle or a high-tech fighter plane, that price was affordable. And in spending that money, they funded companies producing carbon fiber, who learned along the way, competed with one another, and thus brought prices down to the point that professional golfers and Olympic skiers were willing to pay. That in turn drove prices down farther. And now we're entering an age of $5-a-pound carbon fiber, where it can be used in airliners and expensive sports cars. That in turn will drive the price down to $1 or $2 a pound, the level at which it can be used in mid-range and inexpensive cars and trucks. And that, in turn, by reducing weight, will increase the efficiency of transportation.

The trend in increasing efficiency—of travel, of steel production, of food production, of carbon fiber manufacture, or of anything else—happens so slowly that at times we underestimate it. It's an exponential process, not a linear one. The amount of carbon fiber you can buy for a dollar has increased at a rate of somewhere around 9 percent per year. Over a year or two we may not notice it. But in the long term, it works like compound interest. It's an *exponential* process. The gains don't add up year over year. They *multiply*. Over forty years of 9 percent gain, we don't end up able to buy 360 percent more carbon fiber per dollar. We end up able to buy *3,000 percent* more. Inventor and author Ray Kurzweil has argued that we humans have a tendency to look at exponential gains and overestimate the short-term impacts, while under-estimating the long-term impacts. If you'd asked anyone in 1960 or 1970 to predict the food yields, carbon fiber prices, or energy efficiency of lighting in 2010, you're likely to have gotten answers that tremendously underestimated the amount of progress we've made.

Most of the reductions I've mentioned here have been driven by the mar-ket. The cost of fuel drove Boeing to look for ways to make airplanes lighter, which drives innovation in carbon fiber and other lightweight materials, which reduces their long-term cost. Agriculture uses less water, less land, and less energy per calorie produced today because all of those things cost money. Using less means farmers can sell food at lower prices and reap more profit. Steel manufacturers have cut their energy use because energy is a large portion of the cost of turning iron into steel.

The market generally drives reduction in resource use. But sometimes it fails.

Burn On, Big River, Burn On

On June 22, 1969, a rail car crossing a bridge over the Cuyahoga River in Cleveland sent a rogue spark down into the river below. The spark lighted on an inches-thick slick of oil and chemical-soaked debris that choked the river. Flames leapt up as high as five stories. The river was ablaze. As the slick traveled downstream, it passed under two more bridges, singing one and setting the other on fire. Fire fighters in pump boats quickly extinguished the flames, but the damage was done. Cleveland was the laughing stock of the nation that month. *Time* magazine proclaimed that the Cuyahoga "oozes rather than flows." Johnny Carson told jokes about the polluted river on *The Tonight Show.*

Why didn't the market take care of the Cuyahoga's pollution problem before the 1969 fire? Through the 1950s and 1960s, our resource productivity soared. The amount of food we could produce from an acre of land, the amount of steel we could forge from a kilowatt hour of electricity, and a dozen other metrics of the efficiency with which we can use resources all rose in those two decades. Yet, while resource use for any given task went down, pollution rose.

No one owns the nation's rivers, lakes, or skies. In the language of economists they're "commons"—resources that are free for anyone to use without charge. Where market forces are incredibly effective in reducing the need for any resource that costs money—whether that be energy, materials, labor, land, or time—the market is oblivious to harmful side effects that don't come with a price. And so those shared resources are prone to be exploited and damaged in the "tragedy of the commons."

In fact, the Darwinian nature of the market can push toward *more* pollution. If it's cheaper to dump oil in the river than it is to haul it to a safe place for disposal, then any company that tosses their oil into the river has a price advantage. Because they have lower costs, they can charge lower prices to customers. And with lower prices for customers, they're likely to attract more business, which in turn leads to more oil being dumped into the river. The market isn't just neutral to pollution. If that pollution saves a company money, the market *encourages* it.

But the money the company is saving by dumping oil into the river is costing someone else. It's costing fishermen who could once get fish out of the river. It's costing the city in the form of bridges burned, and the cost of putting out the fire. It's costing the rail company whose service was cut off while the bridge was being repaired, and costing their customers who now have their goods shipped more slowly.

These are all *externalities* of the business. They're external side effects of doing business that affect others. A business that dumps oil into a river is saving itself money, but it's costing others. It's exporting its costs. It's privatizing the profits, and socializing the costs.

We've come a long way since Cuyahoga. While the models of *The Limits to Growth* predicted that economic growth since 1970 would lead to a quadrupling of pollution levels by now, the trend has, for most pollutants, been in the opposite direction. Our rivers and lakes are cleaner now than at any point in generations. Our skies have less smog. Acidic rain no longer falls on our forests. Innovation has produced ways to reduce pollutants of all sorts, or to replace polluting substances with others that serve the same purpose but don't damage the environment.

The numbers tell the tale. Emissions of sulfur dioxide, the chemical that causes acid rain, are less than half of what they were in 1970, and are down to levels not seen in the United States since 1910.[7] Carbon monoxide emissions are down to half of what they were in 1970.[8] Mercury emissions have dropped by half since 1990. Lead concentrations in the atmosphere are just *one-tenth* of what they were in 1980, and new emissions of lead have dropped to near zero.[9] Emissions of particulates, polychlorinated biphenyls (PCBs), and nitrogen oxide are all down by roughly half. Worldwide emissions of ozone-destroying chlorofluorocarbons (CFCs), once used as refrigerants, have plummeted to nearly zero. The Antarctic ozone hole is now recovering, ahead of schedule. Even the Cuyahoga is in fair health now, with more than forty species of fish occupying it, a massive increase from the two that could be found there in 1969.

Yet our cars and trucks haven't stopped running. Their engines haven't seized up. Our power plants have kept producing valuable electricity. And our refrigerators haven't stopped working. In every case we've found a way to reduce the amount of a pollutant we emit, or to replace the substance with something more benign, without stopping industry or growth. Innovation has driven down pollution while keeping our economy running, and in fact *doubling* per capita wealth since 1970. Innovation has the power to decouple economic growth from pollution.

That hasn't happened on its own. The market has played a key role in each of those reductions of pollution, but it hasn't been the driver.

The Cuyahoga fire, the thirteenth recorded on that river since the 1800s, served as a wake-up call. In 1970, Richard Nixon signed a law creating the Environmental Protection Agency. In 1972, the U.S. Congress enacted the Clean Water Act, giving the EPA the power to regulate pollution in the nation's rivers, lakes, and streams. That led to the Cuyahoga's recovery. But it wasn't the end.

Nixon signed the Clean Air Act, which regulated smog, particulates, and other air pollutants. Under the Nixon administration, the EPA created regulations to phase out leaded gasoline. Ronald Reagan signed the Montreal Protocol that phased out CFCs and saved the ozone layer. George Bush senior pushed for and signed amendments to the Clean Air act that placed restrictions on acid rain–producing sulfur dioxide.

Markets are made of rules. Laws we've created make it illegal to steal from a supplier, to defraud a customer, to break a contract. I can't dump waste created by my business into my next door neighbor's yard. And so we've evolved those rules to take care of problems that the market doesn't inherently take care of on its own.

Not every environmental regulation is a good one. The best regulations determine the *goal*, the thing that the market often can't determine for itself, but then leave the *implementation*, how and where and with what technology to achieve the goal, up to the efficiency of the market. Not all regulations work that way today. There's room to make them more effective, more efficient, and lower cost by moving most to that basis. Even so, the market by itself is blind to damage to the commons. Over time, we've stepped in through other methods to help. The very visible hand of democracy has guided and improved the invisible hand of economics. In Part IV, I'll talk about the further improvements to our economic system that we need to make to protect the commons that are at risk today, and in particular the climate that we share.

Plenty of Headroom

Across the board, the headroom to increase efficiency and to reduce pollution is enormous. Around 70 percent of the energy stored in an automobile's gas tank is wasted as heat due to the inefficiency of small internal combustion engines. The roughly 30 percent that remains is used to move a vehicle that weighs thousands of pounds, while its cargo—the thing we really want to move—usually weighs hundreds or less. When you accelerate, only about *3 percent* of the energy in gasoline is accelerating you. The rest is lost to engine inefficiency, friction, and moving the weight of the car. When you brake, your car uses friction to reduce the speed of the car, turning the energy of its forward momentum into heat, which is then wasted.[10]

Electric drive trains are 90 percent efficient. Carbon fiber weighs a fifth as much as steel for the same toughness and safety. Regenerative braking—such as that in the Toyota Prius—captures energy from the wheels when the car brakes, and stores it for later use. Together those technologies could improve the energy efficiency of cars by a factor of more than 10, *reducing* the costs of transportation. Those technologies are all expensive today, but time and learning curve driven by consumer demand will bring their prices down rapidly.

Buildings can be improved upon just as much. "Green" office buildings can avoid much of the energy waste of heating and cooling, and can capture energy from the sun and wind around them. A mile south and west of my home, construction is underway on Seattle's Bullitt Center, a six-story, 50,000-square-foot office building designed to capture as much energy as it uses.[11] If it lives up to its design goals, its owners will save close to $100,000 per year in energy costs.[12] Two miles north from my home, on the University of Washington campus, is the university's new Molecular Engineering and Science building. The building's walls have an inch-thick layer of an advanced gel that freezes when exposed to cool air at night, and then absorbs heat from the sun during the day, providing passive cooling for the 90,000-square-foot building and cutting energy costs.[13]

In 2011, a study by the Edison Foundation concluded that increasing efficiency in buildings cost an average of 3.5 cents per kilowatt hour saved. That's around a third of the average retail price of electricity in the United States, meaning that every dollar spent on increased efficiency of buildings *saves* three dollars in energy bills.[14] In 2012, the American Council for an Energy-Efficient Economy released a report estimating that efficiency investments could cut American energy use by half by 2050, with a net *savings* of $400 billion per year.[15] The cheapest energy technology we know of is energy efficiency.

Pollutants are just as prime for reduction. The thirty least-polluting coal-fired electrical plants in the United States produce around one-fifth the nitrogen oxide pollution (per unit of electricity created) of average coal plants in the United States. They produce *one-tenth* the amount of acid rain–causing sulfur dioxide, per megawatt hour of electricity, as average coal plants.[16]

Even with the technology we have today, the headroom to increase efficiency and reduce pollution, *if* we create the right incentives and rules to encourage that, is large. New ideas can drive us even further. Knowledge accumulates over time. Where it's applied, it can reduce the need for resources and pollution of any sort. Furthering innovation in efficiency and pollution reduction is our best tool for continuing to grow our wealth while reducing our impact on the planet.

eleven the recycler

Not a Drop to Drink

"Water, water, everywhere, nor any drop to drink." So the ancient mariner lamented in Samuel Taylor Coleridge's most famous poem. We live on a water world, yet we fear water shortage. Seawater is poison to us. We can't drink it. We can't feed it to our livestock. We can't water our crops with it.

Yet this poison is a vast, barely untouched resource. Ninety-seven percent of our planet's water is salty. Another 2 percent is locked up in frozen (for now) polar ice caps and high-altitude glaciers. We can access, at the very most, 1 percent of the world's water for food and agriculture, and in reality, much more like 0.1 percent.

References to desalination abound throughout history. In the Bible, Moses led the Israelites to the edge of the waters of Marah, which were "too bitter to drink." Exodus has this passage: "Then Moses cried out to the Lord, and the Lord showed him a piece of wood. He threw it into the water, and the water became sweet."[1] We could use that technology today. In the third century BC, Aristotle described a way to remove salt from water by boiling it.[2] In 1791, Benjamin Franklin, then secretary of state of the United States, presented a technical report describing a way to distill salt water to make freshwater for ships at sea. He ordered the report printed and displayed on ocean-going ships to ensure that there would always be a way to produce freshwater onboard.[3]

For years since then, the dream has been that we could efficiently desalinate large enough quantities of seawater to provide enough freshwater to ensure that everyone has enough to drink and enough to grow food, while reducing pressure on our dropping aquifers and increasingly over-pumped and dried-up rivers. Yet desalination has a negative reputation in environmental circles. It's too energy intensive, goes the story. The coal or natural gas burned to power desalination of seawater pumps too much carbon into the atmosphere.

In 1970, desalinating water was indeed incredibly energy intensive. The most common method was to boil the water, turning it completely into steam (and thus freeing it from the salt) and then letting that steam condense into a separate chamber, producing freshwater. The energy needed to not only bring water to a boil, but literally turn all the water one wanted to desalinate into steam made it prohibitive.

Newer desalination technologies borrow tricks from nature and from materials science. Biologists have long understood that nature has semi-permeable membranes that can let some fluids and dissolved substances through, while keeping others out. The walls of every cell inside a human body are an example of such a membrane. Starting in the 1960s, Stanley Loeb and Srinivasa Sourirajan of UCLA began experimenting with a form of desalination that mimicked the function of biological membranes. They used acetate—the plastic used in photographic film—to perform a similar task.[4] Their initial systems were flimsy, costly, slow, and inefficient. But as always, innovation has pressed on. Since Loeb and Sourirajan's first experiments, a series of advances in the physics and chemistry of permeable membranes have revolutionized desalination. Instead of boiling water, modern desalination plants push water through advanced membranes that filter out salt, other minerals, and even bacteria.

The result is that, we've reduced the amount of energy it takes to desalinate a gallon of water by a factor of 9 since 1970.[5]

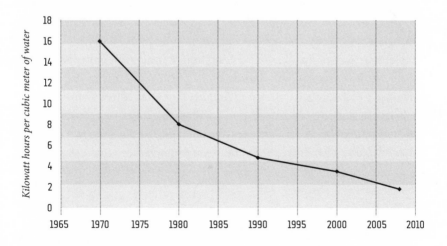

Figure 11.1. Energy required to desalinate water. The energy needed to desalinate seawater has been reduced by nearly a factor of 9 over the last forty years. Data from Menachem Elimelech and William A. Phillip.

The improvement in energy efficiency of desalinating water has made it suddenly viable and affordable in the last few years. The Singapore-Tuas seawater desalination plant, for example, which is still only half as efficient as the best laboratory systems, provides 10 percent of Singapore's water needs, at a price of $0.49 per cubic meter, which equates to one-fifth of a cent per gallon.[6] Israel's massive Ashkelon Sea Water Reverse Osmosis plant, the largest in the world, produces 84 million gallons a day, enough to provide water for 1.4 million people in southern Israel, at a similar price.[7]

Even at today's incredibly improved efficiency, desalination still consumes significant power. To get 100 percent of the water the average American consumes directly and indirectly through agriculture, drinking, and industrial uses, we'd need to produce an extra 900,000 kilowatt hours of electricity for that person each year. If that electricity came from coal-fired power plants, that would result in the emission of two additional tons of carbon dioxide into the air each year for that hypothetical American, on top of the seventeen tons he or she already emits each year.

Realistically, though, we don't need to produce all our water from desalination. It will help most in areas that are close to the ocean. In most areas it will supplement water withdrawn from rivers and lakes at sustainable rates. And even as we get better at desalinating water, more efficient farming techniques will reduce the amount of it that we need to use in agriculture, the world's largest single user of water.

Perhaps most importantly, as better technology allows us to transition away from coal-electricity and toward solar, wind, and other renewable sources, the energy cost of desalination will no longer mean CO_2 emissions. If we think of the energy required to desalinate water in terms of the amount of solar collection it requires, the numbers look far better. Using current efficiencies, the solar cells needed to collect enough electricity to desalinate 500,000 gallons of water per year—the amount that the average American uses—would cover an area about fourteen feet on a side. That area, around nineteen square meters, is one-sixtieth the size of the plot of land it takes to feed the average person.

Through innovation we've dropped the energy needed to turn salt water into fresh by a factor of 9. Through other innovations we've gone from needing to burn coal and heat our planet to gather that energy, to being able to do it sustainably, in a compact enough area, from the plentiful light of the sun.

This Place Is a Dump

Houthalen-Helchteren is a sleepy municipality in the east of Belgium, about an hour's drive from Brussels, and home to just under 30,000 people. Until recently, the town's greatest claim to fame was as the site where, in 1702, French and Spanish armies faced off during the War of Spanish Succession and *almost* fought a battle.[8] Soon, the region may have a new place in history, as the first place that trash was turned to value on a mass commercial scale.

Just outside the town is the Remo Milieubeheer landfill, a fifty-year-old site where seventeen million tons of trash have been deposited over the years. In 2006, the operators of the landfill began collaborating with the University of Hasselt and the Flemish Institute for Technological Research to find ways to better manage the site. The result is a plan that, over twenty years, will recycle an estimated 45 percent of the material in the landfill, and use the rest as fuel to provide seventy-five megawatts of electricity to the region for the lifetime of the project.[9]

Mining landfills was first attempted on a small scale in Tel Aviv in 1953, where a project filtered dirt from garbage dumps to use as soil in citrus groves. The value derived was modest. The project remained small scale. It was attempted in the United States in the early 1970s, and again in the 1990s, but failed to take off due to a combination of high cost, fires that plagued the processing centers built in landfills, and insufficiently advanced technology.[10] Now, however, the idea's time may have come.

The world's landfills contain tens of billions of tons of waste worldwide. That material includes valuable metals, plastics, glass, and more. For example, Alcoa, the world's largest aluminum company, believes that landfills already contain more aluminum than can be produced by the world's mines. Indeed, aluminum makes up a larger fraction of the weight of most landfills than it does of bauxite, the ore from which aluminum is extracted.[11] A paper in 2004 estimated that the world's landfills contained 225 million tons of refined copper, an amount that, if brought on the market, would allow the world's copper mines to completely shut down for ten to fifteen years, and that would fetch a total market price of more than $2 *trillion* at 2011 prices. Another paper in 2006 estimated that in the United States alone, landfills contained 850 million tons of iron and steel, about ten times as much as the United States produces each year.[12] Undoubtedly, since 2004 and 2006, both numbers have increased.

In Britain, recycling experts estimate that the country's landfills contain around $100 billion worth of discarded plastics that could be recycled or converted into oil or natural gas.[13] Recent analysis in Japan has found that landfills in that country contain 300,000 tons of rare earths,[14] as much as Japan consumes in a decade.[15] Those landfills in Japan alone are estimated to contain three times more gold, silver, and indium than the world consumes in a year.[16]

Retrieving those valuable materials from landfills hasn't been economically feasible until now. Separating the useful materials from the non-useful ones has been too energy and labor intensive. In recent years, though, rising commodity prices have reignited interest, and innovations in processing technology have brought mining landfills to the brink of feasibility.

Over the last few years, for instance, recyclers have pioneered the use of spinning rotors of magnets that can not only extract iron and steel, but can create currents in other conducting metals such as iron and rare earths, which then cause those metals to eject themselves from the heap. Alcoa, meanwhile, has reported efficiency gains in fractional crystallization, the chemical process it uses to separate metals from one another. Both of those innovations reduce the amount of time, labor, and energy needed to separate useful materials from landfills and sort them out from one another.[17]

Landfills also contains organic matter that, if left alone, will decompose into methane, a gas that warms the planet thirty times more than carbon dioxide in the long run, and 100 times more in the short run. The EPA describes landfill methane release as the largest source of human methane release and the third largest overall human global warming source in the United States. Around the world, the methane released from landfills contributes a long-term climate heating effect equivalent to around a billion tons of CO_2 a year. Because methane has most of its effect on the climate quickly, in the short term that heating effect is even larger, on the order of three billion tons of CO_2 or more. That is a major cost the world pays for food and other organic matter decaying in landfills.[18]

Methane is the prime constituent in the natural gas burned in many homes. Burning it releases useful energy and also releases CO_2. But the CO_2 released from burning methane has only 3 percent of the climate-warming power that the methane itself would have had. Burning methane not only provides useful energy, it's also cleaner than letting the methane enter the atmosphere unburned. And capturing the 600 billion cubic feet of methane released from landfills in the United States alone would provide enough energy to power millions of homes.[19]

We're learning, once again, to turn waste into something of value. Fittingly, the International Energy Agency titled its 2009 report on landfill gas "Turning a Liability into an Asset." Through innovation, we can do that again and again.

The innovations in mining landfills aren't just valuable for the trash already in landfills, of course. The world dumps an additional 1.6 billion tons of material into the trash each year. By mid-century that could be 3 billion tons. While recycling programs that encourage residents to separate recyclables from trash help, most potentially recyclable materials still end up in the trash. Better technology for extracting the valuable materials out of waste will help address that, and slowly narrow the gap between what it means to recycle something (to intentionally set it out for recycling) and to throw it away (to put it into a mixed stream that someone will eventually recycle it from). It will often be more energy and labor efficient to separate out the valuable materials from the waste at the source, but reaching the point where that's universally done will take time. And for some materials, like the rare earth metals inside consumer electronics, there is no easy way to separate materials on the horizon. Fortunately, for the foreseeable future, innovation will make it progressively easier and cheaper to extract the valuable materials from the things we throw out, whether they're intentionally recycled or not.

Other examples of new technologies allowing us to capture waste abound. In 2011, Virgin Airlines announced an alliance with a New Zealand company called LanzaTech to capture carbon monoxide produced by steel mills and convert it, through the use of engineered microbes, into jet fuel. The process could save as much as fifteen billion gallons of jet fuel per year.[20]

In the same year, a handful of companies announced projects aimed at bringing thermoelectric systems to markets. Thermoelectrics are devices built like computer chips that use the difference in temperature between two conductive plates to create an electrical current. In so doing, they can capture waste heat and turn it directly into electricity. They can work at any scale, from capturing the excess heat produced by a cell phone and using it to recharge the battery, to capturing the heat given off by a factory or power plant, and using that to generate additional electricity.[21] Worldwide, the potential for thermoelectric capture of waste heat amounts to at least terawatts of electricity. That's a gain equivalent to building more than a thousand large coal-fired power plants, and it comes not from burning any new fuels, but simply from capturing heat that we're giving off as waste through inefficient processes. New ideas and new discoveries continually turn waste into value.

Metals, plastics, and energy aren't the only valuable things we can extract from waste. One of the more frightening future shortages that's been postulated is that of phosphorous. Without rare earth metals, we might have to use fewer gadgets, or find some other way to manufacture solar cells. But all plants fundamentally, biologically, need phosphorous to grow. And the fertilizer we use to boost yields doesn't contain just nitrogen, it contains phosphorous as well. The most productive phosphorous mine in the United States (of twelve), in Florida, is estimated be just twenty years away from having depleted its supplies.[22] And around the world, the phosphorous content of the rocks being mined is dropping.[23] If a "peak phosphorous" exists in our future, it could dramatically drop food production, or at least dramatically raise the price of food production, neither of which would be good for the world.

Yet, as the Global Phosphorous Initiative notes, the phosphorous we consume in food eventually comes out of us as well. A human being's urine contains somewhere between 50 and 100 percent of the phosphorous needed to grow food for that person, using current farming technology.[24] And just as over time we've reduced the amount of water we need to use to produce the food for one person, over time we'll do the same for phosphorous. In 2009 a research group in the Root Biology Center of South China Agricultural University published results showing that they could tweak the genes of plants to make them twice as efficient in utilizing phosphorous in the soil.[25] Ultimately, if we make it a priority, innovations in recycling phosphorous from waste can meet innovations in reducing the need for phosphorous in plants, bringing us to a point of sustainable phosphorous use.

Nature abhors waste. Anywhere in the natural world that one finds resources, one will eventually find life. Evolution will select for organisms that can thrive in the environment and efficiently make use of the resources available. The same, it seems, is true of innovation in a finite world. Anywhere we find resources that are being wasted, eventually new ideas will come along to capture, tap into, and make use of those resources.

In 2002, German chemist Michael Braungart and American architect William McDonough wrote their manifesto, *Cradle to Cradle: Remaking the Way We Make Things*. Braungart and McDonough made a compelling case that we should build buildings, cars, planes, electronics, and products of all sorts, with a designed-in plan for what happens to them and their pieces at the end of their useful lifetimes. We live on a finite world, after all. That means that, in the final equation, there's only so much useful material out there, and so much room to dump things we no longer want. Better to design things such that the useful parts of them can easily come back into circulation. I wholeheartedly agree.

Until that happens, though, innovation will keep on finding ways to take one person's waste and turn it into another person's value.

The Fallacy of Finiteness: Part 1

What does it mean to say that we live on a finite world? We apply the word to indicate limits, to indicate the worry of running out. But it means different things in different contexts.

A finite amount of food or fuel can only last so long. It's chemically changed by use, and the stored-up energy in it is lost. Whether it's a morsel or a month's supply, a thimble-full or a barrel, the value it produces comes from its combustion, whether in our bodies or in our engines.

But what about a finite amount of land? Or a finite amount of steel? The value either of those can provide isn't fixed. The steel can be forged into a sword or a plowshare. It can be made into a pot or a horseshoe. And, given energy, it can be changed from one form into another. It can even be repaired if broken, if energy is available.

Energy sources and raw materials behave very differently. When we burn up oil or coal, they're lost to us. But as far as raw materials go, very little is truly lost. The water that we use to irrigate our fields isn't destroyed. It sinks into the soil and eventually makes its way to rivers and to the sea, or it evaporates and comes down as rain, mostly into the world's oceans.

The metals, glass, plastic, minerals, and so on that we throw away don't cease to exist. They're just moved from one place to another. The materials that make them up have been disorganized, scattered, and mixed with other materials. Usually, that dilutes them. Sometimes (as in the case of piles of thrown-out electronics, or in the case of copper) the process actually concentrates valuable things beyond the levels at which they're found in nature. Either way, those materials still exist. They're still there, a resource for us to exploit.

The idea of running out of raw materials doesn't quite capture the dynamic. We could run out of *energy* in principle, but until we do, we can use energy to reform raw materials into new shapes and uses, or to retrieve them from the places they've wound up after they've been "thrown away."

The total amounts of all minerals in the Earth's crust is astounding. At current rates of extraction, it would take fourteen million years to deplete the Earth's crust of iron, two million to deplete it of phosphorous, one million to deplete it of copper, four million to deplete it of tin, and *billions* of years to deplete it of titanium. The limiting factors in mining are innovation and energy, not raw materials.

We'll never get to those points of extraction. Because raw materials are nearly infinitely reusable, and because it takes *less* energy to reuse already processed materials than to mine and refine new ones, we're gradually becoming a society that reuses materials as much or more than we extract new materials from the land. More than half of the copper[26] and aluminum[27] used in the United States, and two-thirds of the lead,[28] is produced from recycling rather than mining. More than half the paper used in the United States is produced from recycled paper or waste from other processes.[29] Around 40 percent of the steel produced worldwide starts with recycled scrap steel rather than iron ore.[30]

As the technology of mining dumps and waste streams improves, those numbers will rise. And they bring with them, and indeed are motivated by, tremendous energy savings. Recycling steel reduces the energy needed to make new steel by 60 percent. Recycling aluminum reduces energy needed by an incredible 95 percent.[31]

Ultimately, our world is a nearly closed system for materials. But the vast quantity of raw materials we possess, combined with their nearly infinite reusability, makes the value we can extract from that finite resource nearly limitless.

twelve the multiplier

A Scenic Drive

Driving back toward Seattle one evening from a long trip, I came upon a beautiful sight. I was in northern Oregon, headed north toward the border with Washington, still three hours from home. Washington and Oregon meet at the Columbia River Gorge, an eighty-mile long canyon, in places thousands of feet deep, where the river flows west until it eventually empties out into the Pacific. The Gorge makes for incredible scenery. As you approach it from the north or south, you come over a rise several miles from the river. The land just falls away and a vista opens up before you. In the western parts of the two states, the slopes on both river banks are green and verdant, covered with the trees of the Gifford-Pinchot National Forest to the north, and the Mount Hood National Forest to the south. Further east, where I was crossing, it's high desert, with a starker but no less gorgeous beauty brought by amber grasses and reddish-brown rock walls. As you descend into the gorge, the fast flowing river looms larger and larger in your sight, until suddenly you're on a bridge above it, with the waves crashing below you, and the opposite slope rising ahead.

And then there are the wind surfers. On a sunny day in summer you can see dozens of them, standing upright on their boards, holding up their triangular sails in blue and red and green and orange, skimming at high speed across the surface of the river. The unique geography of the Gorge creates strong, sustained, reliable winds, making it one of the best places in the world to windsurf.

Those winds also make the Columbia River Gorge one of the best locations in the world for something else: harvesting energy from the wind. And as I came over a ridge that evening I got my first view of the wind turbines that have sprung up in this sleepy, rural stretch of the Pacific Northwest. Dozens of them, tall, majestic, their rotors slowly turning as they captured a small fraction of the energy in the Gorge's winds and turned it into electricity for the West Coast.

The potential is huge. The National Renewable Energy Laboratory estimates that Washington and Oregon have enough potentially harvestable on-land wind energy to meet all of their electricity needs, even *after* excluding the 70 percent of the land area of the states that hosts homes, cities, forests, and airports.[1] If the potential of wind energy just offshore on the Pacific coast is added, the two states have enough available wind to meet their total electricity needs *five times over.*[2]

The Fallacy of Finiteness: Part 2

We were lucky enough to be born on a planet with a tremendous abundance of energy. We live on a planet that is a mostly closed system for raw materials. For the most part, we don't destroy or create materials. We shift them around, changing their form and concentration. There's no obvious limit to the value we can get out of the raw materials the world supplies us with. Our challenge is to move them from the bowels of the Earth to the surface more efficiently, and then to reuse them more frequently.

By contrast, the energy sources we use are destroyed. They're chemically changed. The atoms that they're made of aren't destroyed, but the chemical energy that held them together is released, and lost to us. Every barrel of oil or ton of coal we burn is one less on the planet.

But the Earth is not a closed system for energy. We have a huge and continual *influx* of energy. The sun strikes our planet with around 160,000 terawatts of energy. All human energy use today, from coal, oil, natural gas, nuclear energy, hydro, wood, geothermal, wind, solar, and every source combined, totals around 17 terawatts. The sun's input of energy is almost 10,000 times the amount of energy humanity uses from all sources combined. In nine seconds, the sun strikes the Earth with as much energy as we use in a day. In less than an hour it strikes the Earth with as much energy as we use in a *year.*[3]

In a few days, the sun delivers more energy to the Earth than is contained in all known reserves of coal, oil, and natural gas today.

In a single week, it delivers more energy to our planet than humanity has used through the burning of coal, oil, and natural gas through *all of human history.*

And the sun will keep shining on our planet for billions of years.

Our challenge isn't that we're running out of energy. It's that we're tapped into the wrong source—the small, finite one that we're depleting. Indeed, all the coal, natural gas, and oil we use today is just solar energy from millions of years ago, a very tiny fraction of which was preserved deep underground. Our challenge, and our opportunity, is to learn to efficiently and cheaply tap into the *much more abundant* source that is the new energy striking our planet each day from sun.

The sun's energy manifests itself in several ways. Some is reflected back into space. Some heats the atmosphere, creating wind. Some drives the evaporation of water into the atmosphere, which then comes down as rain and snow that feed the flow of rivers. And some of the sun's energy reaches the ground, where it powers photosynthesis in plants and heats whatever it touches.

We can capture the Sun's energy by harnessing the power of rivers, harnessing the wind, and collecting the sunlight that falls to Earth. Those three sources range from large, to vast, to incredibly vast.

Hydropower from the planet's rivers today generates around 1 terawatt of energy out of the 17 terawatts that the world uses. The International Energy Agency estimates that another 1.6 terawatts of capacity could be tapped into. That additional amount of energy would be larger than the total consumption of all the world's automobiles combined.

The planet's winds are a much larger source. Worldwide, winds in the lower layers of the atmosphere carry more than 800 terawatts of energy, more than forty times as much energy as humanity uses today. Estimates of the amount of wind power the world can capture on land and near shore range from 1 terawatt (with extremely conservative assumptions about technology) to 72 terawatts (with much more optimistic assumptions). Most middle-of-the-road estimates show that the world could capture 20 or more terawatts with current and near-term technologies, or slightly more energy than we use today from all sources combined.

But the real champion of available energy is the direct power of the sun's rays. Eighty-six thousand terawatts of power, or 5,000 times the amount that humanity uses from all sources, strikes the surface of the Earth. Around 30 percent of that energy, still more than 1,000 times humanity's energy use, strikes land.

Here's how abundant the sun is. To collect enough energy to provide for all of humanity's current needs, using *current consumer-grade solar technology*, it would take only 0.6 percent of Earth's land area.

If world energy demand doubles by 2050, then using *today's* consumer solar efficiencies, we'd need 1.2 percent of the world's land area. How much is 1.2

percent of Earth's land area? It's about 700,000 square miles, or a square 860 miles on a side. In absolute terms, that's a vast area. Yet as compared to the amount of land available, it's tiny, around one-twenty-fifth of the amount of land we use for agriculture. It's around one-sixteenth the size of the world's deserts. The Sahara Desert, alone, is more than five times the area we would need to capture enough energy to power humanity in 2050, using 2010 consumer-grade technology.

And the fraction of the sun's energy that solar panels capture is continuing to rise. All of the numbers I've just given assume cells that capture just over one-eighth of the energy of the sunlight falling on them. The theoretical best cells we could build would capture five times as much.[4] At those efficiencies, powering the world in 2050 would take around a quarter of a percent of our land area, or one-one-hundredth the amount of land we use to grow food.

The Learning Curve

The problem with wind and solar, to date, hasn't been the amount of energy we have available. There's plenty of that. It hasn't been the amount of land it would take to capture that energy. There's a huge amount of available space

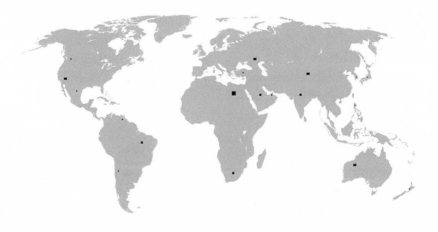

Figure 12.1. Surface area required to power the world with solar. Black squares represent the 0.6 percent of the land area on Earth required to capture enough solar energy to meet current demands. Image courtesy of the Land Art Generator Initiative (www.landartgenerator.org).

for solar in the world's deserts and unused land in sunny regions, and on the rooftops of homes and businesses. There's a tremendous amount of room for wind energy in places like the Columbia River Gorge, and just off shore all along our coasts. Wind turbines can happily coexist with farms, capturing energy from the winds above them as plants grow below. Solar and wind can even coexist with each other, capturing even more area per area of land.

The primary problem hasn't been energy or space. It's been cost.

When Ronald Reagan took office in 1980, average retail electricity costs in the United States were around 5 cents a kilowatt hour (in today's dollars).[5] Electricity produced from wind power, on the other hand, cost around ten times more, at 50 cents a kilowatt hour. And electricity from solar power cost 30 *times* more, at around $1.50 per kilowatt hour.[6]

How the times have changed. Today, new wind power installations in good locations are producing electricity at a cost of 5 cents per kilowatt hour, competitive with the wholesale prices of coal and natural gas at the power plants.[7] While the price of wind has remained flat for the last decade, it's flat at a level that makes it a good option in many parts of the world. Solar prices have dropped as much since 1980, and are still dropping fast. Large-scale solar installations in the very sunniest areas are down into the ballpark of 10–15 cents per kilowatt hour, on the edge of being competitive with the retail price of electricity customers pay at their buildings and factories.[8] In 2011, General Electric announced that it intended to have solar photovoltaic systems at costs at or below current retail electricity prices (a point known as "grid-parity") for sale by 2015.[9] An analysis by researcher Joshua Pearce goes a step further, and argues that current solar prices assume that panels break and wear out far faster than they actually do, and that with more realistic assumptions, solar is already as cheap as grid electricity in sunny places like Texas, Nevada, New Mexico, and Southern California.[10]

The single largest factor in those price declines is the dropping cost of the components. The first solar photovoltaic panel, built by researchers at Bell Labs in 1954, cost a whopping $1,000 per watt of electricity produced. The cost at the beginning of 2012 was around $1 per watt. The price of solar technology has dropped by a factor of 1,000 in less than sixty years.[11]

Solar energy has a substantial learning curve. As the solar industry grows, prices drop. For every doubling of the amount of solar energy built, prices drop around 20 percent.[12] In the last few years, the price of solar has dropped even *faster* than usual. Photovoltaic cell prices dropped in half between 2009

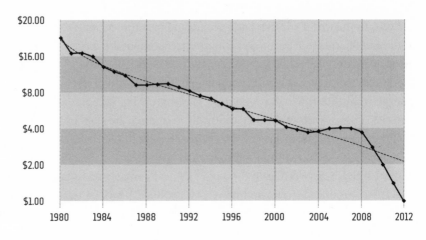

$20.00

$16.00

$8.00

$4.00

$2.00

$1.00

1980   1984   1988   1992   1996   2000   2004   2008   2012

Figure 12.2. Plummeting cost of solar PV modules (cost per Watt in 2012 dollars). The cost of electricity from solar photovoltaic cells has dropped by a factor of 20 in the last thirty-two years. Sources: DOE NREL Solar Market Report, SolarBuzz Retail Environment

and 2011.[13] In 2012, solar prices were about half of what the long-term trend projected. The rapid drop has spurred deployment. Jim Rogers, CEO of Duke Energy, one of the largest utilities in the country, told me in early 2012 that his company was now aggressively installing solar, years ahead of schedule. "We've been able to deploy solar at prices we didn't expect to see until 2018 or 2020."

To put this in context, consider the price of natural gas. With a recent surge of shale gas bringing U.S. production back up toward its former highs, the price of natural gas has dropped sharply in the last few years. Newspapers and magazines have proclaimed that natural gas is a game changer in energy. But a closer look turns up a slightly different picture. Natural gas prices, after plunging from their 2008 highs, are just back to where they were in 2000. Solar cell prices, on the other hand, are at one-quarter of their year 2000 prices, and still dropping.

Rising Returns

Solar cells, in turn, have dropped in price so rapidly because of increases in efficiency and reductions in the energy and materials needed to manufacture them. As recently as 2000, for every watt of electrical power that a solar cell could produce, its manufacturing required 16 grams of pure silicon.[14] Today some companies claim less than 3 grams of silicon per watt of electrical power in their solar panels, and at least one company is targeting 1.5 grams per watt—a reduction of ten times since 2000, by 2014.[15]

Using fewer raw materials and less energy to manufacture each cell means that the return on investment of solar energy is rising. The first photovoltaic cells built in the 1980s consumed more energy in their constructions than they could ever capture from the sun in their lifetimes. Typical solar photovoltaic cells manufactured in 2010, by contrast, capture as much solar energy as it took to build and install them before the end of the first three years of their estimated thirty-year lifetime,* giving an Energy-Return-on-Energy-Invested (EROI) of 10.[16]

Better is on the way. In late 2011, Norwegian firm REC started selling a solar panel that they claimed has an energy payback time, in areas of relatively normal amounts of sunlight, of just *one year*.[17] That means that over a thirty-year lifetime, the panels will have an EROI of 30, paying back the energy used to create them thirty times over. That's roughly on par with the EROI of natural gas and of conventional oil around the world today, and dramatically higher than the EROI of shale oil or tar sands.[18] Wind already has payback times of around a year.

Every solar panel made *decreases* the price of future solar panels through the magic of the learning curve and the Darwinian creation of and competition between new ideas. Those accumulating ideas reduce the amount of labor, time, energy, and materials needed to build each new solar cell.

Fossil fuel technologies have learning curves as well. But the learning curves for coal, natural gas, and oil are much slower—around 3–4 percent improvement in price and efficiency per doubling.[19] And those technologies are growing far more slowly. Worldwide use of coal has doubled over roughly the last thirty years. The amount of solar energy deployed has doubled in the last eighteen *months*.

While fossil fuels don't get much advantage from the learning curve, they suffer from a depletion curve. Every ton of coal, barrel of oil, or cubic foot of natural gas taken from the ground leaves behind a supply that's just a bit

*This assumes these cells are installed in a location with sunlight similar to the average amount in the United States.

more difficult to extract. We take out the easy stuff first—the coal near the surface, the large high-pressure fields of oil and gas. What remains is farther away, under less pressure, in smaller fields, and harder to get out.

Every solar panel built makes solar energy cheaper. Every barrel of oil extracted makes oil more expensive.

In the long run, which of those would we rather have our wagon hitched to?

Storing the Wealth

A Tesla Roadster is a gorgeous piece of driving machinery. It's a sleek, exotic-looking sports car. Everything about it screams "speed." It seems totally at home among Ferrari and Lamborghinis, with its low-to-the-ground body and its aggressively aerodynamic shape. You don't just get into a Tesla Roadster. You have to lower yourself down into it, carefully, sinking your body into the deep bucket seats in the fighter jet–like interior.

When a friend offered me a ride in his, conveniently parked right outside my home, I jumped at the chance. I eased myself into the passenger seat, closed the door, and buckled my belt, chattering away the whole time on the topic of battery energy density and electric motor power curves. Then he hit the gas, and I was struck dumb as the acceleration slammed me into the back of my seat.

A Tesla Roadster is a completely electric vehicle. Its power is provided by a 115-pound electric motor that delivers 288 horsepower to the wheels. While even high-performance internal combustion engines in traditional sports cars need to rev up their engines before they can deliver high torque to drive the wheels, the electric drive train of a Tesla delivers 100 percent of the torque, right from the instant you step on the gas pedal. The result is instant acceleration. Bone-shaking acceleration. Zero to sixty miles per hour in 3.7 seconds acceleration. Acceleration that beats most Ferraris, Lamborghinis, and Porsches. From an *electric* car that's *six times* as energy efficient as other cars of its class.

Tesla salesmen have a little trick they like to play to demonstrate what a Roadster can do. Get the passenger into the car. Suggest that the passenger play with the radio. Then, just as she stretches out her arm, accelerate. The passenger is thrown back into her seat with three-quarters of a G of acceleration. Her fingers never touch the radio.

My friend didn't suggest I reach for the radio. But his foot on the gas pedal silenced me, instantly. It's one thing to talk about energy densities of 250 watt-hours per kilogram of battery and a motor that can turn 900 amps and 375 volts of electricity into wheel power at 90 percent efficiency. It's another thing to *feel* it.

Collecting energy from the sun and wind is only one half of the battle. To use that energy to drive our cars or to power our cities and factories when the sun isn't shining and the wind isn't blowing, we need to be able to store the energy for later.

And storage is a substantial challenge. The batteries in a Tesla Roadster weigh around 1,000 pounds, or nine times as much as the car's engine. In comparison, the gasoline in a fifteen-gallon automobile tank weighs around 100 pounds. And the Tesla's high tech, top-of-the-line batteries cost an astounding $36,000 per car in 2009.

Battery storage for the electrical power grid isn't much better. Today, the batteries to store a day's worth of energy output from a typical solar or wind installation would cost as much as the solar cells or wind turbines they provided storage for.

Fortunately, human ingenuity is dropping the price of batteries, as well, and increasing the amount of power that can be stored. Between 1991 and 2005, the price of storing a watt-hour of electricity in a lithium-ion battery dropped by a factor of around 10, from $3.20 per watt hour to just over $0.30 per watt hour. In the same time frame, the amount of energy that could be stored in lithium-ion batteries of a given weight (their energy density) more than doubled, from under 90 watt hours per kilogram to more than 200 watt hours per kilogram.[20]

That pace of improvement of both price and density is *faster* than the corresponding pace of improvement of solar and wind. In a typical fifteen-year period, the price of solar cells falls by around a factor of 3, while the prices of batteries have fallen by around a factor of 10. If the learning curve of battery technologies can be maintained, the ability to store energy will advance faster than the ability to collect it, and overall prices will keep falling.

The history of batteries gives us reason to be optimistic. Lithium-ion batteries themselves are one of a long line of successive battery technologies, each of which has had higher energy densities than the last. A lead-acid battery (the kind used in cars) can store around 40 watt hours per kilogram. A "NiCad" nickel cadmium battery can store around 60 watt hours per kilo. NiMH batteries, nickel metal hydride, can store around 90 watt hours per

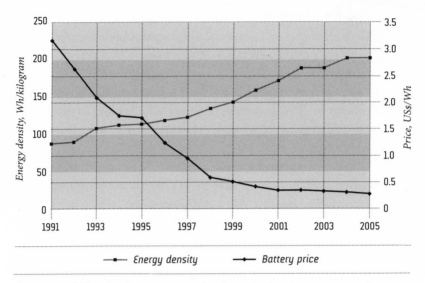

Figure 12.3. Lithium-ion battery energy density and price. Between 1991 and 2005, the price of laptop batteries dropped by nearly a factor of 10, and the amount of energy stored per weight more than doubled. Data from David Anderson and Dalia Patino-Echeverri, Duke University.

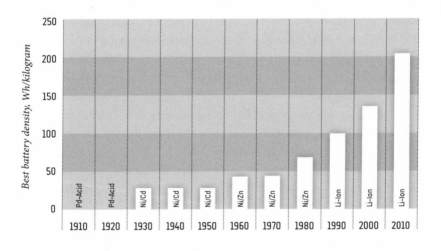

Figure 12.4. Rising battery energy densities over time. Each successive battery technology has had a higher energy density (in watt hours per kilogram) than the ones before it. Zinc-air and lithium-air batteries (not shown) could drive this dramatically further forward. Data from Chen-Xi Zu and Hong Li.

kilo. Lithium-ion batteries have a theoretical cap at around 300 watt hours per kilo, with the best on the market now, such as those in the Tesla Roadster, reaching 250 watt hours per kilo.

Eventually, new battery technology will succeed Lithium Ion. In late July 2008, for instance, the Zephyr-6 solar plane flew a record breaking three days at 60,000 feet, powered by solar cells during the day, and overnight on lithium-sulfur batteries charged during daylight. The lithium-sulfur batteries stored 600 watt hours per kilo, or more than twice that of the very best lithium-ion batteries available today.[21] And solid state batteries, built using techniques more similar to those of computer chips than traditional batteries, could achieve energy densities approaching 1,000 watt hours per kilo.[22] That would quadruple the range of an electric car.

Also on the horizon are metal-air batteries. One type of these, zinc-air batteries, could store as much as 2,000 watt hours per kilogram, eight times as much as the best battery on the market today. Pennsylvania startup EOS claims that it will soon start selling a zinc-air battery for electrical grid storage at a price of $160 per kilowatt hour, or half the price of the cheapest suitable batteries today.[23]

Even higher-capacity lithium-air batteries could practically store as much as 4,000 watt hours per kilogram, sixteen times as much as the best battery on the market today, with a theoretical max as high as 12,000 watt hours per kilo, another three times higher. Such batteries would bring down the cost of storage along with the weight. They'd make it feasible for solar and wind power systems to cheaply store sufficient surplus power to get through nights, cloudy days, and periods without wind. They'd make it possible for electric cars to go for a thousand miles on a single charge.[24]

Mining the Air

The other option for storing energy is making fuel. Gasoline, today, carries thirty times as much energy per weight as the best lithium-ion batteries. That means a vehicle can be lighter. That's important in automobile range, and even more important in air travel, where weight is at a premium. While metal air batteries have the potential to eventually equal gasoline's ability to store energy densely, they're not there yet today.

The fuels we burn today are hydrocarbons. They're made from hydrogen atoms and carbon atoms linked together. We get energy out of them by breaking the links between those atoms, turning the energy that once linked them together into heat. But we can also run that process in reverse, capturing carbon and hydrogen from water and the atmosphere, and adding energy to turn them into fuel. Think of it as solar powered mining of the air for its valuable carbon.

In fact, this is what plants do when they photosynthesize. Sugar is a fuel that plants make by combining sunlight, carbon dioxide, and water. If plants can do it, we can do the same, or we can utilize the ability that plants already have.

The world already produces half a billion barrels of biofuels each year, making up almost 3 percent of the fuel burned on our roads. Eighty percent of that biofuel is corn ethanol. Corn captures solar energy, CO_2, and water, and combines them to make sugar inside its kernels. That sugar is then fermented to produce ethanol, an alcohol.

In theory, biofuels should be effectively carbon neutral. The carbon that's released when they're burned is the same carbon that's captured from the air when the fuel crop is grown. If we replaced all oil and coal with ideal biofuels, we'd be sucking carbon dioxide out of the air as fast as we're pumping it into the air. The same technologies that capture carbon from the air and energy from the sun to create fuels could also create all the other petroleum products that we depend on—plastics, synthetic rubber, lubricants, and chemicals of all sorts that enrich our lives. And the ultimate energy source powering the creation of both this new breed of plastics and the fuels we depend on would be the sun. And that energy source is good for another few billion years.

Corn ethanol, unfortunately, is an extremely poor technology. An acre of corn produces the equivalent of around 200 gallons of gasoline per year.[25] The world uses around 1.4 trillion gallons of gasoline per year. That means, to grow enough fuel using corn to power the world, we'd need to plant 7 billion acres, or more than twice as much farmland as the world has. Along the way, we'd use nearly as much energy to grow the corn as comes out in the ethanol on the other side.[26] And every acre of corn planted for ethanol (about a third of U.S. corn land today[27]) reduces the acreage available to grow food for people, contributing to food price spikes and hunger around the world.[28]

Other crops like sugarcane or palm trees get better yields when converted to fuel, but still far too low to replace oil. And planting of those crops for fuel also competes with food for humans and increasingly drives deforestation.

Fortunately, we can do better. Dismissing biofuels on the basis of corn ethanol (or even sugarcane or palm oil) would be like dismissing solar technology because the first solar cells cost $1,000 a watt. Corn ethanol is merely the beginning of the biofuel story, not the end.

Termite Mounds . . .

In December 2010 I found myself on a photo safari in South Africa's Kruger National Park. One afternoon, as we were headed back to the lodge, our guide pulled the jeep to a stop by an impressively large mound of dirt, just to the side of the grass-and-mud-rut road we were driving down. "Termite mound," he said. "Climb up!"

Climbing up, of course, entailed getting out of the jeep. And since we'd seen leopards, lions, and hyenas in this stretch of jungle, I wasn't really keen on this idea. Nor do bugs excite me. Quite the opposite, really. Nevertheless, I went along with it. Scrambling up the mound, my mind flipped back and forth between images of a leopard bounding out of the jungle and pouncing on me from behind and equally horrifying images of hundreds of thousands of termites swarming out of their home and consuming me. To this day I'm not really sure which would have been worse. The leopard probably would have been a quicker way to go.

I didn't die, of course. The mound was fascinating. Deep inside, hordes of worker termites, with help from microbes that live in their guts, digested bits of wood and then regurgitated them to feed the other members of the colony. The unique ability of termites and their gut bacteria to digest wood is a bane to home owners. In the United States alone, termites cause $5 billion dollars in home damage each year.

Yet that ability is also a potential asset in creating a second generation of biofuels.

Plants make sweet sugars that can be readily turned into ethanol. But they also make stalks, husks, trunks, branches, and leaves—structures that are mostly made of cellulose. Cellulose contains energy, but it can't be easily broken down in chemical refiners. And so all of that energy, which plants have soaked up from the sun, is wasted.

Enter the termites. Or rather, their microbes.

Researchers around the world are now experimenting with using genes found in termites and their gut flora to create enzymes that can more easily break cellulose down, making the energy contained in most of the plant available for making fuel. For example, a company called ZeaChem announced in 2011 that, using bacteria that grow in termite guts, they'd reached levels of 2,000 gallons of ethanol per acre of poplar tree per year, including the time for the poplars to regrow. That's the equivalent of 1,400 gallons of gasoline, or seven times better than normal corn ethanol.[29] Other companies using left-over plant stalks and husks from cornfields and wheat fields, wood chips from lumber mills and paper mills, and other sources are close behind.

. . . And Pond Scum

Breaking down cellulose is the second generation of biofuels. The *third* generation is all about pond scum.

Near my home in Seattle is the Washington State Arboretum, a mile-long park a few hundred feet wide lined with trees of all sorts, brought from various parts of the world. It's a lovely place for a walk to clear one's head, and I've gone there often while writing this book. Near the south end of the park there's a small pond, which in the fall accumulates a slimy layer of algae. That algae might just be transformed in the coming decade into a pivotal source of cheap fuel.

Algae are simple, one-celled creatures of amazing variety and importance to life on earth. Various strains grow in freshwater, waste water, and salt water. More than half the oxygen we breathe is produced not by plants, but by algae, most of them in the oceans.

Algae are also incredibly efficient in capturing the sun's energy in ways that are relatively easy for us to extract. Because they don't build complex structures, they devote most of the energy they collect directly to reproducing or to storing up energy for future use. Unlike most biofuel crops, algae store much of the energy they save up as fats. That makes algae good candidates not just for generating ethanol, but also for generating biodiesel. In essence, the algae fats are extracted as algae oil, which can then be refined in a process similar to that of refining petroleum.

Algae has three big advantages over current biofuels. First, the fuel yields from algae could be as high as 6,000 gallons per acre, or thirty times the yields of corn ethanol. Second, algae don't compete with food for land. Algae can be grown on salt water and on waste water where food crops won't grow. In June of 2011, for instance, scientists at Los Alamos National Laboratory announced that they'd successfully grown biofuel algae on the non-potable water pumped out of oil wells.[30] Other groups have grown biofuel algae on city waste water and on ocean water. Third, while corn ethanol produces just a tiny bit more energy than is put into it, estimates show that algae biofuels should be able to produce at least five times as much energy as goes into growing and refining them.[31]

Algae biofuels aren't in mass production yet. Current costs are $9 per gallon of fuel and up. Not a cost people are willing to pay. Just like solar electricity, though, solar fuels via algae have learning curves. And progressive stages of innovation look set to bring their prices down.

A company called Solix Biofuels, for example, believes they can get the price of production, after taking into account other outputs of the algae that they can sell, down to less than $2 per gallon.[32] A different startup, Aurora Biofuels, believes that they can have yields of 6,000 gallons per acre and a wholesale price of $1.30 per gallon by 2015.[33] The Algae Biomass Organization, a group that represents the staggering 170 start-up companies and laboratories working on algae biofuels, believes that those fuels will be competitive with the current price of oil before the end of the decade.[34] If the price of oil rises, that day will just come sooner.

In 2010, Barbara McQuiston, then an official at the Defense Advanced Research Projects Agency, and now an assistant secretary of defense, stated that the U.S. Department of Defense expected to see algae biofuel prices at $2 per gallon soon, on the way to an eventual price of $1 per gallon.[35] Why does the Defense Department care? Because fuel in warzones must be transported, and that process is dangerous and costly. In 2011, the *Wall Street Journal* reported that delivering fuel to advanced bases in Afghanistan could cost as much as $400 per gallon.[36] The Defense Department foresees a day when U.S. forces in hostile territory can generate their own fuel—or at least some of it—from the sun.

Even more radical approaches to generating fuel from the sun are in the works. Traditional algae biofuels require periodic harvesting of the algae. Every few days, most of the algae is pulled out from the tanks, then processed to extract the oils and carbohydrates inside, which must then be refined to create ethanol, diesel, or gasoline. The remaining, less crowded algae then use the sun's energy, carbon extracted from the air (or the smokestack gasses from the nearby power plant), and hydrogen from the water to reproduce, grow in number, and fatten themselves. The whole process adds inefficiencies.

In the last few years, two of the pioneers of modern gene sequencing have proposed another route. George Church is one of the scientists who originally proposed sequencing the human genome and one of the most respected re-searchers in genomics. Craig Venter is the researcher and entrepreneur who led the private team that finished the first human genome sequence, faster and at lower cost than the public, government-run approach. Both are working on heavily modifying single-celled organisms so that they produce desired fuels directly, without the need for any further processing or refinement.

The company George Church is involved with, Joule Unlimited, has genet-ically engineered cyanobacteria (blue-green algae) to produce fuel directly, without the need for a refinery. Instead of periodically harvesting the organ-isms, processing them, and refining the output, Joule slowly siphons fuel out of the algae tanks and replaces it with water. That saves them the energy and time it takes to regrow the algae population. Venter's company, Synthetic Genomics, which received $600 million from ExxonMobil in 2009, goes even further, starting with a synthetic, single-celled creature with the smallest possible genome, and then adding in genes to produce fuels. The logic, Venter says, is that their synthetic organism has no unnecessary functions that could draw energy off from its primary task. It's a stripped down biological factory whose only purpose is to produce fuel.[37]

Joule has stated that their process can directly, without any external refin-eries or processing, produce 15,000 gallons of diesel fuel per acre or 25,000 gallons of ethanol per acre, with a projected cost as low as $0.60 per gallon.[38] In a peer-reviewed paper published in the journal *Photosynthesis Research*, Church and others showed that it was feasible to achieve more than 7 per-cent efficiency in photosynthesis—turning 7 percent of the sun's energy that strikes their cyanobacteria tanks into fuel. That's still well below the 13 per-cent efficiency that biologists have determined is the theoretical maximum for photosynthesis, but it's close to 100 times the efficiency of corn ethanol. Capturing just 7 percent of the solar energy striking a biofuel tank would give us the ability to capture more than enough fuel in the world's deserts to meet the planet's energy needs, even if every person on Earth burned twice as much fuel as the average American.

Dominoes

If we can crack energy, beating the challenge of peak oil and peak fossil fuels, while simultaneously driving our greenhouse gas emissions close to zero, then most of our natural resource and environment problems become tractable.

Energy prices affect the price of everything else. It's not surprising, then, that spikes in the price of oil seem to predict recessions.[39] Cheaper energy would make it cheaper to mine or recycle minerals; cheaper to build a factory; cheaper to plow a field; cheaper to make fertilizer; cheaper to manufacture cars, appliances, homes, office buildings, airplanes, trains, buses, and more. It'd make it cheaper to operate those factories, buildings, and vehicles as well. All of that translates into cheaper goods, cheaper travel and transportation, and lower investment costs to start new businesses—all forces that can help continue economic growth in the rich world as well as the poor.

With enough energy, we can meet the world's water needs sustainably, by desalinating a tiny fraction of the vast supplies in the world's oceans. We could meet the water needs of nine billion people with roughly .001 percent of the energy the sun delivers to our planet.

With enough energy, we can further boost food yields. A project at the University of Minnesota has demonstrated that wind power can be used to harvest nitrogen from the atmosphere and create fertilizer, right on the farm. "It's an elegant concept," Mike Reese, the director of the project, says. "Farmers raise grains underneath wind turbines, which capture the energy to make fertilizer to feed the crop." In areas without much wind, solar panels atop barns could do the same.[40]

Energy, in the words of economist Julian Simon, is the master resource. With energy, you can increase your access to almost any other resource. And through innovation, we have the potential to tap into the vast, multi-billion-year energy resources of our sun.

A Better World

In the hills of India, in the state of Orissa, there's a tiny village called Tinginaput. Journalist Alex Renton describes it as, "two rows of neat mud houses, a couple of water pumps, a mango tree where people gather to talk." Tinginaput is about as poor and as far off the grid as one can get. It's also a story of the power of this new sort of energy.

In 2007, a program run by the state government of Orissa trained local women to assemble, install, and repair small solar panels—each the size of two hardback books—on local rooftops. Each panel produces just a few watts of power, but those watts are enough to charge a few mobile phones and to power bright LED lights at night. Those phones connect Tinginaput to the world. And that light allows children to study, boosting their education. It saves local families on kerosene—a large expense for a villager, and a fire risk in each home. It lets local women do handicrafts at night, and allows men to stay out longer in the fields before coming home, both of which boost family income. Five solar street lamps now light the town at night, boosting safety and discouraging local bears—who once routinely wandered into the village—from visiting.[41]

The women who assemble and install the solar panels are known as the "barefoot solar engineers." Most of those barefoot solar engineers are illiterate. They were never taught to read as girls. Yet now, in part because of the night-time lights and the new income that the solar panels have brought, their daughters are learning. Where access to energy spreads, education, wealth, and a reduction of poverty follow.[42]

Wind and solar not only have the power to help us collect more energy. They have the power to *decentralize* the collection and generation of energy. They can democratize the means of production. Most solar and wind farms in the decades to come will be large ones. Economies of scale and the existence of prime locations mean that it will be more cost effective, in most cases, to build large installations.

But in the cases where no power grid exists, like Tinginaput, solar or wind can be deployed at a fraction of the price and time it would take to extend the grid to the region. That's good news for the developing world.

It's also good news for the world as a whole. Today, the world's stores of fossil energy are distributed unevenly. Saudi Arabia, with just 0.4 percent of the world's population, produces 12 percent of the world's oil. The nine top oil-producing countries of the Middle East, with less than 3 percent of the world's population between then, produce 30 percent of the world's oil. That oil has brought money that has strengthened dictatorial regimes and that has often been spent spreading hatred of the United States. In 2009, Russia became the world's top oil producer, with oil exports producing half of government revenues, and propping up the administration of Vladimir Putin. Russia, in turn, has used oil and natural gas supplies to intimidate neighboring Ukraine, Georgia, and Europe. "Don't cross us, or we'll cut off your energy supplies," Putin has all but said year after year.

These are the countries that profit from U.S. and worldwide dependence on foreign oil.

With advances on the horizon in wind, solar, and biofuels, the United States has the ability to generate many times more energy than it needs. Europe, China, and even densely populated Japan could as well. Some countries would still choose to purchase energy from a neighbor that's better endowed with wind, sun, or rivers, but overall, energy dependence on a small number of nations would decrease. That shift would change the dynamics of world power tremendously, and for the better.

That, then, is the world we could have. It's a world where plentiful energy, continually *dropping* in cost, could fuel tremendous growth and help us meet the world's demand for food, water, and minerals. It's a world where the energy poor aren't any more—where they have access to the energy they need to build, farm, cook, clean, communicate, and learn. It's a world where the United States and other countries don't put trillions of dollars in the hands of a few nations who despise them.

But can we get there? And when?

Speed and Scale

Wind and solar energy have surged across the world at an incredible rate over the last decade. The total amount of wind energy available in the world rose by a factor of 10 between 2001 and 2011, to 240 gigawatts.[43] The total amount of solar PV electricity available worldwide rose by a factor of *30* over the same decade, to end at more than 60 gigawatts.[44] The growth rate is incredible. Between 2009 and 2010, the total amount of installed solar in the United States doubled. Between 2010 and 2011, it doubled again.

Renewable energy is a disruptive technology. No one expects the amount of solar to continue doubling each year. But projections of 40–50 percent growth per year—about what solar averaged over the last ten—is common. That mirrors the growth rate of cell phones in their first twenty years. From being large, clunky, expensive, and only for a few rich users, cell phones transformed themselves into cheap, small, versatile, mass consumer devices. And in so doing, they spread like wildfire and have eclipsed their older, well-established cousin, land lines. We're seeing what looks like the beginning of that process for wind and solar today.

These trends have generated optimism. The IPCC, even after assuming that the price trends and deployment trends of solar and wind will slow substantially, believes that renewable sources can meet 80 percent of the world's energy needs by 2050.[45] Energy consulting company Ecofys has published a report proposing a mechanism to get to 100 percent renewable energy by 2050.[46] In 2011, Stanford researcher Mark Jacobson and UC Davis scientist Mark Delucchi published a detailed study in *Energy Policy* that predicted that, by 2030, solar and wind would eliminate the profit in building any further coal and natural gas plants, and that by 2050 the price advantage of renewables would make it profitable for utilities to shut down existing coal and natural gas plants and switch to wind and solar.[47]

Yet there are reasons for concern, or at least, not to take these gains for granted. Exponential curves tend to eventually flatten out in nature. History is littered with examples of trends that *didn't* continue. For a while in the 1940s, 1950s, and 1960s, you could draw a graph of the maximum speed a human had ever traveled at, rising astronomically as the sound barrier was broken in 1947 up through May 1969, when Apollo 10 carried three astronauts at speeds close to 25,000 miles per hour. At that rate of growth, we should now be able to travel at around 26 million miles per hour. Needless to say, we're not.

And there are concrete challenges ahead. Ecologist Vaclav Smil points out that the last energy transition, from wood to fossil fuels, happened at a time when the world used less than one terawatt of power. Today we use seventeen. The sheer scale of the amount of new equipment that must be built and deployed makes the transition from fossil fuels to wind and solar possibly the largest industrial challenge of all time.

Along the way, we'll run into numerous problems. Some are on the horizon now. Silicon photovoltaic cells use the rare earth element indium. Thin film cells use the rare earth tellurium. Both are currently in short supply in global markets. Supply will very likely ramp up in response to price, but it's hard to know how soon. Researchers have also shown that it's possible to build cells that *don't* need rare earths, for example by using carbon nanotubes, but those techniques are new and still extremely costly. How rapidly will they catch up in price?

The price of other components that go with solar panels is also becoming an issue. While solar cells themselves have generally dropped in price by about 20 percent per doubling of capacity, the invertors that convert the DC electricity of the solar cells to the AC used throughout the world are decreasing in price at only half the rate. Other parts of the *total* cost of installing a solar system, including the labor, permitting, and whatever structure the cells are mounted on, are declining in price more slowly than the core technology of solar cells. Can we reduce those prices more quickly?

Second- and third-generation biofuels look extremely promising. On paper they look capable of making a major dent in and eventually replacing the use of oil, at a fraction of the current price. The science says this is totally possible. But from a practical perspective, these technologies are new. No one has taken them to the scale of billions of gallons of gasoline each day that's necessary to have a meaningful impact. Undoubtedly, we'll hit problems along the way.

I doubt that any of these problems is insurmountable. Time and again we've found ways to reduce the cost, energy, time, labor, and raw materials involved in accomplishing tasks that we care about. Within the sphere of renewable energy, there's a terrific amount of Darwinian creation of and competition between new ideas. Hundreds of companies have been formed. Dozens of variants of technologies I've described are being tried as ways to more efficiently and reliably capture energy from sun, wind, waves, tides, and geothermal heat of the Earth. I've had time here to explain just a few that currently appear most likely. That Darwinian competition will kill off a tremendous number of companies along the way. The failure of solar company Solyndra in 2011 persuaded some that solar was just a pipe dream, but it's the other way around. Solyndra went under because it couldn't compete with the incredible cost reductions other companies were achieving. In a young, highly competitive industry, fierce competition will cause many businesses to fail. But that process will also produce better, stronger ideas that can deliver useful energy to us in larger quantities, more cheaply.

Not Sit Idly By

Yet every obstacle to be overcome will take resources and time. And time may be the ultimate constraint. I said early on in this book that we're in a race, between the rate at which we're damaging or depleting natural resources and the rate at which we're learning to use them more effectively and efficiently. Nowhere is that more true than in energy.

Sudden shocks in the price of oil cause global recessions. Higher oil prices run the risk of igniting conflict. And growing worldwide demand for oil, coupled with stagnating supply, makes oil price spikes more likely, and possibly far larger, than ever. Will we get new, high-yield, food-friendly biofuels online before the next major spike? Before spikes larger than what we've seen so far?

Meanwhile, carbon dioxide emissions from fossil fuel power plants—and especially coal—are warming the planet, threatening to set off a time bomb of buried methane in the Arctic. Will we transition off of coal and natural gas in time to prevent that ignition? On current course and speed, even with the tremendous price reductions in renewable energy, the planet will soar past the levels of CO_2 in the atmosphere that climate scientists consider safe.

Every passing year *without* a transition away from fossil fuels increases the risks to the global economy and to the health of the planet we depend on. As I mentioned toward the beginning of this book, we humans have invented a way to deal with risks. It's called insurance.

In 2010, the world spent more than $4.3 *trillion* dollars on insurance of all sorts—health, home, vehicle, life, and others. That amounted to 6.9 percent of global GDP. That's what insurance is worth to us.

It's time to take out just a little bit of insurance against the risks that fossil fuels create. And the best way to insure ourselves against that risk is to invest in boosting our rate of innovation.

Indeed, across all of the world's challenges—energy, climate, water, food, minerals, forests, fish, and the others—it makes sense to focus on boosting our rate of innovation in solving those problems. We are in many ways the most innovative society that has ever existed on this planet. We have more brains, with more education, better tools, faster and richer means of communication, and greater incentives to innovate than ever. But that is no guarantee of success. The choices societies make impact their rates of innovation. Just as Europe of the Renaissance made choices that led to its innovation and growing wealth while China and other parts of the world stagnated, we can make choices today that maximize our odds of innovating rapidly, solving our problems, and growing our wealth.

What do we need to do to flourish? We need to invest in innovation. We need to invest in human capital that increases the power of minds to innovate. We need to fix the flaws that remain in our markets, so that those markets protect our commons. And we need to embrace the technological innovations that hold the promise of making our world a better place, even when those technologies at first seem alien or frightening. If we do those things, there's every possibility that our power to innovate can overcome the damage we're doing to our natural resources and environment.

Those are the topics of Part IV of this book: boosting innovation, fixing the flaws in our market, embracing powerful technologies that we fear, and the ultimate limits of growth and prosperity that innovation can take us to, if we make the changes necessary to fully embrace it.

part four
unleashing innovation

thirteen investing in ideas

Innovation Nation

What do the Internet, the Green Revolution that boosted crop yields since the 1960s, and the Human Genome Project all have in common? They were all produced, in part or in whole, by government-funded projects.

I've sung the praises of the market through this book, and will continue to. Markets are incredibly effective, and businesses produce a huge number of innovations. But not all of them. Governments have certain advantages over private investors. They can invest in projects that have a payoff farther in the future, without worrying about the immediate bottom line. They can invest in projects whose payoff might be too small for any one company, but huge for an entire industry, and for the nation as a whole.

Today, government funding for clean energy and energy efficiency research is around $5 billion per year. By comparison, the country spends $1 trillion a year, or 200 times as much, on energy consumption. The returns on those R&D dollars, so far, have far outweighed the costs. In 2011, for instance, the National Renewable Energy Laboratory unveiled a new device for making solar photovoltaic cells called an Optical Cavity Furnace. The furnace costs between a quarter and a half of current solar PV manufacturing furnaces and produces cells that can produce around 25 percent more electricity.[1] That one innovation is worth more in long-term benefits than the entire annual clean energy R&D budget of the United States.

The situation is similar elsewhere. A 2011 estimate found that the U.S. government's $3.6 billion investment in the Human Genome Project resulted in $800 billion of activity in the U.S. economy, and nearly $50 billion in additional tax revenue. The return on investment, for both the nation and the government itself, is tremendous.[2]

The return on investment of the Green Revolution is even harder to quantify. The government of Mexico and the Rockefeller Foundation (persuaded by U.S. Vice President Henry Wallace, then serving in the Franklin Delano Roosevelt administration) spent a few million dollars on Norman Borlaug's research into higher-yielding varieties of wheat. Those few million dollars saved *billions* of lives.

What's puzzling is, given how high the return on investment of government research is, how little we spend. The United States spent $337 billion on oil *imports* from foreign sources in 2010,[3] compared to the only $5 billion the DOE spent on clean energy R&D of all sorts. The United States spent $2.6 trillion on health care in 2010, but only $31 billion, or 2 percent of that, on the National Institutes of Health, the major source of funding for medical research in the United States.

Economist Alex Tabarrok explains it thus: We think of ourselves as an innovation nation, but "at the level of government, the innovation nation competes with the warfare and welfare state."[4] That is to say, between the top four programs of Medicare, Medicaid, Social Security, and the Department of Defense, the U.S. government spent $2.2 trillion in 2010, around two-thirds of the federal budget, and about forty *times* more than it spent on all forms of research spending excluding the military. We think of ourselves as an innovation nation, but that's not where our tax dollars go.

We've seen that innovation can be the ultimate reducer of cost and multiplier of value. More dollars spent on producing new and useful technologies could dramatically magnify the value that those $2.2 trillion buy, or reduce the amount we need to spend to get the same results. If innovation is the ultimate source of human progress, as I've argued through this book, then our priorities at the level of our national government are out of whack. We should be spending more on generating new and useful ideas, in smart, measurable ways, that harness the power of incentives and competition between ideas, in order to *increase* the value we get from every other dollar spent, or reduce the need to spend them in the first place.

Education Nation

Of all the investments that a society makes, none is more focused on future innovation than the investment on education. Human minds are the root source of new ideas, for the betterment of both themselves and others.

And increasingly, what our economy values is intellectual output. One of the top political issues of the last two years has been the rise in income inequality in the United States. Much of the ire has gone toward the top 1 percent of earners, who've seen their share of income rise. But there is another factor at work here—the growing gap between those engaged in manual labor and those engaged in innovation. Between 1979 and 2009, the incomes of college graduates (after inflation) rose more than 25 percent. The incomes of holders of advanced degrees (beyond a bachelor's degree) rose around 50 percent. Meanwhile, the incomes of high school graduates without any college education dropped by close to 10 percent, and the incomes of those without a high school degree dropped by around 25 percent.[5]

This effect is far *more* important than the rising wealth of the 1 percent. It affects far more of the country. And quantitatively, it's responsible for a larger share of the rising income inequality in the United States. Harvard Economists Claudia Goldin and Lawrence Katz calculate that the growing gap in income between the highly educated and the less educated accounts for two-thirds of the increase in income inequality in the United States since the 1970s.[6]

Not only does education increase wages, it also provides some degree of protection against downturns. During the peak of unemployment in late 2010, unemployment rates reached around 5 percent for those with bachelor's degrees, around 10 percent for those with only a high school diploma, and 15 percent for those who hadn't graduated high school. Increasingly we value the creation and improvement of new ideas, rather than manual labor.[7] In a world where wealth is created through innovation, we need to increase our focus on empowering people through education.

Those numbers account for a large fraction of the growth of income inequality in the United States over the last few decades. They account for *all* of the income stagnation of the middle class. For holders of college degrees, there has been no stagnation: incomes have steadily risen. This is not to say that everyone who holds a college degree has seen their wages rise, but most have, and the average and median wages for college degree holders has risen. The most pervasive economic gap in the United States is increasingly based on one's education. That growing wage gap reflects, in part, the value different workers created for others. Wages are higher for holders of college degrees and advanced degrees because they, on average, produce more services and more *innovations* that produce value for others. That benefits the entire world.

Yet in the United States, 25 percent of students do not graduate from high school.[8] And American students, on average, get mediocre results on international tests of reading and math when compared to students in other developed countries. Goldin and Katz, in their book *The Race between Education and Technology*, make a case that between 1900 and the 1970s, American K–12 education improved rapidly, empowering more children with the skills demanded by an increasingly skills- and technology-focused market. But since the 1970s, U.S. schools have fallen behind.

If the minds of the young are the ultimate resource for future innovation, then we should be doing a better job than this.

The problems in education run deep. Many of them reflect experiences children have before they even enter school. The gap between students in families in the top 10 percent income bracket and students from families in the bottom 10 percent income bracket is around two grade levels. It *starts* at two grade levels when the students enter kindergarten, and it remains steady at that level (on average) all through their academic career.[9] Studies show that preschool education closes that gap between children of rich and poor students, by boosting the performance of poor students in particular. And because the academic achievement of these children helps determine not only their own future wealth and well-being, but that of the nation as a whole and the world as a whole, investment in improving that situation isn't just charity. It's a benefit not just to the child, but to all of us. Investing in helping every child reach their full potential is an act of enlightened self-interest.

Within the school system itself, a different problem rears its head. We're a nation founded on competition and experimentation. The lesson of Europe's success in the Renaissance and the stagnation of China, Japan, and the Ottoman Empire teaches us the value of decentralized systems, with competition between ideas and between people, with incentives for hard work and innovation.

None of these are emphasized in our education system. At the school level, competition and choice between schools is the exception rather than the rule. At the teacher level, incentives for good teachers are scarce to nonexistent and firing bad teachers is notoriously difficult. At the level of curriculum, text books and core classes are often chosen by state school boards and dictated, in a top-down fashion, to schools and teachers throughout the state. Everything about the school system of the United States more closely resembles late Middle Ages China than Renaissance Europe. This is despite the fact that evidence shows that the best teachers produce value for their students in the hundreds of thousands of dollars, and that, where school choice exists, it has proven effective.

How could we improve this system? The core concepts we have to embrace are competition and experimentation. Parents and children should have a choice of schools. Schools should compete for those children, receiving funding for each child that attends, and no funding for children who don't attend. Principals and teachers need to be given more leeway to experiment with different curricula, to choose their own textbooks and lesson plans, and their own ways of teaching. School administrators need to have the freedom to hire, fire, and reward teachers on the criteria that they decide—just as happens anywhere in the private sector.

The ultimate endpoint of such a system would be the elimination of "public schools" entirely. There is a very good reason for the government to ensure that every child has the opportunity of a good education. Indeed, we should be willing to fund education far more than we do now, if those dollars can be spent in a manner that's effective.

But providing the funding for that education is not the same thing as doing the teaching. Funding education for all children is an issue of social justice and of investing in the children who will create the wealth of future decades. Doing the teaching is something else entirely. It's the creation of a state-run monopoly. And monopolies, history has taught us, tend toward stagnation rather than innovation. If we want to see education improve, we'd do well to provide the funds and let parents and children take them to any school they choose, including schools operated by the private sector. And we'd do well to regulate those schools lightly. Ensure that they're not mistreating children, assess them on objective tests of quality and publish that information for parents, but also give them a great deal of leeway in experimenting with and improving on current teaching methods.

What does this have to do with catching up to other nations in K–12 education? Europe and Japan don't use a system like this, after all. That's very true. What I'm proposing here isn't an approach for catching up to other nations in K–12 education. It's an approach for *leapfrogging* the rest of the world, using a tried-and-true method—the power of evolving ideas fueled by diversity, competition, and incentives.

Higher Education Nation

While the high schools of the United States are, at best, mediocre on an international scale, our universities are the envy of the world. Every year, tens of thousands of foreign-born students come to the United States to attend our colleges, the best on the planet. Unlike our grade schools and high schools, our universities *do* embrace competition and experimentation. They compete heavily with one another for the best students, and each university has tremendous leeway in what and how they teach. By comparison, the rest of the world, where the university system is often much more top-down, have *less* of the experimentation, diversity of ideas, and competition that make American universities great.

But there are problems at the university level as well. If we want to boost innovation in the science and technology that will multiply the value of our natural resources, find substitutes for the scarcest, and reduce the amount we need to use of all the rest—then we will need more college graduates with degrees in science and engineering. But those graduates are becoming increasingly scarce.

In the United States, the fraction of college graduates receiving degrees in an engineering discipline has dropped by nearly half since the mid-1980s, from a high of 9.8 percent down to 5.3 percent in 2009.[10] That's movement in the wrong direction. Government can and should do more to encourage students to enter fields that are vital to our future. Doing so would increase our rates of innovation in energy, materials, efficiency, and other fields that we need to accelerate innovation in.

Doing so would also help those students. Data from the Georgetown Center on Education and the Workforce shows that students with degrees in mechanical engineering had a 2010 unemployment rate of 3.8 percent. Students with degrees in physics, electrical engineering, and environmental science all had unemployment rates of 5 percent or lower. By contrast, graduates with degrees in library science, fine arts, and clinical psychology all had unemployment rates of 15 percent or more.

Yet financial aid programs don't differentiate between those fields of study. Student loans are agnostic to a student's major. While the long-term economic reward is far greater for choosing an engineering degree than a fine arts degree, the upfront signals—the amount of money available to pay for the education—mask that from students. It's easy to put off dealing with that long-term issue, since there's almost no financial impact on the short term.

The result is an ever-increasing amount of student loan debt, with more and more college educated Americans discovering that the field of study they chose makes it difficult or impossible to repay that debt. The result for the nation as a whole is fewer potential innovators in energy, climate, and other environmental and resource issues. Surely it's in the best interest of both students and the country to encourage students to choose the majors that earn them the most and that deliver much needed skills to the country and the world.

How could we do this? Give better terms and financial incentives to students entering science and technology fields. Give *less* favorable terms to students entering majors where unemployment is high or wages are low. Giving large loans to someone entering school for a fine arts degree doesn't make sense for the student or for society. It saddles the student with high debt while their degree means they're less likely to be able to pay that debt off. And because that debt is less likely to be paid off, and because the student will generate less tax revenue and activity throughout the rest of the economy, society gets paid back less in other ways. Loaning young people money to gain degrees that don't earn them enough money to pay off those loans helps no one, neither the students who are saddled with enormous debts nor the society that needs more innovation in science and engineering.

A society that provides its children a high-quality education and gives all of them a shot at a college degree is a just and healthy society. That should absolutely be our goal. But it's reasonable at the same time to help funnel some of those minds toward the areas that are in greatest demand and stand the best chance of producing the innovations we need to overcome the challenges that face us now and for the decades to come.

Increasing our governmental investments in R&D, introducing competition and incentives into schooling, and funneling more college students into science and engineering are all key steps to boosting our long-term rate of innovation. Yet there's something else we have to do on top of that. We have to address the limitations and flaws of the market itself. And that is where the next two chapters will take us.

fourteen the flaw
in the market

"To get rich is glorious." With these words, Deng Xiaoping, premier of China, leader of the most populous Communist nation on Earth, ushered in the global capitalist era.

In 1976, Mao Tse-tung, who'd exiled Deng for his pragmatism and openness to Western economic ideas, died, opening the door for the reformist Deng's rise to power. Deng returned from his exile to Beijing's halls of power in 1977 and seized the reins of China just a year later.

Deng Xiaoping's first actions after being restored to the leadership of China were remarkable departures from China's Communist past. In 1977, he successfully pushed to allow Chinese capitalists to join the Communist Party. In 1978, he opened China to foreign corporations, purchasing aircraft from Boeing and allowing Coca Cola to begin selling its products in the country. In 1979 he began to unravel the system of communal farming in China. He lowered minimum quotas on Chinese farmers, gave them more control over what was planted, and allowed them to keep whatever profits they could garner from selling any production above and beyond their quota. In the next few years he would open China to foreign investments, create incentives for local managers based on the success of their state-run operations, and allow private businesses to operate for the first time since the Communists had taken over the country in 1949.[1]

Deng's rise to power and his reforms, in a manner rather unnoticed by the West, heralded the end of the era of state-run economies and the final phase of capitalism's takeover of world economies. Eleven years after Deng's reforms in China, Mikhail Gorbachev's attempts at political reforms in the USSR would lead to its disintegration and the end of the richest state-run economy on the planet. Two years later, in 1991, a nearly bankrupt India, in a move of desperation, dramatically loosened economic controls, allowed foreign companies in, and embraced capitalism. In those short thirteen years, more than a third of humanity would go from living in a state-run economy to living in a market-driven economy.

Markets drive more of what happens around the world today than governments do. Virtually all of the world's $73 trillion in economic activity goes through markets of some sort. By contrast, the world's governments spend around $25 trillion a year. And much of that they spend by buying goods and services on the open market.

Nor is this a bad thing. In fact, in almost every case, the arrival of markets—when coupled with property rights, the rule of law, and good governance—has led to massive reductions in poverty and increases in living standards.

In 1978 China had an estimated 270 million people living in poverty. Seven years later, that number was less than 100 million. Deng's reforms amounted to the largest and fastest sweep of poverty reduction ever seen within a single generation.[2] India's reforms may have topped it. In 1990, 50 percent of Indians lived in poverty. Today it's less than 25 percent, and the UN believes that number will be 22 percent in 2015.[3] Per capita economic growth rates doubled in China and increased by half in India after their markets were opened and competition was introduced. Even in Russia, which had the rockiest road to reform, the transition to capitalism has roughly doubled per capita wealth.

Wherever market-based systems have gone head-to-head with command economies, the market-based systems have come out on top, with greater innovation, greater economic growth, and greater welfare for the people within the system. Consider the Cold War between the USSR and the United States of America.

On paper, the USSR and the United States started out at the end of WWII as well-matched rivals. Indeed, the USSR had larger stockpiles of coal and iron, two and a half times the land area, a 20 percent larger population, more college graduates, more scientists, more engineers, and vastly more oil than the United States. By most measures, the USSR had the upper hand. If we were predicting the future based on natural resources, we would have predicted that today the Soviet Union would be the dominant super power.

Yet in the forty-five years that followed, the two countries diverged significantly in the health of their people, in their rates of innovation, and in the growth of their economies. By 1990, when the USSR collapsed, it was nearly bankrupt. Its economy was one-quarter the size of the United States' economy.

Or compare West Germany and East Germany. In 1946 they had similar natural resources, similar education rates, similar culture, similar infrastructure, and identical life expectancies. By 1990, West Germans earned two and a half times what East Germans did, and lived an average of three years longer.

South Korea and North Korea are another example of the relative power of markets as compared to top-down economies. They started as a single nation, with a single culture, and nearly identical human capital. Yet they've chosen different paths. South Korea ranks at number 35 on the Heritage Foundation's 2011 Index of Economic Freedom. North Korea ranks dead last, at 179. South Korea's economy, per capita, is 20 times the size of that in the North. Hunger is basically unheard of in South Korea, but repeatedly, the United States and others have been forced to offer food aid to North Korea to prevent starvation.

If North Korea is too extreme an example, compare South Korea to my birth country of Egypt. In 1960, South Korea adopted a market-based economy, while Egypt became a client state of the USSR. At that point the two countries were similar in GDP per capita, in literacy, in life expectancy. Now, the average South Korean earns five times more than the average Egyptian and lives ten years longer. Egypt has fourteen times the illiteracy rate of South Korea.

Market forces empower people. They create incentives to deliver value to others. They reward hard work, creativity, and innovation. In all those ways, they give people more power to improve their own lives and those of others.

Markets also heighten the Darwinian competition among ideas, technologies, and the most Darwinian entities of all: corporations. Businesses are intense competitors. While they can, in theory, live forever, the average corporation lives for just forty years, around half the lifetime of an individual.[4] For example, a full third of the companies listed on the S&P 500 stock index in 1970 no longer exist. In the last few years, the trend appears to be toward companies living an even shorter time, with some researchers claiming a trend toward an average lifespan of just fifteen years.[5]

Businesses exist in a do-or-die environment. Those that bring in profits, largely by selling products and services that consumers and other businesses value, thrive. Those that don't, perish. And unlike most biological life on Earth, businesses can evolve themselves. The successful ones seek out and absorb the most effective ideas, technologies, business models, and even employees from their competitors. In evolutionary terms, corporations actively seek out and absorb the genes that they think will best help them thrive.

All of that means that corporations are ruthless competitors, constantly looking for ways to improve the bottom line. While at times that leads to behavior that's bad for the world, so long as the best way to generate a profit is to provide something of value to consumers or other businesses (who in turn provide something of value to consumers) and at a low cost, the fierce Darwinian competition drives them toward positive contributions.

In a Communist system such as the USSR or pre-Deng Xiaoping China, corporations and private businesses didn't exist. There was no way to get rich by building a business that provided value to others. Institutions didn't compete to maximize sales and lower cost. A whole level of evolution was missing.

And even at the level of individuals, many of the incentives to perform are gone. Personal wages in the USSR were much more homogenous and not linked directly to performance. The notion of "from each according to their ability, to each according to their needs" effectively decoupled output and reward. The consequence was a far lower incentive to produce valuable output. Partially as a result, per worker productivity grew twice as fast in Western nations as in the USSR between 1950 and 1989.

How powerful is this effect of self-interest? Consider the example of agriculture in the Soviet Union. Despite the USSR's high level of education and industrialization, Soviet farmers produced only about 25 percent of the crop yields of the United States.[6] Soviet farms produced output similar to those from a third-world nation, not what we'd expect from the most powerful political and military competitor to the United States. While most farmland in the Soviet Union was farmed collectively, around 3 percent of it was held and farmed privately. That private land produced an estimated 25 percent of all of the agricultural output of the Soviet Union.[7] Its productivity was around eight times that of collectively farmed land, putting it on a par not just with average yields in the United States, but with the yields of the very best and most productive farms in the United States.

The major difference between those private farms in the Soviet Union and the collective farms that made up the bulk of the nation's agriculture was self-interest, pure and simple. Farmers who owned their own land pocketed the profits they reaped from increased yield. That gave them tremendous incentive to work harder and smarter. On collective farms in the USSR, by contrast, there were no individual incentives for success.

Finally, consider the impact of capitalism on innovation. Through most of the twentieth century, the majority of the world's people lived in state-run economies. The USSR and its client states had a population somewhat larger than that of the United States and its allies, and similar levels of education and industrialization. Despite that, a staggering majority of the innovations of note during the twentieth century came from market economies. Henry Ford's first commercial automobile, the Wright brothers' heavier-than-air flight, the assembly line, radio, television, plastics, Penicillin, the transistor, the personal computer, the Internet and World Wide Web, mobile phones. All of those inventions came from the United States or market-oriented Western Europe, where a strong *incentive* to invent useful technologies existed.[8] Most of those came from within corporations.

I've extolled the incredible takeover of the world by capitalism and the tremendous power of the free market and self-interest for two reasons. First, at this late date, there can be no denying that the market is the fundamental system—the software, if you will—that runs our civilization. It is the system that governs what happens in human society, and the approaches we pick to solve our problems and continue the growth of our prosperity have to acknowledge that.

The second is that I want to reinforce that, not only has the market won, it's won by being, by all objective measures, far superior to any competing system for producing innovation, for reducing poverty, for growing wealth, and for increasing productivity. Capitalism is, in effect, a new technology we've created. It's a technology for organizing the flow of resources and labor, and it's proven itself to be incredibly effective in doing so. It's a technology for accelerating the Darwinian process of innovation, and it's proven itself remarkably effective in that regard as well. And one of the core elements that have driven capitalism's success is its incredible power to tap into human self-interest through properly aligned incentives.

Selfish interest isn't the only motivator of human behavior, of course. Far from it. Men and women perform altruistic, courageous, noble deeds without any thought of personal gain quite frequently. We act out of love, out of concern for our children and family members, out of a sense of duty, out of friendship, out of a sense of justice, out of a sense of charity. All of those drives are real, and we should welcome and embrace them.

But self-interest, on a global scale, is the most *consistent* driver of human behavior. While many drives besides self-interest have helped make the world a better place, virtually no society that has failed to leverage self-interest has thrived. Those that *depended* on motivating their citizens primarily out of duty, honor, or service to their countrymen have crumbed or, at best, found themselves languishing in relative poverty. Meanwhile, the civilizations that have tapped into the power of self-interest to drive people to act in the common good—rewarding them for and incenting them toward behaviors that meet the needs and desires of others—have seen themselves grow more prosperous over time. They've seen themselves innovate.

If we want to solve our problems today, then, we must make sure that the power of self-interest is fully engaged. If we want to save the world, we have to make sure people can get rich—or at least make a good living—by doing so.

There's just one problem. Capitalism has a fatal flaw. And that flaw can't be fixed by the market itself.

Who Owns the Air?

When the *Mayflower* pilgrims arrived in Plymouth in December of 1620, they faced long odds in a strange new land. The first winter the Pilgrims spent in Plymouth was a brutal one, killing 45 of the 102 men and women who'd survived the journey across the Atlantic. Had history gone differently, the small remaining colony could easily have perished.

Instead, in March of 1621, the Wampanoag chieftain Massasoit met with them for the first time, bringing a hundred of his warriors, a set of gifts for the pilgrims, and a peace pipe with him. Within hours, he and John Carver, the governor of the young colony, agreed to a treaty of peace and mutual support between the Wampanoag and the pilgrims. After the signing of the treaty and the ritual smoking of the pipe, Massasoit left another Native American, Tisquantum, with the pilgrims that spring and summer, teaching them how to survive in the land they'd found themselves in. Over the following months, Massasoit sent other Native American tribes to them with offers of peace and mutual respect. When the first Thanksgiving was celebrated that fall, it was with the fifty-three remaining pilgrims and ninety of Massasoit's men. The Wampanoag brought deer and waterfowl to the feast. The peace between the pilgrims of Plymouth and the Wampanoag would last another fifty years. Without the friendship of Massasoit and his confederation of tribes, the fragile colony at Plymouth might not have survived even a second winter, and the *Mayflower* might be just another ship, her name hardly remembered by anyone.[9]

Massasoit is perhaps the first Native American whose views of the land, property, and the environment were captured by Europeans. He's reputed to have said, "What is this you call property? It cannot be the earth, for the land is our mother, nourishing all her children, beasts, birds, fish and all men. The woods, the streams, everything on it belongs to everybody and is for the use of all."[10]

That line of thought has wound its way through history. In 1754, the philosopher Jean-Jacques Rousseau, who would later help inspire the French Revolution and influence the thinking of Karl Marx, wrote "the fruits of the earth belong to us all, and the earth itself to nobody."[11] He warned that the first men to divide land up into private property had brought with them murder, rape, and destruction, and that the very idea of private property was poisonous to humanity.

Yet if the Earth and its fruits belong to us all, collectively, who has the incentive to care for it? Who has the incentive to not pollute it? Where is the power of self-interest?

We might think that we *all* have a vested interest in seeing our planet healthy. And that's true. But that was just as true of the serf farmers of thirteenth-century England, the Soviet workers on low-productivity communal farms in the 1980s, and all the citizens of India and China prior to their economic reforms. All of those individuals had an interest in seeing their farms, their manors, their state-run businesses, and their command economies flourish, or at least survive. Yet none of them had very *much* self-interest at stake. If a hundred serfs farmed a manor communally, and one of them put in exceptional efforts, only one one-hundredth of those efforts would return to him or her. Why should that one serf work hard or take risks to increase production, when the returns are spread so thinly?

The more people the value of a common resource is spread across, the less incentive there is for each person to care for it, to protect it, to take pains not to damage it, or to work to improve it. That's true of a field, a river, a budget, a public park, an ocean full of fish, a rainforest, or a planet's atmosphere.

Long before this notion would be codified as the "tragedy of the commons" by Garrett Hardin in 1968, the ancient Greek philosopher Aristotle would see it clearly. In the fourth century BC, he would write, "That which is common to the greatest number has the least care bestowed upon it. Everyone thinks chiefly of his own, hardly at all of the common interest."[12]

More than 2,300 years later, in 1985, Mikhail Gorbachev would note that, "In a family you feel it when something is taken from your pocket, but if it's the state's pocket nobody feels it directly."[13] Gorbachev was thinking of how the communist system of the USSR diluted incentives, personal responsibility, and accountability over millions of people. Today the effectively communist treatment of our oceans and our air dilutes incentives, personal responsibility, and accountability over *billions* of people.

If something is taken from your pocket, you feel it. If it's the planet's pocket, no one feels it directly.

This, then, is the glaring flaw in the market. Our economy rests upon a foundation of a stable ecosystem on which we depend. Our rivers, lakes, forests, oceans, and our atmosphere are resources that we simply can't live without. The value they provide us is astronomical. Yet because no one owns them, and no one manages them, no one feels the full brunt of loss when they are damaged. No one feels a concentrated self-interest proportional to the value these resources provide us. Instead, all the signals, all the incentives, all the self-interest, both good and bad, are diluted across billions of people.

Today, for example, if a factory emits carbon dioxide that warms the atmosphere—doing millions of dollars' worth of harm to others around the world by contributing to more fires that destroy forests and homes, more droughts that wreck fields, more floods that cover whole countries, devastated crops at the levels of whole states or countries, and steadily rising seas—no one holds that factory accountable. That factory, as a by-product of providing real value to customers buying its goods, is producing what economists call a negative externality—a negative side effect of its business that is *external* to the market mechanism and thus not governed, controlled, optimized, or reduced by normal market forces.

The factory is privatizing profits from what it's making and selling, but socializing the costs of pollution.

From an evolutionary standpoint, so long as those externalities are completely free to factories, power plants, airlines, automobile drivers, and others, there is absolutely no pressure to develop a technology that reduces carbon emissions. Darwinian evolution—the force that has driven innovation throughout history—is completely oblivious to carbon emissions so long as they come without apparent cost.

I'm a capitalist. I make no bones about that. Looking at the arc of history, it's abundantly clear to me that the market is an incredibly powerful tool. It's an algorithm—a way of organizing the flow of information, of raw materials and goods, and of human labors in such a way that they produce far more value than they did under any previous system. It's the most effective way we've ever seen to boost productivity, to boost wealth, to reduce poverty, to boost human well-being, to get the most possible value out of the resources that we have. Compared to its most recent competitors—socialism or communism, capitalism has proven itself tremendously, paradoxically, almost unreasonably superior to anything that's come before it.

Yet the market is limited in what it can do. It can only optimize the use and protection and improvement of goods that have prices, that have buyers, that have sellers. Some of the things we care about most—things like a stable climate for our planet—don't have buyers or sellers or prices. They are, literally, priceless. Those things—parts of a global commons—aren't even parts of the market system. They're impacted by the market system—generally quite negatively. Yet that negative impact is because they're treated as *socialist* resources, free for anyone to use, exploit, or damage without direct repercussions to themselves. And when the profit-seeking mechanisms of the market intersect with a commons that they can exploit without cost, they do so.

It's tempting to blame corporations for this. But they're simply following the path that the system we've created has dictated for them—maximize profit, without regard for externalities. The problem is with the system itself. It's with the algorithm we've designed. It's an algorithm that's proven its worth for hundreds of years, but it's not perfect. There are parameters—like the value of the environment—that it can't easily set for itself. It needs our help in order to do so.

My education and most of my career has been as a computer scientist. I've spent more years designing computer software than anything else. And there's a saying in that field: "garbage in, garbage out." What that saying means is that no matter how smart an algorithm or a formula or a piece of software is, if you feed it data that is wrong or that has crossed signals or that has any sort of significant error, the results you'll get out on the other side will be full of errors as well.

The market is in a sense a kind of software. It's the operating system that runs most of our world. Its inputs are the demand and supply of various goods, the desires that billions of men and women around the world have, the skills that those men and women have to offer. Its outputs are the consumption and creation of raw materials and goods all around us, the changes in income and wealth that we see all around the world. And as we've seen, the market is incredibly effective at producing positive outputs.

Yet some of the inputs the market gets today are little better than garbage. By failing to put a price on a stable climate or a cost on the amount of carbon in our atmosphere, we're conveying to the market that the climate has *no* value, that damage to it has *no* cost, that the atmosphere can absorb an *infinite* amount of carbon without any penalty to us.

And so the market is encouraging our current behavior of burning finite fossil fuels, pumping carbon into the atmosphere, and increasing the twin risks of an abrupt scarcity of the fuel that's driven our society and an even more abrupt blowback in the form of a rapidly destabilized climate.

Garbage In, Garbage Out

A Full Accounting

If we want to stop the mistreatment of our common resources, we need to create powerful direct incentives for every man, woman, and business to do the right thing. We need to change the evolutionary landscape so that businesses, technologies, and behaviors that maximize the wealth created for all of us and that minimize the damage done to our shared resource—the Earth—evolve. We want to still take advantage of the enormous power of evolution, of course. But we need to guide it.

If we want to evolve the technologies that can drive our future prosperity while preserving our planet, then we need to appeal to the most base self-interests of men and women, and even more so to those of businesses. We need to make it more profitable to take care of our shared resources than to abuse them. We want to make it more attractive to start a new business that improves the state of the planet than to start one that damages it. And we want to draw the smartest, most ambitious, most entrepreneurial minds to the task of preserving and expanding our natural resources.

We want to make it just as possible to get rich at a solar startup or a high-density battery company or a next-generation biofuels corporation as it is to get rich at the next Facebook or Google. That is how we drive the changes in fossil fuel consumption and efficiency. And, more importantly, that is how we continue to fuel further innovation in creating new technologies that allow us to live richer, healthier, wealthier lives while ratcheting down and eventually eliminating and even reversing the damage we do to our planet.

The key to that—to all of that—is to make sure the market directly values the natural resources we care about. Damage to those resources must cost. It must cost as much as the value being subtracted from the lives of others, both now and in the future. And, in complement to that, steps that improve the state of our natural resources or that reduce the damage occurring to them must come with substantial financial rewards.

This applies to damage to the fish in the deep ocean, to nitrogen and pesticide runoffs from our farms, and to pollution of all sorts. What I'm about to describe is a model that applies to *all* externalities and *all* impacts on the commons. The most important of those externalities today is climate change. So that's where we'll focus.

In the case of climate change, fixing the flaw in the market means putting a price on the emissions of carbon dioxide and other greenhouse gasses. When I talk to groups about this topic, as soon as I mention putting a price on carbon emissions, part of the audience goes frosty. So let me state one thing up front. In an intelligently designed system where we charge companies for releasing carbon dioxide and other greenhouse gasses, all of that money raised would go to *you*. For every dollar that carbon emitters pay, a dollar goes back into the pocket of taxpayers. The nation's citizens, after all, are the ones who own its air.

Pricing carbon isn't a big-government initiative. It's a way to *improve the market* by giving it access to information it doesn't have—the external costs of carbon emissions. The government doesn't need to hold on to any of that money to achieve that goal. It can return every cent of it to the nation's taxpayers. In fact, it works best, and is the fairest, if all that money goes back into taxpayer pockets.

I'll explain more in a few pages. But first, I want to tell you a bit about the history of pricing pollution. There are two commonly discussed ways to do that. One is cap-and-trade. The other is a tax on pollutant. And both of them, amazingly enough, have their roots in the presidency of Ronald Reagan.

fifteen market solutions

The notion of market-based techniques to reduce pollution first picked up momentum in the final months of Ronald Reagan's last term. In late 1988, after the election that made George H. W. Bush the president-elect, Reagan administration attorney C. Boyden Gray received a call from Environmental Defense Fund president Fred Krupp. Krupp knew that Gray was slated to be George H. W. Bush's White House Counsel. He had also heard Bush say on the campaign trail that he wanted to be known as the "Environmental President." Would Gray and Bush consider a novel way to take on the problem of acid rain?

Acid rain is hardly something we hear about today. Emissions of sulfur dioxide, the pollutant that causes it, have plunged by more than 50 percent since their highs in the late 1980s. But at the time, acid rain was a source of considerable concern. Brian Mulroney, the first Conservative prime minister of Canada in decades, declared that acid rain had destroyed 14,000 Canadian lakes and streams. And since most of the sulfur dioxide causing that rain was coming from the United States, the issue was perceived in Canada as one of Mulroney being unable to influence Canada's powerful neighbor to the south. Perhaps in an attempt to bolster his conservative ally north of the border, Ronald Reagan had gone along with a proposal to devote funds to research the problem and had declared his support for finding a solution to it. But he'd resisted any specific proposals to regulate sulfur dioxide emissions. So had Congress, which over the course of Reagan's two terms had proposed and voted down seventy bills to regulate acid rain.

Sulfur dioxide is a by-product of burning coal. Then, as now, the bulk of the electricity in the United States was produced by burning coal. A number of critics of regulation to curb acid rain by controlling sulfur dioxide emissions, including prominent Democrats such as Virginia Senator Robert Byrd, cited the economic cost and the job-destroying potential of such legislation as a major concern. Electricity prices were sure to rise. Trade groups estimated that such regulation would cost utilities $25 billion a year.

Power companies assumed that any sulfur dioxide law would include hundreds if not thousands of pages of rules, costly inspections, a virtual army of regulators and inspectors visiting sites, and mandates to make specific and costly changes to equipment, procedures, and operations. One-size-fits-all rules would be imposed on different utilities with different circumstances. Decisions would now need to be approved by regulators. Flexibility and the ability to adapt to changing conditions would disappear. That's how environmental regulations had always taken shape before.

The potential solution that Fred Krupp proposed to C. Boyden Gray was rather different, though. Instead of telling utilities exactly *what* to do—what sort of equipment to install or what changes to make to their operations—it simply put a cap on total sulfur dioxide emissions. Every company would receive a certain number of sulfur dioxide emission permits—the right to emit so much, free of charge. The initial number of permits would be set based on a simple formula that factored in their emissions over the past few years. That number would then shrink year over year, pushing down the total amount that the entire industry could emit.

To reduce sulfur dioxide emissions, utilities could use any technique they could devise. They could purchase and install any of a number of sulfur-scrubbing technologies. They could switch to different grades of coal that had lower sulfur contents. They could employ technologies that cleaned high-sulfur coal before burning. They could retire their oldest, dirtiest coal power plants early. They could work with local communities to increase efficiency and reduce demand. They could build more natural gas plants to replace coal plants, or purchase electricity from other utilities that produced it via natural gas, nuclear power, or hydro power.

The flexibility for individual utilities and power plant operators to choose the approach with which to meet the mandated goal allowed each operator to use the technique or set of techniques that best applied to local conditions. It also put the various technologies for reducing sulfur dioxide in competition with one another, encouraging innovation to improve effectiveness and reduce cost.

Sulfur dioxide emissions permits could even be bought or sold. If one coal plant was able to reduce emissions faster than expected, they could sell the unused permits on the market to other utilities, some of whom were going more slowly than expected in reducing emissions. Sulfur dioxide emissions would now be a market. And in theory, according to economists, that market would find the most efficient and lowest cost way of reducing the emissions. Rather than depending entirely on the intelligence of regulators to assign emissions perfectly to each area, the market approach allowed the details of where the emissions occurred to vary. Those areas that had the greatest need for additional power—from a growing population, say, or increased industrial demand—could purchase the ability to emit from areas that had smaller demand. At the same time, the total emissions would be capped by the absolute number of emissions permits issued that year. The emissions would go down. The market would find the cheapest, most efficient way to get them down.

The ability to buy and sell emissions permits created a new way for a coal plant to make money. If it could drop its sulfur emissions *faster* than mandated by law, it could sell the remaining emissions permits. That, in turn, poured money into development of better technologies to reduce sulfur. With billions of dollars a year on the line, a better sulfur-capturing technology could bring a huge return to its developer.

Cap-and-trade found little initial love. In fact, it enraged people on *both ends* of the political spectrum. Republicans in Congress, and Democrats from coal-heavy states, hated that it added new regulation and new cost to coal plants. Utilities repeated their claim that it would cost them $25 billion a year. John Sununu, George H. W. Bush's Chief of Staff, said that the cap would "shut the economy down."

And cap and trade outraged environmental groups. Sulfur dioxide emissions were a public health issue, an environmental health issue, a *moral* issue. Selling off the right to damage people and the environment struck them as a relinquishment of environmental values, as bad as selling permits to commit murder or rape. As Richard Conniff noted in an article on the history of cap-and-trade in *Smithsonian Magazine*, "some people called it 'morally bankrupt' or even 'a license to kill.'"[1]

Yet, largely through the personal commitment of George H. W. Bush and the unlikely alliance of Republican White House Counsel C. Boyden Gray and Environmental Defense Fund President Fred Krupp, the capping and trading of sulfur dioxide emissions went into law in 1990. The first cap became effective in 1995, and that year sulfur dioxide emissions dropped by 3 million tons. While in 1990 the United States pumped more than 15 million tons of sulfur dioxide into the atmosphere, by 2010, emissions had declined to less than 7 million tons, and still dropping. The EPA now projects that by 2025, they'll be under 4 million tons.[2]

Cap and trade is itself an innovation in how we operate as a society. It combines the best traits of the market—the rapid rate of innovation and the ability to find ever more efficient ways to do things—with the unique ability of government to set goals around things that the market is blind to, like damage to the environment. And it's worked. Not only has it brought down the emissions of sulfur dioxide, it's done so at a fraction of the expected cost.

Industry groups predicted that the sulfur dioxide cap-and-trade program would cost them $25 billion per year.[3] The EPA disagreed, projecting that the cost would be only $6 billion per year. The almost two decades of experience since the program went into effect have allowed us to see the real cost. It was only *$3 billion* per year, just one-eighth of the industry estimates, and half of what the EPA estimated.[4] And the benefits? In addition to protecting lakes and forests, the regulations saved an estimated $118 billion per year in reduced health expenses.[5]

The market does wonders. We just have to point it in the right direction.

Even Simpler: The Pollution Tax

In 1987, Ronald Reagan signed the Montreal Protocol, which would lead to the phasing out of Freon and other CFCs that deplete the planet's ozone layer. In doing so, he overrode the objections of his secretary of the interior and former chief of staff, Don Hodel. He went against the advice of some of his "closest political friends," as the U.S. ambassador who had negotiated the agreement would later write.

The ozone layer in our atmosphere is essential for life on Earth. It filters out 99 percent of the UV radiation—the same radiation that causes skin cancer—before it can reach the planet's surface. Without it, the planet would have a massive and deadly case of sun burn. Almost no plant or animal on land or that swims close to the surface of the water could survive the radiation we'd be exposed to without the ozone in our atmosphere.

Reagan didn't come into office intending to address ozone depletion. While he at times said that he saw himself as an environmentalist, he was also fiercely anti-regulation and pro-business. His first secretary of the interior, James

Watt, eased restrictions on mining and oil drilling on public land, rolled back environmental regulations, and explored the possibility of de-authorizing some National Parks to allow logging.[6] Reagan's first EPA Director, Anne Gorsuch, described ozone depletion as a scare tactic and a nonissue.[7]

Reagan was also initially skeptical. Then, in 1985, three British scientists discovered the Antarctic ozone hole, a continent-sized patch of the atmosphere where ozone levels were already sharply down. The ozone hole captured the public's imagination and drew attention to the much broader problem of ozone depletion over the entire planet. To stop ozone depletion, it was clear that the world needed to stop the release of Freon and other CFCs, and do it within a decade or two. It wasn't a problem that any one country could solve. All the industrialized nations needed to work together to tackle it.

Don Hodel, who'd become secretary of the interior after James Watt had been forced to resign for making off-color comments, objected strenuously. He argued that any near-term risk of thinning ozone layer could be handled by telling people to wear hats and put on more sunscreen. Industry groups had long agreed. In the late 1970s, DuPont's chairman of the board had asserted that any connection between CFCs and ozone depletion was "science fiction." The company warned in the 1980s that phasing out CFCs could cost the United States more than $130 billion and that "entire industries could fold."[8]

George Schultz, secretary of state at the time, took the other view. The United States needed to show leadership on this issue, Shultz argued. The science was sound. The ozone layer was being depleted, and posed a long-term global risk. Without the United States leading the way, no international deal would get signed. The common global good of the ozone layer would be degraded faster and faster, as industry released more Freon and other CFCs each year.

No one can say exactly what changed Reagan's mind, but two things may have played a role. First, Reagan's Council of Economic Advisors gave him a cost-benefit analysis that showed that, even using the most conservative estimates, the cost of the future skin cancer cases that would result from a thinned ozone hole drastically outweighed even the highest estimates of the cost required to fix the problem. Even without factoring in *environmental damage*, Reagan's economic advisors projected that phasing out CFCs was the smart thing to do. Delaying action would be penny wise but pound foolish.

The second factor is that Reagan himself was a skin cancer survivor. He'd had a cancerous patch removed from his face in 1985 and another in 1987, just months before the Montreal Protocol meetings.[9] Did that affect his decision? We'll never know.

Ultimately, Reagan signed the protocol, and sent it to the Senate, which ratified it unanimously. Creating a law to actually get CFC emissions down would take another two years. In the new CFC regulations, passed as the 1990 amendments to the Clean Air Act during George H. W. Bush's term in office, the EPA used another new market-oriented approach. In addition to tradeable emissions permits, it would levy a tax on the production of all new CFCs. If you wanted to manufacture substances that depleted the ozone, you had to pay. The cost would start at $1.37 a pound* and then ratchet up each year, increasing the pressure to find alternatives. The EPA expected the phase-out to cost a total of $28 billion to the U.S. economy.

DuPont, by this time, and to their credit, had dropped their objections to a CFC phase-out. Other companies weren't as supportive. At a congressional hearing, a representative of the Air-Conditioning and Refrigeration Institute (an industry lobbying group) testified that if CFCs were phased out on the proposed schedule, "We will see shutdowns of refrigeration equipment in supermarkets. . . . We will see shutdowns of chiller machines, which cool our large office buildings, our hotels, and hospitals."[10] As late as 1994, the Competitive Enterprise Institute was claiming that phasing out CFCs would cost the country between $45 billion and $99 billion.[11]

Pressured by the threat of high costs and a cap on the amount of CFCs they could manufacture, companies rushed to find substitutes, to increase recycling of CFCs (which didn't incur the tax), and to use them more efficiently. In 1990, there were no good substitutes for CFCs on the market. None were expected to arrive for another eight or nine years. Yet by 1992, new substitutes were available that had less impact on the ozone layer, and that soon cost *less* than Freon and other CFCs had. Some companies saved money as a result. Nortel, for example, estimated that it spent $1 million buying new equipment, and saved $4 million by eliminating CFC purchases and reducing the cost of disposing of chemical waste. According to an analysis by the Economic Policy Institute, the actual cost across the entire U.S. economy turned out to be less than $10 billion.[12] And the country's air conditioning and refrigeration kept on working without disruption.

---

*The cost for a baseline CFC was $1.37. Since some types of CFC are more dangerous than others, those had higher costs, proportional to the amount of ozone they destroy.

That $10 billion was less than a tenth of what DuPont had estimated, less than a quarter of the lowest end of the cost estimates from the Competitive Enterprise Institute, and only slightly more than a third of what the EPA itself had estimated.

In fact, in almost every case that the EPA has worked to lower emissions of a pollutant by setting a price or a target—but staying out of the details of exactly what technology is used, or where, or how—prices have come in lower than expected.

In the 1970s, when the EPA began to put limits on the amount of cancer-causing benzene that could be released, chemical companies forecast that it would cost $350,000 per plant to install equipment to meet the new targets. A few years later, new processes that eliminated benzene entirely reduced the cost to zero.

During the CFC phase-out debate, U.S. automakers predicted that it would cost $650–$1,200 per car to fit new vehicles with air conditioners that didn't use Freon. In 1997, the cost was estimated at between $40 and $400 per car, less than a third of the initial projections.

In the 1970s, OSHA, the Occupational Health and Safety Administration, estimated that ending the use of asbestos in manufacturing and insulation would cost $150 million. A few years later, the cost was found to be half that, at $75 million.

In 1987, the EPA estimated that reducing air pollution from the steel industry's coke ovens (where coal is cooked as part of the process of making steel) would cost $4 billion. By 1991, experience had dropped the cost estimate to less than $400 million, a tenfold reduction.

Everywhere we look, the cost of reducing either resource use *or pollution* drops through innovation. Even the cost estimates of regulators turn out to be too high. And necessity—or *profit*—is the mother of innovation. If we want industry to produce less carbon dioxide, all we need to do is put a price on it.

Clarity

We have two models to choose from. In option A, we auction off the right to emit carbon, and *shrink* the amount auctioned off each year. In option B, we charge a fee for every ton of carbon emitted, and *raise* that price each year. Either will reduce carbon emissions. And based on the experience we have from the last twenty years of market-based and target-based environmental regulation, either is likely to do it at a small fraction of the price that anyone, *including the EPA*, is likely to project.

There are three keys to making either system work right. One is a clean, level system devoid of loopholes or giveaways. The second is giving every dollar brought in through auctions or a carbon tax back to the taxpayers. And the third is clarity on the long-term plan.

First, the level playing field. In 2009 the U.S. House of Representatives passed a bill (later defeated in the Senate) that would have created a national carbon cap-and-trade system. Unfortunately, that bill didn't auction off the carbon emissions rights. It didn't even allocate them via an impartial algorithm. Instead, the bill specifically allocated 85 percent of initial emissions permits to utilities and industries picked by hand, at no cost. Because those initial allocations didn't necessarily match the most efficient way to bring CO_2 emissions down, the bill almost certainly would have resulted in costs higher than the market could do on its own. Yes, it would have brought CO_2 down. But it would have done so at a higher total cost to the country than if the emissions permits were auctioned on an open market. With any cap-and-trade or carbon tax proposal, there will be a strong temptation to hand out initial breaks to chosen industries and companies. I'm realistic enough to know that some of that will happen. Would I accept an imperfect plan with some handouts and special breaks? Yes. That would be better than no plan at all. But every bit of initial handout is both a subsidy to business *and* a market inefficiency that raises costs for the whole country. If we want to address climate, insulate ourselves against fossil fuel prices, and do it with as little impact on our economy as possible, the best approach is a level playing field.

Second, give the money back to taxpayers. A price on carbon—imposed either by a tax or by auctioning off emissions permits—will raise the price of fossil fuels. Gas prices will go up. The price of heating a home through natural gas will go up. The price of electricity from coal or natural gas will go up. Those price increases, unfortunately, make life harder. They raise household bills. They slow economic growth.

Many proponents of a carbon price—either through a tax or a cap-and-trade system—point out that higher energy prices drive down energy use. When the price of gas is up, people drive less. When electricity prices are up, people turn the lights off more conscientiously. With a carbon price, consumers and businesses will be more motivated to invest in energy efficiency through more fuel-efficient cars, better insulation, newer furnaces, and so on. That impact, particularly the efficiency gain, is important.

But there's another benefit to a carbon price. In addition to reducing energy use, it can *shift* energy use to non-carbon forms, like solar and wind. If a carbon price makes coal more expensive than solar, then consumers, businesses, and utilities will choose solar. Even if total energy consumption remains exactly the same, the shift to the endless supply of climate-benign solar is a positive effect. Indeed, it's the effect we were looking for.

By shifting dollars toward solar and wind, a carbon price engages the power of the learning curve, driving the cost of renewable energy *down*. That acceleration of innovation is arguably the most important benefit of a carbon price. Every dollar we shift toward harvesting energy from the far larger source in the sky brings us closer to the point when we have energy *cheaper* than today, without any impact on climate.

From that standpoint, government doesn't have to hold on to the money raised. In fact, if the dollars *aren't* returned to tax payers, a carbon price drags the economy down, by raising prices. And it hits the poor, who spend the highest fraction of their incomes on energy, the hardest.

So long as a carbon price makes fossil fuels more expensive *in comparison to* non-fossil energy, it's doing its job. If that money flows back to tax payers, it gives them more ability to invest those dollars in non-fossil energy, in energy efficiency, and in the overall course of their lives. The best model is for consumers and businesses to pay more at the pump and in their energy bills, and to have 100 percent of that money distributed back, evenly, to the country's tax payers.

In that model, those who reduce their carbon usage the fastest, by investing in efficiency or by switching to non-carbon energy, would end up getting more money back than they spend on the added carbon price.

We need new names for these plans that capture this. It's not just a carbon tax. It's a carbon *dividend*. It's not just cap and trade. It's cap and *dividend*. The net cost to the economy is nearly zero.

Third, long-term clarity. Jim Rogers is the CEO of Duke Energy. When Duke completes its acquisition of Progress Energy, he'll be the executive chairman of the second-largest utility in the United States and the second-largest CO_2 emitter in the country. If the combined utility were a country of its own, it would rank forty-first in the world for energy production, just behind South Korea and ahead of Mexico.

Rogers, like a growing number of utility CEOs, accepts the science on climate change. He's actively campaigned for Congress to pass a cap-and-trade bill. And Rogers made it clear to me that for any carbon price bill to be effective, it has to lay out a long-term roadmap.

"I build power plants that last forty years," he told me in early 2012. "I need as much clarity as possible about what the rules are going to be. The clearer the roadmap, the better able I am to make good decisions that will still be good a decade from now or three decades from now."

Energy infrastructure is a long-term investment. Energy prices help guide what sorts of power plants are built. The investments in those plants are then slowly defrayed over forty or even fifty years. When you pay for electricity, you're paying more for the cost of the power plants than you are for the coal or natural gas that's being burned.

With so much money sunk in infrastructure, sudden shifts in energy policy can be incredibly costly. They can leave tens of billions of dollars of equipment sitting idle, wasting the money that went into them. If we want to make the transition to much more abundant non-fossil-fuel sources of energy, and we want to do so cheaply and efficiently, we'd do best by laying out a clear roadmap.

A Simple Plan

Here's a plan. It's not the only possible plan, by any means. But it's a stake in the ground for something that can get us shifted over to new, nearly unlimited sources of energy quickly enough to have a chance of avoiding the worst dangers of climate change. It's neither a big government plan nor a small government plan—it's a "just as big as it has to be" government plan. It's not a plan that pits government against the market—it's a plan where government *uses* the market to achieve a public good.

First, tax carbon. For the first five years after the law is passed, the tax is 0. This is a time for industry and consumers to get ready. In year six, start the tax at $10 per ton of CO_2. That's equivalent to ten cents per gallon of gasoline and roughly 0.7 cents per kilowatt hour of electricity (1 cent for coal, half a cent for natural gas).

Second, raise the price until you've met your goal. Every year that the United States is not on target for reaching an 80 percent reduction in CO_2 emissions by 2050, raise the price by another $10 per ton. If the United States *is* on target, leave the price where it is. If the price gets to a ceiling of $100 per ton, or $1 per gallon of gasoline and 7 cents per kilowatt hour, stop. Adjust all these prices for inflation.

Third, put a tax on any imports from countries that *don't* have a carbon price, to level the playing field. Calculate the tax by dividing a country's carbon emissions by the fraction of its manufactured goods that are shipped to the United States, and applying our rates. Conversely, if a U.S. export is going to a country that *doesn't* have a carbon price, refund the carbon tax to the U.S. manufacturer. Those two steps keep U.S.-manufactured products on a level playing field with products manufactured in countries that don't have a carbon price.

Fourth, give all the money back to tax payers. Divide it up evenly between every man, woman, and child in the United States. For convenience sake, this would probably be done as a *reduction* in payroll tax and income tax, showing up as lower withholding in each paycheck, and more take-home pay. Economists encourage us to tax the bad rather than the good. In this plan, we'd be shifting some of the taxes *away* from income, and onto pollution.
    That's it.

The Impact

Here's what would happen if this bill were passed.

First, there wouldn't be any immediate impact on prices. There would be a five-year period before even the first dime of gasoline price increase and first penny of electrical price impact went into effect. In that time, consumers and businesses would have time to prepare.

Second, from the day this bill was passed, no more coal plants would be built in this country. Because coal plants operate for forty years or more, the cost of energy fifteen years out matters to them. At an added price of 10 cents per kwh fifteen years from now, coal is no longer viable. No one wants to build a coal plant today and scrap it fifteen years from now. Even building new natural gas plants, which emit half as much CO_2 per kwh, would start to look like a dicey proposition.

Third, money would pour into clean energy, energy storage, and efficiency. Money would pour into deployment of solar, wind, hydro, biofuels, grid storage batteries, electric cars, more efficient home insulation, and more. It would pour into R&D in all of those areas. And all of that would drive new innovations that would *lower* prices.

Fourth, you'd start to see both your paycheck and your power bill creep up, at about the same rate. Energy bills would rise, though more slowly than the carbon price. Even as the price of carbon went up, increased efficiency and switchover to green sources would reduce the amount of carbon released in driving a mile or in powering a home, office, or factory. On average, after-tax paychecks would rise by the same amount as energy bills. And for those who produce less carbon than average—either by driving less, buying better insulation, using a more fuel efficient car, or switching to solar or wind—paychecks would rise *faster* than energy bills.

Fifth, and finally, as renewable energy prices drop, and batteries become cheap enough for night-time storage, we'll cross the point where it makes more sense to shut coal plants down than to keep operating them. The dirtiest, least-efficient plants, that release the most CO_2 per kwh generated, would be the first to go. Then the newer coal plants. And eventually, even most of the natural gas plants. All of those plants would be in the second half of their natural lifetime, and most would be in the last decade of their planned lifetime when they're shut down. Some infrastructure would be written off early, but mostly, by signaling prices clearly ahead of time, we'd avoid the building of expensive new infrastructure that would later get shut down early.

Along the way, at every step, we'd be reaping benefits. We'd be slowing and eventually halting climate change. We'd be reducing the money we send to the Middle East and Russia for oil. We'd be insulating ourselves from the effects of sudden shocks to the price or supply of oil or coal that could cause recessions. We'd be *reducing* the price of nearly limitless energy through innovation and learning curve effects funded by the dollars we spent on renewables instead of on fossil fuels. And through that, we'd be setting ourselves up for cheap access to water, minerals, food, and everything else that bountiful cheap energy can help us get. At the other side of our transition to renewables, energy, and everything that depends on it will cost *less* than they do today.

And what would it cost us in the short term? Not much. We can't say that it's zero, exactly, but if solar prices continue to decrease—something that a carbon price would accelerate—the cost would indeed by close to zero. It won't drag the economy substantially, as Americans using fossil fuels will have the same amount in their pocket after taxes. The price rise in fossil energy and in manufactured goods will be exactly matched by the dollars distributed to taxpayers. The switch to efficiency will *help* the American economy overall, by reducing the cost of everything. And the switch to solar and wind will push those technologies along their learning curves, driving their prices down. It won't hurt the poor—if anything, because they emit less carbon than the rich, their dividends will be greater than their increased costs. They'll come out of this ahead. It won't put American industry at a disadvantage internationally, because imports and exports with countries that don't have a carbon price will be adjusted at the border.

In fact, we have an example to look at to see how such a policy would affect the economy. Just north of Washington State is the Canadian province of British Columbia. In 2008, it introduced a province-level carbon tax of $10 per ton of CO_2, rising by another $5 per ton each year. Canada's prime minister, Stephen Harper, warned that year that a proposal for a national carbon tax in Canada would "screw everybody." But British Columbia is doing just fine. Unemployment is slightly lower in the province than in Canada as a whole, and economic growth is slightly faster. And residents of British Columbia now pay the *lowest* income taxes in Canada.[13] A carbon tax wouldn't wreck our economy. It would tax the bad instead of the good, leaving the overall tax burden the same, while shifting us to larger, nearly endless, ever-*cheaper* sources of energy.

That's not to say that there would be no downsides at all. A carbon price *would* cause a shift in our economy. There would be fewer jobs for coal miners or oil workers. But there would be more jobs for wind and solar technicians and installers—hundreds of thousands of them. It would cause hardships for those whose livelihoods are tied to fossil fuels. Those hardships would be buffered by the fifteen-year phase in of the tax, but they'll still exist. At the same time, it will also create new opportunities, in new industries that are higher paying, friendlier to the planet, and that ultimately tap us into *more* energy than fossil fuels, and that will help drive our growth through this century.

This is the way we take out insurance against the risks of peak oil, rising coal prices, and climate change. Compared to the trillions of dollars the world spends every year—6.9 percent of all spending in the world—on insuring homes, health, and cars, this nearly free insurance policy is an incredible bargain.

Other Approaches

There are other approaches that have been proposed to help us switch to abundant zero-carbon sources of energy. Let's grade them on a scale from A+ to F.

The "A+" goes to increasing Federal R&D into clean energy and energy efficiency. As a strategy, it is incredibly effective. As implemented, with the tiny amounts we spend, it earns a "C" instead. Clean energy is vital to the national interest. Our investment in producing innovations to accelerate its adoption could and should be far higher.

A "B+" goes to the CAFE fuel mileage law that governs cars and to the state renewable energy portfolio standards, which specify that a certain fraction of electricity production must be from wind, hydro, or solar. Both are good policies. Both have made a difference in energy efficiency and in encouraging clean energy. But they don't get an "A" because, even combined, the policies are incomplete in their coverage of energy, and they don't work as efficiently as a carbon price. California has the most ambitious renewable energy portfolio standard, mandating that 33 percent of its electricity must come from renewables by 2020. My hat is off to Californians and Governor Schwarzenegger for putting this in place. Even so, while the law changes electricity generation, it doesn't create incentives for consumer efficiency or conservation. It doesn't differentiate between coal, natural gas, and nuclear, even though coal produces twice the CO_2 as natural gas does, and nuclear produces almost no CO_2 emissions at all. It's a good law, and it should be continued, emulated, and improved upon. But it doesn't substitute for a carbon price.

CAFE fuel efficiency standards have also been successful, but have similar limitations. They encourage car makers to manufacture more fuel efficient cars but don't give consumers an incentive to choose higher fuel efficiency. They don't encourage consumers to drive their current or future cars less. They don't impact the price of driving an older less fuel-efficient vehicle less, or to car pool or use public transit more. And CAFE covers only 60 percent of the oil consumed in the United States. It doesn't cover the other 40 percent consumed in trucks, vans, shipping, trains, air freight, and air travel. CAFE has brought real benefits and should continue to be ratcheted up and expanded to cover more categories. It doesn't, however, substitute for a carbon price.

A "C" goes to wind and solar energy subsidies, where governments pay part of the cost of buying or using renewable energy. When first introduced, these were an "A." They were absolutely essential in encouraging early deployments of wind and solar, and thus driving down the nonsubsidized price for later customers through the learning curve. But, like renewable energy portfolio standards, they don't encourage energy efficiency. They don't prioritize replacing coal over replacing natural gas, despite the fact that coal produces twice as much CO_2. And, conceptually, they work in the opposite direction to a carbon price. Instead of making polluters pay to pollute, and then returning that money to the tax payers, they go the other way. They require the tax payers to pay for cleaning up after the polluters. That's backwards. And eventually, that bill will grow too large. Already, governments around the world are beginning to roll back subsidies due to their costs. That, in turn, causes chaos for utilities and renewable energy companies, who need the sort of long-term clarity that Jim Rogers talks about in order to have the confidence to invest in expensive infrastructure.

The "F" goes to biofuel subsidies. The United States has spent $30 billion from 2005 through 2011 subsidizing the production of corn ethanol, which, because it's so energy and land intensive to grow and process, saved almost no energy for the country, prevented almost no carbon dioxide emissions, and *raised* the price of food for billions of people around the world. Fortunately, those subsidies expired at the end of 2011. They should stay that way.

The EU's mandate for biofuels has been as bad. It's encouraged the use of palm oil, which also takes a tremendous amount of land to grow and other fossil fuels to refine into biodiesel. The result has been the deforestation of 6 million acres of rainforest in Indonesia, and the emission of *more* CO_2 than would have been emitted by burning diesel from traditional oil wells. Picking winners is dangerous. Governments do a poor job at it. The best thing to do is to specify the goal—eliminating carbon emissions and getting to nearly infinitely renewable sources of energy—and let the market find the implementation.

What about China?

In 2010, China passed the United States to become the number one source of carbon dioxide emissions in the world. That's part of a larger trend. The market revolution in China, India, and the rest of the world has pulled those countries out of poverty and into an industrial era. In 1980, the developing world produced 20 percent of the world's CO_2. Rich countries produced 80 percent of it. In 2012, developing countries produced *60 percent* of worldwide CO_2 emissions.

The Kyoto Protocol put no binding limits on the CO_2 emissions of developing world nations. That, to many, looked like a fatal flaw. Even if developed countries drove their CO_2 emissions down to zero, the amount coming from the China, India, Brazil, and other developing countries would drive temperatures up by several degrees this century, possibly enough to reach the tipping point where stored-up methane accelerates warming out of our control.

Despite this, I believe the United States should press ahead with adopting a carbon price and driving our emissions down by 80 percent by 2050, even if China and India don't. Why? Three reasons.

First, we created this mess. Carbon dioxide lingers in the air for an average of 100 years before breaking down. The heating of the world *this year* depends not on this year's emissions, but on the total amount of CO_2 still in the air from the last century of emissions. On that basis, the rich countries (the United States, Canada, Europe, and Japan) are responsible for two-thirds of the heating of the planet that is happening *today*. The United States alone is responsible for more than a quarter of the warming that will happen this year. China is responsible for around 10 percent. India for less than 3 percent.[14] We made this mess. We need to show leadership in fixing it.

Along those lines, I asked Jim Rogers of Duke Energy how he, the chairman of a company that emits more carbon dioxide than Mexico and depends heavily on coal, had come to view climate change as an issue that needed to be addressed. What he told me was that, "Once you've identified a problem, and that you're part of the problem, you need to be part of the solution. You need to go to work on it, rather than being in denial of it." We created this problem. We need to show leadership in fixing it.

Second, it's in our own best interests. Shifting away from oil and coal will shield us from recessions caused by global oil and coal price spikes. It'll reduce the dollars we send to the Middle East and Russia. It'll drive our long-term energy costs *down* by further fueling innovation in capturing the nearly endless supply coming from the sun. If we want energy independence, healthy economic growth, and long-term *cheap* energy, a carbon price is the way to go.

Third, the best way to get China, India, Brazil, and the rest of the developing world off of fossil fuels is to drive down the price of alternatives. If it's cheaper to produce electricity from solar and wind than it is from coal, and if that electricity can be supplied 24/7, then countries will switch. Make it cheaper, and they will come. And the best way to make it cheaper is to invest in R&D in those areas, and to shift business and consumer spending into them, igniting the power of Darwinian innovation and the learning curve. As a side benefit, as we encourage innovation in clean energy technology at home, we stand to benefit economically by becoming exporters of that technology to the rest of the world.

Ultimately, China may well get there before we do. Unlike in the United States, in the halls of power in China, there is no debate as to whether climate change is happening or is manmade. Those are both accepted as scientific facts. That's not surprising given that eight of the nine members of China's Politburo are engineers.

China is now the world's leader in renewable energy. China is the world's largest manufacturer of solar panels.[15] Sinovel, the world's second largest manufacturer of wind turbines, is a Chinese company, and has announced its intent to be the world's largest producer by 2015.[16] China overtook the United States in the total amount of installed wind power in 2010, becoming the number one nation in the world in wind power capacity.[17] While the United States was the first country to introduce fuel economy standards for cars, China's fuel economy standards are now *higher* than those of the United States.[18] With an economy less than half the size of the United States, the Chinese surpassed the U.S. investment on renewable energy in 2009 and 2010. The United States just barely clawed back the lead in absolute dollars invested in 2011, but China still invests almost three times as large a fraction of its economy.[19]

And, in early 2012, China, for the first time, created caps on CO_2 emissions for four cities: Beijing, Shanghai, and the industrial hubs of Shenzen and Chongqing. The United States has never done anything like that with greenhouse gases. Those caps aren't yet national, but in a policy paper in 2011, the Chinese government argued that only through hard caps on CO_2 emissions could the country effectively combat climate change. We may be seeing the first moves on China's part toward a national cap-and-trade system.[20] There are fair odds that in China's 2016–2020 economic plan, it will adopt national greenhouse gas emissions caps for the first time.

In short, China is acting more aggressively against climate than we are, even though the problem is one of our making. We should worry a little less about whether China and the rest of the developing world will address climate. They will, especially if we show leadership on the global stage and in driving the price of clean energy down through innovation.

A Snowball's Chance in Hell?

Is there any realistic chance of enacting either a fair cap-and-trade proposal or a reasonable carbon tax in the near future? Do we have any chance of enacting one globally? Could we even enact one within the United States? We might look to the nation that emits the most CO_2 per capita as a lesson in possibility.

What country is that? You may have guessed the United States. That's understandable. The United States has been the largest overall emitter for most of the last half century. You might have guessed China. That's farther from the mark. Per person, China still emits only a third as much as the United States.

The nation that emits the most per person—at least among the industrialized countries of the world—is actually Australia. Australia is, in many ways, a smaller, Southern Hemisphere reflection of the United States. Like the United States, it's a young nation, highly educated, made up of immigrants, and with a population that continues to grow. Like the United States, Australia has a frontier mythos that celebrates the rough-and-tumble individual and shrugs off the importance, if any, of social cohesion and central government. That's reflected in Australia's politics and economy. According to the Heritage Foundation, Australia ranks number one among large nations in terms of economic freedom, meaning that it has relatively loose regulations, a business-friendly and trade-friendly set of policies. The United States is also in the top ten of that list. Germany, the economic powerhouse of Europe, comes in twenty-third. England comes in sixteenth. France, the other major player in the Eurozone, comes in sixty-fourth. Australia's federal government spends less, as a fraction of the country's GDP, than that of the United States, and far less than the major governments of Europe.[21] All of that makes Australia far more like the United States than like Europe. Indeed, in many ways, growth rate, economic freedom, and government spending among them, Australia is more American than America.

Which perhaps makes it a shock that in late 2011, Australia became the latest in a long list of nations to place a price on carbon dioxide emissions. The Australian carbon tax will start in 2012 at a price of around $25 per ton of CO_2. In 2015, it'll switch to a cap-and-trade scheme, with emissions permits auctioned off to the highest bidder. Australia will return 40 percent of the money raised directly to tax payers through lower taxes. It'll use another 50 percent of the revenue to assist existing polluters in transitioning to cleaner energy sources. And it will funnel around $10 billion into research and development of improved solar and wind energy.[22]

If Australia, a nation that is even more small-government, anti-regulation, and pro-business than the United States can pass a carbon tax, it's certainly not out of the realm of possibility that the United States could as well.

And there's precedence. The United States did, after all, pass a cap-and-trade bill for sulfur dioxide to combat acid rain, even over the staunch objections of prominent Republicans like Bush chief of staff John Sununu and coal-state Democrats like Senator Robert Byrd. Ronald Reagan did sign the Montreal Protocol, even over the objection of other Republicans and cries from industry that it would have an incredible price tag.

Majorities of Americans now support acting on climate in various ways. According to the November 2011 Yale/George Mason poll, 65 percent of Americans believe that developing sources of clean energy should be a high or very high priority for the president and Congress. According to the same poll, 55 percent believe Congress should do more to address global warming; 60 percent of Americans believe the United States should reduce its greenhouse gas emissions, regardless of what other countries do; 66 percent of Americans believe their country should make at least a medium-size effort to tackle global warming, even if it has moderate economic costs; 66 percent of Americans would support the United States signing an international treaty that requires the nation to cut emissions of carbon dioxide by 90 percent by the year 2050; and 73 percent support regulating carbon dioxide as a pollutant.[23]

In short, public support exists, precedent within the United States exists, and precedent in countries with an even stronger individualist streak than the United States exists. Indeed, the U.S. Congress almost passed a cap-and-trade bill in 2009. The House of Representatives passed the American Clean Energy and Security Act (also known as the Waxman-Markey Bill), largely, but not completely, along party lines. While the bill died in the Senate, the number of additional votes needed to have brought it to the floor and passed it was a handful, a number small enough that a single election could cause that significant a swing in Congress.

Will the odds of passage of such a bill change in the future? I believe they will. As extreme weather events become more frequent, public belief in climate change as an important issue will rise. The Cuyahoga River fire galvanized environmentalism in the United States. Further extreme weather events may do so for climate.

And on the other side, as solar and wind drop in cost and hybrids and electric vehicles improve in their range and become more common, the idea of weaning ourselves off of fossil fuels will begin to seem more natural. Texas now leads the country in wind power. In the next few years, rooftop solar is likely to soar in deployment in the American South and West. Solar and wind will start to seem less like science fiction, and more like a practical and affordable way to get electricity.

As the impacts of climate change grow more evident and the costs of halting it drop, resistance will fade.

The Problem with an Inconvenient Truth

Political leaders can and should do some things to push this forward. Democrats who favor climate legislation need to get behind and clearly articulate a revenue-neutral form of it. The strongest ideological opposition to a carbon price (and indeed, the strongest ideological opposition to climate change) is that it's a left-wing plot to enlarge government. Some readers of this book will be for larger government. Some will be for smaller government. Pricing carbon needn't be *either*. Mixing it with other political issues will just increase opposition to it. The point of a carbon tax is that when a consumer or a business executive decides how to spend their dollars, they become more likely to spend them on goods or services that emit less or no carbon, and that, in so doing, they drive the competitive marketplace to emit less carbon overall and to innovate in ways to reduce carbon at ever lower prices. That's it. Mixing the issue with anything else only muddies the waters.

Republican leaders who believe or have at least at one point believed the abundant evidence about climate change, including Arnold Schwarzenegger, John McCain, Mitt Romney, George Schultz, and others, have a different task. While a majority of Americans believe that climate change is real and that businesses, citizens, and the federal government should all take more action against it, opinion is still polarized around party lines. So is opinion of climate change in general. In 2010, for instance, a Gallup poll found that two-thirds of Democrats believed that negative effects of climate change were already happening. Only one-third of Republicans believed the same, and another one-third believed that negative effects of climate change would never occur.[24]

Why is this divide so stark? Dan Kahan at Yale has done research that points to a key factor. Kahan ran an experiment where he brought in vaccine experts to present arguments to mixed audiences of conservatives and liberals* that vaccination against HPV was safe or not safe. The audience got to see both views. When the two views were presented by supposedly neutral experts, 56 percent of the conservatives thought the vaccine was safe. After the same presentation of views, where the expert presenting the vaccine as safe was presented as a liberal and the expert presenting the view that the vaccine was unsafe was a conservative, the results were different. Only 47 percent of conservatives thought the vaccine was safe. When Kahan switched the roles, so that the apparently conservative expert presented the "it's safe" view and an apparently liberal expert presented the view that the vaccine wasn't safe, the conservatives swung toward they expert whom they believed they agreed with politically. Sixty-one percent of the conservatives seeing that debate decided that the vaccine was safe.[25]

So hearing the exact same position presented by a perceived political ally or a perceived political foe swung opinions by 14 points. The lesson, Kahan says, is that people respond to an argument an expert makes in large part based on whether they think they agree ideologically and politically with that person. Hearing about an important problem from an expert they agree with will increase their belief. Hearing about it from someone across the political divide may actually be worse than never hearing about it at all. It may well *reduce* their belief in the problem.

In that vein, UCLA geographer Laurence Smith noted in 2011 that "[t]he problem with *An Inconvenient Truth* (the 2006 documentary that helped raise awareness of climate in the United States) wasn't its science, but that it was Al Gore."[26] Smith isn't trying to disparage Al Gore here. The point he's making is that Gore's campaigning for climate made the issue an even more political one than it already was, and may have inadvertently reduced the extent to which conservatives are willing to believe that climate change is a problem.

The burden, then, is on leading conservatives—the ones who acknowledge that climate truly is changing, and that the changes pose dangers to both humanity and the planet—to actually lead. There is plenty to like for conservatives about a revenue-neutral carbon price. Lower payroll and income taxes. Less money sent to Russia and the Middle East. The creation of new, higher-paying green energy jobs. More opportunity for investors and

---

*Kahan actually classified his subjects as "egalitarian-communitarianists" (whom I've called liberals) and hierarchical-individualists (whom I've called conservatives).

entrepreneurs to flourish in this new industry. A new wave of market-led approaches to environmental protection that got their start under Ronald Reagan.

Indeed, even before signing the Montreal Protocol, Reagan prided himself on his record on the environment. As Governor of California he'd worked to reduce air pollution and tighten vehicle emission standards, something he talked about in later years. And in a 1984 speech commemorating the opening of a new headquarters for the National Geographic Society, Ronald Reagan drew the connection between conservative political philosophy and protecting the environment.

> You are worried about what man has done and is doing to this magical planet that God gave us. And I share your concern. What is a conservative after all but one who conserves, one who is committed to protecting and holding close the things by which we live? . . . This is what we leave to our children. And our great moral responsibility is to leave it to them either as we found it or better than we found it.[27]

In his State of the Union address of that year, Reagan put the politics of it clearly: "Preservation of our environment is not a liberal or conservative challenge—it's common sense." He made that statement just before asking for a budget increase for the EPA, even as he was cutting federal spending overall.[28]

It's time for Republican leaders to stand up, make the case for a market approach to weaning ourselves off of finite and dangerous fossil fuels, and work with their colleagues across the aisle to address the largest challenges facing our nation and our world today.

It's time for Republican voters to do the same, making it clear to their friends, neighbors, and their political representatives that this is an issue that goes beyond politics. Climate change is real. Fossil energy supplies are limited. It's time to take out a little bit of insurance against both. Especially when that insurance is nearly free.

Republican voters and leaders both need to step up on climate and energy. Getting climate legislation passed is probably going to require a bipartisan consensus, and that means some Republicans will have to join in. Along the way, they have the opportunity to help craft the legislation in a market-oriented mold that will encourage entrepreneurial approaches, create jobs, and keep the overall cost of addressing climate near zero. But if Republicans stand by the side, the odds of getting *any* legislation passed to address climate are far lower.

So, if you are a conservative who believes in climate change, or even that there's a small *chance* of climate change that is worth insuring against, then much of the responsibility for political action is on your shoulders. Al Gore is not going to convince your fellow conservatives on climate change, the risks of dependence on foreign oil, or the potential of clean energy. You can.

Fixing the flaws in the market, bringing externalities into its scope so that market forces can properly weigh them and can work to protect and *improve* the commons is vital. There is no greater task before us in converting our incredibly successful model of market economics into a *sustainable* model that preserves our common resources even as it creates wealth and encourages innovation.

Yet, in many important cases, innovations are here or on the horizon that we are turning a blind eye to, or actively rejecting. If we want every tool in our arsenal available in fighting the challenges of energy, climate, and meeting the food and resource demands of a growing and increasingly wealthy global population, we need to look rationally at a wide range of ideas and technologies, even those that some would call unthinkable. And that's what we'll do over the next three chapters.

sixteen the unthinkable
here there be dragons

At the eastern edge of Death Valley, where the barren desert crosses from California and into Nevada, lies a testament to the current state of nuclear power in the United States and much of the world. A twenty-five-foot-wide tunnel gapes into the sun, a train track emerging from its mouth. The tunnel bores in a U-shape 5 miles into the heart of Yucca Mountain. Here, until recently, the United States planned to store the radioactive waste produced by its 104 operating nuclear reactors. It now seems likely that day will never come. After years of construction, widespread opposition in Nevada led President Obama to shut down the project in 2009.

Six thousand miles west of Yucca Mountain lies the symbolic other half of the story: the devastated Fukushima Daiichi plant in northern Japan, the site where the Tohoku tsunami set off the worst nuclear accident since Chernobyl, flooding television stations and websites around the world with images of blown off roofs, twisted pipes, devastated buildings, and radioactive steam being released into the air.

One of the technologies environmentalists and the general public fear most is nuclear energy. While in 2010 there was talk of a "nuclear renaissance," the disaster at the Fukushima-Daiichi nuclear plant brought much of that talk to a halt. Within months, the governments around the world announced plans to halt the construction of new nuclear power plants, or to decommission existing ones.

The response was understandable. Nuclear catastrophes strike fear deep into our hearts. Watching the steam rising from the reactors at Fukushima; tuning into the news each day to hear of more explosions, radioactive leaks, and increased contamination of the already devastated countryside; contemplating the potential sacrifice the "Fukushima Fifty," the workers struggling to get the reactors back under control, were making—all of this made a deep emotional impression on viewers, including me.

Given those challenges, it'd be tempting to rule nuclear power out. But doing so would be turning our back on a tremendously powerful energy source. There's enough uranium in known deposits to provide all of humanity's electrical needs for centuries. And unlike wind power and solar power, nuclear power can be delivered 24/7, with no regard for whether the sun is shining or the wind is blowing.

We *might not* need nuclear power. Innovation in other areas might eventually make it completely unnecessary. If energy storage technology moves forward quickly enough, providing cheap high-capacity storage for wind and solar, we'd have a way to provide zero carbon energy overnight. But it's never safe to bet on just one option. No investor puts all his or her money down on a single stock, or even a single industry. The more options we have for the future, the better.

Nuclear power, if it could be made safe and kept affordable, would be a huge asset for humanity. Today nuclear reactors supply 20 percent of the electricity used in the United States and 14 percent of the electricity used in the world. The world's on-land uranium reserves could fuel those reactors for at least another 200 years, and possibly as much as 500 years with small improvements to how the uranium is processed. Yet conventional nuclear reactors use only a small fraction of the energy in uranium. Breeder reactors, which consume most of the fuel rather than leaving it as waste, could match today's nuclear output using known uranium supplies for an estimated 30,000 years.

The on-land supplies of uranium, though, are dwarfed by the amount dissolved in sea water. The world's oceans contain more than 100 times as much uranium as the deposits known to exist on land. Harvesting uranium from the seas would allow breeder reactors to provide the current level of electricity for millions of years, and to supply 100 percent of humanity's present electricity needs for at least hundreds of thousands of years.[1]

Aside from the power of the sun, and the as-yet-unrealized dream of practical nuclear fusion, there is no energy source that we have access to that amounts to even 1 percent of the total energy of nuclear fission.

And all the electricity produced by nuclear power is very nearly free of carbon emissions. The only carbon dioxide released by nuclear energy is that involved in the construction of nuclear power plants, an amount that is less than a tenth of that released by the operation of coal-burning power plants.

Nuclear energy is a natural complement to wind and solar. It can provide "baseload" electricity that is "always on," while wind and solar add to that energy while they're available. Eventually, as grid storage becomes available and drops in price, nuclear may become completely irrelevant. Looking at the trend in battery technologies and prices, I believe that will happen. But if we take the current green energy and energy storage cost trend lines and project them out, the point at which solar or wind becomes cost competitive with current nuclear plants in providing electricity twenty-four hours a day, seven days a week is around 2030. That's a nearly twenty-year gap within which nuclear power could uniquely provide nearly carbon-free electricity 24/7. The only other energy technology that can do this on a large scale is hydro power, and the best spots for dams are already occupied in the United States and, to an only slightly lesser degree, worldwide. Hydro power growth can't replace coal and natural gas. Solar and wind can *only* if our pace of innovation continues in energy storage technologies, and even then, only in around 2030. Nuclear, if it is made safe enough, could make a significant dent *today*.

Can nuclear be made safe enough to substantially reduce the burning of coal and natural gas? I would argue that it already is.

Real and Perceived Risk

Former U.S. president Jimmy Carter seldom speaks about the day he was exposed to nuclear radiation. It happened at a place called Chalk River Laboratories. Chalk River is a sleepy Canadian town of 800 people, 110 miles northwest of Ottawa. There's not much to the town—one Catholic school, two restaurants, a gas station, a public library. And the laboratories, just two miles out of town.

Chalk River Laboratories grew out of the World War II effort to build an atomic bomb. The lab opened in 1944. In September of 1945, it became the site of the first nuclear reactor outside of the United States, the NRX. In 1952, a series of human errors led to an explosion that shot the concrete dome above the reactor four feet into the air and resulted in a partial meltdown at the site.

Carter at the time was a lieutenant in the U.S. Navy, working in Schenectady, New York, under Admiral Hyman Rickover on the nuclear propulsion system for the USS *Seawolf*, the world's second nuclear-powered submarine. He was slated to be her engineering officer when the *Seawolf* went to sea, though the death of his father would lead him to resign his commission instead. When the NRX meltdown occurred, the future president and his men were ordered to rush to Chalk River, 200 miles away, to assist in stabilizing the reactor. Carter and the twenty-three men under his command drilled on a mock-up of the reactor, then put their lives on the line, rushing into the radioactive core, armed with wrenches to remove critical plates necessary to stop the release of radioactive steam and water. Later estimates reveal that the men that went into the building were exposed, in a matter of hours, to 200 millisieverts of radiation, around fifty times the amount of radiation the average American is exposed to in a *year*.

Despite this, Jimmy Carter is still alive as of this writing. None of the workers involved in the emergency response or cleanup of the NRX reactor have died in a manner attributable to radiation from the incident. And the amount of radiation that workers stabilizing the Fukushima power plant were exposed to is roughly equivalent to the amount Jimmy Carter was exposed to.

Radiation kills. Radiation causes cancer. Radiation can cause sterility and birth defects. All of these things are true. But how much? How many deaths? Nothing in this world is perfectly safe. Oil kills. Coal kills. Is nuclear more dangerous, or less? Is it safe *enough?* Would its widespread deployment be safer than climate change? Would it be safer, even, than other side effects of burning coal?

As the world sat transfixed, watching the evolving disaster at Fukushima, it was easy to lose perspective. Yet while Fukushima made for excellent television, coal-burning power plants around the world continued to pump fly ash, carbon monoxide, mercury, and other pollutants into the air. Those pollutants, in the United States alone, are estimated by the Clean Air Task Force to result in the death of more than 13,000 Americans each year.[2] Worldwide, particularly in the developing world, where power plant emissions are less controlled by environmental regulation, the burden is far higher. Some estimates place the number of annual deaths from coal-produced pollution as high as 170,000 people worldwide each year.[3] Is that because there are more coal plants than nuclear? No. Even looked at on a per-energy basis, coal kills more. Per terawatt hour of energy produced, coal kills an estimated 161 people worldwide. Nuclear, even after adding up all the potential future deaths attributed to every nuclear accident that has ever occurred, comes in at less than one-tenth of a death per terawatt hour.

By contrast to the massive death toll of coal, not a single person died at Fukushima. Estimates of the health impact of the radiation released are that no one *will* die as a result of the accident. Nearly 20,000 people died in a matter of hours as a result of the massive earthquake and tsunami that rocked Japan, mind you. But no lives were lost as a result of the accident at the reactor.[4] Yet the nuclear accident commanded far more news attention, in the long run, than the far more deadly tsunami that caused it.

We're wired to focus on such spectacles. The threat of radiation seems so alien, so powerful. When it appears in the form of a crisis at a nuclear reactor, it's a potent, concentrated drama. By contrast, thinly spread deaths from respiratory disease and heart attacks caused by coal-created pollution are mundane. The deaths caused by coal are so diffuse that they're hard for us to detect or attach to. Was this heart attack caused by exposure to air pollution from a coal-fired electrical plant? What about this one? There's nothing as obvious or as spectacular as the spectacle of a nuclear meltdown.

Yet the deaths are just as real, and far more numerous.

The worst nuclear disaster of our time, the Chernobyl disaster, still rings in our memories. In 2003, the World Health Organization convened a panel of experts to assess the long-term human impact of Chernobyl. What the experts concluded was that Chernobyl had directly killed fifty-seven people. Twenty-eight of them were fire fighters and others who worked to put out the fire at the reactor and who died on the spot or in the months that followed. The rest were among the other workers who'd responded to the scene and assisted with the cleanup in some way.

The long-term impact of Chernobyl is much larger, of course. Radiation is a risk factor for cancer. Nearly 200,000 workers assisted in the cleanup of the site between 1987 and 1988, and 135,000 local residents were evacuated from a thirty-kilometer radius around the reactor. Another 7 million or so people lived within areas where they could have conceivably received a low dose of radiation from Chernobyl. Summing up all these individuals, the radiation they've received, and statistics about their death rates from cancer before, since, and in comparison to other areas, the World Health Organization estimates that the disaster will ultimately cause up to 9,000 deaths from cancer.[5]

Those 9,000 deaths are 9,000 separate tragedies. Yet that number means very little out of context. Cancer is the number two cause of death in the world. Of the 7 million people living in the areas surrounding Chernobyl, had the disaster never happened, WHO reports that they'd expect to see roughly 900,000 cancer deaths over their lifetimes. Those 9,000 additional deaths represent a 1 percent increase in the cancer death rate, spread out over thirty or forty years. Over those decades, at the current rate, coal-produced air pollution will kill millions of people worldwide.

Coal is by far the more deadly technology.

Other estimates have been made of the death toll, some of which are much higher. Greenpeace estimates that between 93,000 and 200,000 cancer deaths will ultimately occur due to Chernobyl. Their report depends upon the "no threshold" model of radiation, which holds that even extremely small amounts of radiation exposure increase cancer risk. The Greenpeace estimate is based on a projection of increased cancer risk based on that theoretical model. The WHO report is based on more concrete data—how many more cases of cancer have been seen. Even if the more speculative Greenpeace numbers are correct, however, the death toll from coal will still be far higher. Coal kills roughly as many people *each year* as Greenpeace estimates that Chernobyl, the worst nuclear accident is history, is likely to kill over half a century.

Nuclear accidents like Chernobyl, Fukushima, and Three Mile Island have economic costs, through the deaths they cause and the property they destroy. Even after we factor those in, coal is far worse. Nuclear disasters over the past thirty-five years have cost around $700 billion dollars—a huge sum. But over that time, nuclear power has generated around 70 *trillion* kilowatt hours of electricity. The cost of disasters totals around 1 cent per kilowatt hour of nuclear electricity. By comparison, a 2011 study from Harvard found that the externalized health costs of coal, even after *ignoring* CO_2 emissions and climate change, was anywhere from 9 to 27 cents per kwh.[6]

Not only does coal kill more people than nuclear energy, it also releases more radiation. The fly ash released from coal-burning power plants carries with it radiation. How much? Per megawatt of power produced, coal-burning plants release 100 times as much radiation as nuclear power plants.[7]

We fear nuclear power because the deaths it causes come in spectacular accidents, with our eyes glued to the television screen, anxiety pounding in our chests. We fear it because, like genetic modification technology, it seems in some way unnatural. It's still new to us. The idea of radiation isn't intuitive. We don't understand it the way we understand burning wood or coal or even natural gas to produce heat.

But the cold hard facts don't lie. Coal kills hundreds of times more people than nuclear energy. Nuclear energy kills when it fails. Coal kills when it runs perfectly smoothly.

Eternal Waste

What about the waste? Nuclear reactors produce radioactive waste that re-mains dangerous for millennia. The prospect of taking something toxic and storing it away safely for tens of thousands of years is a daunting one. We've only had agriculture for 10,000 years, writing for less than that. The light bulb for even shorter. How can we design a system that will store waste for longer than our civilization has existed? Storing that waste in the heart of a mountain, contained by miles of rock, had a certain primal appeal. It at least reduced the risk that the waste would leak out on its own, or that some future civilization would stumble into our toxic mess by accident. The end of the Yucca Mountain project means that the United States now has no plan.

The best plan may be to turn nuclear waste into value, as we have with so many other waste products. The 'spent' fuel from conventional reactors still contains roughly 99 percent of its original energy. While we typically see that energy and the resulting radioactivity as a liability, it's also a source of potential value.

Fast neutron reactors are reactors that can consume nuclear waste. In the 1950s and 1960s, nuclear physicists and engineers dreamed of using them to extract dramatically more energy than current nuclear reactors do from their fuel, and to burn up the vast majority of nuclear waste. Fast neutron reactors use up virtually all of the long-lasting radioactive materials in nuclear waste, leaving behind a smaller amount of waste that is radioactive for decades rather than millennia. Even that poses a challenge for storage, but far less of one than waste piles that remain radioactive for longer than our civilization has existed.

The problem with fast nuclear reactors, or breeder reactors, as they were originally conceived of, was that they required the separation of waste into actinides (one sort of waste product) and pure plutonium. And plutonium can be turned into nuclear weapons. Creating and transporting plutonium increases the risk that it could be stolen, lost, or hijacked, and eventually be turned into a weapon in the hands of terrorists or rogue nations.

Modern fast nuclear reactors, however, don't require this. A technique called pyrometallurgic recycling keeps all the waste products together while reforming them into fuel rods that fast neutron reactors can burn. At no step along the process is any fuel created that is any closer to a nuclear weapon than the spent fuel stockpiles that already exist. And at the *end* of the process, the total amount of nuclear material remaining has been reduced a hundredfold, *reducing* the risk of it leaking out into the environment or being converted into weapons. Fast neutron reactors eat nuclear waste and spit out valuable, nearly zero-carbon electricity.[8]

Fast reactors can be used to turn fresh nuclear fuel into 100 times as much electricity as current reactors do, with 1 percent of the waste output of current reactors. Perhaps more importantly, they can be fueled by all the *existing* waste that fifty years of nuclear power has created. As with the contents of landfills, the phosphorous we emit from our bodies, and the carbon dioxide in our atmosphere, our ability to innovate can extract the value from something we now consider waste, making us better off, and reducing damage to the environment. Today it is still cheaper to run a conventional reactor than a fast breeder reactor, but eventually the rising price of uranium ore may make breeder reactors more expensive. Or government policy could create economic incentives to reuse fuel in fast reactors rather than storing it indefinitely. That would be both far cheaper and far more useful than Yucca Mountain.

Until then, keeping waste in dry cask storage is fairly safe. Safer, at any rate, than the waste from coal burning power plants. The editors of Scientific American note that, "ounce for ounce, coal ash released from a power plant delivers more radiation than nuclear waste shielded via water or dry cask storage."[9]

Other options exist as well. Seattle-based TerraPower, a company Bill Gates has invested in, is developing a "traveling wave" reactor that consumes almost all of its waste as it operates, leaving behind only short-lived and low-level nuclear waste with a small fraction of the radioactivity of traditional waste. Others advocate turning to thorium as a nuclear fuel instead of uranium, pointing out that the world has more thorium ore than uranium ore and that thorium waste is far less radioactive than uranium waste, and extremely difficult to weaponize. Both are options for the decades ahead. In short, waste is not the problem it appears at first blush.

Small, Safe, Fast, and Cheap

Economically, unfortunately, the nuclear industry has been going backward rather than forward. While solar, wind, and battery technologies have been dropping in cost, nuclear has actually been *rising* in cost.

A 2009 study from MIT on the future of nuclear power found that the average price of electricity delivered by building a *new* nuclear plant (as opposed to operating a current one) was 8.4 cents per kilowatt hour, up nearly 2 cents from the price estimated in 2003.[10] Other analyses have gone further. A review by the Rocky Mountain Institute of published cost data concluded that electricity from new nuclear plants would cost twice what MIT projected.[11] A study by attorney Craig Severance, widely circulated in environmental circles, claimed that, based on rapidly rising construction costs and increasing delays, the cost of electricity from a new nuclear power plant in the United States would be even higher yet, at 25–30 cents per kilowatt hour.[12]

The highest end of price estimates put electricity from new nuclear plants at more costly than coal electricity, even *after* adding in a sizeable carbon tax. If future nuclear plants cost as much as their detractors say, the technology is dead in the water, economically.

Estimates of the cost of nuclear power seem, to me, to correlate with how pro- or anti-nuclear the source is. Pro-nuclear sources often point out that the operating costs for an already running nuclear plant are in the ballpark of 1 cent per kilowatt hour. Nuclear opponents tend to highlight the very highest estimates.

Yet there's no denying that nuclear prices are *rising* rather than falling. The most neutral, balanced, apples-to-apples assessments, such as MIT's 2009 study, all find that.

The price rise in nuclear has been driven by skyrocketing construction costs of nuclear plants. Once, nuclear plants cost an estimated $1,000 per kilowatt of capacity to build. Today some estimates are on the order of $8,000 per kilowatt.

In general, the more a manufacturer or industry makes of a product, the cheaper it gets. The learning curve—the steady accumulation of knowledge about how to build the product most efficiently—continually drops cost. Manufacturers learn how to build the same product in fewer steps. They find places to reduce the amount of energy, labor, and raw materials needed. They invest in innovation that simplifies their manufacturing process. It's difficult, in most industries, to *avoid* the learning curve. It happens naturally, in everything from pocket knives to automobiles to solar cells. Certainly it happens much *faster* in some areas than others. In solar photovoltaics, innovation has proven more powerful in substituting for energy and raw materials than in wind power, for instance. In computing, innovation has had an even larger effect. In gene sequencing, even larger yet. But in all these areas, the learning curve exists. Not so in nuclear reactor construction.

The problem is that nearly every reactor is built from scratch, on site. There are no factories for nuclear reactors. There are no assembly lines. In the United States, most reactors don't even conform to a widely used design—each is a bit different than its predecessors. Because a nuclear reactor can take a decade from proposal to approval by the Nuclear Regulatory Commission, the project managers who manage a nuclear reactor construction, the crews who work on one, and everyone else involved may work on only a few, or even just a *single* reactor in their entire careers, eliminating the opportunity for applying any lessons learned. Because of the mammoth size of reactors, there are only a handful of companies in the world who can build the steel pressure vessels that contain the reactor core. Only one company in the world, Japan Steel Works, can build the pressure vessels out of a single piece of metal with absolutely no welds—the safest way to ensure that radiation stays inside. As a result, Japan Steel Works has a three-year waiting list.

One of the best ways to drive down the cost of nuclear reactors, then, would be to mass produce them. Build them small, build them in factories, and ship them to their location. Tap into the learning curve so that each unit produced is cheaper than the last one. And that's just what a handful of new reactor companies do.

Galena, Alaska, is one of the most remote towns in the United States. 300 miles northwest of Anchorage, Galena has no roads that connect it to the outside world. For three months of the year, barges can make their way up the Yukon River to deliver supplies. The other nine months of the year, the only way in or out is by plane. No power grid comes here. Electricity for the 600 or so residents is provided by gasoline-powered generators. Flying the fuel in makes that electricity fiendishly expensive—at times over 50 cents per kilowatt hour, or four times the national average. And so, in 2004, this tiny town did something radical—it accepted a proposal to build the world's smallest commercial nuclear reactor.

The Toshiba 4S reactor stands for Super, Small, Safe, and Simple. It's been called a nuclear battery. It's a cylinder 60 feet long, 8 feet in diameter with almost no moving parts. Rather than being built on site, it's assembled in a factory, and shipped by train, truck, or, in Galena's case, barge. There it will be lowered into a 100-foot-deep concrete-lined cylindrical hole in the ground. The nuclear fuel for the reactor is loaded in at the factory where it's assembled. That fuel will produce electricity for thirty years. When the fuel is depleted, a new reactor is installed in the old one's place, and the old reactor is shipped back to the factory for refueling and refurbishing. It is, indeed, quite a bit like a nuclear battery.

The 4S is a tiny, puny sort of reactor. The reactors at the Fukushima Daiichi plant produced a combined total of 4,700 megawatts. By comparison, the 4S produces only 10 megawatts. And the 4S could be installed as soon as 2013.

The U.S. Nuclear Regulatory Commission has a pipeline full of design reviews for similar (though mostly slightly larger) mini-reactors. Nuclear startup Hyperion Power Generation is taking advanced orders for its Hyperion "Power Modules," hot-tub-sized mini-reactors just five feet across and less than ten feet tall that produce twenty-five megawatts of power. NuScale's 45-megawatt reactor is fourteen feet wide and sixty-five feet long. The 125-megawatt Babcock and Wilcox mPower, the heavyweight of the bunch, is twelve feet wide and seventy feet tall. All of them can be shipped by train, boat, or heavy truck.

What all of these reactor designs have in common is that they leverage the learning curve. Instead of each reactor being a custom design, depending on one-of-a-kind parts built to order for the site, reactors would become mass-produced products.

There's a rule of thumb in engineering that the larger a project is, and the more unique a project is, the later it will be. Today almost every nuclear reactor is a mega-project, with the mega-complexities, mega-problems, and costly mega-delays that brings. MIT's cost analysis shows that, if construction delays didn't occur, new nuclear plants would provide electricity at an estimated 6.6 cents per kilowatt hour, making it competitive with coal even *before* adding the cost of a fair carbon tax to coal. Mini-reactor manufacturers believe they can hit costs in the 6–9 cents per kilowatt hour range with their first generation products. Hyperion Power has already announced buyers for its first six power modules, at a cost substantially below that of megalithic nuclear reactors, even before the NRC finalized approval of the reactor design.

Standardizing reactor design also means greater safety. Designs can be thoroughly tested with problems worked out once, and solutions rolled out across an entire product line.

Indeed, if there's one area the nuclear industry has learned quite a bit, it's safety. Unfortunately, the lessons from that haven't been rolled out to older reactors—and in many cases, the designs of old reactors make it impossible to do so.

Nuclear reactors work by generating heat, which is then used to create steam, which drives an electric turbine, generating electricity. Cooling fluid circulates through the reactor, picking up heat from the core, pushing the turbine, and then cooling and returning to the core. The circulation both creates electricity and drains heat away from the reactor core, keeping it from overheating and melting through its walls.

The tragedy in Fukushima came about because the pumps that normally circulate water through the core had their power sources knocked offline by the tsunami, which wiped out both the electrical grid connections and the backup generators. Without the pumps pushing in cold water, the reactor cores grew hotter and hotter. As the water in the reactor was turned to steam and evaporated, water levels dropped, exposing nuclear fuel rods to air. Their coatings, never meant to be exposed to air, reacted with air and steam to produce hydrogen gas. It was that hydrogen gas that eventually exploded in three reactors, tearing off their roofs and releasing radiation into the nearby area.

It's deeply ironic that the Fukushima meltdown was caused by a lack of electricity, when the plant itself generated hundreds of thousands of times more energy than was necessary to run the pumps. That, however, is one of the risks of active safety measures. Older plants such as Fukushima require active steps to cool them and render them safe in the event of an emergency. If the plant must be shut down, and those active steps can't be followed, the risk of a meltdown becomes real.

One of the most important innovations in nuclear reactor design in the past decade has been the creation of passive safety measures. Often called "walk away safe," reactors with passive safety are designed to simply stop producing electricity and go into a dormant state if not kept actively running. Instead of pumps to circulate water, new reactor designs are built such that condensation and gravity work to continue to circulate water, even if all power fails. Virtually every new reactor design going through approval today uses passive safety.

Finally, if a mini-reactor does suffer an accident, the consequences are far smaller than with a massive reactor. Most mini-reactor designs have the reactor core deep inside a concrete well drilled into the ground that can be capped and sealed if necessary. When multiple mini-reactors are together at the same location, they're each inside their own concrete hole deep underground. And the sheer scale of possible radiation release from a mini-reactor is dramatically smaller. A mishap of a Toshiba 4S (something *less likely* to happen than a mishap at a large, one-of-a-kind reactor) would release only about 2 percent of the radiation that Fukushima released.

There's a saying that you can't make things foolproof, because fools are so ingenious. That's true in anything we humans build. We won't ever build a totally failsafe nuclear reactor. We won't ever build a totally failsafe *anything*. We can reduce the risk of accidents—and new reactor designs do so—but we should also be realistic that there will be accidents in the future. Just as plane crashes don't mean we shouldn't build new planes, nuclear accidents don't mean that we shouldn't build new nuclear plants. The issue isn't whether an accident is possible or not—it's the odds of an accident occurring, the damage done when one does occur, and the trade-off vs. the alternatives.

In this case, the alternative we're concerned about is primarily coal. Coal mining kills thousands. Coal pollution kills more. Coal CO_2 emissions are the leading contributor to climate change. Coal *will* kill. And by all measures it kills more than current nuclear power, let alone newer, more standardized, more passively safe, smaller scale mini-reactors of the future.

Market Forces

Perhaps energy storage technology and solar and wind power will improve quickly enough to render the nuclear question moot. I hope so, though the current trends suggest that for the next twenty years or longer, nuclear—if construction costs can be kept down—will have an advantage in price.

Do we care about price? Yes, we do. The cheaper an alternative to coal is, the faster it will spread. Whether we're dealing with deployment funded by private investors or deployment funded by governments, the cheaper a carbon-free energy technology is, the more of it our dollars will buy, and thus the more impact it will have on reducing carbon building up in the atmosphere.

We can also, if we're smart, use market forces to *increase* nuclear safety. Nuclear power opponents have frequently pointed out that today, the U.S. government assumes the liability in the case of a major nuclear accident. Without this, nuclear opponents say, no nuclear reactors could ever be built because no one would be able to afford the insurance necessary to cover the possibility of an accident, or be willing to risk bankruptcy in the case of one.

The Price-Anderson Nuclear Industries Indemnity Act protects nuclear reactor operators against ever paying more than $12 billion in damages in the case of an accident. All costs beyond that would be paid for by the federal government or passed on to the nuclear industry as a whole.

I've made the point throughout Part IV of this book that market forces affect the evolution of businesses, behaviors, and technologies. I've also made the point that externalities and tragedies of the commons disrupt that function of the market, and often cause the market to fail in ways that harm us all. The Price-Anderson Act creates a new externality. It lets a nuclear plant operator and manufacturer export the financial risk to the nation as a whole. And as a result, it reduces the effectiveness of the market in driving up safety for nuclear plants.

If nuclear power plant manufacturers and operators had to assume all the liability for their accidents, they would do so by relying more heavily than they do now on private insurers. (They do rely on private insurers now, but those insurers know that their liability is capped at $12 billion per accident.) To build a plant, they'd be required to find an insurer that they could convince of the inherent safety and low maximum danger level of their reactor. Insurers might well refuse to cover reactor designs they considered insufficiently safe, keeping those reactors off the market. Even the premiums insurers charge would likely vary by reactor design, with the safest reactors getting the lowest insurance prices. That would create a market incentive toward safety and would help drive the entire industry toward safer designs.

Hard Choices

I realize that for many readers, the notion of supporting nuclear technology will be a difficult one. We have a long association with nuclear technology as inherently dangerous. It's hard to separate nuclear energy from nuclear weapons, which are surely the largest threat humanity ever created to its own existence and the health of the planet. Yet if we step back, and try to measure the risks with our heads rather than our hearts, things look different. Nuclear has risks, yes. But those risks are smaller than the certain damage we're creating with coal. Until solar and wind are paired with future storage technologies to provide 24/7 energy, nuclear is our best hope for reducing the amount of carbon we emit.

Greenpeace International, on the homepage for their campaign to eliminate nuclear energy, has a prominent quote from one of their founders, Patrick Moore. "Nuclear power plants are, next to nuclear warheads themselves, the most dangerous devices that man has ever created."

Actually, it turns out, that mantle should be given to coal plants, the devices that already kill far more people than nuclear power ever has, which contribute more than any other devices to climate change, and which newer, safer, cheaper reactors could displace.

Ironically, Patrick Moore himself has come to realize that. After campaigning for years against nuclear power, the challenges of climate and coal have changed his mind. These days he campaigns for increased nuclear power as a way to save our planet. "Nuclear energy," the Greenpeace founder told me, "is the best technology we have today to replace fossil fuels and reduce greenhouse gases."

seventeen the unthinkable climate engineering

There are two more backup options for climate change that we should have in our pocket. Neither of them is a sustainable solution, but either might play a vital role in the coming decades of transitioning away from fossil energy.

The first is to contain the problem of carbon dioxide, by capturing it from power plants or from the open air, and storing it in some form where it won't warm the planet or acidify the seas.

The second is to reflect some of the energy of the sun back into space, reducing the warming of the planet.

Containing the Problem

In eastern Germany, between Berlin and Dresden, is the town of Schwarze Pumpe. Since September 2008, German energy company Vattenfall has been operating an experimental power plant in the town. The coal-fired plant produces 30 megawatts of power, making it a baby compared to its 1,600 megawatt cousin nearby. What's unique about the planet is that it emits virtually no carbon dioxide into the atmosphere. Instead, the CO_2 produced by burning the coal is captured, condensed into a liquid, and injected into container trucks. Those trucks transport the liquefied CO_2 to a site outside the town of Ketzin, just west of Berlin.

At the Ketzin site, the liquefied CO_2 is inserted into something rather like the opposite of an oil or natural gas well. Rather than pull fossil fuels out of the ground, the equipment at the site pumps the liquid CO_2 half a mile down, into a natural sandstone cavern capped by a 700-foot-thick layer of impermeable clay, with additional layers of sandstone and clay, above that. There, if all goes well, the CO_2 will remain trapped for millions of years.[1]

The Schwarze Pumpe/Ketzin project runs at a tiny scale, capturing less than

100,000 tons of CO_2 per year, compared to the more than 30 *billion* tons of CO_2 that humanity emits each year. Its goal is to prove that the technology, carbon capture and sequestration, works.

And it does appear to work, though not without its challenges. Carbon capture requires extra energy and extra equipment. That means greater costs. A landmark paper from Harvard, surveying all current carbon capture proposals estimated that the first projects would cost roughly $100–$150 per ton of CO_2 captured, dropping over time to a range of $30–$50 per ton as experience and scale brought costs down.[2]

At that long-run cost, the cost of coal electricity would rise by 3 to 5 cents per kilowatt hour, and natural gas electricity by about half that.

The more options we have to address climate, the better. Batteries or next-generation nuclear power may provide us baseload power for the times when the sun isn't shining and the wind isn't blowing. Or they may be slower to develop than we expect. Judging by the current course and speed, it will still be twenty years before battery technologies have matured to the point that they can handle the grid's needs for overnight power at a reasonable cost. And if unexpected hiccups appear, it could take longer.

Carbon sequestration would give us a way to meet that baseload power need for those intervening decades.

The challenge is enormous. Because CO_2 is only a third carbon by weight, and condenses down to a liquid that is only about half as dense as oil and a third as dense as coal, the total volume of liquid CO_2 that would need to be pumped underground to capture all of the world's carbon emissions is on the order of ten times as much as all the oil the world pumps out of the ground today. Building that infrastructure would require a massive initial outlay of capital, manpower, and energy, to build ships, pipelines, wellheads, pumps, and so on to move and sequester that carbon, none of which will happen quickly.

In addition to the difficulty of the task, storing high-pressure carbon dioxide underground brings with it the danger of leaks into drinking water or back into the air. A 2010 Duke study, for instance, found that in some areas, high levels of CO_2 deep underground could slowly bubble into drinking water, bringing with them dangerous heavy metals.[3] Even worse would be a catastrophic release of major amounts of carbon dioxide. In addition to undoing the benefit of capturing CO_2 underground, a leak of a large amount could be deadly. In 1986, the release of a large amount of CO_2 in a natural reservoir under Lake Nyos in Congo suffocated 1,700 nearby villagers, killing them.[4]

Even so, the U.S. Environmental Protection Agency, the International Energy Agency, and the UN's Intergovernmental Panel on Climate Change all believe that there are enough natural caverns and reservoirs far from water sources and fault lines to store at least one trillion tons of CO_2, and possibly as much as ten trillion. The proof of principle is existing oil and natural gas fields, which have held hydrocarbons under similar or higher pressures for millions or tens of millions of years. We know geological formations are capable of that. What we need to do is select them carefully. If the EPA, IEA, and IPPC's projections of at least one trillion tons of safe CO_2 storage capacity underground are correct, then there's enough storage underground, if we can make use of it, to delay further CO_2 buildup in the atmosphere for at least another thirty years at current rates of emissions, and possibly much longer. At the high end of estimates, those geological formations could store all the emissions humanity will produce in the twenty-first century.

Spurred on by the challenges of underground storage of liquid CO_2, researchers have proposed new ideas over the last few years. As limestone weathers, it absorbs carbon dioxide from the atmosphere, in a process that takes millennia but that captures the carbon for millions of years. Some proposals, called "advanced weathering," involve chemically accelerating that process to speed up the rate at which CO_2 can be absorbed into the earth's crust. The authors of one such proposal from Harvard estimate that it would use roughly 400 kilowatt hours per ton of CO_2 sequestered, increasing energy costs by around 25 percent.[5]

Another approach, proposed by Greg Rau at the University of California, Santa Cruz, involves running the carbon dioxide plumes of power plants through a mixture of sea water and crushed limestone, which it will react with to create calcium bicarbonate, which can then be injected back into the oceans without raising ocean acidity, a process that should be cheap in terms of energy but that may only work near large bodies of water.[6]

Yet another approach, championed by a venture-backed company called Calera, would use waste CO_2 from power plants, combined with waste water and fly ash from coal, to manufacture cement that would bind up the carbon dioxide for its lifetime. Calera points out that the world consumes more than twelve billion tons of cement each year, enough to capture virtually all of the CO_2 emissions from today's power plants.[7]

For most of these approaches, it's simply too early to know how they'll pan out. Carbon sequestration in underground formations is the furthest advanced, yet also presents risks in storage and challenges in the scale of operations needed. The more recently proposed solutions don't have the risk of CO_2 suddenly escaping underground storage. They look attractive, but are far younger and far less tested. Yet the more such ideas we try, the more likely it is that we'll hit upon a solution that works cheaply, safely, and at a volume high enough to make a dent.

The more options we have, the better.

The Elephant in the Room

For the last million years, the amount of carbon dioxide in the atmosphere never went above 280 parts per million. We are now at 390 ppm. Opinions differ on the level that we can safely stabilize at without a major risk of hitting a climate tipping point. The most talked-about number right now is 450 ppm, a level that would keep average planetary warming below 2 degrees Celsius, or 3.6 degrees Fahrenheit. Others, concerned that we're already in uncharted waters, and by the evidence of methane release from melting tundra and from the Arctic seabed, are urging a return to a level around 350 ppm, lower than today, but still higher than the planet has seen during the lifetime of our species.

The elephant in the room is this: We're not going to halt the accumulation of carbon dioxide in our atmosphere at 350 ppm or even 450 ppm, even with the most aggressive ramp up of clean energy we could imagine.

In 2010, three eminent climate scientists wrote a paper in *Science* posing the question "what if we stopped building CO_2 emitting devices today?" That is to say, what if, in 2010, we'd put a halt to the construction of all coal and natural gas plants and all gasoline-powered cars, trucks, and planes. Their answer was that we'd reach 430 ppm. And today, the world hasn't stopped building coal or natural gas plants, or cars, trucks, and planes. Deployment of all of those is going *faster* than ever.

The world needs energy. People need it to come out of poverty, to achieve the type of comfort and health that we have in the rich countries of the world. They're going to keep clamoring for electricity, for cars and trucks, for manufactured goods. We will, eventually, replace the way that we provide that energy. But even in the most optimistic scenario I can muster, the world as a whole will keep building new coal-fired power plants until at least 2020, and quite possibly longer. We'll keep growing the number of cars on the world's streets for a lot longer than that.

Clean energy will eventually win out. The issue is one of time. And right now, it looks like it won't be fast enough to avoid the danger zone. Indeed, we may be in that danger zone already.

In 2009, U.S. energy secretary and Nobel Prize winner Steven Chu echoed this when he told *Rolling Stone*, "The fact is, we're not going to level out at 450 ppm. . . . I hope we hit 550 ppm. Who knows?"[8]

So we need one more tool in our tool belt. I've argued since the beginning of this book that the way to think about climate and energy isn't in terms of certainty—it's in terms of risk and the need to insure against that risk. We need one more piece of insurance. We need a way to cool the planet, either globally, or in select parts.

One approach is to use carbon sequestration to capture CO_2 from the open air. That would allow us to collect CO_2 that's built up from past years of burning fossil fuels, and from current emissions of cars, trucks, and planes. There's wide disagreement about how feasible CO_2 capture from the open air is. The physics indicates that it's definitely possible to do with a relatively small amount of energy. At the theoretically best possible efficiency, using 4–8 percent of the energy originally released by burning fossil fuels, we could capture and compress the CO_2 they emitted. Some people question whether coming anywhere near that is practical, but in other areas of science and engineering we've come within a factor of 2 of the best efficiency the laws of physics allow. If we can do that again, we can capture old emissions at a cost of 8–16 percent of the energy we gained from burning them in the first place. If the climate situation becomes dire, it may make *more* sense to use wind, solar, and nuclear to capture carbon dioxide, either from power plants or from open air, than to replace current coal and natural gas plants. A one-gigawatt nuclear reactor or solar or wind farm could capture and sequester the carbon released from six similar-capacity coal plants or twelve similar-capacity natural gas plants.

And if those plants have already been shut down, or are already sequestering their own carbon emissions, then, every year of operating that solar, nuclear, or wind installation could recapture the cumulative carbon emissions of six years of a similar-sized coal plant or twelve years of a similar-sized natural gas plant.

These systems haven't been built. This is just theory at the moment. But it's a capability we *should* invest in, as a backup we may well need at some point in the future. It's an area that we should be aggressively funding the research in. It's an area that we need to be sure our carbon prices support. Every ton of CO_2 pulled *out* of the atmosphere should be rewarded by a bounty. The same price it costs to emit a ton of CO_2 is the price that should be paid to anyone who *improves* our atmospheric commons by sucking CO_2 out of it. If we put that profit incentive in place, do the research on safety and sustainability of carbon sequestration, and invest in early basic research to bootstrap the field, then we'll see innovation bloom. And if some day we need to use this technology—which is not at all unlikely—then we'll be happy that we nurtured it well in advance.

The Solar Shield

In the early morning hours of June 12, 1991, Mount Pinatubo erupted in an explosion ten times larger than that of Mount St. Helens. The eruption sent a column of superheated steam and ash 12 miles high into the atmosphere above the Philippines. Friction from the column ignited lightning storms in the sky. The explosion was so powerful that it knocked out the seismographs at Clark Air Force Base, 20 miles away. A cloud of ash covering 50,000 square miles descended on the Philippines, bringing total darkness to much of the country's largest island, Luzon.

Over the next two years, the eruption of Mt. Pinatubo did something else. It cooled the Northern Hemisphere of the planet by nearly a degree Fahrenheit. In the ash released by the volcano were an estimated 17 million tons of small sulfur dioxide particles that reached the upper atmosphere, and then lingered there for the next two years. Once in the stratosphere, those particles were too high up to cause acid rain. But they did alter the environment in another way: they reflected just a small fraction of the sun's light back into space, thus cooling the planet.

In 2006, Nobel Prize–winning chemist Paul Crutzen, who won his Nobel for work on the ozone hole, proposed a radical idea in the journal *Climate Change*: We could use the cooling effect of aerosols in the upper atmosphere to fight climate change.[9] The idea was controversial enough that many climate scientists argued against publication. Had it been proposed by anyone with less credibility than Crutzen, the idea might have been dismissed as science fiction. But with a Nobel Prize winner as the source, the idea had to be at least looked at it. Since then, dozens of scientists have proposed variations on the idea.

The idea of reflecting more sunlight into space by injecting small particles into the stratosphere—solar radiation management, as it's called—is deeply imperfect. The particles will only stay in the atmosphere for a year or two, meaning that we'd need to constantly keep injecting new particles if we want to keep the cooling effect. Even if we cool the planet in this way, the buildup of small particles in the upper atmosphere will cause changes to rainfall patterns, with results that aren't fully predictable. If sulfur dioxide is used, there's a chance that some of it will drift down low enough to cause acid rain before it's destroyed in the upper atmosphere.

Most seriously, solar radiation management doesn't slow down ocean acidification. The CO_2 we emit still ends up dissolving in seawater to create carbonic acid, which breaks down coral reefs and the calcifying phytoplankton at the bottom of the ocean food chain. If we keep pumping CO_2 into the atmosphere and compensating for it by pumping aerosols into the upper atmosphere, we'll eventually kill off much of the life in the ocean.

For these reasons, many climate scientists and activists—maybe most of them—oppose this approach.

But the dangers of solar radiation management have to be weighed against the dangers it guards against. In the Arctic, we're at risk of hitting a climate tipping point. As the tundra thaws, buried vegetable matter decays and releases methane. As the ice cap over the Arctic Sea melts, it exposes dark water underneath that absorbs more sunlight, warming the shallow sea above a trillion tons of frozen methane. It's a ticking time bomb.

We can't depend on solar radiation management forever. It's not a full solution to the climate problem. But using it selectively, to cool the Arctic and stabilize the methane there, would reduce the risk of hitting a climate tipping point. It'd lower the risk of tremendously *more* carbon entering the atmosphere, and eventually finding its way into the oceans. It could be a very useful part of our global insurance plan.

What we need now is further research into both carbon sequestration from the air *and* techniques to reflect more sunlight into space. We don't want to be forced to use either, but we'd rather have them and not need them, then need them and not have them.

eighteen greener than green

I grew up by a cornfield. In the early 1980s, my parents came to the obvious conclusion that the United States was a better place to live and raise a child than Egypt. Immigration law didn't make it easy to stay. The normal requirement of the law was for us to return home to Egypt after my mother finished her studies. Then, after two years in Egypt, U.S. law would allow us to apply for the lottery of a small number of immigration visas allocated to Egyptian nationals. With fifty applicants for every visa issued, the odds were slim.

Fortunately, the law had one provision that might allow us to stay in the United States. A physician providing a critically needed service in a community where no one else provided that service was eligible to apply for a "sixth preference" green card, of which a very limited number were available. So it was that we packed up and moved to tiny Flora, Illinois, population 5,000, where my dad would set up shop as the only surgeon in the surrounding county.

When I say that I grew up by a cornfield, I don't mean that a cornfield was just nearby. I mean that our yard ended, and a cornfield began. There wasn't a fence or a gate or a marker of any kind. There was just an invisible line. On one side of that line, I mowed the grass. On the other side, a combine harvester reaped and threshed the corn.

Of all the things that have changed about how humans live since the dawn of our species, how we get food may be the largest. Food is the first and most fundamental energy source for humans. For most of the history of humanity, everyone in the tribe, except for the very young and very old, worked to bring in that energy. The advent of industrialized farming has changed that. A combine harvester does the work of hundreds of men. Fertilizer added to the land doubles its outputs. Pesticides keep insects at bay and kill off weeds that once had to be pulled by hand. Now, less than 2 percent of the citizens of industrialized countries farm, while producing more food per person on the planet than ever before.

The industrialization and intensification of agriculture has been a blessing. In the last fifty years alone we've tripled food production. We've managed to feed billions of people that experts told us we had no chance of feeding. And amazingly, we've done it without chopping down the world's remaining forests and turning them into farmland. The Green Revolution that boosted yields has been a tremendous success. It's one of the clearest stories of innovation overcoming apparent limits that we've ever seen. But it's not without its downsides.

Nitrogen runoff from U.S. farms in the Midwest has created an 8,000-square-mile dead zone in the Gulf of Mexico, an area roughly the size of New Jersey.[1] Runoffs of pesticides are the number one source of pollution in U.S. lakes and rivers.[2] Farm irrigation uses 70 percent of the world's freshwater, draining rivers, and drawing down aquifers on every continent that humans farm. Agriculture remains the number one cause of deforestation in the tropics, where farmers burn down tropical rain forest to plant crops, releasing CO_2 in the process. Synthesizing fertilizer, running farm combines, and operating other machinery release more CO_2. On top of that is the worst climate impact of agriculture: cows and sheep on farms around the world release 80 million tons of methane. Those emissions from livestock alone account for an estimated 18 percent of the world's greenhouse gas output. That's more than all the world's cars combined.[3]

In the next forty years, the demand for food around the world is expected to rise by 70 percent, with much of that being demand for more meat and dairy products. At the same time, extreme weather, with droughts, floods, and heat waves, is likely to become more intense. And we must reduce the environmental damage that agriculture accounts for.

We face not just one challenge with agriculture, but four: How do we grow 70 percent more food? How do we do so in the face of climate risks? How do we do so without chopping down the rest of the world's rainforests? And how do we do all of that, while reducing carbon emissions, nitrogen runoff, pesticide use, freshwater depletion, and all the other environmental externalities of industrial farming?

The Dream of Organic

A few blocks from my home is Madison Market, an iconic Seattle organic foods store. In the summer, the city boasts not one, not two, but at least six different farmers markets where local farmers offer up mostly organic fare.

The countryside just beyond Seattle is dotted with small organic farms. You can even sign up for a "community-supported agriculture" service, where a network of local farms will deliver fresh organic produce to your door.

Organic farming is the fastest growing food trend in the United States today. It offers the promise of an environmentally friendlier way to grow tastier, more nutritious food.

And organic farms succeed in several important ways. They use less pesticide and less fertilizer. There's less nitrogen runoff from them. Organic farms use less fossil fuels per acre of crops. And a 2012 survey of the evidence by Stanford University found organic food, on average, to be roughly as nutritious as non-organic food.

But organic foods have a tremendous downside. They grow less food per acre. And as a result, they use more land.

Organic yields per acre have been an area of debate for more than a decade, with agronomists showing that organic farms have lower yields, and organic farmers and organic food advocates replying with examples of organic plots matching conventional ones. For example, the Rodale Institute, which is credited for introducing organic farming into the United States, has reported that, in their thirty-year side-by-side trial of organic farming versus conventional farming, their organic and conventional test plots produced equal yields.

Unfortunately, larger-scale evidence doesn't back that up. In 2008, as part of its Census of Agriculture, the USDA conducted the Organic Production Survey, the largest ever study of organic farming yields. The study surveyed all of the 14,450 organic farms in the United States, covering a combined 4.1 million acres.[4]

By covering the overwhelming majority of organic production in the United States, the survey gave the first clear view of how organic farming compares on a large scale to conventional farming. And one of the things it found is that organic farms in the United States have lower yields than conventional farms. Organic corn has around 70 percent of the yield of conventional corn. Organic rice has 59 percent of the yield of conventional rice. Organic spring wheat has 47 percent of the yield of conventional spring wheat. Organic cabbage has 43 percent of the yield of conventional cabbage.[5]

Across the board, it takes one and a half times to two times as much land in the United States to grow food organically than it does to grow food via conventional methods. That, in turn, puts more pressure on farmers around the world to grow more. In the developing world, that often means slashing and burning forest into farmland, a process that emits a tremendous amount of carbon dioxide into the atmosphere and harms both the water cycle and species that live in forests.

Organic farming is environmentally kinder to every acre of land. But it requires *more* acres. The trade-off is a harsh one. Would we rather have pesticides on farmland and nitrogen runoffs from them? Or would we rather chop down more forest?

How much more forest would we have to chop down? If we wanted to reduce pesticide use and nitrogen runoff by turning all of the world's farmland to organic farming, we'd need around 50 percent more farmland than we have today. Nobel Prize winner Norman Borlaug, whose work helped triple crop yields over the last fifty years and arguably saved billions from starvation, estimates that the world would need an *additional* 5 to 6 billion head of cattle to produce enough manure to fertilize that farmland. There are only an estimated 1.3 billion cattle on the planet today.[6]

Combined, we'd need to chop down roughly half of the world's remaining forest to grow crops and to graze cattle that produce enough manure to fertilize those crops. Clearing that much land would produce around 500 billion tons of CO_2, or almost as much as the total cumulative CO_2 emissions of the world thus far. And the cattle needed to fertilize that land would produce far *more* greenhouse gasses, in the form of methane, than all of agriculture does today, possibly enough to equal all human greenhouse gases emitted from all sources today.[7]*

That's not a viable path.

Undoubtedly, innovation in organic farming will increase yields on organic farms. But we need to produce 70 percent more food than we do with today's *conventional* yields to feed the world in 2050. Starting with conventional agriculture we'll need to boost yields by 70 percent. Starting with organic agriculture, we'd need to nearly triple yields in that time—a much larger challenge.

Is there a way to get the best of both worlds? Can we find a way to grow more food, on the same land, with less pesticides, and less nitrogen runoff?

*Eating a vegetarian organic diet offsets the low crop yields. However, the use of livestock to produce organic manure still requires the clearing of a large fraction of the world's remaining forest in order to produce fertilizer. And those livestock would still produce more greenhouse gases in the form of methane than climate projections show we can safely produce from *all* sources.

Can we meet one of the original goals of organic farming, to provide food that's more *nutritious* as well?

I believe we can.

Bright Green Agriculture

Vitamin A deficiency is one of the little-talked-about killers of children in the developing world. Every year, between two and three million children under the age of five die from a lack of vitamin A. Half a million children go blind, permanently. Much of the death and blindness happens in Asia, where the staple crop is rice.

Rice is the world's most eaten food. More people depend on it than on wheat, corn, fish, or any other crop or wild food. Rice, unfortunately, carries no vitamin A.

That may change soon. In the rice paddies of the Philippines there are test plots run by the International Rice Research Institute. There, a new type of rice, which carries vitamin A, is being grown for testing. The rice grains of the plant have an orange-ish tint, which has given the new strain its name: Golden Rice.

Golden rice is a genetically modified plant. Of the 50,000 genes in a rice plant, just two have been changed to allow the plant to produce beta carotene—a substance the human body can turn into vitamin A. It's been in development for more than twenty years, and in testing for eight. And while much of the work to develop it has been done by biotech firm Syngenta, and some of that used patents owned by Monsanto, both companies—and others—have agreed to give the rice away to farmers in the developing world. Any farmer who earns less than $10,000 a year—meaning almost all farmers in the developing world—can freely plant golden rice, grow it, sell it, and save seeds to plant again the next year.

Golden rice could save millions of lives. It fulfills one of the goals of organic farming—more nutritious food. It can, in fact, be grown organically, with only organic pesticides and manure. And it's a GMO.

Inspired by golden rice, a team of Australian researchers in 2011 created an experimental rice breed that boosts vitamin A and also quadruples the amount of iron and doubles the amount of zinc in rice grains.[8] An international team has taken the same ideas and applied them to Africa's most common staple crop, cassava, which feeds 700 million people, and created

BioCassava, a variant that has increased levels of vitamin A, iron, and dietary protein.[9]

In labs around the world, there are other works in progress that could feed more people, with greater nutrition, less fertilizer, less irrigation, and less use of pesticides.

Consider the C_4 rice and wheat projects. Corn and sugarcane grow like weeds. They typically get yields that are about 70 percent higher than those of wheat or rice. They need less water than wheat or rice. They need less nitrogen than wheat or rice. They're less vulnerable to the droughts that are rising in frequency around the world.

Corn and sugarcane have the advantage of a new, better form of photosynthesis called C_4. C_4 evolved in the last thirty million years.[10] Plants that use older C_3 photosynthesis have to open their pores to absorb CO_2 during the heat of the day, while the sun is shining on them. As a result, they lose moisture to the warm air. Plants that use C_4 photosynthesis inhale carbon dioxide at night, when it's cool, and save it for combining with sunlight during the day. By doing that, they hang on to more water and capture almost twice as much of the sun's energy as calories than do C_3 plants. And the system they have to turn CO_2, water, and sunlight into sugars needs 30 percent less nitrogen than the system in C_3 plants.

Now an international team of scientists funded in part by the Bill and Melinda Gates Foundation is working to move the genes for C_4 photosynthesis from corn and sugarcane into rice.[11] Another team of scientists is working to do the same for wheat.[12] If the projects succeed, we'll have rice and wheat that produce one and a half times the yield per acre, that require *less* water per calorie, that need *less* fertilizer per calorie, and that are more resistant to drought. They'd allow us to feed more people, on the same land, with less stress on aquifers and rivers, less energy used to create synthetic fertilizer, and less nitrogen runoff. They'd be achieving some of the goals of organic farming—growing food in a more environmentally friendly manner, while still feeding the world.[13] And those strains will be free for farmers in the developing world.

The C_4 genes are totally natural. What the C_4 rice project is doing, in a sense, is cross-breeding rice with the plants that have evolved to use C_4. The resulting crop will be more than 99.9 percent rice, but with the energy capturing genes that evolved in thousands of other plants, and have been present in nature for thirty million years. It's no different than other sorts of hybrids we create through selective breeding, except that it's done at a dramatically accelerated rate.

Other scientists are working on an even more ambitious idea: eliminate the need for fertilizer altogether. Legumes, such as beans and peas, get their nitrogen directly from the abundant supply in the air, with the help of bacteria that grow inside the plants. Indeed, their ability to do so is what inspired the Haber-Bosch process that pulls nitrogen from the air to create synthetic fertilizer. In April 2011, the Gates Foundation convened a small group of researchers to discuss approaches to move this ability into grains like wheat, rice, and corn. Several scientists have suggested paths forward.[14] Success would eliminate the need for synthetic fertilizer—and the carbon emissions and ocean dead zones it causes—entirely. If we'd like to see lower use of synthetic nitrogen fertilizer (with good reason) then surely this would be a welcome step as well.

Other groups in industry, academia, and national laboratories in the United States, India, China, and Australia are working on drought-resistant wheat[15] and corn,[16] flood resistant crops of all varieties,[17] rice that can grow in saltier water and soils,[18] and canola and yeast that produce healthful long-chain omega-3 fatty acids (previously only found in fish).[19]

Finally, let's come back to greenhouse gas emissions. After deforestation, the worst environmental impact of agriculture is likely the emissions of greenhouse gasses from cows, sheep, and pigs. Those greenhouse gas emissions—because they come in the form of methane, a far more powerful greenhouse gas than CO_2—are far larger than the warming effect from creating synthetic fertilizer or operating farm machinery.

But there may be a way to address this. Wallabies, small kangaroo-like animals that live in Australia, have digestive systems that are similar to those of cattle, but they emit only one-fifth as much methane. In 2011, researchers in Australia pinpointed the bacteria in wallaby intestines that keeps methane production down, and the enzyme they produce which may be the key to this process.[20] The next step is to see if that can be introduced to cattle and other livestock. If so, it could cut livestock greenhouse emissions by 80 percent.

An even more radical proposal is to grow meat in laboratory dishes, outside of any animal. Mark Post, a physiologist at the University of Maastricht in the Netherlands, is working on doing exactly that. The technology is extremely young, but if successful, it could create meat far more efficiently than any natural animal—cutting the amount of food and water that goes into creating every pound of meat, and thus making it more ecologically sound. It would entirely eliminate the suffering of animals in the creation of meat. And because the laboratory meat wouldn't be digesting food in any normal sense, it wouldn't emit the large amounts of methane that cows, pigs, and sheep do. And the process, of course, depends on genetic techniques.[21]

In short, genetically modified foods could achieve many of the goals of organic agriculture. They could reduce the amount of energy we need to use, the emission of greenhouse gasses, the amount of water drained from rivers and aquifers, and the runoffs that enter the water. And they could do this while raising yields, feeding more people, and sparing the world's forests.

The Effect So far

The few genetically engineered crops we've deployed so far are already proving themselves to be environmental wins. Roundup Ready soybeans, corn, cotton, and other variants are crops that have been engineered to be resistant to the plant-killing qualities of the herbicide glyphosate (sold as Roundup). They're widely decried because they encourage farmers to spray their crops with glyphosate, since farmers can now do so in larger amounts, killing off weeds, but leaving their crops intact. And it's true that glyphosate usage has gone up. But glyphosate is incredibly safe compared to previous generations of herbicides. Despite hundreds of studies, no sign of toxicity from eating foods sprayed with glyphosate has ever been found. And in the ground, glyphosate binds to soil particles, meaning that very little of it winds up in groundwater.

The result has been that, while Roundup Ready crops have increased the use of glyphosate, measurements of agricultural runoffs in the Midwest show lower levels of herbicides in general than at any point in the last twenty years. And the decline in some of the most dangerous herbicides, those that can enter drinking water, has been the most impressive. Midwestern river concentrations of the water-contaminating herbicide alachlor, for example, dropped by a factor of around 30 over the course of the 1990s.[22] Concentrations of atrazine, another herbicide far more dangerous than glyphosate, have also plummeted.[23] All told, on soybean farms, the use of other herbicides, which the National Research Council call "more toxic than glyphosate" has dropped by a factor of 10 since the mid 1990s.[24] On cotton farms, which are also heavily planted with Roundup Ready crops, use of more toxic herbicides has dropped by a factor of 3. They've dropped by around half on cornfields.

Glyphosate also helps encourage the use of conservation tillage and no-till techniques that are more environmentally friendly. On most farms, a tractor will make five passes—one to plant the seeds, one to harvest the grain, and three after the harvest to destroy weeds. Those passes use fuel. They release carbon trapped in the soil into the atmosphere, contributing to global warming. And they accelerate evaporation from the soil, meaning that more water must be used in irrigation. Because heavily tilled soils form a crust on top, that additional irrigation also produces more runoffs that enter rivers, lakes, and oceans. Broad-spectrum herbicides like glyphosate eliminate the need for the passes that destroy weeds, encouraging no-till techniques that require only two tractor passes. As a result, the farm uses less energy, releases less carbon, uses less water, and produces less runoffs.[25]

On top of that, in the United States, genetically modified crops such as Bt corn, which resists insect pests like corn earworm, have made it possible for farmers to spray less. As a result, over the last thirteen years, the amount of insecticide applied per acre of corn and cotton in the United States has dropped by a factor of 5.[26]

By improving resistance to weeds and insects, Bt crops have also increased yields. The National Research Council in 2010, after reviewing fifteen years of studies, found that GM crops in the United States had lifted yields of corn by 5–10 percent and yields of cotton by as much as 20 percent.[27]

In the developing world, where pesticides are more expensive and agriculture is less mechanized (making it more labor-intensive to spread pesticides over the fields), the difference is even larger.

In India, for example, before 2002, infestations of bollworm regularly destroyed half the cotton crop. K. R. Kranthi, director of India's Central Institute for Cotton Research, tells an interesting story about how farmers viewed GM crops in those days. In 2001, he says, farmers endured incredible 118 degree heat to make the trek to a cotton seed testing facility at his institute in the city of Nagpur. Kranthi recalls meeting a group who'd traveled 800 miles from the Gujarat region, bringing with them sealed aluminum pouches with cotton seeds. What they all wanted to know was—were these seeds genetically modified to contain the Bt gene?

Kranthi writes, "By end of that day, when they saw the results, they were all smiles and suddenly looked well-fed, despite having eaten just a banana and samosa that day. All of the seed packets tested positive for the presence of the Bt toxin."[28] That is to say, all the seeds had been genetically engineered. That was one year *before* India approved Bt cotton for use in the country. The farmers didn't care. They just wanted to produce viable crops.

Since its introduction to India, Bt cotton has doubled cotton yields per acre, and cut the use of insecticides by half. The most dangerous insecticides have fallen in use by 70 percent. Writing in 2011 in the journal *Ecological Economics*, German researchers estimated that by reducing the use of toxic insecticides in India, where cotton is harvested by hand, Bt cotton was preventing at least 2.4 *million* cases of insecticide poisoning per year, and possibly as many as 9 million per year.[29]

What's the Resistance?

So GM crops have already reduced insecticide usage, reduced insecticide poisoning, encouraged soil conservation, reduced usage of the most dangerous herbicides like atrazine, reduced pollution of drinking water with herbicides, increased profits for developing world farmers trying to pull themselves out of poverty, and moderately increased yields.

And GM crops of the future could save hundreds of thousands of lives a year (in the very near future), could boost yield per acre dramatically, could feed the planet, could boost nutrition, could reduce the use of synthetic fertilizer, and could save millions of square miles of forest from being turned into farm land.

Yet environmentalists and Europeans resist them. In 2004, Greenpeace successfully campaigned to stop the introduction of Roundup Ready wheat into the United States and Canada, an action that has resulted in millions of pounds of atrazine entering our waterways. More damagingly, Greenpeace and Friends of the Earth have successfully campaigned to keep GMOs of all sorts out of most of the countries in Africa, the countries that need it most.[30] Greenpeace, Friends of the Earth, and other organizations based in rich countries with plenty to eat have done this largely by spreading disinformation and exploiting local fears. The consequences at times are deadly.

In 2002, for instance, Southern Africa was struck by a severe drought that left fifteen million people without enough food to eat. Robert Paarlberg talks about what happened in his book *Starved for Science: How Biotechnology Is Being Kept Out of Africa*:

In May 2002, just as this crisis was intensifying, the government of Zimbabwe decided to turn away a 10,000-ton shipment of un-milled U.S. corn, expressing an official concern that some of the GM kernels might be planted rather than eaten. . . . Zambia, however, took even stronger action. In August 2002 the vice president of Zambia provisionally turned down all imports of GM maize, even though nearly 3 million of his citizens faced a pressing need. . . . Zambian president Levy Mwanawasa later commented, "Simply because my people are hungry, that is no justification to give them poison, to give them food that is intrinsically dangerous to their health."[31]

Where did the notion that GM corn is poison come from? It came from Greenpeace. In September of 2002, the organization published a featured article on Greanpeace.org praising Zambia's actions and criticizing the United States for sending genetically modified corn as aid (virtually all corn grown in the United States is genetically modified). The article called Zambia's decision to ignore the starvation of three million of its citizens a "brave choice." It characterized the U.S. donation thus: "The US donation was an ultimatum: 'eat our unwanted genetically engineered food or die.'"[32]

Meanwhile, managers of food aid programs and refugee camps were forced to sit on stockpiles of food aid from the United States that they were forbidden from distributing. Government radio broadcast messages informing Zambians that the GMO food was poison. Yet in some areas, villagers ransacked warehouses to get to the food—which they knew was GMO. The *New York Times* described a woman, Josephine Namangolwa, shouting at aid workers in a famine refugee camp that she and her eight children were dying, that they wanted to eat.[33] But all the food the camps had they were forbidden to distribute, despite the lack of any evidence that it would harm Zambians, and the abundant clarity that without food, Zambians would die. Finally, in September of 2002, Zambia allowed food aid groups to distribute GMO food to refugees who'd entered Zambia from other countries—but not to Zambian citizens.[34] Eventually, the food crisis passed, but not before an estimated 20,000 Zambians died—preventably—of famine.[35]

What accounts for this intensity of opposition to genetically modified foods? Even if GMOs produced, say, a small negative impact on health (a claim for which there's no credible evidence), surely that would be preferable to starvation? Yet Zambia's leaders kept the food away even from people on the verge of death, and Greenpeace cheered them on.

Is the resistance to GMOs well founded on the basis of human health? Are GMOs poison, as Greenpeace and Zambia's president Levy Mwanawasa have said? No. Despite fifteen years of research, hundreds of studies, and hundreds of billions of meals containing GMOs, there is no credible evidence of harm to humans or animals. The most widely cited studies that purport to show harm to rats fed Monsanto Bt corn (in the form of toxicity and slightly enlarged livers) were conducted by Gilles-Eric Séralini in 2007 and 2009. However, other studies show that eating a diet made up primarily of corn, whether genetically modified or not, show the same symptoms. Multiple panels that have reviewed the data, including scientists from France, Germany, Canada, the United States, Australia, and New Zealand, have *all* come to the conclusion that the Monsanto corn posed no additional risk.

In 2008, a report authored by Alberta Velimirov and Jürgen Zentek at the Free University of Berlin made waves when it purported to show that mice strains fed another variety of GMO corn for four generations showed signs of reduced fertility. But in 2009, the Austrian government, which had commissioned the study, announced that due to calculation errors and problems with the experiment itself, the study had been withdrawn, and that the results were invalid.[36] As always, bad news travels faster than good. In November 2008, Greenpeace issued a press release pointing to Zentek's study as demonstrating the dangers of GMOs. They made no comment on the retraction of the study's findings.

While the few studies pointing to any risk to animals have been retracted or shot down, no paper showing harm to humans has ever been published. Conversely, a number of large studies and reviews of the hundreds of smaller studies have found no health impact to humans. In 2004, a report from the U.S. National Academy of Sciences said that "To date, no adverse health effects attributed to genetic engineering have been documented in the human population."[37]

In 2008, a review published in the *Journal of the Royal Society of Medicine* found that there were no credible claims of health damage from GMOs, stating, "Foods derived from GM crops have been consumed by hundreds of millions of people across the world for more than fifteen years, with no reported ill effects (or legal cases related to human health), despite many of the consumers coming from that most litigious of countries, the USA."[38]

In fact, GMOs are tested far more thoroughly than any other food. In the United States, they're tested more like new medicines. First, scientists look at the genome of any new GMO to ensure that the new gene has gone in cleanly and not obviously disrupted any other gene. Second, scientists analyze the plant's metabolism and study the chemical composition of the resulting food, looking for any sign of a change other than the one that was intended. Along the way, they measure the level of every vitamin, mineral, toxin, and other substance in the food. Third, the new food is tested for the presence of around 500 known allergens. Fourth, it's fed to animals in amounts many times higher than humans will ever eat it. A GMO passes testing only if, at every one of these stages, it's found to be safe, with only the genetic changes that were intended, no impact on allergies, equal or better nutrition to the old food, no dangerously elevated toxin levels, and no sign of any health impact on animals, even when the new food is the *only* thing they eat for generations. Only after it passes all of those tests to the satisfaction of the Food and Drug Administration is a GMO ever fed to humans in the United States. In other countries around the world, the testing is similar.

And in more than a decade of doing these sorts of tests, no health impact has ever been found.

If the resistance to GMOs is based on concerns over human health, it's ill founded.

Is resistance based on damage to the environment? The National Academy of Science's 2010 report, *Impact of Genetically Engineered Crops on Farm Sustainability in the United States*, found that GM crops planted to date had *reduced* insecticide use, *reduced* use of the most dangerous herbicides, increased the frequency of conservation tillage and no-till farming, reduced carbon emissions, reduced soil runoffs, and improved soil quality. The report said, "Generally, GE [GMO] crops have had fewer adverse effects on the environment than non-GE crops produced conventionally."[39]

In 2011, the government of Spain, long opposed to genetic technologies, released its own report on Bt corn, finding that GMO corn had no adverse effect on the environment, and that glyphosate was significantly *less* toxic and *better* for the environment than the herbicides it replaced.[40]

What about pesticide resistance? It's a real problem, but one that's far older than GMOs. Any time a pesticide is used, whether on an organic farm, a conventional farm, or a GMO farm, there's a chance of insects or weeds developing resistance. Over the course of the twentieth century, that happened many times. We know good practices that help slow down the development of pesticide resistance: plant more than one type of crop, use more than one type of pesticide. Both the problem and the solutions are far older than GMOs. What we need to do is actually encourage the solution. Recently, that's begun to happen. In 2000, the EPA began requiring that all corn farmers who plant genetically modified Bt corn plant at least 20 percent of that land with non-Bt corn. Instead of eating Bt corn, the pests that are susceptible to Bt now eat the unmodified corn, delaying the advent of resistance. More practices like that can and should be encouraged, and in some cases required.

The most vivid claim of environmental harm from genetically modified crops is that Bt corn kills monarch butterflies. Even that finding was quickly refuted by other researchers, who pointed out that the monarch study was done entirely in a laboratory rather than natural settings, and who conducted field tests that showed no detectable harm to monarchs at all.[41] Seldom mentioned in environmental concerns raised over Bt corn is the fact that Bt is an *organic* insecticide, sprayed onto crops on thousands of organic farms today, and used in agriculture since the 1920s.[42]

The European Union is notoriously opposed to GMOs. But in 2010, looking at all of this data, the European Commission released a report admitting that, "The main conclusion to be drawn from the efforts of more than 130 research projects, covering a period of more than 25 years of research, and involving more than 500 independent research groups, is that biotechnology, and in particular GMOs, are not per se more risky than e.g. conventional plant breeding technologies."[43]

In 2011, the French Supreme Court struck down a French ban on a Monsanto GMO corn on the basis that the government had shown no evidence that the corn posed any risk to either humans or the environment.[44]

So GM crops, in many ways, are kinder to the environment than non-GM crops. And as future GM crops raise yields—by upgrading photosynthesis, making extraction of nitrogen more efficient, or other routes—they'll spare tremendous amounts of forest and other land from conversion to agriculture. That alone will be a tremendous environmental benefit.

◇ ◇ ◆

As I've made this case to people over the last year, I've had the "unknown unknowns" problem brought up. GMOs could be causing problems to human health or the environment that we simply haven't observed yet. There could be an impact waiting for us years or decades down the road.

We can never rule out some subtle effect that we haven't seen yet, but we can put constraints on it. Given that hundreds of millions of people in the United States, at all ages from infant to elderly, have been eating genetically modified food for two decades now, with no evidence of ill effects, any negative effect on health would have to be very small to have avoided detection so far. On top of that, the hundreds of studies that have been done on animals have failed to detect any harm from GMOs, even when fed to them for their entire lives, and fed to multiple generations in a row for their entire lives. Again, we can't ever rule out that there is *some* problem that appears only in humans and only after thirty or forty years of diet containing GMOs. But if there is such a problem it would be nearly unique in the medical literature. If it will be significant after thirty or forty years, it should at least be detectable today, and it isn't.

In the end, on the topic of safety, we're faced with the fear that there is some unknown, yet-to-occur problem we haven't detected yet. And on the other side are known and clear benefits—higher yields, less use of insecticides, less use of highly toxic herbicides like atrazine, more use of conservation tillage. And looming in the future: better nutrition; dramatically increased yields; drought resistance; and less need for nitrogen fertilizer, water, and other inputs. We have very real, measureable, concrete benefits for people and the environment stacked against hypothetical harm that has never been seen.

Greenpeace founder Patrick Moore, who split from Greenpeace over this issue and others, expressed it to me thus, "You can't base your decisions today on some unknown risk that's never been seen. You have to weigh those unknowns against real issues, against the lives of millions."

The other complaint about GMOs that's frequently cited is about the business practices of companies like Monsanto, who require farmers to buy new seed each year rather than replanting seed harvested from the crop, and who've been known to prosecute farmers for violation of their agreements or even for seeds from GM crops accidentally spreading to the fields of farmers who haven't planted them. And I agree that Monsanto's practices are overly aggressive in many cases. Farmers who haven't planted GM crops shouldn't be held legally responsible if seeds of other farmers spread on the wind to their fields. The burden of proof should be on Monsanto, not on the farmers. If

GMO seeds find their way into organic farmers' crops, organic farmers ought to be able to get compensation for that from Monsanto or from GM farmers. A system like that exists in Denmark. The dollar quantities paid have been small, because actual spread of GMO genes is rare and seldom widespread.[45]

And Monsanto should find a way to offer its seeds in a less restrictive way to poor farmers in the developing world. Pharmaceutical companies struck deals that made HIV drugs available at dramatically lower prices in Africa. Monsanto can and should take a similar approach, making its products freely replantable for low-income farmers in the developing world, while using whatever pricing and replanting model it likes for farmers in rich nations like the United States, who can afford to buy new seed each year, and who generally do anyway.

Yet Monsanto is not the whole of the GM world. In 2014, Monsanto's patent on Roundup Ready soybeans will expire—the first of a wave of patent expiries that will let *anyone* take advantage of that gene to create new seeds that can reduce the use of toxic pesticides like atrazine, while being licensed in much more open ways.

At the same time, a host of other competitors have biotech crops that have recently come onto the market or will in the next few years. And nonprofits and universities are producing GM crops that will be free to the poor and that are often developed in the "open source" model. Golden rice and C_4 rice are being co-developed by a network of universities and nonprofits, for example, and will be available free of charge to farmers in the developing world.

In the early days of computing, the only computers were giant IBM mainframes that cost millions of dollars. Today, you have more computing power in your pocket than the entire planet possessed forty years ago. The dramatic decline in the price of computing over those decades has democratized computing tremendously. Proverbial "garage start-ups" like Apple, Google, and Facebook start with humble resources but can revolutionize the world. Open source networks of unpaid developers build software used by hundreds of millions.

That revolution is on the very edge of hitting biotechnology. The cost of gene sequencing has dropped by a factor of *1 million* over the last twenty years. That's faster than the cost of computing has ever dropped. Research is dropping in price. The ability to create new GM foods, tailored exactly for local conditions and needs, is growing. Already there are dozens of different projects to create GM crops that deliver better nutrition, higher yields, or lower need for pesticides or fertilizer underway. Some are from private companies, who'll compete with one another to provide the best products, prices, and terms. And many more are from nonprofit foundations and universities.

What we're going to see in the future is not a monopoly on the technology of food. We're going to see wide open competition between dozens of companies, hundreds of universities, and some day thousands of different GM foods. And that is exactly what we want. We don't want the world's food supply to be controlled by any one company. We don't want monocrops that are all genetically homogenous and vulnerable to the same diseases. We want a wide variety of seeds being offered, planted, and grown to be consumed.

There's an association today between genetically modified crops and large, faceless companies and heavily monocultured agriculture. If the computing revolution is any guide, then the future will be one of more riotous diversity, with thousands of genetically modified food strains available for planting and eating, many of them originating from small start-up companies and many of the rest from academic labs and nonprofit organizations.

The real reason so many people fear genetically modified organisms, I suspect, has little to do with rational assessment of the data, and everything to do with our hardwired emotional responses. Humans (and other animals) have evolved a high disgust instinct. That instinct may have evolved to protect us from disease. We're instinctively disgusted by blood, by bodily waste, by rotting food, by the stench of death. All of those, for our ancestors, were potential threats to survival. Any of them could have carried a contagious disease. In the days before antibiotics and other modern medicines, that could be fatal. The disgust mechanism drove early opposition to vaccination, to blood transfusions, and to other medical technologies that seemed "gross." The smallpox vaccine, blood transfusions, organ transplants, and fertility treatments all suffered from this early on. All are now accepted in society.

Genetic modification of plants and animals, something few people truly understand, seems alien in many of the same ways. It's a tinkering with our food, not in a mechanical sense, but in some mysterious biological sense.

For others, perhaps, the issue is one of associating science and industry with damage to the environment and ourselves. It's plain to see that industrialization has produced a tremendous amount of pollution. Toxic chemicals really can make people ill and kill them. At some point, those factors may tar someone's perception of science so much that they reject other products of science, even if those stand to improve both human health and the environment.

I believe opponents of genetically modified foods are doing what they're doing out of the best of intentions. I think their judgments are driven by a highly selective sort of caution, however. As we look at the facts, look at the potential gains, the real gains already achieved, and the way that losses and harms seem to recede into the distance as we investigate them, using genetic technology to improve our farming seems more and more attractive.

Will genetic technologies fix all the problems of agriculture by themselves? Absolutely not. We need policies to discourage the externalities of agriculture, just as we need them to discourage the externalities of burning fossil fuels. We should be adopting rules that encourage crop diversity, discourage nitrogen and pesticide runoffs, and encourage the practices that slow pesticide resistance. All of those are places where intelligent policy choices can help. But in the context of those policy improvements, GMOs can play a vital role in actually achieving those goals of greater diversity, lower pesticide resistance, and reduced runoff. GMOs aren't the whole of the solution to agriculture's problems, but they're a key piece.

Garden Earth

There's a logical extension of what we could do with increased yields that all environmentalists should be delighted by. That's the prospect of shrinking the amount of *land* needed for agriculture. Land use is by far the worst ecological impact of farming. Of all the things we've done, it's farming, and not CO_2 emissions or pollutants, that has changed the land surface of the Earth the most. Our planet has half as much forest now as it did prior to the advent of agriculture. The only thing that's kept that remaining half of the world's original forest intact has been our ten-thousand-year process of boosting yields per acre.

What happens if we keep on boosting those yields? The maximum efficiency of photosynthesis is believed to be around 13 percent. That is the highest fraction of the sun's energy that can be captured by a process of combining sunlight, water, and CO_2 to make sugars. Today, a typical field of crops captures only around 0.1 percent of the sunlight striking it. Ten billion people on the planet all eating diets as resource intensive as that of a typical American would need a little less than five times as much food as is produced today—or around 0.4–0.5 percent of the sunlight that strikes our farmlands. If we grew our food in a manner that captured the full 13 percent that is physically possible, we'd be producing nearly thirty times as much food as would be required to feed 10 billion Americans. We could, in theory, feed *300 billion* people on this planet an American-style diet, *if* we boosted overall crop yields by another factor of 100 or so. That may sound like a tremendous task, but it's just a fraction of the 10,000 times multiplier of yield that we've achieved over the course of our history.

There's no sign that this planet will ever host 300 billion people. On current trajectory, it appears that our population will peak at or below 10 billion people and then, unless steps are taken, decline.

Let's assume for the moment that rather than shrinking, we stabilize our population at 10 billion. In that world, if we raised crop yields to their physical maximum, and everyone on the world ate an American style diet, we could *shrink* the amount of land needed to grow food by a factor of 30. That is to say, we could reduce agricultural land by 97 percent.

What would we do with all that land? Perhaps we'd build parks. Perhaps we'd return it to nature. The back yard I mowed as a child in Flora, Illinois, and the cornfield next to it were both once covered in ancient forest. Perhaps they could be again.

Of course, that will not happen with today's crops. Any yield increase of that magnitude—or anywhere close to it—will come only through crops that we've modified. Genetic engineering has the promise to meet the needs of billions of people, while saving the forests that remain. And beyond that, it holds out the promise of going further and returning huge fractions of the world to nature. Genetic technologies may someday be viewed as one of the most environmentally friendly innovations of all time.

Embracing the New

In 984 AD, the Viking leader Erik the Red led 500 Norse men and women north to a new land he'd discovered. He called it Greenland. In that time, during an era now referred to as the Medieval Warm Period, Greenland was likely a warmer, gentler place than it is today. It may even have been green.

Erik the Red's Norse followers brought with them the technology they knew and understood. Wood longhouses provided shelter. Wood hearths provided heat to forge iron tools. Fields, turned by iron plows, were planted with oats, wheat, and barley. Sheep, goats, pigs, and cows provided milk, cheese, and beef. Hunted caribou supplemented the diet. For hundreds of years, that pattern worked. A small settlement of 5,000 or so Norse made a living.

In the 1300s, the situation changed. The Medieval Warm Period came to an end. Worldwide climate cooled. The world entered the "Little Ice Age." Throughout history, the areas closest to the poles have consistently proven the most sensitive to climate change. Today, the Arctic is heating up faster than anywhere else on Earth. In the 1300s, Greenland cooled far more quickly and far more dramatically than the rest of the world, dropping in temperature by around 7 degrees Fahrenheit.

The traditional technology the Norse had brought with them turned out to not be up to that challenge. Greenland, cold already, became colder. Already fragile soils became marginal. Crop yields declined. Trees, which had always grown slowly there, began to barely grow at all. Wood with which to build homes and heat up forges with which to make iron tools became increasingly scarce, and then completely absent. The cows and pigs died. Eventually, with nothing to feed off of, the sheep and goats died too. We don't know exactly when the Norse settlement as a whole died. We do know that when the missionary Hans Egede journeyed to Greenland in 1721, he found no surviving Norse there. He did find the Inuit.

The Norse and Inuit coexisted in Greenland for at least 150 years. Yet they interacted with the world around them in very different ways. While the Norse had brought with them a set of technologies that had worked for them in the conditions they'd encountered in the past, the Inuit had a different technology base, one oriented toward the conditions of Greenland, and that better prepared them for a colder future. The Norse depended on crops that grew poorly in the thin soils, on buildings and tools that required a tremendous amount of wood to create, and on livestock that proved difficult to feed in the harsh conditions. The Inuit, by contrast, lived off of fish, seals, and whales. They had mastered the construction of kayaks that stretched waterproof seal hide over a minimal wooden frame, and from these they could hunt by harpoon. They burned whale blubber for both fuel and illumination. They built their igloo homes from plentiful ice and snow.

The Inuit weren't necessarily the technological superiors of the Greenland Norse in all ways. They didn't know how to work iron, for instance, and that has been a major differentiator between societies throughout the world. The Inuit knowledge base wouldn't have been particularly useful in Europe, where wood abounded and metal could be worked and whales were nowhere in evidence. But in the near-arctic climate in which the two societies met, the Inuit undoubtedly had the superior knowledge base, enabling them to extract more resources from their surroundings and making them less dependent on highly scarce resources like wood.[46]

Why didn't the Norse adopt the Inuit technologies? Perhaps the cultures remained too hostile to each other. Perhaps the Norse settlement was just too small to produce enough "early adopters" willing to try out new ways of doing things. Perhaps the Inuit technologies just seemed too alien, too strange and different.

What we do know is that the Norse stuck stubbornly to their own ways. Perhaps a few adventurous souls tried something new, but if so, the archeological evidence from the Norse settlements doesn't show it. By and large, until the end, the Norse were trying to eke out a living using the same crops, the same types of livestock (those that survived), and the same sorts of tools. And they paid the price for that stubbornness.

The Inuit are still there, in Greenland. The Norse are not.

Sometimes, new technology, even though it looks different or frightening, is exactly what we need to embrace in order to survive and thrive.

nineteen the decoupler

There's a story about the invention of chess in ancient India. When the inventor of the game, a great sage, showed his invention to the king, the king was extremely pleased. He asked the sage to name his reward. The sage, who was very wise, asked for a seemingly modest gift. Give me one grain of rice for the first square on the board, he asked. Then two for the second. And four for the third, and so on, doubling each time, until all sixty four squares on the board had been accounted for.

The king, amazed that the sage would ask for so humble a reward as a few grains of rice, agreed. He ordered his treasurer to see to it.

The treasurer returned, fear in his eyes. I can't do it, Your Majesty. There isn't enough rice in the whole kingdom.

The story is one of the power of exponential growth. The fourth square on the board represented only 8 grains of rice. The eighth square represented four more doublings, bringing it to 128 grains of rice. By the end of the second row, the tally was up to more than 32 thousand grains.

By the end of the third row, the tally had reached more than 8 million grains.

By the end of the fourth row, halfway through the board, the king owed the sage 2 *billion* grains of rice.

At the three quarter mark, it was 140 *trillion* grains.

And by the end of the board it was 9 quintillion grains of rice, a pile that would weigh 400 billion tons, or a thousand times more rice than the world produces each year. If heaped in one place, that pile would be larger than Mount Everest.

The king, not amused at how he'd been tricked, had the sage beheaded.

The full story is one of exponential growth, *and* the reckoning that it eventually brings. When Thomas Malthus, in 1800, warned that the world would collapse, the reason he cited was the "geometric growth" of human population. In his view, world population was advancing along the squares of that chess board, growing exponentially, while the amount of food we grew advanced only "arithmetically," adding one unit per square. At square six, food production would be up by a factor of 6, but population would be up by a factor of 32, far outpacing food. Paul Ehrlich saw much the same problem, as world population doubled before his eyes.

Most of our concerns about the limits to growth of humanity come down to this problem. If we keep growing exponentially, even by just a few percent each year, we'll eventually reach the absurd levels of consumption of the second half of the chess board. And since those levels are so far beyond anything that our world could possibly sustain, we'll collapse. Like the sage in the story, our reward for inventing exponential growth will be to have our head cut from our shoulders. And as with the sage, it'll happen suddenly. We'll be at the height of our wealth, satisfied with ourselves for our cleverness, and then it will all come to an end.

This is the narrative of collapse. Of the foolishness of believing in exponential growth. It tells us that if we keep on going the way we are today, it's all going to come crashing down around us. It's the core narrative of the computer simulations of *The Limits to Growth*.

It's also untrue.

Or at least, it doesn't need to be true. We can keep growing as far into the future as the eye can see *if* we make some intelligent decisions.

I've made most of the case for this in the previous pages of this book. To bring that case together, we need to understand what we mean by growth. And, in general, the term is used to mean three different things:

First, growth of population.

Second, growth of consumption of resources, and its flip side, pollution.

And third, growth of wealth and well-being.

Let's look at those one at a time.

Population

The IPAT equation claims that environmental Impact (I) is equal to Population (P) times Affluence (A) times Technology use (T). All else being equal, a growing population will use more resources. A population that grows exponentially, like the grains of rice along the chess board, will ultimately use all available resources.

And for quite some time, human population did grow exponentially. But those days appear to be over.

In Brazil, two generations ago, the average woman had 6 children over the course of her lifetime. Now, the average woman in Brazil has just 1.8 children over her lifetime. That number isn't enough to even maintain the population. If fertility doesn't rise, Brazil's population will *shrink* over time.

Brazil is just one example. Everywhere that incomes rise, that education rises, and that women gain more opportunity outside of the home, fertility rates drop. European women now have around 1.5 children on average over the course of their lifetimes. Russian women are similar. South Korean women have only 1.3 children, on average, over the course of their lives.

Around the world as a whole, the average number of children a woman will have in her lifetime has dropped in half over the last fifty-odd years, from 4.9 children per woman in 1960 to 2.5 children per woman around the world in 2011. When fertility drops below 2.1, population stops growing.

As a result, between 2050 and 2100, something almost unprecedented in the history of the world is likely to occur. The world's population is likely to plateau between 9 and 10 billion people. And after that, so long as wealth and education continue to rise, the world's population is likely to drop.

Consumption

Population is stabilizing. But, as we grow richer, consumption and pollution—the true measures of impact—may still increase. The A and T terms in the IPAT equation, Affluence and Technology, say it will. So does the Limits to Growth model first published in the 1970s, and revised since then. The model predicts that as wealth grows, pollution and depletion of resources will inexorably grow with it, eventually leading to collapse.

We've seen already that technology can often reduce the resources required to perform any given task. But increasing efficiency may also lead to more consumption, as it lowers prices and makes it possible for individuals to afford bigger houses, richer diets, larger cars, and so on. This is the so-called Jevons Paradox—the idea that efficiency can actually *increase* consumption.

So which of these things has a bigger impact? Does greater efficiency win out, or does greater consumption enabled by that efficiency win out?

The evidence now is that, after a nation reaches a certain level of wealth, the consumption of each person in the nation starts to level off and, perhaps, decline.

Consider oil. In 1972, the average American consumed more than thirty barrels of oil per year. In 2002, with oil at a historically low price of $30 a barrel and both the U.S. and global economies roaring, oil consumption was down to less than 25 barrels per person per year. In 2010, driven by high prices and a slow global recovery, consumption was down to less than 19 barrels per capita per year. As the global economy recovers, oil consumption may rise temporarily. Even so, the International Energy Agency projects that in 2030 the average American will consume only 17 barrels of oil per year, just over half the amount consumed in the early 1970s.[1]

Nor is the change limited to the United States. France, Germany, Great Britain, and the OECD as a whole have all seen their consumption of oil per capita drop by anywhere from 30 to 40 percent since the peaks of the 1970s.[2]

That reduction in per capita oil consumption has not been a result of halted growth. The average American lives six years longer, in a larger home, with a larger television, more computing power, a higher likelihood of owning a car (or two cars), higher likelihood of having an air-conditioned home, and higher likelihood of owning all sorts of appliances and conveniences

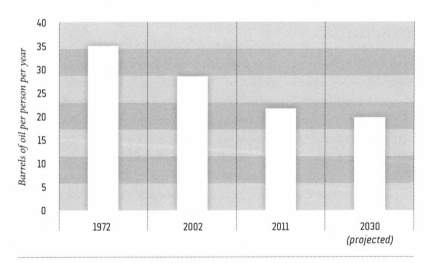

Figure 19.1. U.S. oil consumption per capita. The average resident of the United States used one-third less oil in 2011 than in 1972. Source: EIA

than he or she did in the 1970s. We've gotten richer, by any measure, while consuming less oil.

If we look at *all* energy sources, per capita use in the United States is flat since 1970. If we look at all CO_2, per capita emissions in the United States are down slightly since 1970.

Some of that is a result of outsourcing manufacturing to China and the rest of the developing world. How do we really know if we've reduced our CO_2 emissions? In 2009, scientists Steven J. Davis and Ken Caldeira set out to measure this. They looked at the manufactured goods Americans imported from China and other countries around the world, as well as the energy required to transport those goods and raw materials. They looked at flows of cars, machinery, electronics, clothes, toys, and so on. What they found was that the average American was responsible for about 2.5 tons of CO_2 emissions per year that happened in other parts of the world. That brought the per capita CO_2 emissions of an American up to 22 tons per year. But that level was still lower than the 23 tons of CO_2 the average American emitted *domestically* (not counting any imports) in 1973.[3]

Even including globalization, American CO_2 emissions have been effectively flat, if not slightly declining, for the last forty years. They're still too high, and they need to be brought down, but it's clear that economic growth—a near doubling of U.S. GDP per person since then—doesn't necessarily depend on either more energy consumption or CO_2 emissions per person.

Water use per person has dropped as well, thanks largely to the increases in the efficiency of water use in farming. According to the U.S. Geological Society, water use per person in the United States, for all uses, peaked at just shy of 2,000 gallons per person per day in 1975 and steadily declined to around 1,400 gallons per person per day in 2005, a level not seen since the 1950s, and a decline of about 1.2 percent per year.[4]

What about pollution? Pollution is certainly part of the *I* for Impact in the IPAT equation. The *Limits to Growth* model projects that, as economies grow, their levels of pollution will grow. It predicted that overall pollution levels would roughly quadruple between 1970 and 2010. But the reality is that, for those pollutants we've *decided* to regulate, absolute levels have dropped tremendously. Emissions of lead and CFCs have dropped to nearly zero. Emissions of sulfur dioxide, carbon monoxide, mercury, PCBs, and nitrogen oxide have all dropped by half.

Water use, energy use, and CO_2 emissions have all held steady or dropped

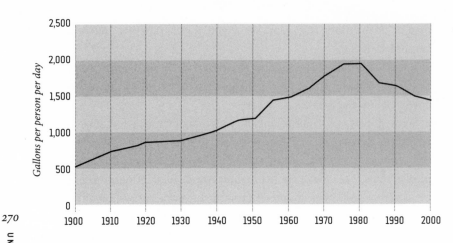

Figure 19.2. Per capita water withdrawals in the United States. U.S. per capita water consumption, after rising for decades, has dropped sharply since the late 1970s, returning to levels not seen since 1950. Data from Pacific Institute.

purely due to the market. Efficiency there has been an issue of cost savings. CO_2 emissions have held steady or dropped slightly as a result of energy efficiency.

Pollution is different. Because it's an externality, there's no economic incentive to reduce it in most cases. Where it's dropped sharply, it's done so because we've made a collective decision, through legislation, to constrain it. We haven't done that with CO_2 yet, but if we do, we have every reason to think emissions of it will come down in the same way that emissions of other pollutants have, and that the economy will keep on growing, just as it did when we limited CFCs or sulfur dioxide. The amount of pollution we create isn't inexorably linked to our rate of economic growth. It's a function of the policies we choose.

In short, in the rich world, our levels of consumption and pollution have leveled off and in many cases dropped over the last forty years. And while consumption is still rising in the developing world, it looks like it too will level off in time.

Wealth: The Great Decoupling

This is the great decoupling. At a certain point in the history of the United States, Canada, Europe, and Japan, resource use has leveled off, even as wealth has continued to grow.[5]

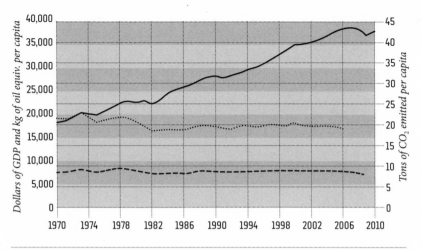

───── *U.S. GDP per capita* ·······*U.S. CO₂ emissions per capita* ─ ─ ─ *U.S. Energy use per capita*

Figure 19.3. U.S. GDP has pulled away from CO_2 and energy use. U.S. per capita GDP, adjusted for inflation, has doubled since 1970 while per capita CO_2 emissions and energy use have stayed flat. Including globalized CO_2 emissions from China would move the CO_2 line up very slightly, with the overall trend remaining flat. Data from the World Bank.

Wealth, in the rich countries, is decoupling from energy use and CO_2 emissions, even *after* including the energy used to manufacture and ship goods from overseas. The per-person *A* for Affluence in the IPAT equation is rising, but the per-person *I* for negative Impact on the world is not.

This effect is not limited to the rich countries. Decoupling is happening everywhere on the planet. In still-developing countries, energy use per capita and CO_2 emissions per capita are still growing. But wealth is growing far faster. Over the last forty years, CO_2 emissions per capita worldwide have grown by 10–15 percent. Energy use per capita has grown by around 50 percent. GDP per capita has grown by around 80 percent.

Wealth is pulling away from physical constraints. More and more, we're getting richer not by using more resources, but by using resources more intelligently.

Average incomes around the world are roughly twice as high now as they were in the 1970s. Global life expectancy has grown around twelve years, from fifty-seven years in the early 1970s to sixty-nine years today. Infant mortality has fallen by half. The fraction of the world that lives in hunger has dropped

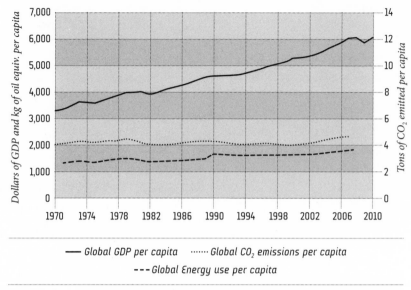

- Global GDP per capita   ⋯⋯ Global CO_2 emissions per capita
- - - Global Energy use per capita

Figure 19.4. Worldwide GDP is also decoupling from CO_2 and energy. On a global basis, per capita GDP, adjusted for inflation, has risen far faster than per capita energy use or per capita CO_2 emissions. Data from the World Bank.

by half. The number of people with access to electricity has soared. Yet we've done this while barely increasing CO_2 emissions. Even *without* any policy to contain those emissions.

Richer, More Efficient

Affluence, thus, does not always increase consumption or impact. In fact, affluence, by enhancing technology, brings greater efficiency.

In the fields of India, farmers flood the fields to irrigate the crops. In high tech farms in the United States, Europe, and Japan, farmers water the crops by drip irrigation. And so it is that American farmers use half the water that Indian farmers do (and a quarter of the land) to produce the same volume of crops.[6]

In the steel mills of China, steel is made mostly through powerful, inefficient blast furnaces. In the steel mills of developed nations, steel is made mostly through newer, twice-as-efficient electric arc furnaces. And so it is that making a ton of steel in China takes twice the energy and releases twice the CO_2 as in a steel mill in the United States, South Korea, Japan, or Germany.[7]

As countries grow richer, they're more able to invest in newer technology that allows them to use resources more efficiently. Building a drip irrigation system takes more up-front time and energy than flooding the fields. Converting to electric arc furnaces for steel production is an up-front cost. But both pay dividends in the long run. The market drives quick and dirty approaches early on, then more efficient approaches as nations and businesses have the resources to invest for the long term.

That effect is what's allowed the rich countries to level out in their use of energy and their emissions of CO_2 per capita, even as we've grown wealth. And as China, India, Brazil, and the rest of the developing world rise up in wealth, they're becoming more efficient as well. Even now, China is deploying electric arc furnaces to replace blast furnaces, India is investing in more efficient irrigation, and countries all over the world are switching to more efficient technologies.

China and the rest of the developing world benefit from a late-mover advantage. They benefit from research and development that's happened in the developed world to create more efficient technologies—ways to farm with less energy, water, and land; technologies like the electric arc furnace that reduce the amount of energy needed for manufacturing; and so on. They benefit from the knowledge that's accumulated, that can be tapped into without having to re-create it. As a result, they are far more efficient in their use of energy, water, land, and other resources than the United States was when the it was at the same stage of economic development that China is at now.

By the time China and India are as rich per capita as the United States is today, they'll be far *more* efficient in the use of resources than we are today, having benefited from the accumulation of new innovations that transform, reduce, substitute for, and recycle resources of all sorts.

We *all* benefit from that. Because ideas can increase the efficiency with which we can use natural resources, the spread of those ideas can increase the size of the global pie.

Richer, Cleaner

Richer countries, in many ways, aren't just more efficient. They're greener. They pollute less. They destroy the environment less.

Consider deforestation. Even as the world struggles to stop deforestation in the tropics, forests in the rich world are growing. The UN's Food and Agriculture Organization reports that, between 1990 and 2010, the amount

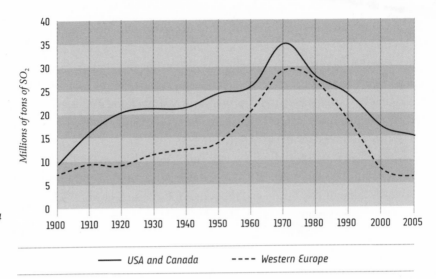

— USA and Canada   ---- Western Europe

Figure 19.5. Sulfur dioxide emissions. Acid rain–causing sulfur dioxide emissions rose until 1970, and have now dropped to levels not seen since 1910. Data from S. J. Smith, J. Aardenne, Z. Klimont, R. J. Andres, A. Volke, et al.

of U.S. land covered by forests grew by roughly 3,000 square miles.[8] Europe has increased its forest area even faster, adding almost 6,000 square miles of forest in that time.[9] The two richest regions in the planet have added forest, rather than destroying it.

Consider this list of countries that gained or held steady in forest cover between 1990 and 2010: Iceland, Spain, Denmark, Italy, the United Kingdom, France, Switzerland, New Zealand, Portugal, Sweden, Germany, Austria, the United States, Finland, Japan, and Canada.

Now compare it to a list of countries that lost forest cover in the same time period: Comoros, Togo, Nigeria, Burundi, Niger, Uganda, Honduras, Ghana, Pakistan, Nicaragua, Zimbabwe, Nepal, Armenia, El Salvador, Guatemala, Cambodia, Sri Lanka, Indonesia, Tanzania, Myanmar, Ethiopia, Somalia, Namibia, Mongolia, Haiti, Sierra Leone, Liberia, Chad.

Could this be simply the result of rich countries exporting their deforestation to poor ones by importing wood, food, and other materials that result in the chopping down of forests from developing countries? If so, we'd expect deforestation to be continuing unabated. But that's not what's happening. The rate of deforestation between 2000 and 2010 was just over 1 percent per decade, or *half* of the 2 percent per decade deforestation rate between 1990

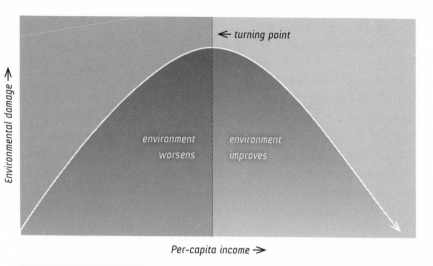

Figure 19.6. The environmental Kuznets curve. Rising incomes first lead to more environmental degradation and resource consumption, and then eventually bring levels of environmental damage back down.

and 2000. As countries get richer, they become more interested in preserving their forests. As the world as a whole has grown richer, global deforestation has dropped in half in the last twenty years, and looks likely to drop further.[10]

Or consider acid rain–causing sulfur dioxide emission. Countries that are extremely poor, with no industry at all have very low levels of sulfur dioxide. They simply don't have any factories or coal-burning power plants to produce sulfur. Countries that are *rich* have very low levels of sulfur dioxide as well. They have coal-fired power plants and factories, but they also have laws and technology that reduce emissions. Countries in the middle, that are rushing into industrialization, but haven't yet adopted strict environmental standards, have the highest levels of sulfur dioxide emissions.

We can see this in the trend of sulfur dioxide emissions in the United States, Canada, and Europe. They started out very low at the beginning of the twentieth century, soared until the 1970s, and have now plunged back to levels not seen since 1910 or earlier.[11]

Environmental economists refer to this as the Environmental Kuznets Curve, named after Nobel Prize–winning economist Simon Kuznets, who pioneered the process of actually measuring what happens in an economy.

The Environmental Kuznets Curve states, broadly, that the poorest countries will have very little pollution. Countries that have recently risen out of poverty and that have used the fastest and frequently dirties technologies to do so will have the most pollution. And after a peak during the period of heavy industrial development, pollution will come down.

The Environmental Kuznets Curve is a theoretical model. It's not a perfect prediction of what happens. All sorts of factors can affect real rates of resource consumption and pollution. Examples of it have been found in numerous places, though. Looking at trends within countries and comparisons between them, researchers have found evidence for the Environmental Kuznets Curve in sulfur dioxide emissions, deforestation, nitrous oxide emissions, lead levels, DDT use, sewage production, release of ozone-depleting substances such as CFCs, and more.[12] In all of those cases, pollution rises until a country reaches a certain level of wealth, and then pollution comes down.

Why does this happen? Some of it is made possible by increased technology. Scrubbers can stop sulfur dioxide emissions before they leave power plants. Less toxic additives have replaced lead in gasoline. Newer types of coolants have replaced CFCs.

But technology is only the *how*. It's the method by which rich countries reduce their environmental impact. It's not the *why*. It's not the reason they do it.

The reason has little to do with technology, and everything to do with relative priorities. People who have just recently come out of poverty, who remember a time when there wasn't enough to eat, who are still trying to save up to buy their first car or expand their home or ensure that their children can get an education just don't prioritize environmental protection highly. But as people get richer, they begin to care. When we have our material needs met, the pollution of our waters, skies, and forests begins to matter. And so we act.

The market increases the efficiency with which we use any resource that has a price. Pollution seldom comes with a price. And so the market seldom takes care of pollution on its own. But when a collective decision is made to restrict that pollution—by passing laws mandating it—the market finds the way to bring the levels down. The Environmental Kuznets Curve is real, but only where we intentionally work to employ it. As countries like China get richer, they'll enact more stringent controls on pollutants like sulfur dioxide.

Advocates of the *Limits to Growth* model have pointed at our levels of carbon dioxide as an indication that growth can't continue. But the history of dealing with pollution in general tells us that any pollutant we *decide* to reduce, we eventually do. We'll come back to the topic of how we get to that decision in the final chapter of this book. But for now the point I want to drive home is this: We haven't yet found a pollutant that we were unable to reduce, or one whose reduction halted our economic growth. Growth does not inherently mean more pollution. Pollution often happens as a side effect of growth, but once nations decide to act against that pollution, they conquer it within a matter of years or decades, and keep on growing in that time.

What Are the Limits to Growth?

So what, then, are the true limits to growth? The physical resources of our planet are enormous. Farming at the highest possible efficiency, on the current amount of farmland, could provide an American-style diet to 300 billion people. The crust contains every mineral we use in quantities that will not be exhausted for thousands of years at our current rates of mining (even the so-called "rare earths"), even *before* considering our growing ability to reuse minerals. The planet's oceans contain thousands of times more water than we need, and the water we use is constantly recycled back into them. And energy—the resource that can unlock so many others—is available from our sun in quantities 10,000 times greater than we consume today from all sources combined.

The planet is finite. There's only so much water and so many mineral resources we can have in circulation. And we only receive so much new energy each year. But those limits are vast. There's more than enough energy, water, land, and raw materials to provide 10 billion people lifestyles every bit as rich as those enjoyed by wealthy Americans.

Our problem in the near term is not that resources are in short supply. It's that we use those resources incredibly inefficiently, with side effects we have yet to eliminate. We're tapped into small, polluting, depleting sources of energy, while a much more abundant, clean, multibillion-year supply goes relatively untapped. Our industries produce pollutants that, history teaches us, we can almost entirely eliminate, and at a cost far lower than we're likely to predict.

Resources aren't the problem. It's the way we go about getting and using those resources. And that we can change.

Yet even with 10,000 times as much energy coming in from the sun than we use today, there are limits to exponential growth. Like the grains of rice doubling for each square on the chess board, exponential growth in our energy use would eventually consume all the energy that strikes the Earth from the sun. If our population stabilizes around 10 billion people, and after that point we grow our energy use per capita by 1 percent per year (about the rate of per capita energy growth around the world in the last few decades), then we'll be using all of the energy the sun delivers to the Earth within 900 years. If we want to, say, limit our use to 10 percent of the energy the sun strikes the Earth with (leaving the rest for nature), growing our energy use at 1 percent per year, we'd hit that limit in just 700 years.

And exponential growth makes a mockery of even cosmic scales. One percent annual growth in energy use would lead us to use the energy of every star in our entire galaxy in just 5,000 years, less time than has passed since the invention of agriculture. In less than 8,000 years, we would be consuming the total energy of every star in the visible universe.

Those limits are close in historical and astronomical terms, but still distant in comparison to our planning horizons. It will be people far removed from us, and a society likely far smarter than we are, who will have to wrestle with them. It's tempting to just dismiss those limits entirely on that account. For the next century or two, at least, we can grow energy use exponentially without any obvious cap in sight.

But there's another message of this chapter. *Economic* growth—the growth of comfort, convenience, prosperity, health, well-being, and all the things that come with it—is decoupling from the growth of consumption. In the United States, Canada, Europe, and Japan, wealth has doubled in the last forty years, with almost no change in the use of energy, even *after* adjusting for globalization and the import of manufactured goods from places like China.

How far could innovation take us? If our incoming supply of energy each year were capped, how much richer could we become?

The answer is that we just don't know. Consider the lowly iPhone. It uses *less* energy and *less* raw materials than the supercomputers of the past, yet it provides tremendously more computing power, communication abilities undreamt of decades ago, and dozens of other capabilities that were nearly impossible to purchase through most of the twentieth century. New knowledge has reduced the resources necessary to calculate and communicate. Using fewer resources than earlier technologies, the iPhone can do far more. That is the power of innovation.

Looking around, it's hard to see any limit on our ability to generate ever more new and useful ideas that increase the comfort, convenience, health, and richness of our lives, even within the confines of finite physical resources. It may be that no such limit on the power of ideas exists. If it does exist, it's astronomically far from where we are today.

For all practical effects and purposes, our growth is unbounded. If we choose wisely, and tap into the right resources, while acting together to put limits on the negative side effects and externalities of our actions, then we can grow for at least centuries to come, and perhaps far longer.

Our only limit, for the foreseeable future, is our collective intelligence in innovating, and in putting in place the systems to guide our collective behavior.

twenty of mouths and minds

The Virtue of People

At the Central Drug Research Institute, a team of scientists has developed a drug that has the potential to improve the lives and health of diabetics. The drug shows promise in both controlling blood sugar and insulin levels and in preventing the cholesterol abnormalities that frequently come with diabetes and that can lead to heart disease. Twenty-six million Americans suffer from diabetes. The U.S. National Institutes of Health and the Centers for Disease Control have described it as an epidemic.[1] In 2010 diabetes was the seventh-leading killer of Americans, and caused more than $200 billion in damage to the U.S. economy.

The team of scientists who've come up with this new potential treatment for diabetes is led by Dr. Atul Kumar. The Central Drug Research Institute isn't in the United States. It's in the city of Lucknow, India.[2] India's rise in wealth and education may soon pay dividends for Americans in the form of lower health costs and longer lives.

We live on a world with more than seven billion people on it. Only one billion of those people live in the rich world. But the remaining six billion are rapidly rising in wealth. That's happening most notably in China and India.

How are we to view the rise in wealth of other countries? Are they competitors? Are they allies? Does the growing wealth of consumers in Shanghai or Mumbai reduce our own wealth, or does it increase it?

There is no doubt that rising wealth in the developing world contributed to a surge in prices between 2008 and 2011. Worldwide production of steel, copper, food, coal, and a host of other commodities has risen continuously to new records, yet their prices also soared due to ballooning demand in the developing world, and especially from China.

Yet in the long term, in the absence of physical constraints, demand creates supply. In the case of oil we may truly be up against physical constraints. In the case of all other commodities, production has kept increasing at a rapid pace, and investments to bring more supply onto the market have also soared. And in the case of energy, the one physical resource that can do the most to liberate other resources, we are nowhere near the physical constraints. The lesson of history is that, as resources rise in price, innovation will lower the cost of producing almost all of those resources, find substitutes for others, and overall bring the supply up and the prices back down.

At the same time, ideas created by people in China, India, or anywhere else, have a nearly unlimited ability to enhance the lives of people in the United States, Europe, or anywhere on Earth. The richer those countries become, the richer *all* of the developing world becomes, the greater the likelihood that they'll produce new innovations that benefit us.

The six billion people in the developing world represent a huge untapped force. The entire population of Europe during the Renaissance was less than 100 million. If we can unlock the potential human capital in the developing world, then it's a potential source of the next Leonardo da Vinci, the next Albert Einstein, the next Norman Borlaug who'll kick off the next Green Revolution. The next Thomas Edison or Bill Gates or Steve Jobs of clean energy, food, or water could emerge from Africa or India or China, *if* those places see their human capital rise.

There are excellent, simple, and profoundly human *moral* reasons to want to see the world's developing nations continue to rise out of poverty and into affluence. Virtually every religion on Earth emphasizes helping the poor—that theme unites Christianity, Judaism, Islam, and Buddhism. The overwhelming majority of men and women alive would regard a world with less hunger and less poverty as a better world, purely on the basis of an innate sense that suffering, hunger, and poverty are bad, and that everyone deserves at least a chance at well-being. From a purely moral and compassionate standpoint, we'd like to see the poor grow richer.

But there is an entirely separate reason. From a purely *selfish* standpoint, we should want to see the poor grow richer. Properly empowered with adequate nutrition, education, and access to the fruits of modern civilization, minds anywhere on the planet become a huge potential asset for *you*. An Indian chemist could be the person who develops a drug that saves you or a loved one from cancer. A Chinese physicist could be the one who finds a way to produce super-strong and light plastics at cheap prices—a discovery that would enrich your life in myriad ways. An African biologist might be the person who develops a vaccine against HIV or a cure for the common cold.

Or, to the point of resource usage and the environment, that Indian chemist could be the one who develops a new process for creating solar fuels cheaper than gasoline. That Chinese physicist's new plastic might make wind turbines lighter and wind electricity cheaper, and reduce the fuel consumption of cars and planes. That African biologist might invent a new strain of wheat that produces more food with less need for water, fertilizer, or pesticides.

Innovations add to our wealth and well-being. Innovations multiply resources, allowing us to grow richer while using less. Innovations, once created, have no nationality. They may bring their inventors revenue, may make them fortunes, but the knowledge itself, if it's useful, will find its way to every corner of the world given time. Indeed, the only way an innovation *can* bring wealth to its inventor is by its dissemination to others.

The Chinese invented rag paper and block printing, but it was in Europe that those two inventions, along with others, combined to make Gutenberg's moveable type printing press. Ultimately, the whole world benefited from those inventions in China and the new idea they helped create in Germany. Penicillin was discovered by the Scottish biologist Alexander Fleming. The first functioning technique for sterilizing food was produced by a French man, Louis Pasteur. The first practical electric light was produced by an American, Thomas Edison. The first solar photovoltaic cells were created by a trio of Americans working at Bell Labs. Fiber optics were developed by a Chinese scientist, Charles Kao, during his time in England. The Green Revolution wheat varieties and breeding techniques were created by American Norman Borlaug while working in Mexico, his research funded in part by the Mexican government and in part by an American foundation. All these innovations spread to the world, bringing benefit to millions, if not billions. In some cases, their inventors grew rich off patent rights or through savvy commercialization of the idea. In *all* cases, the benefit to the world was far greater than the benefit to the inventor.

In the long term, it doesn't matter where an innovation comes from. The best of them will spread. What matters most is that we encourage more innovation, period. And the best way to do that is to see the developing world rise out of poverty and into wealth. We should think of the rising wealth of China and India as a great future blessing for Americans. We should view the task of reducing poverty and growing nutrition, health, literacy, education, and wealth in the developing world as not just a humanitarian cause, but a selfish cause. The more innovators there are in the world, the better off we will all be.

Nor is the effect limited to innovators. More *consumers* also help make the world better, by increasing the incentives for innovation. Consider this. If you're diagnosed with a disease, would you rather it be a rare disease that only a few people suffer from? Or would you rather it be a fairly common disease? The fairly common disease will have had more effort put into curing it. The incentive to innovate is proportional to the financial rewards of innovation. And that, in turn, is proportional to the size of the market. The more well-off consumers in the world market there are, the greater the rewards of producing a new idea, and the greater the fraction of the world's resources that are turned to innovation.

If there are only five potential buyers for a new idea or a product based on it, the potential rewards are smaller than if there are 500 or 5 million potential buyers. Perhaps that, in part, explains the increase in innovation in developed countries. Economist Charles Jones has calculated that in the combined economies of the United States, the United Kingdom, France, Germany, and Japan, the total number of people working in research and development has risen four to five times *faster* than the population has increased since 1950.[3] A larger market has increased the rewards for innovation, drawing more people and resources to it. And growing wealth for the world means a larger market for any new innovation. As economist Alex Tabarrok has pointed out, "If China and India were as rich as the United States is today, the market for cancer drugs would be eight times larger than it is now."[4] And that larger market for new goods of *all* sorts would draw more people and more resources, and produce more innovations. As the poor world gets richer, the rewards for innovation *anywhere* in the world will grow, continuing that trend, and further fueling innovation.

Is More Better?

Innovators are good, and innovators are people. A larger market encourages even more innovation, and markets are made of people. So would having more people on the planet be better? Of course, there's huge untapped brainpower in the world already. There are billions of people who haven't had the opportunity to meet their full potential and contribute to the world's store of ideas. Fixing that has to be the top priority when it comes to increasing the planet's brain power. Addressing poverty and boosting education in the developing world should be a top foreign policy priority for the United States and other rich nations.

But what about beyond that? How many people should the world have on it? It's a given in most environmental and natural resource discussions that overpopulation harms the planet and increases poverty. I was educated to believe that overpopulation was a great ill, and that population growth was at the heart of most of the world's problems. But is that really true?

Consider this thought experiment. Would your life be better off if only half as many people had lived before you? For fairness and simplicity, assume that those people were evenly removed from history from all corners of the world. You can't pick and choose which ones lived. It's a random reduction.

Would you be better off?

I've asked this question to dozens of people over the course of writing this book. The answers vary wildly. But those who think about the benefit they've accrued from science, medicine, and inventions of all sorts invariably answer that their lives would be worse off if fewer people had lived before. There would be fewer medicines, less food, fewer symphonies and books. There might be no such thing as antibiotics or telephones or automobiles. We owe past generations a debt for their production of ideas that enrich our lives today.

There's an American Indian saying that we do not inherit the Earth from our ancestors. We borrow it from our children. The proverb is an exhortation to leave the world in good shape so that future generations can prosper. It's a wise saying, and one that we haven't lived up to. In numerous ways, we're leaving the planet's air, land, and seas worse off than when we found them. We're depleting one-time resources. That needs to stop. We can and should protect our shared, common resources. We can and should transition to sources of prosperity that can be maintained nearly indefinitely.

Yet in other ways, we're leaving future generations an inheritance richer than the one that we received. We're leaving them a richer store of knowledge about the world—knowledge that enhances and enriches their lives. Isaac Newton once wrote, in a letter to his contemporary Robert Hooke, "If I have seen farther, it is because I have stood on the shoulders of giants." In a sense, we all stand on the shoulders of the generations before us, the discoveries they made, and the innovations they produced. That's true for those, like Newton, who developed revolutionary future ideas atop those of the ones who came before them. And it's also true of those of us—all of us, really—who reap the benefits of those past ideas.

So, if we are better off for having had more people before us, what does that say about our population today? What does that say about what's best for future generations?

The Knowledge Commons

The phrase "The Tragedy of the Commons" comes to us from an essay that ecologist Garrett Hardin wrote in the journal *Science* in 1968. Hardin saw, perceptively, that common resources that were open to unlimited use and exploitation without cost would be degraded. He failed to grasp the many ways in which small-scale commons are regulated by the social webs between people, the study of which won Elinor Ostrom her Nobel Prize in economics. But for large, anonymous commons like the world's oceans and its atmosphere, the problem he saw exists.

Hardin's prescribed cure was to hold down the number of people on the planet. "Freedom to Breed is Intolerable," he titled one section of the essay. Yet as we've seen, there are other ways to protect the commons, by making it in everyone's personal and direct self- interest to deplete them less and to restore and improve them more. In areas where we've enacted regulations or changed our economic system to reflect the value of the commons—like the sulfur dioxide emissions that cause acid rain, or the CFC emissions that deplete the ozone layer—things are turning around. Those commons are improving. Acid rain is no longer a scourge of North America. The ozone hole is recovering more quickly than expected. The physical commons we share can be protected and can, in some cases, be repaired.

The complement to the physical commons is the knowledge commons, the sum set of knowledge that humanity has created. While physical commons can either be depleted or restored, the knowledge commons changes in only one direction—toward a greater wealth of ideas.

And knowledge, unlike physical resources, is non-rival. It can be used in as many times and places as we care to, without depleting it. Its value to us is multiplied by the number of people who put it to work. In 1813, Thomas Jefferson wrote in a letter that "[h]e who receives an idea from me, receives instruction himself without lessening mine; as he who lights his taper at mine, receives light without darkening me."[5]

Economist Paul Romer puts it less poetically, but more plainly in the context of population. Do more people hurt our prosperity, or increase it? He says, "If everything were just objects, like trees, then more people means there's less wood per person. But if somebody discovers an idea, everybody gets to use it, so the more people you have who are potentially looking for ideas, the better off we're all going to be."[6]

Even for those ideas that are still in their twenty-year patent lifetime, and even with the many ways in which the patent system should be improved, the unique qualities of ideas lead to their spread, intersection, and continual improvement. Edison patented his light bulb, but that didn't prevent electrified lighting from spreading. By 1899, the last year of Edison's patent, millions of people in the United States, Canada, and Europe were using electrified light. And new advances such as tungsten-based bulbs were on the market. Those new bulbs were informed, in part, by Edison's carbon-filament bulb. His patent prevented others from producing the same bulb, but in the process of filing it, Edison, as all other inventors who file patents do, was forced to reveal its construction and design. And that knowledge, loose in the world, enriched the knowledge commons, and led to the creation of newer and better bulbs, even *during* the lifetime of Edison's patent.

Physical commons can go either direction—toward degradation and destruction, or toward restoration and improvement. Knowledge commons almost always grow richer over time. Each additional idea is a gift to the future. Each additional idea *producer* is a source of wealth for future generations.

If we can improve the ways in which our economic system regards the commons, we can protect and restore them. We know that the physical resources of the planet are abundant. The key is to make use of them efficiently, while minimizing or eliminating the collateral damage we do along the way. Enriching the knowledge commons with new ways to use resources more efficiently, multiply their value, and replace the scarcest of them is the ultimate way to go about that. And the knowledge commons is the fruit of human minds. More minds—when they're empowered to innovate, and encouraged to improve rather than destroy the commons—means more ideas and more wealth for us all.

The Shrinking Global Brain?

Yet in many parts of the world, the number of minds that actively contribute to innovation is set to shrink in the years ahead.

As a fraction of population, the number of people of working age is already shrinking in some parts of the world. In Japan, in 1990, 70 percent of the population was of working age. Today that number is 65 percent and shrinking. Europe and China will start seeing their working age populations decline as a percentage of total population in this decade, putting more pressure on pensions and safety nets for the elderly, which must be funded by those who are employed.

But the decline will not just be as a percentage. It will come in absolute numbers. The only major economic powers in the world that will have larger workforces in 2050 than today, if current trends hold, will be the United States and India. The *total number* of working-age people in the other economic powers of the world—Japan, Europe, and China—are all declining or about to decline.

In 1995 Japan had a working-age population of around 85 million people. Today it's less than 80 million. By 2050, it's projected to be only 55 million people.[7]

Europe today has a working age population of around 310 million people. By 2020 that population will be 5 million smaller. By 2050, on current trends, Europe's working age population will have shrunk to around 260 million people, 50 million less than today. And a largest-ever fraction of those will be workers in their fifties and sixties, rather than the most innovative workers in their twenties, thirties, and forties.[8]

China will fare little better. China's working age population, in both absolute numbers and as a percentage of the country, is peaking right now. Demographers expect it to reach its all-time high in around 2013, just shy of 1 billion people, after which it will begin to shrink.[9] In 2050, China will have just over 800 million people of working age, 200 million fewer than today. The country will have 1.6 working-age people per retiree, down from its present ratio of 5.4 working-age people per retiree.[10]

Is that the world we want? Much has been written about the challenges of having more elderly per worker. Pensions, social security, and health care for the elderly don't come for free. They're paid for by younger men and women still in the workforce. As the number of retirees grows and the number of workers—the *absolute numbers*—shrinks, fewer workers will be supporting more retirees. That poses huge challenges to the world.

But even if the remaining workers *didn't* have to support retirees, it's not clear that a shrinking number of people producing new goods, services, and ideas for others would be a better world. With fewer people alive, working, and innovating are we more or less likely to produce a cure for cancer? A cure for Alzheimer's disease? A new technique for harnessing more of the abundant energy from the sun at a lower cost?

Less, of course. People are the ultimate source of innovations, and innovations are the source of our present prosperity.

Can those innovations compensate for the ecological damage that we've done? Contrary to what Malthus would have expected, it appears that the innovation people produce routinely outstrips the ecological cost of those additional people. Evidence from both ancient civilizations and modern civilization suggests that, as the number of people in an area rise, their total rate of innovation rises *faster* than the population and *faster* than consumption.

The Anti-Malthus

In 1993, economist Michael Kremer published a paper provocatively titled "Population Growth and Technological Change: One Million B.C. to 1900."[11] Kremer was interested in the idea, recently promoted by Paul Romer, that people, by producing innovations, were the primary source of human wealth.

Kremer set out to test this by looking back in history at civilizations that had no contact with each other, and thus had access only to the ideas they produced internally. He chose five: The Old World, comprising Europe, Asia, and Africa; the New World of North and South America; Australia; Tasmania; and the tiny civilization of Flinders Island.

He then reasoned that, all things being equal, a larger contiguous area should be able to support a larger initial population. That larger population should then produce more ideas, which would show up as more advanced technology and the ability to support higher population densities.

What he found supported that conclusion.

By the time Columbus discovered the Americas, the Old World, with a larger starting land area, had a substantially higher population density and greater technology. Europe, which had benefited from ideas originating in China and Africa, had the highest technology level on the planet—steel, firearms, ocean-going ships, the wheel, and so on. It had a population density of five people per square kilometer, at least twice that of the Americas, and possibly far higher.

The Americas, the second-largest land area, came in second in both population density, at perhaps one to two people per square kilometer, and second in technology, with agriculture, stone tools, writing, and calendars among the Maya of Central America.

Australia, the third-largest land area, came in third in population density, with a third of a person per square kilometer. The Australians, despite having reached their home at least 20,000 years before the residents of the Americas, had never developed agriculture. With fewer minds, there had been fewer innovations.

Australia did have some powerful tools—the spear thrower, the boomerang, fire-making, stone tools with handles, and bone tools like needles. Australia's smaller neighbor Tasmania, an island the size of Ireland, lacked even these. And on tiny Flinders island, the population had gone extinct soon after rising seas had separated it from Tasmania.

Jared Diamond, in *Guns, Germs, and Steel*, articulated that European progress came so much faster than that in the Americas and Africa because of Europe's greater endowment of useful plant and animal species that early humans could domesticate. He may well be right. Kremer's thesis, however, is even simpler. More land area means more minds can be supported with the most primitive technology. Having more minds means faster progress.

The notion is provocative. The greater the population, the faster technological innovation occurred. And that innovation increased the effectiveness with which people could harvest resources from their land, letting more people live on the same area of land, in greater wealth. The presence of more minds in a region *increased* the carrying capacity of that region, through their innovations.

It makes one wonder—would the Easter Islanders still be alive if their island had been larger? Would the added brainpower have allowed them to innovate their way out of their problems? Would it have allowed them to find ways to use less wood? Would they have created the social and economic systems necessary to protect their forests and use them sustainably?

Metropolis Earth

The notion that as populations grow, the rate of innovation rises *faster* than population is a challenging one. Yet the evidence of it comes from more than just ancient history. We can see signs of it today, all around us.

In 2008, humanity hit a pivotal milestone. For the first time ever in our history, more people live in cities than in the countryside. We've become an urban species. Call us *homo urbanicus*.

In 2002, a physicist named Geoffrey West set out to try to quantify the behavior of cities in a way that would allow scientists to predict and understand it. West had made his career in physics. He'd started and led the high-energy physics group at Los Alamos National Laboratory and had become one of the lab's ten Senior Fellows. In 1993, when Congress killed funding for the Superconducting Supercollider that would have shed more light into the behavior of fundamental particles and forces of nature at high energies, West decided to leave the field. He ventured into biology, where he and his colleagues wrote a seminal paper that is now one of the most cited in the field.

That paper showed that, in general, the larger an organism is, the slower everything in it runs. An elephant, for example, may weigh 10,000 times what a guinea pig does, but it needs to eat only 1,000 times as much food. Building on research done in the 1930s by Max Kleiber, West and his colleagues showed that just about everything about animals is "sub-linear" with respect to size. That is to say, just about every measure you can take of an animal goes up less rapidly than does its size. In general, for every 10 times multiple of size, total metabolism goes up by a factor of just under 6. While a few animal species are exceptions, the vast majority follow this rule.[12]

Seeing how universal this rule was, West wondered if it would apply to other systems. And so in 2003, he turned his attention to cities. Would they behave like organisms? Would they be governed by simple scaling laws?

What West and his colleague Luis Bettencourt found was a deep similarity between cities and biological organisms in some ways, and a surprising and far-reaching divergence in others.

In some ways, cities also slow down as they get larger. A ten-times increase in the size of a city means a roughly six-times increase in the number of gasoline stations and the amount of gasoline sold. That means that, per person, a ten times larger city is only using six-tenths as much gasoline as a city one tenth its size. Similar patterns apply to the total amount of road surface in a city, the total length of electrical cables, and so on. All of these show increasing efficiency and decreasing per-person consumption as cities grow. The larger a city, the *less* of many resources it uses per person.

But in other ways, cities behave quite differently. As the size of cities rises, their economies and their rates of innovation rise even faster. Increasing the size of a city by a factor of 10 increases the number of patents it produces each year by a factor of 19 and the size of its economy by a factor of 18. They increase *faster* than the size of a city. Innovation and economic activity don't show diminishing returns with respect to size at all. They show *accelerating* returns.[13]

It wouldn't be so surprising to find that innovation scaled at the same rate as a city's population. After all, human minds are the source of innovation. A city with ten times as many minds should, we'd think, produce roughly ten times as many innovations. But why does it produce nearly twenty times?

Computer scientist Manuel Cebrian's simulations may show an answer. Attempting to build a model of a city that explained West's results, Cebrian found that as the population of a city rose, the number of connections between people in the city rose faster than the population. It rose at a rate nearly identical to the rate at which West and his colleagues saw innovation rise. The implication is that innovation isn't just about the number of minds. It's about the connections between those minds. It's about the speed with which information flows between minds. And it's about connections that are formed from the bottom up, through diverse individual choices rather than a central plan.[14] And all of those things are amplified inside a city.

Some of the effects Geoffrey West found in cities appear to exist in whole nations as well. In 2002, Francisco Alcalá and Antonio Ciccone found that, after controlling for trade and other variables, increasing the number of workers in a national economy by 10 percent produced a 2 percent rise in GDP per worker. A ten-times multiple of workforce produced a sixteen-times larger GDP overall. Larger economies generated *more wealth* from *each* worker.

The whole world is becoming a city now. The technology of the Internet, mobile phones, and a million spinoffs of that are networking us all together. We're drawing more connections, exchanging more insights, innovations, and information. Minds are the source of wealth and innovation. But their production isn't linear. It scales with the number and quality of connections. And so, the more minds we have—educated minds, empowered minds, interconnected minds—the more *each* produces.

Our planet is like a giant living brain. Each mind added to it is a neuron. Each connection between those minds is a synapse. As we grow larger, we grow denser in connections, and so we grow smarter, more able to innovate, at rates faster than we consume.

And this brings us back to Malthus. Malthus said that population rises geometrically while production of food rises linearly. But what we've learned from recent history, from ancient civilizations, and from the nonlinear behavior of cities and economies is something else. As population rises, consumption rises. But it's innovation that rises geometrically with respect to population. A world with twice as many people may consume more. But its innovation will rise faster than its consumption. And in that lies a tremendous amount of hope, and a reason to revisit our views of population.

We should hope to reduce population growth rates in the poorest parts of the world, as those nations are under the greatest ecological stress and are the least well equipped to accommodate and empower new children. At the same time, we need to rethink what we want for population worldwide. We may very well want to work to at least *maintain* the population of developed countries, if not slowly grow it. We have the natural resources to support more people, so long as we keep innovating. And the evidence suggests that more people, so long as they are educated, empowered, and connected to one another through the webs of technology and the market—innovate more rapidly than they consume.

On the event of the seven-billionth person being born, William McGurn wrote in the *Wall Street Journal* that we should view it as an opportunity rather than a cost. "Malthusian fears about population follow from the Malthusian view that human beings are primarily mouths to be fed rather than minds to be unlocked. In this reasoning, when a pig is born in China, the national wealth is thought to go up, but when a Chinese baby is born the national wealth goes down."[15]

People aren't just mouths. They're minds also. Each of us is both.

Left in hunger, poverty, and without education, we are primarily mouths. Adding people to the poorest nations, where human capital is least developed, helps no one.

Fed, educated, empowered, and guided by a future iteration of capitalism that values *all* of our resources and aligns incentives to protect them, our minds produce far more than our mouths consume.

If we fix our economic system and invest in the human capital of the poor, then we should welcome every new person born as source of betterment for our world and all of us on it.

twenty-one
easy way, hard way

Crisis, Danger, Opportunity

The natural resources of our planet are incredibly abundant. As I've tried to show, the amount of energy we could capture, food we could grow, water we could access, and minerals we could use and reuse are all vast. All of them are at least a hundred times greater than our current needs. And in the case of energy—the resource that can increase access to so many other resources—the amount available is thousands of times greater than what we currently take advantage of.

Innovation is the ultimate source of our wealth. New ideas have multiplied the resources we have access to; have reduced the amount of land, energy, and raw materials we need to accomplish any task; have created substitutes for every resource we've been in danger of exhausting in the last 500 years; have grown our ability to recycle waste into things of value; and have, in recent years, begun to decouple our economic growth from our levels of consumption and environmental damage.

Even as our store of new ideas is expanding, our population is leveling off—if not on its way to a long-term decline—and consumption in the rich countries appears to have leveled off as well. Not only are the material resources of the planet vast, but on current trajectory it looks like our consumption will reach a plateau far below what the planet is capable of offering, even as our rates of poverty shrink, our health improves, and our wealth grows.

But there are dangers. Just because a path to continually expanding our wealth while preserving and restoring our planet exists, doesn't mean that we'll take that path. We need to transition from finite supplies of fuels—almost the only material resource that is actually *consumed* by use—to the thousands-of-times greater, multibillion-year supply of the sun. The sooner we transition, the less painful the process will be. If we don't do it proactively, rising fossil fuel prices may well force our hand, making the transition bumpier and more economically costly than if we'd driven it ourselves.

Market forces will help in the transition. The rising price of oil and coal encourage investments in energy efficiency and green energy. But the market isn't perfect. There's always a lag between when a price rises and when the market produces a solution. We'd rather not experience that lag and the price spikes and recessions that come with it.

The real systematic problem isn't with the resources the market governs today, though. It's with all the parts of the world the market *doesn't* govern. It's the market's propensity to ignore or even actively consume and pollute the shared resources that *don't* have either a price or laws protecting them. Wherever it's cheaper to pollute than to reduce pollution, the market actively selects for pollution. Doing things cheaply is an economic advantage. But the true costs are carried in impact to all of us.

The market is the most effective system of encouraging innovation and hard work that we've ever seen. It's a brilliant tool for aligning personal self-interest with the interests of others. But it has that fatal flaw in how it deals with the commons, how it deals with damage and costs that are externalized to others. Fixing that flaw would complete the market-economics revolution that has swept the planet. It would make preserving and improving the environment a self-interest of businesses and individuals everywhere. It would make the market a tool for protecting and improving our shared environment, rather than one that tends to damage them.

This isn't an issue of a limit to growth. Growth without any practical bound is possible given our resources and the right system. But our system is flawed. We have to fix it. Innovation is important not just in technology, but in social structures. The market was an innovation. Democracy was an innovation. Now we have to use democracy to create a new version of the market rules.

For me the story of ozone depletion sums things up well. It was a global threat that truly could have wreaked havoc on the planet. Destruction of the ozone layer was actually a far *larger* threat to humanity and the planet than climate change. Left unaddressed, it would have eventually ended nearly all life on the surface of the planet, and most life in the oceans.

Industry, ironically enough, claimed that stopping ozone depletion *would* impose a limit to growth—that cooling systems would stop working, that it would cost Americans over $100 billion. But both business groups and the EPA underestimated the power of innovation. The true cost of phasing out

CFCs turned out to be less than a tenth of the highest estimates, and less than half of the EPA's own estimates. Once we engaged the market in finding a solution, it did so, with its typical efficiency. That's how it's been with every pollutant we've seen. Once we've engaged the power of innovation, solutions to reduce emissions of a pollutant have *always* lowered the cost substantially below even the lowest estimates.

Climate change is the biggest threat we face today. It's the latest in a long string of unintended consequences we've had on the planet. And it's a problem that's caused by an incredibly pervasive activity—burning fossil fuels. This is going to be harder to fix than ozone depletion was. But the history of emissions reductions tells us that it's going to cost far less than mainstream estimates.

And if you aren't fully convinced on the danger of climate, I urge you again to think about it in the context of insurance. I don't know that my home will catch fire in the next year or that I'll suffer a heart attack. Those both seem pretty unlikely to me. But I have insurance in case either happens. Even a small risk of a terrible event is worth investing some amount to protect ourselves against.

Climate change and peak oil are the "danger" half of crisis. On the other side of the transition to renewables is the opportunity: energy far more abundant than the sources we depend on today, distributed broadly around the world rather than concentrated in a few hands, getting *cheaper* with each successive unit rather than more expensive. Energy that can power our world, power the reduction of poverty, power the fulfillment of human potential, power our global growth and prosperity, as far as the eye can see.

What You Can Do

There are no certainties about the future. We could succeed or we could fail. The opportunity for future growth is nearly unlimited, but whether or not we seize it depends on our actions.

So what can we, as individuals, do?

First, be open to new ideas. GMOs, nuclear energy, and climate engineering are all technologies that produce strong reactions of fear and distaste. The truth is that no technology is perfect. But we shouldn't let the perfect be the enemy of the better-than-we-have-today.

Nuclear energy is less deadly, less polluting, and less costly to the planet as a whole than coal is. It can play a valuable role in transitioning from fossil fuels to renewables. GMOs *reduce* the use of the worst pesticides, encourage no-till farming, and will soon boost both nutrition and yields, saving millions of lives and sparing billions of acres of land. Carbon sequestration and techniques to reflect more sunlight into space are far from perfect, but we'd rather have carbon in the ground than carbon in the atmosphere, and we'd rather have the option to cool the Arctic than not have that option.

Across the board, we shouldn't reject new technologies because they're new. Each should be weighed for what they have to offer, and how they compare to what we're using today. With every new technology we'll see fear mongering. Look past that and try to find what the science actually says.

Second, embrace the power of "and." Climate is a large enough challenge that we're going to need multiple approaches. I'm always surprised when I see the vehemence of some climate activists' opposition to nuclear energy or carbon sequestration or solar radiation management. "These can't possibly work," I'm told. Or, "this is just an industry story to distract us from what needs to happen now."

It's true that we need CO_2 emissions reductions now. We can't wait for technologies that are twenty years away. But we shouldn't try to fight climate with one hand tied behind our back. As new, safer, cheaper nuclear reactors come to market, why wouldn't we adopt them? They're not going to be a complete solution to the problem, but they're going to be part of the solution. And the problem is big enough that we need every possible tool available for use.

Future technologies like solar radiation management shouldn't be used as an *excuse* for not acting now. But neither should we discourage research and development into them. Indeed, we should accelerate it.

Third, communicate. This is a big one. For the market to work, people don't need to be in agreement. But for democracy to work, a majority of our elected officials need to be able to come together. And their positions are determined by what will get them elected.

Talk to others. These issues are highly politicized and at times highly divisive, but they don't need to be.

If you're on the left, or talking to someone on the left, talk about how Golden Rice is on the verge of release, and how it could save millions of children's lives. Talk about how GMOs have been found again and again to be safe, about how they reduce the amounts of highly toxic chemicals like atrazine used on fields, and how they could soon boost yields tremendously, allowing us to feed more people without chopping down more forest. Talk about how nuclear energy kills fewer people than coal, and how it could help us reduce carbon emissions as we transition to solar and wind.

If you're on the right, or talking to someone on the right, talk about the ecological actions of Ronald Reagan and George Bush. Talk about how Reagan overrode his chief of staff and secretary of the interior to sign the Montreal Protocol that has halted ozone depletion. Talk about how George H. W. Bush pushed through anti–acid rain legislation even after his chief of staff said it would shut down the U.S. economy. Talk about how, in each of those cases, the price tag has been not just lower than what *industry* claimed, but lower than what even the *EPA* claimed. Talk about how putting a price on carbon could and should be engineered to return that money to tax payers.

Talk about how every barrel of oil pumped raises the long-term price of oil, while every wind farm and solar panel made *reduces* the long-term price of wind and solar. Talk about how market-based solutions that shift our energy use over to the nearly endless supply from the sun and wind are setting us up for lower long-term energy prices, energy independence from the Middle East and Russia, and supplies that can feed a growing economy as far into the future as the eye can see.

Talk about the insurance model of climate risk. Be honest that there are limits to climate modeling. But even if the odds of climate disaster were low, insurance against that sort of event—at the right price—is worth it.

Talk about how free exploitation of the commons isn't the free market. It's a form of socialism. The market only works well in managing those resources that have prices on them. Leaving the commons free to consume or pollute guarantees the destruction of those common assets. Fixing that doesn't harm the market—it extends the reach of the market, allowing it to manage and improve those shared resources.

Talk about what a tiny amount of money we spend on energy and efficiency research and development at the federal level compared to the potential returns.

Don't be afraid. Talk to your friends. Talk to your family. Talk to your coworkers. Talk to people you meet. Don't politicize. Don't insult others or put down their views. Listen. Understand their priorities. And patiently explain the issues. We need people all across the political spectrum to come together on these issues, and especially climate. So reach out. Reach across the aisle to talk to someone who has a different opinion than you do. People don't change their views unless they encounter new information, and they'll accept that information most readily from people whom they already know, trust, or agree with on other issues.

The responsibility is especially on the shoulders of conservatives to persuade other conservatives on the risk of climate, and the need to insure against it. Al Gore isn't going to persuade your fellow conservatives. You can.

Fourth, participate.

Fixing the blind spots in the market is going to have to be done through our other most vital institution—democracy. Our legislators govern by the consent of the governed. They're representatives of the people who elected them. Yet we too-seldom express our opinion via anything other than voting.

Write to your representative in the house. Write to the senators for your state. Call them. You can find contact information for them on the web at house.gov for your representative and at senate.gov for your senator. Be polite and to the point. Let them know that you live in their district or state, that you vote, and that addressing climate change is something you care about.

Do the same at the state level. We often focus on policy at the federal level to address climate and energy, but today, there's been far more done in the individual states of the Union than by the federal government. Twenty-nine states have renewable energy portfolio standards that mandate that a certain fraction of electricity must come from hydro, wind, and solar. If you're in one of those states, drop a line to your state representative, state senator, and governor's office, letting them know that you support those laws and want to see them strengthened. If you're in a state that *doesn't* have a renewable energy portfolio standard, write your elected leaders and say that you live in their region, you vote, and you want to see a renewable energy standard in the state.

And do it again at the city level. Half of the world's population now lives in cities. Cities are responsible for 70 percent of manmade greenhouse gas emissions. And increasingly, mayors and city councils are starting to take note, and starting to set greenhouse gas reduction targets. Find out what's happening in your city, and make your support for addressing climate change known to your mayor's office and your city council.

Finally, have hope. We've done this before. We removed lead from our gasoline. We stopped the release of benzene from our chemical plants. We eliminated the use of asbestos in construction. We've cut the emissions of acid rain–causing sulfur dioxide by half, with more on the way. We eliminated the production of CFCs that were destroying our ozone layer and endangering our planet.

At every step, the industries that had the most to lose from reducing our levels of pollution have cried foul. They've lobbied elected officials. They're taken out newspaper and television ads. They've claimed that change would cripple industry, stop the economy, or cost unbelievable sums. In every case, accumulating evidence and rising concern from voters has overcome that opposition. And in every case, fixing the problem was far less expensive than anyone imagined.

All those past solutions to environmental problems took time, continued campaigning, and stamina. Some of them only happened after visceral evidence of the danger. Ozone depletion was only tackled after the discovery of the Antarctic Ozone Hole. It took the Cuyahoga River catching on fire—for the thirteenth time—before we created the EPA and passed the Clean Air and Clean Water acts. It may take more disasters that are linked to climate change before enough Americans are convinced to act. I hope not, but that's a possibility.

But we've done it before. As renewable energy gets cheaper, as second- and third-generation biofuels come to market, as wind farms and solar panels sprout—out of pure economic self-interest—across Texas and California and much of the rest of the country, a large part of the resistance to acting against climate will fade away. Innovation will make it easier to get the nation across the threshold of action.

We've done it before. Keep your eyes on the future. Keep hope. And keep talking about these issues to your friends, your family, your colleagues, and your elected representatives.

Man and Nature

As I've talked about this book over the course of writing it, I've at times been confronted by others' deep pessimism about the human race. We destroy everything we touch, I've been told. Our basic tendency is to expand and consume, until nothing is left. Humans, unlike nature, know no limits. Plants and animals self-regulate their growth to fit the ecosystems they're part of. Humans, on the other hand, grow their consumption without limit. Humans are a virus.

This attitude, I fear, gives nature too much credit, and humans too little. Far from being the species that expands without limit, we humans are the species that have best displayed the ability to restrain and redirect our urges. We've lived with the power to destroy ourselves in nuclear war for more than sixty years now, and have somehow pulled back from that brink each time. We've learned to restrain our urge to violence, and reduced our deaths by warfare and murder. We've invented laws and market mechanisms that have reduced the amount of pollution we release into our air and water—whether it be lead, acid rain–causing sulfur dioxide, carbon monoxide, ozone-destroying chlorofluorocarbons, or toxic atrazine. We've even slowed the growth of our population—the force that we were once assured would destroy us.

Among all the animal species on our planet, we alone have the ability to reason about our urges and behaviors and to invent ways to channel and guide them. And we've used that ability. If we'd acted without restraint, the world as we know it wouldn't exist today.

We appear so rapacious not because we're unable to restrain ourselves, but because we're so powerful. We enjoy an advantage in capabilities over all other life and inanimate matter that is orders of magnitude larger than any species before us on this planet.

Yet with that great power comes great responsibility. We've shown that we can restrain our urges and behaviors, but we haven't gone far enough in that yet. We have to fix the flaws in the systems that now govern us. We have to turn our incredible capabilities increasingly toward creation, not depletion. We have to shift our consumption toward resources that are plentiful, that can be tapped into without destructive side effects. We have to teach the market to care for and husband those shared resources of ours that today don't have a price.

Easy Way, Hard Way

Ultimately, there are two paths forward for us, the easy way and the hard way.

In the easy way, we acknowledge the evidence that we are causing real harm to our planet, leaving it worse off for future generations, and flirting with the possibility of sudden and dramatic consequences. We retain our optimism, that we can both address these problems and be far richer in the future than we are today. We take our wildly successful economic system and we fix it so that it recognizes the value of our shared resources and encourages their protection, restoration, and careful, efficient, sustainable use. We invest in insurance against the risk of disasters caused by our actions. Nothing is certain in life. But on that path, the most likely outcome is that we'll solve the problems that plague us and grow progressively richer and richer even as we reduce and eventually reverse our negative impact on the planet.

At the other end of the this path is a world of 9 or 10 billion people, the large majority of them living lives of greater wealth, health, comfort, and freedom than the richest Americans live today, on a planet that is growing cleaner and greener with each passing year.

The other path, the hard way, isn't so pleasant. On that path, we continue to deny the damage we're doing, the very real consequences, and the risk of much worse if we continue along this path. We keep on acting in the way we have, pumping carbon into the atmosphere, warming the planet, acidifying the oceans, hunting fish toward the brink of extinction, depleting the last fossil water buried under our lands. On that path, we'll eventually come to realize that we've made a mistake. When the rivers and wells run dry, when we can no longer find the type of fish we used to eat, when the corals we used to admire have all bleached, when droughts and floods and storms wreck our cities and fields, when the price of a barrel of oil climbs into the multiple hundreds of dollars, then we'll realize that we've taken the wrong path.

And then we'll respond.

I'm an optimist. I believe in humanity's ingenuity. Even on the path of the hard way, I think we'll prevail. We'll scramble and find solutions. Yet the cost will be far higher a decade or two from now than it would be if we started today. And the scars will run deeper, in species lost, in acidified seas, in forests chopped or burned down, in climate-created famines and pestilence, in wars and conflicts born of resource scarcity.

And I could be wrong in thinking that we'd prevail. My optimism could be misplaced. The Romans had their share of optimists, who thought that all Rome had to do was win one more battle, reconquer one more lost province, put down one more rebellion, and all would be fine. I imagine the Maya had their optimists as well. Perhaps the Easter Islanders did too. And who could blame them? They were at the very peaks of their civilizations. Their accomplishments dwarfed those of previous generations. Surely they could overcome this little problem.

Optimism doesn't mean complacency. Optimism means hope. But hope must be joined with action to produce results.

Easy way or hard way. Simple, gradual, manageable changes to the systems that drive us now, or harder, more urgent, more costly changes later. A clear path to sustainability *and* incredibly growing wealth prosperity, as far into the future as the eye can see. Or more flirtation with disaster.

Easy way or hard way.

The choice is ours.

coda living in the twenty-first century

In 2009, a team of demographers and physicians studying aging published a paper showing that if trends in life expectancy continue, more than half of all children born in rich countries since 2000 will live to see the year 2100.[1]

What will that world look like?

I've outlined four things in this book that we, as a society, need to do in order to thrive through the twenty-first century:

1. Fix our markets to properly account for the value of the commons.
2. Invest in R&D to fund long-range innovation.
3. Embrace the technologies that stand poised to improve our lives while bettering our planet, even when they seem alien.
4. Empower each of the billions of minds on this planet, to turn them into assets that can produce new ideas that benefit all of us.

If we do those things, the twenty-first century is likely to be the richest, most prosperous century humanity has yet seen.

Let me take you on a tour of that world—the world we *could* build, *if* we make the right choices.

We start in the countryside. The first thing we might notice is that the areas outside cities are more sparsely populated in 2100 than in 2013. Humanity has all but completed the transition away from spending its time hunting or farming food and toward other professions. Where in our time 1.3 billion people still farm the Earth, and half of those eke out barely enough to survive, by 2100 there will be less than one-tenth as many farmers on the planet, as machines take over the tasks of sowing and reaping in every corner of the world.

The world's populace, by 2100, will have concentrated in the cities. Today roughly half of the world's population are city dwellers; in 2100 more than 80 percent will be. Those nine or ten billion people will be rich. Each of them, on average, will be as rich as today's Americans or Europeans. With their wealth they'll demand more and richer food—roughly three times as much as the world consumes now. Yet as we look around the countryside, we'll find that farms use up far less of the land than they do today. If we triple the yields of farms in the rich countries by 2100 (roughly what we did from 1950 to 2010), and if the rising wealth of today's developing countries brings their yields to parity with the rich countries, then the world will produce *six times* as much food per acre as it does now. We'll be able to meet the food demands of humanity with only half the land we use today. And if other trends continue, and if we embrace next-generation genetically modified crops, we'll grow that food with the use of less pesticide, less nitrogen fertilizer, and less water than ever before.

All that land and the lakes and rivers that flow through it will be cleaner than at any time since the start of the 1900s. The rising wealth of people worldwide will shift their concerns towards environmental protection, just as has happened in rich countries to date. Already, today, the land and water in every rich country are cleaner than they have been for at least forty years. That trend will continue, driving pollutant levels down in the countries that are already rich and in all those that have become rich by 2100. Rivers will be running higher than they have in decades as well, as more water-efficient crops have reduced the amount of water needed on our farms, and smarter market-based pricing of our freshwater commons has increasingly shifted water production toward desalination, rather than draining down the world's freshwater rivers, lakes, and aquifers.

Other sorts of farms will dot the landscape—energy farms that pull power out of the wind and from the sun's rays. If per capita energy needs continue to increase around 1 percent per year, those nine to ten billion rich people alive in 2100 will demand roughly three times the amount of energy that we use today. We'll meet the bulk of that demand through these energy farms—wind farms in the world's windiest places, solar farms in the world's deserts—with plentiful energy storage to capture energy for use when the sun doesn't shine and the wind doesn't blow, and a grid that ships energy from where it's collected or stored to where it's needed. Some energy will be collected in more distributed fashions, on the rooftops of homes and factories, on wind turbines above fields, and so on. But the economies of scale and the advantages of the best locations mean that concentrated energy farms will produce the bulk of the world's energy. Those energy farms will occupy less than 1 percent of world's land area and capture less than a tenth of a percent of the energy the sun strikes the Earth with, with headroom to grow our energy use at that pace—if, indeed, the pace hasn't slowed—for another few centuries yet.

Now let's continue our tour of 2100 by venturing into the wilderness. The world's forests and savannahs will be regrowing and healthier than they have been in decades. Some of the land once used for farming will be given over to parks and forests once more. That wilderness will bear scars, to be sure. The marks of millennia of human impacts will be there. The impact of the rapid warming of the late twentieth and early twenty-first century, in particular, will be apparent. Some species—many, many species—will be lost to us forever. Others may still be on the edge as we nurse them back to health. The world will likely be a warmer place in 2100, no matter what we do now. The species that do remain will be shifted in their distribution, all of them pushing toward the poles, some through simple adaptation, and others because we deliberately helped them along to save them from the impacts of the warming world.

Even so, as we walk through the forests and jungles and savannahs of the world, we'll see that they have turned a corner and are finally growing in size rather than being whittled away by human farming. They are on their way toward better health rather than worse.

From the forests and jungles we might venture out toward the oceans. Along the shores we'll see fish farms aplenty—now the source of the large majority of the world's fish protein. These will not be dirty, disease-spreading fish farms—they'll be separated tanks, with water filtered between ocean and farm, and with fish production far greater per acre than could ever happen in the wild.

When we reach the ocean itself we'll see good and bad. As with the on-land wilderness, there will be scars. But there will also be more life thriving in the seas than there has been in decades. Massive schools of deep-ocean fish will have returned around the world. The transition from fish-hunting to fish-farming will have given them time and space to heal. Coral reefs will also have benefited from the decline in fishing, which will remove the greatest pressure on them. Some reefs and some calcifier species will have suffered greatly from the acidification of the oceans that happened in the early twenty-first century. But where they've suffered the most, new coral species, transplanted from the areas where corals have shown the greatest ability to withstand heating and acidification, will be taking hold. Our oceans will be scarred, but healing, and healthier than they have been in almost two centuries.

Finally, we'll return to land and move in toward the cities. At the outskirts of those cities we'll find waste reclamation plants, where those materials that have been thrown out come to be put back into circulation. By 2100, the concepts of "garbage" and "recycling" will have merged. Just as in nature evolution selects for the rise of species that can extract value from any wasted resource, so too our market economy, with the tweaks we've made, will select for the extraction of any value we can find in materials that are thrown out. Farther away, we'll still have mines, of course. Powered by the plentiful energy of the day, they'll be pulling mineral resources out of the almost unthinkably vast resources in the Earth's crust—resources large enough to meet the material needs of 9 or 10 billion people living like today's billionaires. But by 2100, we'll have found it more efficient and more cost effective to recycle the materials we throw out. The large majority of almost every mineral resource put on the market will be recycled from a previous use.

Inside the city we'll find wonders. Technological wonders, to be sure. Most of those, I can't even hazard a guess at. But the most wondrous thing of all will be the people, the ways they connect to one another, and the incredible pace at which they produce new ideas.

These people will be the most affluent humanity has ever seen. Over the course of the twentieth century, the purchasing power of a typical American—measured as the amount of food, energy, housing, transportation, or consumer goods they could buy with an hour of their labor—increased by a factor of more than 20. Touring the world of 2100, we'll find that the purchasing power of the average resident of a rich country has increased by that much again, and the purchasing power of the average resident of today's poor countries will have increased even more, dramatically cutting the gap in wealth between nations today. As we walk through the streets of this city, whether it's in Europe or the Americas or Asia or Africa, we'll find that people spend less and less of their income on what they *need,* and more and more of it on what they *want.* The world's people will be more freed then ever from the chains of meeting their base necessities, and more able to engage in their desires.

As we look around, we'll note that the people of 2100 are the healthiest and longest lived to ever inhabit the Earth as well. By 2100, the average person on Earth will live to be more than 90 years old, and the average person in the currently rich countries will likely live to be 100 or more. We'll do so in greater health, with less pain, less burden of disease, more independence and mobility in our old age.

All that progress in our base physical needs and well-being will provide a foundation for the even more dramatic transformations that are already happening to the way we use the world's minds. We are closing in on a world where everyone can read, where everyone is connected to the Internet, where everyone gets adequate schooling. It will take us decades more to get there, but the trends are all in the right direction. And in connectivity, in particular, the future means of communicating from person to person will likely make our current Internet and mobile phone connections seem as antiquated, slow, and clumsy as hand-copied scrolls.

By 2100, growing wealth, more widespread and effective schooling, and greater automation of farms and factories will free more and more people from manual labor. The result will be an influx of new, educated, incredibly connected brain power larger than any the world has ever seen. Billions of minds that are now disenfranchised, uneducated, undernourished, or trapped in subsistence farming or menial labor will enter the global market of ideas, as both consumers *and* creators.

At the outset of the Renaissance, there were perhaps ten million people in the whole of Europe who could read and write. The printing press tightened the connection between those men and women, accelerating the transmission of ideas and their rate of collision and recombination. The early rumblings of the market and, later, the scientific method helped select for the most effective of those ideas through a process of Darwinian evolution.

We're now on the verge of a world with nine *billion* literate people, nearly 1,000 times more brainpower than those ten million who spurred the Renaissance, wired to one another through much faster, more powerful communication tools, with better scientific instruments and methods, and, we may hope, a market that is even more effective in valuing the things that matter on this planet. As we walk through a city of 2100, we'll be walking through a denser hub of brainpower than has ever existed in human history. Each of thousands of cities will contain more available brainpower than all of Europe during the Renaissance. Between now and 2100, worldwide, the number of men and women who can effectively contribute new innovations will triple, at the very least, and the interconnectivity between each of them, their peers, and the world's stockpiles of knowledge will grow by far more. This is the largest surge in total brainpower humanity has ever seen.

What will all those minds do? We may not be able to guess the specifics, but we can place solid bets on the general patterns. They'll work to provide things that others value. That is, by and large, how they'll make a living. And we all value our health, our comfort, our security, the well-being of our families, our ability to travel and experience new things, our ability to communicate with one another, and to access information of all sorts.

If history is any lesson, the market that wires us all together will select for those things, and the unprecedented brain power of humanity will provide them. Even as we turn the tide for the global commons that is our planet, we'll tremendously enrich the *knowledge commons* that are left to all future generations.

Just as we live with marvels that medieval kings and princes would lust for, our descendants—not so long from now—will live with comforts and capabilities that would amaze us and that will make the large majority of them, in many ways, richer than the richest men and women who live today.

The world I've just described to you isn't the world we're guaranteed to have. But it's not a world out of fantasy, either. It's the world we *can* have, if we work hard and smart to bring it into being.

The human mind is the ultimate source of all wealth. We stand poised on the brink of the largest-ever explosion of human mental power, a second Renaissance, more transformative, more far-reaching, and more inclusive than the first. *If* we make the right choices to empower human minds and encourage innovation, to steer innovation toward the solutions for our planet's problems, and to embrace the fruits that it offers, then the future will be one of almost unimaginable wealth, health, and well-being.

acknowledgments

This book would not exist without the contributions of a number of people.

My agent, Ted Weinstein, helped shape this work heavily at the proposal stage. My editor, Stephen Hull, helped me craft the structure and tone of the book and asked questions that helped me hone my arguments. Ellery Baines, my research assistant, was tireless in tracking down obscure pieces of data to flesh out the figures and examples. Molly Nixon served as frequent first reader and sounding board for ideas of all sorts.

In addition, a host of people read early copies of the manuscript, in part or in full, and offered feedback that's improved the book. I'm indebted to Alexis Carlson, Alison Park Douglas, Alissa Mortenson, Andy Becker, Becky Anderson, Brent Field, Brian Arbogast, Brian Retford, Brooks Talley, Dan Farmer, David Sunderland, Dona Farmer, Gabriel Williams, Gregg Maryniak, Jose Cordeiro, Kathryn Myronuk, Kevin MacDonald, Lars Liden, Leo Dirac, Nancy Linford, Neil Jacobstein, Pat Lasswell, Ratha Grimes, Ryan Grant, Scott Northrup, Suzanne Moon, and Tanya Lasswell.

Thank you all.

This book also owes much to the work of the late Julian Simon and his pioneering efforts to show the ways in which human ingenuity creates wealth and overcomes challenges. While I have placed far more emphasis on the very real problems that beset us and the systematic changes needed to address them, I believe Simon's core insight is as profound and important now as it was during his life. Human minds are, indeed, the source of all wealth. It is up to us to harness and direct that power.

notes

one the rise of innovation

1. Barry Trevelyan, Matthew Smallman-Raynor, and Andrew Cliff, "The Spatial Dynamics of Poliomyelitis in the United States: From Epidemic Emergence to Vaccine-Induced Retreat, 1910–1971," *Annals of the Association of American Geographers* 95 (2005): 269–93.

2. Centers for Disease Control, Division of Reproductive Health, "Achievements in Public Health, 1900–1999: Healthier Mothers and Babies," *Morbidity and Mortality Weekly Report* 48, no. 38 (1999): 849–58.

3. Albert Feuerwerker, *Chinese Economic History in Comparative Perspectives* (Berkeley: University of California Press, 1990).

4. David Landes, *The Wealth and Poverty of Nations: Why Some Are Rich and Some So Poor* (New York: W. W. Norton, 1999).

5. Patricia Ebrey, Anne Walthall, and James Palais, *East Asia: A Cultural, Social, and Political History* (Boston: Houghton Mifflin, 2006).

6. Peter Drucker, "The Next Information Revolution," www.s-jtech.com (accessed March 7, 2012).

7. Landes, *The Wealth and Poverty of Nations*.

8. Ibid.

9. The Applied History Research Group, University of Calgary, "The European Voyages of Exploration," www.ucalgary.ca/applied_history/tutor/eurvoya/columbus .html (accessed March 7, 2012).

10. Ebrey, Walthall, and Palais, *East Asia*.

11. Landes, *The Wealth and Poverty of Nations*.

12. William Rosen, *The Most Powerful Idea in the World: A Story of Steam, Industry, and Invention* (New York: Random House, 2010).

two the incredible present

1. World Health Organization, Global Observatory Data Repository, www.who.int /gho/en/ (accessed January 23, 2012).

2. Ibid.

3. Ibid.

4. Ibid.

5. World Health Organization, *Global Health Risks: Mortality and Burden of Disease Attributable to Selected Major Risks* (Geneva: WHO Press, 2009).

6. National Cancer Institute, *Cancer Trends Progress Report—2009/2010 Update* (Bethesda, MD: National Cancer Institute, 2010).

7. National Institutes of Health, *National Heart, Lung, and Blood Institute Factbook, Fiscal Year 2006* Washington, DC: National Institutes of Health, 2007).

8. Organisation for Economic Co-Operation and Development, *OECD Factbook 2010: Economic, Environmental, and Social Statistics* (Paris: OECD Publishing, 2011).

9. Kenneth Manton and XiLiang Gu, "Changes in the Prevalence of Chronic Disability in the United States Black and Nonblack Population Above Age 65 from 1982 to 1999," *Proceedings of the National Academy of Sciences* 98, no. 11 (2001): 6354–59.

10. Robert Fogel, "Changes in the Process of Aging during the Twentieth Century: Findings and Procedures of the Early Indicators Project," *Population and Development Review (Aging, Health, and Public Policy: Demographic and Economic Perspectives Supplement)* 30 (2004): 19–47.

11. Roderick Floud, Robert Fogel, Bernard Harris, and Sok Hong, *The Changing Body: Health, Nutrition, and Human Development in the Western World Since 1700* (Cambridge: Cambridge University Press, 2011).

12. Xavier Sala-i-Martin, "The World Distribution of Income: Falling Poverty and . . . Convergence, Period," www.columbia.edu/~xs23/papers/pdfs/World_Income_Distribution_QJE.pdf (accessed March 7, 2012).

13. Maxim Pinkovsky and Xavier Sala-i-Martin, "Parametric Estimations of the World Distribution of Income" (National Bureau of Economic Research Working Paper. no. 15433, 2009).

14. Food and Agriculture Organization of the United Nations (FAO), *The State of Food Insecurity in the World: Addressing Food Insecurity in Protracted Crises 2010* (Rome: FAO, 2010.

15. Food and Agriculture Organization of the United Nations, "FAOSTAT," http://faostat.fao.org/ (accessed January 23, 2012).

16. Daniel Cohen and Marcelo Soto, "Growth and Human Capital; Good Data, Good Results," *Journal of Economic Growth* 12, no. 1 (2007): 51–76.

17. International Telecommunications Union, *Measuring the Information Society 2011* (Geneva: ITU, 2011).

18. International Telecommunications Union, "ICT Indicators Database 2011," www.itu.int/pub/D-IND-WTID.OL-2011 (accessed March 7, 2012).

19. David Lam, "Lessons from 50 Years of Extraordinary Demographic History," (Department of Economics and Population Studies Center, University of Michigan, Population Studies Center Research Report 11–743, 2011).

20. Indur Goklany, "Have Increases in Population, Affluence and Technology Worsened Human and Environmental Well-Being?" *Electronic Journal of Sustainable Development* 1. no. 3 (2009).

21. Bureau of Economic Analysis, "Interactive Data," www.bea.gov/itable/ (accessed March 7, 2012).

22. Center for Sustainable Systems, University of Michigan, "U.S. Environmental Footprint Factsheet" (Pub. No. CSS08-08, 2011).

23. Louis Johnston and Samuel H. Williamson, "What Was the U.S. GDP Then?" *MeasuringWorth*, www.measuringworth.org/usgdp/.

24. "Genghis Khan a Prolific Lover, DNA Data Implies, "*National Geographic News*, February 14, 2003.

25. Tahir Shah, "Jewel in the Crown: A Palace Fit for a Nizam," *Guardian*, February 19, 2011.

26. Plutarch, *Plutarch's Lives: Life of Crassus*, Charles River Editors, trans. John Dryden (Amazon Digital Services).

three running out of steam

1. Capital Professional Services, "History of Oil Prices," http://inflationdata.com (accessed March 7, 2012).

2. VOA News, "Oil Industry Set for Record Exploration Spending in 2011," *Voice of America News*, December 29, 2010.

3. U.S. Department of Energy, "Enhanced Oil Recovery/CO_2 Injection," www.fossil.energy.gov/programs/oilgas/eor/index.html (accessed March 7, 2012).

4. Alfred Cavallo, "Hubbert's Petroleum Production Model: An Evaluation and Implications for World Oil Production Forecasts," *Natural Resources Research* 13, no. 4 (2004): 211–21.

5. James Cordahi and Andy Critchlow, "Kuwait Oil Field, World's 2nd Largest, Is 'Exhausted,'" *Bloomberg*, November 10, 2005.

6. Euan Meams, "GHAWAR: An Estimate of Remaining Oil Reserves and Production Decline (Part 2—Results)," The Oil Drum: Europe, www.theoildrum .com/node/2494 (accessed March 7, 2012).

7. British Petroleum, "Prudhoe Bay: Fact Sheet," www.bp.com (accessed March 7, 2012).

8. M. King Hubbert, *Energy and Power* (W.H. Freeman, 1972). www.hubbertpeak .com/hubbert/energypower/ (accessed January 30, 2012).

9. IHS, "IHS CERA: Energy Strategy," www.ihs.com/products/cera/index.aspx (accessed March 7, 2012).

10. Jad Mouawad, "Oil Industry Sets a Brisk Pace of New Discoveries," *New York Times*, September 23, 2009.

11. Ken White, "The Year of Macondo, Brazil Discoveries Set 2010 Pace," *AAPG Explorer*, January 2011.

12. Calatrava Almudena, "Huge Oil Discovery Boosts Argentina's Potential," *Seattle PI*, November 8, 2011.

13. U.S. Geological Survey Department, U.S. Department of the Interior, "3 to 4.3 Billion Barrels of Technically Recoverable Oil Assessed in North Dakota and

Montana's Bakken Formation—25 Times More Than 1995 Estimate," www.usgs.gov /newsroom/article.asp?ID=1911 (accessed January 30, 2012).

14. "Update 4-Statoil: N. Sea Find May Be World's Biggest in 2011," Reuters, August 16, 2011.

15. Herbert Abraham, *Asphalts and Allied Substances* (New York: Van Nostrand, 1920).

16. IHS CERA, "Oil Sands Technology; Past, Present, and Future," www.ihs.com /products/cera/energy-report.aspx?id=1065928651 (accessed January 30, 2012).

17. Cutler Cleveland, "An Assessment of the Energy Return of Investment of Oil Shale," Western Resource Advocates, www.westernresourceadvocates.org/land/pdf /oseroireport.pdf (accessed March 7, 2012).

18. U.S. Energy Information Administration, "Annual Energy Outlook 2010: With Projections to 2035," http://infousa.state.gov/economy/technology/docs/0383.pdf

19. Natural Petroleum Council, "Coal to Liquids and Gas Subgroup of the Technology Task Group of the NPC Committee on Global Oil and Gas," www.npc .org/Study_Topic_Papers/18-TTG-Coals-to-Liquids.pdf (accessed March 7, 2012).

20. Stuart Staniford, "IEA Acknowledges Peak Oil," http://earlywarn.blogspot. com/2010/11/ (accessed January 30, 2012).

21. Steve Connor, "Warning: Oil Supplies Are Running Out Fast," *Independent*, August 3, 2009.

22. Chris Skrebowski, Fatih Birol, Jeremy Leggett, and Jonica Newby, "Peak Oil: Just Around the Corner," *Radio National; The Science Show*, April 23, 2011.

23. James D. Hamilton, "Nonlinearities and the Macroeconomic Effects of Oil Prices," *Macroeconomic Dynamics* 15, no. 3 (2011): 364–78.

24. Kristie Engermann, Kevin Kliesen, and Michael Owyang, "Do Oil Shocks Drive Business Cycles?" Federal Reserve Bank of St. Louis, Working Paper Series, http://research.stlouisfed.org/wp/2010/2010-007.pdf (accessed January 30, 2012).

25. Hillard Huntington, "The Economic Consequences of Higher Crude Oil Prices," Energy Modeling Forum, Stanford University, http://emf.stanford.edu/files /pubs/22457/EMFSR9.pdf (accessed January 30, 2012).

four peak everything?

1. Food and Agriculture Organization of the United Nations, "FAOSTAT," faostat. fao.org/ (accessed January 23, 2012).

2. Food and Agriculture Organization of the United Nations, "How to Feed the World in 2050," www.fao.org (accessed March 7, 2012).

3. Dow Futures, "Historical Copper Prices History," http://dow-futures.net /commodity/historical-copper-prices-history.html (accessed March 7, 2012).

4. International Monetary Fund, "IMF Primary Commodity Prices," www.imf.org /external/np/res/commod/index.aspx (accessed March 7, 2012).

5. Ibid.

6. Ibid.

7. USGS, "Copper Statistics and Information," http://minerals.usgs.gov (accessed March 7, 2012).

8. Dana Cordell, "The Story of Phosphorus: 8 Reasons Why We Need to Rethink the Management of Phosphorus Resources in the Global Food System," *Sustainable Phosphorus Futures*, http://phosphorusfutures.net/why-phosphorus (accessed January 30, 2012).

9. Food and Agriculture Organization of the United Nations, "Fisheries at the Limit?" www.fao.org/docrep/u8480e/U8480Eof.htm (accessed March 7, 2012).

10. Yumiko Kura, Carmen Revenga, Eriko Hoshino, and Greg Mock, "Fishing for Answers; Making Sense of the Global Fish Crisis," World Resources Institute, http://pdf.wri.org/fishanswer_fulltext.pdf (accessed January 30, 2012).

11. American University, "Peruvian Anchovy Case,". www1.american.edu/TED /anchovy.htm (accessed March 7, 2012).

12. George Pararas-Carayannis, "A Year after Johannesburg, Ocean Governance and Sustainable Development: Ocean and Coasts—a Glimpse into the Future," International Ocean Institute, www.drgeorgepc.com/OceanGovernance.html (accessed January 30, 2012).

13. Mark Bittman, "A Seafood Snob Ponders the Future of Fish," *New York Times*, November 15, 2008.

14. FAO Fisheries and Aquaculture Department, *The State of World Fisheries and Aquaculture* (Rome: FAO, 2010).

15. Ruth Thurstan, Simon Brockington, and Callum Roberts. "The Effects of 118 Years of Industrial Fishing on UK Bottom Trawl Fisheries," *Nature Communications* (2010): doi 10.1038/ncomms1013.

16. Sea Around Us Project, "Stock Status in the Global Ocean," www.seaaroundus .org/global/1/101.aspx (accessed March 7, 2012); Boris Worm et al., Impacts of Biodiversity Loss on Ocean Ecosystem Services," *Science* 13 no. 5800 (November 3 2006787–90; Food and Agriculture Organization of the United Nations, "Fisheries at the Limit?"

17. Manjula Guru, "The Ogallala Aquifer," The Kerr Center for Sustainable Agriculture, Inc, www.kerrcenter.com/publications/ogallala_aquifer.pdf (accessed March 7, 2012).

18. David Biello, "Is Northwestern India's Breadbasket Running Out of Water?" *Scientific American*, August 12, 2009.

19. Lester Brown, "China's Water Table Levels Are Dropping Fast," *Grist*, October 26, 2001, http://grist.org/food/table/ (accessed January 31, 2012).

20. Lester Brown, "Aquifer Depletion," *The Encyclopedia of Earth*, January 23, 2010. www.eoearth.org/article/Aquifer_depletion (accessed January 31, 2012).

21. Fred Pearce, "Water Scarcity: The Real Food Crisis," *Yale Environment 360*, June 3, 2009, http://e360.yale.edu/content/feature.msp?id=1825 (accessed February 6, 2012).

22. Sarah Zielinski, "The Colorado River Runs Dry," *Smithsonian Magazine*, October 2010.

23. Philip Whish-Wilson, "The Aral Sea Environmental Health Crisis," *Journal of Rural and Remote Environmental Health* 1, no. 2 (2002): 29–34.

24. World Resources Institute, "Earth Trends: The Environmental Information Portal," http://earthtrends.wri.org (accessed March 7, 2012).

25. Food and Agriculture Organization of the United Nations, *State of the World's Forests* (Rome: FAO, 2011).

26. James Astill, "Seeing the Wood," *Economist*, September 23, 2010.

27. Frank Field, "How You Can Save the Rainforest," *Sunday Times* (London), October 8, 2006.

28. National Footprint Accounts, "Calculation Methodology for the National Footprint Accounts, 2010 Edition," www.footprintnetwork.org (accessed March 7, 2012).

29. Global Footprint Network, "Humanity's Ecological Footprint and Biocapacity through Time," www.footprintnetwork.org/atlas (accessed March 7, 2012).

five greenhouse earth

1. United States Geological Survey, Northern Rocky Mountain Science Center, "Retreat of Glaciers in Glacier National Park," http://nrmsc.usgs.gov/research /glacier_retreat.htm (accessed February 6, 2012).

2. Georg Kaser, Douglas Hardy, Thomas Molg, Raymond Bradley, and Tharsis Hyera, "Modern Glacier Retreat on Kilimanjaro as Evidence of Climate Change: Observations and Facts," *International Journal of Climatology* 24 (2004): 329–39.

3. National Oceanic and Atmospheric Administration, "NOAA Data Set N 09 Area," ftp://sidads.colorado.edu/DATASETS/NOAA/G02135/Sep/N_09_area.txt (accessed March 7, 2012).

4. Intergovernmental Panel on Climate Change, *Climate Change 2001: The Scientific Basis* (Contribution of Working Group I to the Third Assessment Report of the Intergovernmental Panel on Climate Change) (New York: Cambridge University Press, 2001).

5. Geoffrey Lean, "For the First Time in Human History, the North Pole Can Be Circumnavigated," *Independent*, August 31, 2008.

6. Vladimir Romanovsky, "Arctic Theme Page," National Oceanic and Atmospheric Administration, www.arctic.noaa.gov/essay_romanovsky.html (accessed February 6, 2012).

7. Anna York, "Alaskan Village Stands on Leading Edge of Climate Change," University of Carolina at Chapel Hill, http://unc.news21.com/index.php/stories /alaska.html (accessed February 6, 2012).

8. Hinkle Charitable Foundation, "Report: How Real Is Global Warming? The Physical Evidence," www.thehcf.org/emaila1.html (accessed March 7, 2012).

9. Robin McKie, "Natural Signs That Show Spring Comes Earlier," *Guardian*, January 22, 2011.

10. Seth Borenstein, "Spring Keeps Coming Earlier for Birds, Bees, Trees," *USA Today*, March 21, 2008.

11. John Church and Neil White, "A 20th Century Acceleration in Global Sea-Level Rise," *Geophysical Research Letters* 33 (2006). doi:10.1029/2005GL024826.

12. John Tyndall, "The Bakerian Lecture: On the Absorption and Radiation of Heat by Gases and Vapours, and on the Physical Connexion of Radiation, Absorption, and Conduction," *Philosophical Transactions of the Royal Society of London* 151 (1861): 1–36.

13. H. Le Treut, R. Somerville, U. Cubasch, Y. Ding, C. Mauritzen, A. Mokssit, T. Peterson, and M. Prather, "Historical Overview of Climate Change," in *Climate Change 2007: The Physical Science Basis* (Contribution of Working Group I to the Fourth Assessment Report of the Intergovernmental Panel on Climate Change) (New York: Cambridge University Press, 2007).

14. Svante Arrhenius, Svante, "On the Influence of Carbonic Acid in the Air upon the Temperature of the Ground," *Philosophical Magazine and Journal of Science,* April 1896.

15. John Gribbon and Mary Gribbon, *James Lovelock: In Search of Gaia* (Princeton, NJ: Princeton University Press, 2009).

16. Eugene Robinson, "The Scientific Finding That Settles the Climate-Change Debate," *Washington Post*, October 24, 2011.

17. Richard Muller, "I Stick to the Science," *Scientific American*, June 2011.

18. Richard Muller, "Statement to the Committee on Science, Space and Technology of the United States House of Representatives," http://berkeleyearth.org/pdf/muller-testimony-31-march-2011.pdf (accessed February 6, 2012).

19. Robert Rohde et al. "Berkeley Earth Temperature Averaging Process," Berkeley Earth Surface Temperature Project, http://berkeleyearth.org/pdf/berkeley-earth-averaging-process.pdf (accessed February 7, 2012).

20. Kevin Trenberth, et al., "Chapter 3: Observations: Surface and Atmospheric Climate Change," in *Climate Change 2007: The Physical Science Basis* (Contribution of Working Group I to the Fourth Assessment Report of the Intergovernmental Panel on Climate Change) (New York: Cambridge University Press, 2007).

21. Ibid.

22. World Meterological Organization, Press Release No. 935, www.wmo.int (accessed February 2, 2012).

23. Judith Lean and David Rind, "How Natural and Anthropogenix Influences Alter Global and Regional Surface Temperatures: 1889 to 2006," *Geophysical Research Letters* 35 (2008).

24. C. Bertrand, J. P. Ypersele, and A. Berger, "Volcanic and Solar Impacts on Climate Since 1700," *Climate Dynamics* 15. no. 5 (1998): 355–67.

25. NOAA, "Global Climate Change Indicators," National Oceanic and Atmospheric Administration, www.ncdc.noaa.gov/indicators/ (accessed March 7, 2012).

26. John Cook, "CO_2 Lags Temperature—What Does It Mean?" *Skeptical Science*, www.skepticalscience.com/co2-lags-temperature-intermediate.htm (accessed February 24, 2012).

27. Aradhna K. Tripati, Christopher D. Roberts, and Robert A. Eagle, "Coupling of CO_2 and Ice Sheet Stability over Major Climate Transitions of the Last 20 Million Years," *Science* 326. no. 5958 (2009): 1394–97.

28. John Harries, Helen Brindley, Pretty Sagoo, and Richard Bantges, "Increases in Greenhouse Forcing Inferred from the Outgoing Longwave Radiation Spectra of the Earth in 1970 and 1997," *Nature*, May 17, 2000, 355–57.

29. Nate Hagens, "Unconventional Oil: Tar Sands and Shale Oil—EROI on the Web," *The Oil Drum: Net Energy*, www.theoildrum.com/node/3839 (accessed February 2, 2012).

30. Cleveland, "An Assessment of the Energy Return of Investment of Oil Shale."

31. Anthony Stranges, "Friedrich Bergius and the Rise of the German Synthetic Fuel Industry," *ISIS* 75 (1984): 643–67.

32. World Coal Association, "Emissions Reductions from Synthetic Fuels," www.worldcoal.org/coal/uses-of-coal/coal-to-liquids/ (accessed February 24, 2012).

33. Natural Resources Defense Council, "Why Liquid Coal Is Not a Viable Option to Move America beyond Oil," www.nrdc.org/globalwarming/coal/liquids.pdf (accessed February 24, 2012).

34. Jeffrey Kiehl. "Lessons from Earth's Past," *Science*, January 14, 2011, 158–59.

35. A. P. Sokolov, et al. "Probabilistic Forecast for Twenty-First-Century Climate Based on Uncertainties in Emissions (without Policy) and Climate Parameters," *Journal of Climate* 22, no. 19 (2009): 5175–5204.

36. Ibid.

37. Janet Larsen, "Setting the Record Straight: More Than 52,000 Europeans Died from Heat in Summer 2003," Earth Policy Institute, www.earth-policy.org (accessed March 7, 2012).

38. Tania Branigan, "Drought Threatens Chinese Wheat Crop," *Guardian*, February 4, 2009.

39. Jilin Dunhua, "Flood-Hit Families to Get Subsidies from Government to Rebuild Homes," *Xinhua*, August 8, 2010, http://news.xinhuanet.com (accessed March 7, 2012).

40. Lucia Kim and Maria Levitov, "Russia Heat Wave May Kill 15,000, Shave $15 Billion of GDP," *Bloomberg News*, August 10, 2010.

41. "Pakistan Floods Seen as Massive Economic Challenge," *New Zealand Radio*, August 22, 2010, www.radionz.co.nz/news/world (accessed March 7, 2012).

42. Hillary Hylton, "The Great Dry State of Texas: The Drought That Wouldn't Leave Has Lone Star Farmers Scared," *Time*, August 10, 2011.

43. *Texas Business*, "Texas Wheat Crop to Fall by Two-Thirds," www.texasbusiness.com (accessed February 2, 2012).

44. Whitney McFerron and Jeff Wilson, "Drought Withers Smallest Hay Crop in Century to Boost Beef Costs," *Bloomberg News*, July 25, 2011.

45. Bryan Walsh, "Drought Cripples the South: Why the 'Creeping Disaster' Could Get a Whole Lot Worse," *Time*, August 9, 2011.

46. U.S. Global Change Research Program, *Global Climate Change Impacts in the*

United States (New York: Cambridge University Press, 2009). http://downloads.globalchange.gov/usimpacts/pdfs/climate-impacts-report.pdf (accessed February 2, 2012).

47. S. Rahmstorf and D. Coumou, "Increase of Extreme Events in a Weather World," *Proceedings of the National Academy of Sciences* 108, no. 44 (2011): 17905–909.

48. Kerry Emanuel, "Increasing Destructiveness of Tropical Cyclones over the Past 30 Years," *Nature* 436 (2005).

49. P. J. Webster, G. J. Holland, J. A. Curry, and H. R. Chang, "Changes in Tropical Cyclone Number, Duration, and Intensity in a Warming Environment," *Science* 309, no. 5742 (September 16, 2005): 1844–46.

50. National Environmental Satellite, Data, and Information Services, "State of the Climate Wildfires, January 2011," www.ncdc.noaa.gov/sotc/fire/2011/1 (accessed February 2, 2012).

51. Incident Information System, "Texas Initial Attack News Release; Texas Wildfires 2011 Fact Sheet," www.inciweb.org/incident/article/2315/13641/ (accessed February 24, 2012).

52. David Bowman et al., "Fire in the Earth System," *Science* 324, no. 5926 (2009).

53. Aiguo Dai, "Drought under Global Warming: A Review," *Wiley Interdisciplinary Reviews: Climate Change* 2, no. 1 (2011): 45–65.

54. Ibid.

55. Food and Agriculture Organization of the United Nations, "2050: A Third More Mouths to Feed; Food Production Will Have to Increase by 70 percent," www.fao.org/news/story/en/item/35571/ (accessed February 24, 2012).

56. David Lobell, Wolfram Schlenker, and Justin Costa-Roberts, "Climate Trends and Global Crop Production Since 1980," *Science* 333, no. 6042 (July 29, 2011): 616–20.

57. David Grantz and Anil Shrestha, "Ozone Reduces Crop Yields and Alters Competition with Weeds Such as Yellow Nutsedge," *California Agriculture* 59, no. 2 (2005).

58. Food and Agriculture Organization of the United Nations, "Potentially Catastrophic Climate Impacts On Food," www.fao.org/news/story/en/item/54337/icode/ (accessed February 24, 2012).

59. S. L. Lewis, P. M. Brando, O. L. Phillips, G. M. F. van der Heijden, and D. Nepstad, "The 2010 Amazon Drought," *Science* 331, no. 6017 (2011): 554, doi: 10.1126/science.1200807

60. Lauren Morello, "Another Amazon Drought Spurs Greenhouse Gas Emissions," *Scientific American*, February 4, 2011.

61. Global Issues, "Coral Reefs: Ecosystems of Environmental and Human Value," www.globalissues.org/article/173/coral-reefs (accessed February 24, 2012).

62. I. E. Hendriks, C. M. Duarte, and M. Alvarez, "Vulnerability of Marine Biodiversity to Ocean Acidification: A Meta-Analysis," *Estuarine, Coastal and Shelf Science* 86, no. 2 (2010).

63. Justin Ries, Anne Cohen, and Daniel McCorkle, "Marine Calcifiers Exhibit Mixed Responses to CO_2-Induced Ocean Acidification," *Geology* 37, no. 12 (July 21, 2009): 1131–34.

64. Andy Ridgwell and Daniela N. Schmidt, "Past Constraints on the Vulnerability of Marine Calcifiers to Massive Carbon Dioxide Release," *Nature Geoscience* 14 (February 2010), doi: 10.1038/NGEO755. Zimmer, "An Ominous Warning on the Effects of Ocean Acidification," *Yale Environment 360*, http://e360.yale.edu (accessed February 24, 2012).

65. C. Schneibner and R. P. Speijer, *Decline of Coral Reefs during Late Paleocene to Early Eocene Global Warming*, Copernicus Publications, 2008, www.electronic-earth.net/3/19/2008/ee-3-19-2008.pdf (accessed March 7, 2012).

66. Clay Kelly et al., "Rapid Diversification of Planktonic Foraminifera in the Tropical Pacific (ODP Site 865) during the Late Paleocene Thermal Maximum," *Geology* 24, no. 5 (1996): 423–26.

67. Robin Huttenbach, "Cumulative Emissions of CO_2," *A Response to Climate Change*, http://petrolog.typepad.com (accessed February 24, 2012).

68. Drew Shindell et al., "Improved Attribution of Climate Forcing to Emissions," *Science* 326, no. 5953 (2009): 716–18.

69. Global Carbon Project, "Super-Size Deposits of Frozen Carbon in Arctic Could Worsen Climate Change," *ScienceDaily*, June 30, 2009.

70. K. M. Walter et al., "Methane Bubbling from Siberian Thaw Lakes as a Positive Feedback to Climate Warming," *Nature* 443 (2006): 71–75.

71. Torre Jorgenson, Yuri Shur, and Erik Pullman, "Abrupt Increase in Permafrost Degradation in Arctic Alaska," *Geophysical Research Letters* 33 (2006).

72. Arthur Max, "Methane Seeping from Siberian Ice a Climate Concern," Associated Press.

73. Food and Agriculture Organization of the United Nations, "Forests and Climate Change: Better Forest Management Has Key Role to Play in Dealing with Climate Change," www.fao.org/newsroom/en/focus/2006/1000247/index.html (accessed February 4, 2012); Crisis Coalition Team, "Permafrost Methane Time Bomb," www.planetextinction.com/planet_extinction_permafrost.htm (accessed February 4, 2012).

74. Bruce Buffett and David Archer, "Global Inventory of Methane Clathrate: Sensitivity to Changes in the Deep Ocean," *Earth and Planetary Science Letters* 227 (2004): 185–99.

75. National Science Foundation, "Methane Releases from Arctic Shelf May Be Much Larger and Faster Than Anticipated" (Press Release 10-036), www.nsf.gov/news/news_summ.jsp?cntn_id=116532&org=NSF&from=news (accessed February 4, 2012).

76. "'Fountains' of Methane 1,000m Across Erupt from Arctic Ice—A Greenhouse Gas 20 Times More Potent Than Carbon Dioxide," *Daily Mail*, December 13, 2011.

77. "When Crocodiles Roamed the Arctic," *New Scientist* 2661 (June 18, 2008).

78. A. M. Grachev and J. P. Severinghaus, "A Revised 10 4C Magnitude of the Abrupt Change in Greenland Temperature at the Younger Dryas Termination Using Published GISP2 Gas Isotope Data and Air Thermal Diffusion Constants," *Quaternary Science Reviews* 24, nos. 5–6 (2005): 513–19.

79. K. C. Taylor, "The Holocene-Younger Dryas Transition Recorded at Summit, Greenland," *Science* 279, no. 5339 (1997): 825–25.

80. Only Zero Carbon, "Message from Ancient Ice," www.onlyzerocarbon.org
/uploads/Ice_messaging.pdf (accessed March 7, 2012).

81. Global Warming Forecast, "Global Warming Underestimates and Misforecasts:
Global Warming Underestimated," www.global-warming-forecasts.com/under
estimates.php (accessed February 24, 2012).

six end of the party?

1. Bill McKibben, *Eaarth: Making a Life on a Tough Planet* (New York: Times
Books, 2010), 48.

2. Paul Gilding, *The Great Disruption: Why the Climate Crisis Will Bring on the End
of Shopping and the Birth of a New World* (New York: Bloomsbury Press, 2011), 1

3. Richard Heinberg, *The End of Growth: Adapting to Our New Economic Reality*
(Gabriola Island, BC: New Society, 2011), 2.

4. World Resources Institute, "Earth Trends: The Environmental Information
Portal," http://earthtrends.wri.org/ (accessed March 7, 2012).

5. Dianne Schwager, "Trends in Single-Occupant Vehicle and Vehicle Miles of
Travel Growth in the United States," *Transit Cooperative Research Program*, August
1998, http://onlinepubs.trb.org/onlinepubs/tcrp/tcrp_rrd_30.pdf (accessed February
24, 2012).

6. U.S. Department of Energy, "Fact 475: June 25, 2007, Light Vehicle Weight on
the Rise," Vehicle Technologies Program—Facts of the Week, www1.eere.energy.gov
(accessed March 7, 2012).

7. Wards Auto, "Data Center," http://wardsauto.com/data-center (accessed March
7, 2012).

8. Center for Sustainable Systems, University of Michigan, "U.S. Environmental
Footprint," http://css.snre.umich.edu/css_doc/CSS08-08.pdf (accessed February 4,
2012).

9. Gilding, *The Great Disruption*, 1

10. Heinberg, *The End of Growth*, 2

11. Congressional Research Service, "China-U.S. Trade Issues." http://fpc.state.gov
/documents/organization/155009.pdf (accessed March 7, 2012).

12. Anna Ringstrom, "Global Military Spending Hits High but Growth Slows,"
Reuters, April 10, 2011.

13. World Trade Organization, "World Trade Developments," www.wto.org
(accessed March 7, 2012).

14. Brad Johnson, "Pentagon: 'Climate Change, Energy Security, and Economic
Stability Are Inextricably Linked,'" *Think Progress*, February 1, 2010, www.grist.org
(accessed February 4, 2012).

15. Fred Thompson, "The Darfur Genocide and Global Warming," *Townhall*,
June 28, 2007, http://townhall.com/columnists/fredthompson/2007 (accessed
March 7, 2012).

16. David Zhang et al., "Climate Change and War Frequency in Eastern China
over the Last Millennium," *Human Ecology* 35, no. 4 (2011): 403–14.

17. "Unquenchable Thirst: A Growing Rivalry between India, Pakistan and China over the Region's Great Rivers May Be Threatening South Asia's Peace," *Economist*, November 19, 2011.

seven the first energy technology

1. Paul Ehrlich, *The Population Bomb* (New York: Sierra Club/Ballantine Books, 1968).

2. UN Data, "Population Database," http://data.un.org/ (accessed March 7, 2012).

3. Food and Agriculture Organization of the United Nations, "FAOSTAT," faostat. fao.org/ accessed January 23, 2012.

4. Lyn Wadley and Zenobia Jacobs, "Sibudu Cave, KwaZulu-Natal: Background to the Excavations of Middle Stone Age and Iron Age Occupations," *South African Journal of Science* 100 (March 2004): 145–51.

5. Marcus J. Hamilton, Bruce T. Milne, Robert S. Walker, and James H. Brown, "Nonlinear Scaling of Space Use in Human Hunter-Gatherers," *Proceedings of the National Academy of Sciences* 104, no. 11 (March 13, 2007): 4765–69.

6. AgBioWorld, "Iowans Who Fed the World—Norman Borlaug: Geneticist," www.agbioworld.org (accessed March 7, 2012).

7. William Gaud, "The Green Revolution: Accomplishments and Apprehensions," www.agbioworld.org (accessed February 4, 2012).

8. Food and Agriculture Organization of the UN, *The State of World Fisheries and Aquaculture* (Rome: FAO, 2010).

9. Data compiled from multiple sources. Pre-agrarian population density from: Hamilton et al., "Nonlinear Scaling of Space Use." Preindustrial agricultural productivity from B. H. Slicher Van Bath, "The Yields of Different Crops (Mainly Cereals) in Relation to the Seed," In *Acta Historiae Neerlandica II*, ed. J. W. Schulte and J. A. Faber (Leiden, Netherlands: E. J. Brill, 1967). Yields since 1800 from: Food and Agriculture Organization, "FAOSTAT."

10. M. Colchester and L. Lohmann, "The Struggle for Land and the Fate of the Forest," *Forestry* 67, no. 2 (1994): 167–68.

11. Daniel Cantliffe, "Protected Structures for Production of High Valve Vegetable Crops for Florida Producers," The Protected Agriculture Project, University of Florida, http://hos.ufl.edu/protectedag/overview.htm (accessed February 22, 2012).

12. Jesse Ausubel and Dale Langford, *Technological Trajectories and the Human Environment* (Washington, DC: National Academies Press, 1997).

13. United States Department of Agriculture, "Energy and Agriculture," USDA 2007 Farm Bill Theme Paper, www.usda.gov/documents/Farmbill07energy.pdf (accessed February 22, 2012); United States Department of Agriculture, "Agricultural Productivity in the United States," www.ers.usda.gov/Data/AgProductivity/ (accessed February 23, 2012).

14. Jeremy Woods et al., "Energy and the Food System," *Philosophical Transactions of the Royal Society* 365, no. 1554 (2010): 2991–3006.

15. Food and Agriculture Organization of the United Nations, Agricultural and Consumer Protection Department, "Raising Water Productivity," www.fao.org/ag/magazine/0303sp2.htm (accessed February 15, 2012).

16. United States Summary and State Data, "2007 Census of Agriculture," www.agcensus.usda.gov/Publications/2007/Full_Report/usv1.pdf accessed March 7, 2012).

17. Ricegrowers' Association of Australia, "Australian Rice Growers Are Continually Improving Their Water Use Efficiency," www.aboutrice.com/facts/fact01.html (accessed February 23, 2012).

18. USGS, "Management Practices a Factor in Herbicide Declines," http://toxics.usgs.gov/highlights/herbicide_decline.html (accessed February 15, 2012).

eight the transformer

323

NOTES TO CHAPTER 9

1. Paul Romer, "Endogenous Technological Change," *Journal of Political Economy* 98, no. 5 (1990), http://artsci.wustl.edu/~econ502/Romer.pdf (accessed March 7, 2012).

2. David Henderson, *The Concise Encyclopedia of Economics* (Indianapolis, IN: Liberty Fund, 2008).

3. WattzOn, Embodied Energy Database, www.wattzon.com/ (accessed March 7, 2012).

4. Henderson, *The Concise Encyclopedia of Economics*.

5. Stephen Fenichell, *Plastic: The Making of a Synthetic Century* (New York: Harper Collins, 1996).

6. Adrian Kinnane, *DuPont: From the Banks of the Brandywine to Miracle of Science* (Baltimore: Johns Hopkins University Press, 2002).

7. Nylon-Stocking-Society, www.orgsites.com/oh/nylon-stocking-society/ (accessed February 15, 2012).

8. Jeffrey Meikle, *American Plastic: A Cultural History* (New Brunswick, NJ: Rutgers University Press, 1995).

9. P. C. W. Davies and Julian Brown, *Superstrings: A Theory of Everything?* (Cambridge: Cambridge University Press, 1992).

10. Alex Hudson, "Is Graphene a Miracle Material?" *BBC News*, May 21, 2011; and Columbia News, "Columbia Engineers Prove Graphene Is the Strongest Material," www.columbia.edu/cu/news/08/07/graphene.html (accessed March 7, 2012).

nine the substitute

1. Herman Melville, *Moby-Dick; or The Whale* (1851; repr., New York: Library of America, 1983), 1249.

2. Peter Applebome, "They Used to Say Whale Oil Was Indispensable, Too," *New York Times*, August 3, 2008.

3. Hal Whitehead, *Sperm Whales: Social Evolution in the Ocean* (Chicago: University of Chicago Press, 2003).

4. Nathaniel Philbrick, *In the Heart of the Sea: The Tragedy of the Whaleship Essex* (New York: Penguin, 2001).

5. Walter Tower, *A History of the American Whale Fishery* (Philadelphia: University of Pennsylvania, 1907).

6. James Robbins, "How Capitalism Saved the Whales," *New Scotland*, http://newscotland1398.ca/99/gesner-whales.html (accessed February 15, 2012).

7. R. M. Hazen, *The Diamond Makers* (Cambridge: Cambridge University Press, 1999).

8. D. Leckel, "Diesel Production from Fischer-Tropsch: The Past, the Present, and New Concepts," *Energy Fuels* 23 (2009): 2342–58.

ten **the reducer**

1. Ernst Worrell, Paul Blinde, Maarten Neelis, Eliane Blomen, and Eric Masanet, "Energy Efficiency Improvement and Cost Saving Opportunities for the U.S. Iron and Steel Industry," *Berkeley National Laboratory*, October 2010, www.energystar.gov/ia/business/industry/Iron_Steel_Guide.pdf (accessed February 15, 2012).

2. "The Elusive Negawatt: If Energy Conservation Both Saves Money and Is Good for the Planet, Why Don't More People Do More of It?" *Economist*, May 8, 2008; "Appliance Standards Awareness Project," www.appliance-standards.org (accessed March 7, 2012).

3. Office of Energy of Efficiency, "Energy Efficiency Trends in Canada 1990 to 2005," Natural Resources Canada, http://oee.nrcan.gc.ca (accessed February 21, 2012).

4. U.S. Department of Energy, "Energy Intensity Indicators in the U.S.: Residential Buildings Total Energy Consumption," www1.eere.energy.gov/ba/pba/intensityindicators (accessed February 15, 2012).

5. P. M. Peeters, J. Middel, and A. Hoolhorst, "Fuel Efficiency of Commercial Aircraft," *National Aerospace Laboratory (NLR)*, November 2005, www.transportenvironment.org/Publications (accessed February 15, 2012).

6. Airlines for America, "Annual Round-Trip Fares and Fees: Domestic," www.airlines.org (accessed February 23, 2012).

7. S. J. Smith et al., "Anthropogenic Sulfur Dioxide Emissions: 1850–2005," *Atmospheric Chemistry and Physics Discussions* 10 (2010): 16111–151.

8. Joel Schwartz, "Future Air Pollution Levels and Climate Change: A Step Toward Realism," *World Climate Change*, August 10, 2007, www.worldclimatereport.com/index.php/2007/08/10 (accessed February 15, 2012).

9. United States Environmental Protection Agency, "National and Local Trends in Lead Levels," www.epa.gov/air/airtrends/lead.html (accessed February 15, 2012).

10. United States Department of Energy, "Fuel Economy: Where the Energy Goes," www.fueleconomy.gov/feg/atv.shtml (accessed February 15, 2012).

11. Bullitt Center, "Living Building Challenge," http://bullittcenter.org/ (accessed March 7, 2012).

12. Based on national average energy use of 17 kwh per square foot and $.10 per kwh electricity prices.

13. Phil McKenna, "Buildings and Clothes Could Melt to Save Energy," *New Scientist*, January 5, 2012.

14. Consortium for Energy Efficiency, "2011 Annual Industry Report," www.cee1 .org/ee-pe/2011AIR.php3 (accessed March 7, 2012).

15. John Laitner, Steven Nadel, Neal Elliot, Harvey Sachs, and Siddiq Khan, "The Long-Term Energy Efficiency Potential: What the Evidence Suggests," *American Council for an Energy-Efficient Economy*, January 11, 2012, http://aceee.org /research-report/E121 (accessed February 21, 2012).

16. Clean Air Task Force, "SO2, NOx mercury Emissions," www.coaltransition.org /pages/gasification_page_link1/45.php (accessed February 21, 2012).

eleven the recycler

1. Exodus 15:25

2. DESWARE, Encyclopedia of Desalination and Water Resources, "Timelines—Desalination Technology," www.desware.net/Timelines-Desalination-Technology .aspx (accessed February 21, 2012).

3. Ibid.

4. "Tapping the Oceans," *Economist*, June 5, 2008.

5. Menachem Elimelech and William A. Phillip, "The Future of Seawater Desalination: Energy, Technology, and the Environment," *Science* 333, no. 6043 (August 5, 2011): 712–17.

6. Black & Veatch Ltd, "Black & Veatch-Designed Desalination Plant Wins Global Water Distinction," www.edie.net/news/news_story.asp?id=11402&channel=0 (accessed February 24, 2012).

7. "French-Run Water Plant Launched in Israel," *European Jewish Press*, December 28, 2005, www.ejpress.org/article/4873 (accessed February 24, 2012).

8. Spanish Succession, "Cannonade of Helchteren 1702," www.spanishsuccession .nl/helchteren.html (accessed March 7, 2012).

9. Enhanced Landfill Mining Consortium, "Enhanced Landfill Mining and the Transition to Sustainable Materials Management," www.elfm-symposium.eu /downloads.php (accessed March 7, 2012).

10. Kit Strange, "Landfill Mining: Preserving Resources through Integrated Sustainable Management of Waste," *World Resource Foundation*, www.enviroalternatives.com/landfill.html (accessed February 24, 2012).

11. Justin Thomas, "There's Gold in Them Thar Smelly Hills," *Treehugger*, July 29, 2006, www.treehugger.com (accessed February 2, 2012).

12. International Panel for Sustainable Resource Management, "Metal Stocks in Society," www.unep.org/resourcepanel/Portals/24102/PDFs/Metalstocksinsociety.pdf (accessed March 7, 2012).

13. Louise Gray, "Britain 'Could Be Mining Landfill for Gold in a Decade,'" *Telegraph*, October 8, 2008.

14. Hiroku Tabuchi, "Japan Recycles Minerals from Used Electronics," *New York Times*, October 4, 2010.

15. "Rare Element Resources: Potential Short Opportunity," *Shareholder Watchdog*, October 21, 2010.

16. Van Gercen et al., "An Integrated Materials Valorisation Scheme for Enhanced Landfill Mining," International Academic Symposium on Enhanced Landfill Mining, www.elfm-symposium.eu (accessed February 4, 2012).

17. Thomas, "There's Gold in Them Thar Smelly Hills."

18. International Energy Agency, "Turing a Liability into an Asset: The Importance of Policy in Fostering Landfill Gas Use Worldwide," www.iea.org/papers/2009/landfill.pdf (accessed February 4, 2012).

19. Gas Separation Technology LLC, "Landfill Gas," www.gassep.com/lfg.htm (accessed February 24, 2012).

20. R. P. Siegel, "Virgin Atlantic's New Waste Fuel Gas Program Will Save Billions of Gallons," *Triple Pundit*, October 17, 2011, www.triplepundit.com/2011/10/ (accessed February 4, 2012).

21. Katie Fehrenbacher, "Alphabet Energy: Capturing Waste Heat for $1 per Watt," *GigaOM*, May 3, 2010, http://gigaom.com (accessed February 24, 2012).

22. James Elser and Stuart White, "Peak Phosphorus," *Foreign Policy*, April 20, 2010.

23. Sustainable Phosphorus Futures, http://phosphorusfutures.net/ (accessed March 7, 2012).

24. Sustainable Phosphorus Futures, "Phosphorus Recovery," http://phosphorusfutures.net/ (accessed March 7, 2012).

25. Xiurong Wang, Yingxiang Wang, Jiang Tian, Boon Lim, Xiaolong Yan, and Hong Liao, "Overexpressing AtPAP15 Enhances Phosphorus Efficiency in Soybean," *Plant Physiology* 151 (2009): 233–40, www.plantphysiol.org/content/151/1/233.abstract (accessed February 4, 2012).

26. Copper Development Association, "Copper in the USA: Bright Future Glorious Past," www.copper.org/education/history/g_fact_producers.html (accessed February 4, 2012).

27. Earth 911, "Facts about Aluminum Recycling," http://earth911.com (accessed February 24, 2012).

28. Kyle Morris, "Recycling Importance of Gold and Lead," Emporia State University, http://academic.emporia.edu/abersusa/go336/morris/ (accessed February 24, 2012).

29. TAPPI, "Frequently Asked Questions," www.tappi.org/paperu/all_about_paper/faq.htm (accessed February 24, 2012).

30. Bureau of International Recycling, Ferrous Division, "World Steel Recycling in Figures 2006–2010," www.bir.org (accessed February 24, 2012).

31. Ziggy Hanaor, *Recycle: The Essential Guide* (London: Black Dog Publishing, 2005).

twelve **the multiplier**

1. State Master, "Total Electricity Consumption by State," www.statemaster.com (accessed February 24, 2012).

2. Dennis Elliot, Marc Schwartz, Steve Haymes, Donna Heimiller, and Walt Musial, "Assessment of Offshore Wind Energy Potential in the United States," National Renewable Energy Laboratory, www.nrel.gov/docs/fy11osti/51332.pdf (accessed February 24, 2012).

3. Wes Hermann and A. J. Simon, "Global Exergy Flux, Reservoirs, and Destruction," Global Climate and Energy Project, http://gcep.stanford.edu/pdfs /GCEP_Exergy_Poster_web.pdf (accessed February 24, 2012).

4. W. L. Chan et al., "Observing the Multiexciton State in Singlet Fission and Ensuing Ultrafast Multielectron Transfer," Science 334, no. 6062 (2011): 1541–45.

5. U.S. Energy Information Administration, Monthly Energy Review, "Statistical Abstract of the United States, 2008," www.infoplease.com/ipa/A0908464.html (accessed February 24, 2012).

6. National Renewable Energy Laboratory, "Cost Curves 2002," www.nrel.gov (accessed March 7, 2012).

7. Ryan Wiser and Mark Bolinger, "2009 Wind Technologies Market Report," U.S. Department of Energy, www.nrel.gov (accessed March 7, 2012).

8. K. Branker, M. J. M. Pathak, and J. M. Pearce, "A Review of Solar Photovoltaic Levelized Cost of Electricity," Renewable and Sustainable Energy Reviews 15, no. 9 (2011): 4470–82.

9. Brian Wingfield, "GE Sees Solar Cheaper Than Fossil Power in Five Years," Bloomberg News, May 26, 2011.

10. Ibid.

11. Solarbuzz, "Module Pricing," www.solarbuzz.com/node/3184 (accessed March 7, 2012).

12. Intergovernmental Panel on Climate Change, Renewable Energy Sources and Climate Change Mitigation (New York: Cambridge University Press, 2012). http:// srren.ipcc-wg3.de/report/IPCC_SRREN_Full_Report.pdf (accessed February 27, 2012).

13. Solarbuzz, "Module Pricing: Retail Price Summary—February 2012 Update," www.solarbuzz.com/node/3184 (accessed February 27, 2012).

14. Joseph Kanter, Ana Mileva, and Dan Kammen, "Solar Photovoltaics," Gigaton Throwdown, U.C. Berkley, www.gigatonthrowdown.org (accessed February 24, 2012).

15. Evergreen Solar, Inc., "Evergreen Solar and Silpro Announce Polysilicon Supply Agreement," http://renewableenergystocks.blogspot.com/2007/12 (accessed February 24, 2012).

16. National Renewable Energy Laboratory, "PV FAQs," www.nrel.gov/docs /fy04osti/35489.pdf (accessed February 24, 2012); Colin Bankier and Steve Gale, "Energy Payback of Roof Mounted Photovoltaic Cells," Energy Bulletin, June 16, 2006.

17. Renewable Energy Corporation ASA, "REC Produces First PV Modules with One Year Energy Payback Time and Leading Low Carbon Footprint," www.recgroup .com/en/media/newsroom (accessed February 24, 2012).

18. David Murphy and Charles Hall, "Year in Review—EROI or Energy Return on (Energy) Invested," Annals of the New York Academy of Sciences 1185 Ecological Economics Reviews (January 2010): 102–18; Cutler Cleveland, "Net Energy from the

Extraction of Oil and Gas in the United States, 1954–1997," http://citeseerx.ist.psu.edu (accessed February 27, 2012).

19. Parliament of the United Kingdom, "Chapter 3: Technologies for Renewable Electricity Generation," www.publications.parliament.uk/pa/ld200708/ldselect /ldeconaf/195/19506.htm (accessed February 24, 2012).

20. David Anderson and Dalia Patino-Echeverri, "An Evaluation of Current and Future Costs for Lithium-Ion Batteries for Use in Electrified Vehicle Powertrains," http://dukespace.lib.duke.edu (accessed February 24, 2012).

21. Jonathan Amos, "Solar Plant Makes Record Flight," *BBC News*, August 24, 2008.

22. Paula Doe, "Energy Storage Sector Looks to Solid State Solutions," SEMI, www.semi.org/en/IndustrySegments/CTR_037160?id=sguna0610 (accessed February 13, 2012).

23. EOS Energy Storage, "Energy Storage: Opportunity Summary," www .eosenergystorage.com/download/Eos_General0611.pdf (accessed February 14, 2012).

24. Chen-Xi Zu and Hong Li, "Thermodynamic Analysis on Energy Densities of Batteries," *Energy & Environmental Science* 8 (2011).

25. Alexander Farrell et al., "Ethanol Can Contribute to Energy and Environmental Goals," *Science* 311, no. 5760 (2006): 506–8.

26. David Murphy, C.A. S. Hall, and Bobby Powers, "New Perspectives on the Energy Return on Investments of Corn Based Ethanol: Part 1 of 2," *Environment, Development, and Sustainability* 13, no. 1 (July 2010).

27. Tom Doggett, "Ethanol to take 30 percent of U.S. Corn Crop in 2012: GAO," Reuters, June 11, 2007, www.reuters.com/article/2007/06/11 (accessed February 14, 2012).

28. Elizabeth Weise, "Ethanol Pumping Up Food Prices," *USA Today*, February 14, 2011.

29. Jim Lane, "Steel in the Ground," *Biofuels Digest*, www.biofuelsdigest.com /bdigest/2011/03/10 (accessed February 22, 2012).

30. Ibid.

31. David Duncan, "Big Oil Turns to Algae," *MIT Technology Review*, July 22, 2009.

32. Bryan Willson, "Large Scale Production of Microalgae for Biofuels," Solix Biofuels, www.ascension-publishing.com/BIZ/Solix.pdf (accessed February 27, 2012).

33. Concentric Energies & Resource Group, "2008–2009 Review, U.S. Biofuels Industry: Mind the Gap," www1.eere.energy.gov (accessed March 7, 2012).

34. Stacy Feldman, "Algae Fuel Inches toward Price Parity with Oil," Reuters, November 22, 2010.

35. Suzanne Goldenberg, "Algae to Solve the Pentagon's Jet Fuel Problem," *Guardian*, February 13, 2010.

36. Nathan Hodge, "U.S.'s Afghan Headache: $400-a-Gallon Gasoline," *Wall Street Journal*, December 6, 2011.

37. Kevin Bullis, "A Biofuel Process to Replace All Fossil Fuels," *MIT Technology Review*, July 27, 2009. Brendan Borrell, "Clean Dreams or Pond Scum? ExxonMobil and Craig Venter Team Up in Quest for Algae-Based Biofuels," *Scientific American*, July 14, 2009.

38. Joule, "About Joule Unlimited," www.jouleunlimited.com/about/overview (accessed February 10, 2012).

39. James Hamilton, "Nonlinearities and the Macroeconomic Effects of Oil Prices," *University of California, San Diego. Department of Economics*, December 9, 2009, http://dss.ucsd.edu/~jhamilto/oil_nonlinear_macro_dyn.pdf (accessed February 10, 2012).

40. Liz Morrison, "Make Fertilizer from Thin Air?" *Corn & Soybean Digest*, December 15, 2011, http://cornandsoybeandigest.com (accessed February 10, 2012).

41. Alex Renton, "Barefoot Solar Engineers of India," *OneWorld South Asia*, November 9, 2009, http://southasia.oneworld.net (accessed February 10, 2012).

42. Barefoot College, "About Us," www.barefootcollege.org/ (accessed February 27, 2012).

43. John Hanger, "Global Wind Revolution Hits 240,000 Megawatts and to Double Again," *John Hanger's Facts of the Day*, http://johnhanger.blogspot.com (accessed February 27, 2012).

44. ECN, "Global PV Installations to Hit 24 GW in 2011 Predicts IMS Research," www.ecnmag.com/News/2011/11 (accessed February 10, 2012).

45. Intergovernmental Panel on Climate Change, *Renewable Energy Sources and Climate Change Mitigation*.

46. World Wildlife Fund, "The Energy Report: 100 percent Renewable Energy by 2050," http://wwf.panda.org (accessed February 22, 2012).

47. "A Plan for 100 percent Energy from Wind, Water, and Solar by 2050," *Skeptical Science*, March 27, 2011, www.skepticalscience.com (accessed February 10, 2012).

thirteen investing in ideas

1. Bill Scanlon, "Breakthrough Furnace Can Cut Solar Costs," *National Renewable Energy Laboratory*, October 21, 2011, www.nrel.gov (accessed March 7, 2012).

2. Sean Pool, "Investing in Innovation Pays Off," *Science Progress*, May 18, 2011, http://scienceprogress.org/2011/05 (accessed March 7, 2012).

3. Wire Reports, "Pickens Says U.S. Oil Imports Rose 28 Percent in 2010," *Tulsa World*, January 1, 2011. www.tulsaworld.com (accessed February 22, 2012).

4. Alex Tabarrok, *Launching the Innovation Renaissance: A New Path to Bring Smart Ideas to Market Fast* (TED Books, 2011).

5. Bureau of Labor Statistics, "Databases, Tables & Calculators," www.bls.gov/data/ (accessed March 7, 2012).

6. Claudia Goldin and Lawrence F. Katz, *The Race between Education and Technology* (Cambridge, MA: Harvard University Press, 2010).

7. Bureau of Labor Statistics, "Employment Projections," www.bls.gov/emp/ep _chart_001.htm (accessed March 7, 2012).

8. Robert Balfanz, John Bridgeland, Joanna Fox, and Laura Moore, "Building a Grad Nation; Progress and Challenge in Ending the High School Dropout Epidemic," America's Promise Alliance, www.americaspromise.org (accessed March 7, 2012).

9. Sean Reardon, "The Widening Academic Achievement Gap between the Rich

and the Poor: New Evidence and Possible Explanations," Stanford University, http://cepa.stanford.edu/sites/default/files/reardon whither opportunity—chapter 5.pdf (accessed March 7, 2012).

10. National Center for Education Studies, http://nces.ed.gov/fastfacts/display .asp?id=37.

fourteen **the flaw in the market**

1. Lisa Brandt and Thomas Rawski, *China's Great Economic Transformation* (Cambridge: Cambridge University Press, 2008).

2. Gideon Rachman, *Zero-Sum Future: American Power in an Age of Anxiety* (New York: Simon & Schuster, 2011).

3. "India's Poverty Will Fall From 51 percent to 22 percent by 2015: UN Report," *Times of India*, July 8, 2011.

4. Jonah Lehrer, "A Physicist Solves the City," *New York Times*, December 17, 2010; Arie de Geus, *Living Company: Habits for Survival in a Turbulent Business Environment* (Boston: Harvard Business School Press, 2002).

5. John Hagel III, "Running Fast, Falling Behind," *Knowledge @ Wharton*, June 23, 2010, http://knowledge.wharton.upenn.edu/article.cfm?articleid=2523 (accessed February 10, 2012).

6. Michael Ellman, "Soviet Agricultural Policy," *Economic and Political Weekly* 23, no. 24 (1988).

7. Encyclopedia of the Nations, "Soviet Union: Policy and Administration," www.country-data.com/cgi-bin/query/r-12746.html (accessed February 27, 2012).

8. The Great Idea Finder, "20th Century Innovation Timeline," www.ideafinder.com/history/timeline/the1900s.htm (accessed February 10, 2012).

9. Caleb Johnson, "Tisquantum, Massasoit, and Hobbamock," *Mayflower History*, www.mayflowerhistory.com/History/indians4.php (accessed February 10, 2012).

10. Anti-Defamation League, "Lewis and Clark: The Unheard Voices," www.adl.org /education/curriculum_connections/NA_Quotes.asp (accessed February 10, 2012).

11. Kelly Sloan, "'The Fruits of the Earth Belong to Us All' The Left's Hostility Toward Competition," *Liberty Ink*, 2011, www.libertyinkjournal.com (accessed February 27, 2012).

12. Aristotle, *Politics*, ed. Benjamin Jowett (New York: Dover Publications, 2000).

13. Quoted in Rachman, *Zero-Sum Future*, p. 56.

fifteen **market solutions**

1. Richard Conniff, "The Political History of Cap and Trade," *Smithsonian*, August 2009.

2. Steven Hayward, "Energy Fact of the Week: Sulfur Dioxide Emissions from Coal Have Declined 54 Percent," *The American*, April 21, 2011.

3. Roger Raufer and Stephen Feldman, *Acid Rain and Emissions Trading* (Lanham, MD: Rowman & Littlefield, 1987).

4. Environmental Protection Agency, "Acid Rain Program Benefits Exceed Expectations," www.epa.gov/capandtrade/documents/benefits.pdf (accessed February 22, 2012).

5. Ibid.

6. "The Legacy of James Watt," *Time*, October 24, 1983.

7. Dennis Hayes, "Highest Disregard," *Mother Jones*, December 1989.

8. Jeffrey Masters, "The Skeptics vs. the Ozone Hole," *Wunderground*, www.wunderground.com (accessed February 22, 2012).

9. Jessica Whittemore, "Reagan and the Montreal Protocol: Environmentalism at Its Unlikely Finest," *The Presidency*, www.thepresidency.org/storage/documents/Fellows2008/Whittemore.pdf (accessed February 22, 2012).

10. Cry Wolf Project, "Industry Claims about the Clean Air Act," June 16, 2009. http://crywolfproject.org (accessed March 7, 2012).

11. Ben Lieberman, "The High Cost of Cool: The Economic Impact of the CFC Phaseout in the United States," *Competitive Enterprise Institute*, June 1994, http://cei.org (accessed February 22, 2012).

12. Hart Hodges, "Falling Prices: Cost of Complying with Environmental Regulations Almost Always Less Than Advertised," *Economic Policy Institute*, www.epi.org/page/-/old/briefingpapers/bp69.pdf (accessed February 27, 2012).

13. "We Have a Winner: British Columbia's Carbon Tax Woos Skeptics," *Economist*, July 21, 2011.

14. James Hansen, "China Can Slow Global Warming If the US Won't," *Transition Voice*, December 6, 2010, http://transitionvoice.com/2010/12 (accessed February 22, 2012).

15. Keith Bradsher, "China Leading Global Race to Make Clean Energy," *New York Times*, January 30, 2010.

16. Wikipedia, "List of Wind Turbine Manufacturers," http://en.wikipedia.org/wiki/List_of_wind_turbine_manufacturers (accessed March 7, 2012).

17. "Winds from the East," *Economist*, February 3, 2011.

18. Feng An, Robert Earley, and Lucia Green-Weiskel, "Global Overview of Fuel Efficiency and Motor Vehicle Emission Standards: Policy Options and Perspectives for International Cooperation," *United Nations Department of Economics and Social Affairs*, May 13, 2011, www.un.org/esa/dsd/resources/res_pdfs/csd-19/Background-paper3-transport.pdf (accessed February 22, 2012).

19. Todd Woody, "Clean Energy Investment Hits Record in 2011 as U.S. Reclaims Lead from China," *Forbes*, January 12, 2012.

20. Michael Marshall, "China Set to Launch First Caps on CO_2 Emissions," *New Scientist*, January 17, 2012.

21. Heritage Foundation, "2012 Index of Economic Freedom," www.heritage.org/index.

22. "An Expensive Gamble: The Prime Minister Stakes Her Future on a Divisive Scheme," *Economist*, July 14, 2011.

23. A. Leiserowitz, E. Maibach, C. Roser-Renouf, N. Smith, and J. D. Hmielowski, *Climate Change in the American Mind: Public Support for Climate and Energy Policies in November 2011*, Yale University and George Mason University (New Haven, CT: Yale Project on Climate Change Communication).

24. Josh Nelson, "New Gallop Poll Shows Sharp Partisan Divide in Understanding of Climate Change," *Grist*, March 16, 2010, www.grist.org (accessed February 22, 2012).

25. Peter Aldhous, "How Not to Change a Climate Skeptic's Mind," *New Scientist*, March 18, 2011.

26. Laurence Smith, Kistler Book Award Prize Ceremony Speech, 2011.

27. Ronald Reagan, Remarks at Dedication Ceremonies for the New Building of the National Geographic Society, June 19, 1984, www.climateconservative.org /Full_Reagan_Speech_Ad_1.pdf.

28. Jamison Foser, "Flashback: Despite Deficits, Reagan Wanted to Increase EPA Funding," *Political Correction*, July 18, 2011, http://politicalcorrection.org /blog/201107180010 (accessed February 22, 2012).

sixteen the unthinkable: here there be dragons

1. Dean Fetter, "How Long Will the World's Uranium Supplies Last?" *Scientific American*, January 26, 2009, www.scientificamerican.com (accessed February 22, 2012).

2. Clean Air Task Force, "The Toll From Coal," www.catf.us/resources/publications (accessed February 22, 2012).

3. Gideon Polya, "Pollutants from Coal-Based Electricity Generation Kill 170,000 People Annually," *Green Blog*, www.green-blog.org/2008/06/14/ (accessed February 22, 2012).

4. National Police Agency of Japan, "Damage Situation and Police Countermeasures Associated with 2011 Tohoku District," www.npa.go.jp/archive (accessed March 7, 2012).

5. Burton Bennett, Michael Repacholi, and Zhanat Carr, "Health Effects of the Chernobyl Accident and Special Health Care Programmes," *UN Chernobyl Forum*, 2006.

6. Cost of nuclear based on $700 billion in economic damages from disasters, divided by 70 trillion kilowatt hours of energy produced. Social cost of coal: Center for Health and the Global Environment, "Mining Coal, Mounting Costs: The Life Cycle Consequences of Coal," http://wvgazette.com/static/coal tattoo /HarvardCoalReportSummary.pdf (accessed March 7, 2012).

7. Mara Hvistendahl, "Coal Ash Is More Radioactive Than Nuclear Waste," *Scientific American*, December 13, 2007.

8. William Hannum, Gerald Marsh, and George Stanford, "Smarter Use of Fast-Neutron Reactors Could Extract Much More Energy from Recycled Nuclear Fuels, Minimize Risks of Weapons Proliferation and Markedly Reduce the Time Nuclear Waste Must Be Isolated," *Scientific American*, December 2005.

9. Hvistendahl, "Coal Ash Is More Radioactive Than Nuclear Waste."

10. MIT Energy Initiative, "Future of Nuclear Power," http://web.mit.edu /nuclearpower (accessed February 22, 2012).

11. Armory Lovins, Imran Sheikh, and Alex Markevich, "Nuclear Power: Climate Fix or Folly?" Rocky Mountain Institute, www.rmi.org/Knowledge-Center/Library (accessed February 22, 2012).

12. Craig Severance, Nuclear Information and Resource Service, "Business Risks and Costs of New Nuclear Power," www.nirs.org/neconomics/nuclearcosts2009.pdf (accessed February 22, 2012).

seventeen the unthinkable: climate engineering

1. "Pilotstandort Ketzin: Geology," www.co2ketzin.de/index.php?id=13&L=1 (accessed March 7, 2012).

2. Mohammed Al-Juaied and Adam Whitmore, "Realistic Costs of Carbon Capture," *Belfer Center for Science and International Affairs*, July 2009, http://belfercenter.ksg.harvard.edu/publication/19185 (accessed March 7, 2012).

3. Mark Little and Robert Jackson, "Potential Impacts of Leakage from Deep CO_2 Geosequestration on Overlying Freshwater Aquifers," *Environment Science Technology* 44 (2010): 9225–32.

4. Marguerite Holloway, "Trying to Tame the Roar of Deadly Lakes," *New York Times*, February 27, 2001.

5. Kurt House et al., "Electrochemical Acceleration of Chemical Weathering as an Energetically Feasible Approach to Mitigating Anthropogenic Climate Change," *Environment Science Technology* 41 (2007): 8464–70.

6. Greg Rau, "CO_2 Mitigation via Capture and Chemical Conversion in Seawater," *Environment Science Technology* 45, no. 3 (2011): 1088–92.

7. Calera, "Inputs Outputs," http://calera.com/index.php/technology/inputs _outputs/ (accessed March 7, 2012).

8. Jeff Goodell, "The Big Lie in the Durban U.N. Climate Talks," *Rolling Stone*, December 1, 2011.

9. Connor, Steve. "Scientist Publishes 'Escape Route' from Global Warming," *Independent*, July 31, 2006.

eighteen greener than green

1. Joel Archenbach, "A 'Dead Zone' in the Gulf of Mexico," *Washington Post*, July 31, 2008.

2. U.S. Environmental Protection Agency, "Protecting Water Quality from Agricultural Runoff," www.epa.gov/owow/NPS/Ag_Runoff_Fact_Sheet.pdf (accessed February 22, 2012).

3. Food and Agriculture Organization, "Livestock a Major Threat to Environment: Remedies Urgently Needed," November 29, 2006, www.fao.org/newsroom/en /news/2006 (accessed February 17, 2012).

4. U.S. Department of Agriculture, "2007 Census of Agriculture: 2008 Organic Production Survey," www.agcensus.usda.gov/ (accessed February 25, 2012).

5. Steven Savage, "A Detailed Analysis of U.S. Organic Crops," www.scribd.com /doc/47829728 (accessed February 17, 2012).

6. Cattle Today, "Breeds of Beef Cattle," http://cattle-today.com/ (accessed February 17, 2012).

7. Steven Savage, "The Carbon Footprint of Fertilization with Manure and Composed Manure," www.scribd.com/doc/17356325 (accessed February 25, 2012). Steven Savage, SustainABlog, "Putting the 'Carbon Footprint' of Farming in Perspective," http://blog.sustainablog.org/2009/07 (accessed February 25, 2012).

8. David Tribe, "High Iron and Zinc Rice Gives Hope to Micronutrient Deficient Millions," Australian Centre for Plant Functional Genomics, September 10, 2011.

9. Donald Danforth Plant Science Center, "Biocassava Plus Information," www.danforthcenter.org (accessed February 17, 2012).

10. Colin Osborne and David Beerling, "Nature's Green Revolution: The Remarkable Evolutionary Rise of C_4 Plants," The Royal Society 361 no. 1465 (2006): 173–94.

11. International Rice Research Institute, "All About C_4 Rice Consortium Resources," http://irri.org/c4rice (accessed February 17, 2012).

12. David Fogarty, "Factbox: Building a Better Rice Plant," Reuters, June 10, 2011.

13. Debora MacKenzie, "Supercrops: Fixing the Flaws in Photosynthesis," Colombo Herald, September 20, 2010.

14. Perrin Beatty and Allen Good, "Future Prospects for Cereals That Fix Nitrogen," Science, 333, no. 6041 (2011): 416–17.

15. "Drought Tolerant GM Wheat Great Progress in China," Crop Biotech Update, June 17, 2011, www.isaaa.org (accessed February 17, 2012).

16. David Biello, "Coming to a Cornfield Near You: Genetically Induced Drought-Resistance," Scientific American, May 13, 2011.

17. University of California, Riverside Newsroom, "How Plants Sense Low Oxygen Levels to Survive Flooding," http://newsroom.ucr.edu/2769 (accessed February 17, 2012).

18. Darren Plett et al., "Improved Salinity Tolerance of Rice through Cell Type-Specific Expression of AtHKT1;1," PLoS ONE 5, no. 9, September 3, 2010.

19. David Tribe, "Australian Scientific Collaboration Set to Break World's Reliance on Fish for Long Chain Omega-3," GMO Pundit, April 11, 2011, http://gmopundit .blogspot.com/2011/04 (accessed February 17, 2012); Stephen Daniells, "Omega 3 Oil from Yeast Similar to Fish Oil in Safety and Nutritional Effect," GMO Pundit, September 16, 2010, http://gmopundit.blogspot.com/2010/09 (accessed February 17, 2012).

20. P. B. Pope et al., "Isolation of Succinivibrionaceae Implicated in Low Methane Emissions of Tammar Wallabies," Science, June 30, 2011.

21. Alan Boyle, "Lab-Grown Hamburger to Be Served Up This Year," MSNBC, February 19, 2012.

22. United States Geological Survey, "Management Practices a Factor in Herbicide Declines," http://toxics.usgs.gov/highlights/herbicide_decline.html (accessed February 17, 2012).

23. Ibid.

24. Committee on the Impact of Biotechnology on Farm-Level Economics and Sustainability and National Research Council, *The Impact of Genetically Engineered Crops on Farm Sustainability in the United States* (Washington, DC: National Academies Press, 2010).

25. Rick Elkins, "No Till Planting Gaining in Popularity," *Recorder Online*, June 7, 2011, www.recorderonline.com (accessed February 17, 2012); Committee on the Impact of Biotechnology on Farm-Level Economics and Sustainability and National Research Council, *The Impact of Genetically Engineered Crops.*

26. National Research Council, *The Impact of Genetically Engineered Crops.*

27. Ibid

28. K. R. Kranthi, "10 Years of Bt in India: Biotech Seeds Save Indian Market," *Cotton 24/7*, May 1, 2011, http://cotton247.com/news/?storyid=2160 (accessed February 16, 2012).

29. Shahzad Kouser and Martin Qaim, "Bt Cotton Now Helps to Avoid Several Million Cases of Pesticide Poisoning in India Every Year," *Ecological Economics* 70, no. 11 (September 2011): 2105–13.

30. Robert Paarlberg, *Starved for Science: How Biotechnology Is Being Kept Out of Africa* (Cambridge, MA: Harvard University Press, 2009).

31. Ibid.

32. "Eat This or Die: The Poison Politics of Food Aid," *Greenpeace International*, September 30, 2002, www.greenpeace.org/international/en (accessed February 16, 2012).

33. Henri Cauvin, "Between Famine and Politics, Zambians Starve," *New York Times*, August 30, 2002.

34. "Zambia Allows GM Aid for Refugees," *BBC News*, September 8, 2002.

35. Roger Bate, "Political Food Folly: Putting Food on the Negotiating Table," *National Review Online*, August 6, 2004, www.nationalreview.com (accessed February 16, 2012).

36. "Austrian Government Retracts Conclusions Reported in a Long Term Reproduction Study on GM Corn Lines MON810 and NK603," *Food Standards*, April 2010. http://www.foodstandards.gov.au (accessed February 16, 2012).

37. Committee on Identifying and Assessing Unintended Effects of Genetically Engineered Foods on Human Health, National Research Council, *Safety of Genetically Engineered Foods: Approaches to Assessing Unintended Health Effects* (Washington DC: National Academies Press, 2004).

38. Suzie Key, Julian Ma, and M. W. Drake. "Genetically Modified Plants and Human Health," *Journal of the Royal Society of Medicine* 101, no. 6 (2008): 290–98.

39. Committee on the Impact of Biotechnology on Farm-Level Economics and Sustainability, and National Research Council, *Impact of Genetically Engineered Crops.*

40. "Spain Confirms BT Corn Has No Adverse Effects on the Environment," *Crop Biotech Update*, July 22, 2011.

41. Anthony Shelton and Mark Sears, "The Monarch Butterfly Controversy: Scientific Interpretations of a Phenomenon," *The Plant Journal* 27, no. 6 (2001): 483–88.

42. Peggy Lemaux, "Genetically Engineered Plants and Foods: A Scientist's Analysis of the Issues," *Annual Review of Plant Biology* 59 (2008): 771–812.

43. European Commission, *A Decade of EU-Funded GMO Research* (Luxembourg: Publications Office of the European Union, 2010). ftp://ftp.cordis.europa.eu/pub/fp7/kbbe/docs/a-decade-of-eu-funded-gmo-research_en.pdf (accessed March 7, 2012).

44. Sybille Hamaide, "French Court Annuls Ban on Growing Monsanto GMO Maize," Reuters, November 28, 2011.

45. Morten Gylling, "The Danish Coexistence Regulation and the Danish Farmers Attitude Towards GMO," Institute of Food and Resource Economics, University of Copenhagen, www.gmls.eu/beitraege/GMLS2_Gylling.pdf (accessed March 2, 2012).

46. Jared Diamond, *Collapse: How Societies Choose to Fail or Succeed* (New York: Viking Press, 2005).

nineteen the decoupler

1. U.S. Energy Information Administration, "Annual Energy Outlook 2011: With Projections to 2035," April 2011; International Energy Agency, "Statistics & Balances," www.iea.org/stats/index.asp (accessed March 7, 2012).

2. International Energy Agency, "Statistics & Balances."

3. Steven Davis and Ken Caldeira, "Consumption-Based Accounting of CO_2 Emissions," *Proceedings of the National Academy of Sciences* 107, no. 12 (2010): 5687–92.

4. Pacific Institute, "Fact Sheet on Water Use in the United States," www.pacinst.org (accessed February 22, 2012).

5. The World Bank, "Indicators," http://data.worldbank.org/indicator (accessed March 7, 2012).

6. Water Footprint Network, "WaterStat," www.waterfootprint.org/?page=files/WaterStat (accessed March 7, 2012).

7. Taras Berezowsky, "US Steelmaking Only a Small Part of Global Steel CO_2 Emissions—Part One," *Metal Miner*, March 28, 2011, http://agmetalminer.com (accessed February 16, 2012).

8. Food and Agriculture Organization of the United Nations, *State of the World's Forests 2011* (Rome: FAO, 2011).

9. Ibid.

10. Food and Agriculture Organization of the United Nations, "FAOSTAT," faostat.fao.org/ (accessed January 23, 2012).

11. S. J. Smith, J. Aardenne, Z. Klimont, R. J. Andres, and A. Volke, et al., "Anthropogenic Sulfur Dioxide Emissions: 1850–2005," *Atmospheric Chemistry and Physics*, June 30, 2010.

12. Gary Fields, *Distribution and Development: A New Look at the Developing World* (Cambridge, MA: MIT Press, 2002).

1. Centers for Disease Control and Prevention, "Diabetes: Successes and Opportunities for Population-Based Prevention and Control," *CDC*, August 1, 2011, www.cdc.gov (accessed February 16, 2012).

2. Timothy Dall, Yiduo Zhang, Yaozhu Chen, William Quick, Wenya Yang, and Jeanene Fogli, "The Economic Burden of Diabetes," *Health Affairs* 29 (2010): 2297–303.

3. Charles Jones, "Sources of U.S. Economic Growth in a World of Ideas," *American Economic Review* 92, no. 1 (2002): 220–39 www.stanford.edu/~chadj/papers.html

4. Alex Tabarrok, "TED Talk," February 2009, www.ted.com/talks/alex_tabarrok_foresees_economic_growth.html.

5. Thomas Jefferson, *The Writings of Thomas Jefferson*, ed. Andrew Lipscomb and Albert Bergh (Whitefish, MT: Kessinger, 2006).

6. Ronald Bailey, "Post Scarcity Prophet," *Reason.com*, December 1, 2001, http://reason.com (accessed February 16, 2012).

7. "No Sex Please, We're Japanese: Country Heads for Extinction as Survey Reveals Young People Shunning Marriage," *Mail Online*, November 28, 2011.

8. "Demographic Change and Work in Europe," *European Working Conditions Observatory*, August 20, 2010.

9. Haunxin, Zhao. "Working-Age Population Set to Decline," *China Daily*, September 1, 2006.

10. David Pierson, "China's One-Child Policy Causing Working-Age Population to Shrink," *Los Angeles Times*, July 12, 2009.

11. Michael Kremer, "Population Growth and Technological Change: One Million B.C. to 1990," *Quarterly Journal of Economics* 108, no. 3 (1993): 681–716.

12. Jonah Lehrer, "A Physicist Solves the City," *New York Times*, December 17, 2010.

13. Luis Bettencourt, Jose Lobo, Dirk Helbing, Christian Kuhnert, and Geoffrey West, "Growth, Innovation, Scaling, and the Pace of Life in Cities," *Proceedings of the National Academy of Sciences of the USA* 104, no. 17 (April 24, 2007): 7301–06.

14. Wei Pan, Gourah Ghoshal, Sandy Pentland, and Manuel Cebrian, "Urban Economy Scaling: Linking Geography, Population and Social Interactions," web.media.mit.edu/~cebrian/urbanlink.pdf (accessed February 27, 2012).

15. William McGurn, "And Baby Makes Seven Billion," *Wall Street Journal*, October 24, 2011.

coda

1. Kaare Christensen et al., "Ageing Populations: The Challenges Ahead," *Lancet* 374 (October 2009): 1196–208.

index

Berkeley Earth Surface Temperature study (BEST), 65–66
beta carotene, 248
Bettencourt, Luis, 290
biofuels, 168–72, 177, 213
Birol, Faith, 47
bitumen, 45–46
Black, Joseph, 13
blue-green algae, 172
Boeing 787 Dreamliner, 125
Borlaug, Norman, 109–10, 182, 247
Bosch, Carl, 133–34
Braungart, Michael, 154
breeder reactors, 223, 228–29
Bt crops, 252–53, 256–57
Burgan oil field, 43
Bush, George H. W., 145–46, 199, 201, 297
Byrd, Robert, 199–200, 217

C_4 rice, 249, 259
CAFE fuel efficiency standards, 212
calcifers, 78–80, 305
calcium bicarbonate, 239
calories per person, 24, 24
Canada: carbon tax in British Columbia, 211; and Montreal Protocol, 145, 202–5; oil sands in, 45–46. See also acid rain
Cantarell oil field, 43
cap-and-trade, 201–2, 206–7, 215–19
capitalism, 189–98, 292
carbon capture, 237–42, 296
carbon dioxide (CO_2): effect on forests, 78; effect on oceans, 78–81; effect on plant growth, 77; forests' consumption of, 57; liquefied, 237; rate of breakdown, 81; safe levels of, 87
carbon dioxide (CO_2) emissions: in Australia, 216–19; carbon capture, 237–42, 296; climate engineering, 237–43; consequences of, long term, 72–73; consequences of, short term,

73–76; danger zone in halting, 240–42; historically, 63–64, 70; from nuclear power plants, 223; responsibility for, 67–71; and solar shield, 242–43; U.S. reduction of, 269; voluntary reduction of, 90–91. See also cap-and-trade; pollution reduction; pollution tax
carbon dividends, 207
carbon fiber, 125, 141–43, 146
carbonic acid, 78
carbon monoxide emissions, 144, 153, 225, 269, 300
carbon nanotubes, 125–26, 176
carbon sequestration, 237–42, 296
carbon tax. See pollution tax
carrying capacity of planet, 113–15
Carter, Jimmy, 224–25
cassava, 248–49
Cebrian, Manuel, 291
cell phones, 3, 26–27, 26, 33, 120, 175. See also mobile phones
celluloid, 123
cellulose, 169–70
cement, 239
Chalk River Laboratories, 224
Chernobyl nuclear disaster, 226–27
China: economic reforms in, 189–90; efficient use of resources in, 272–73; innovation in, 5–6, 13–19; new wealth and demand for commodities, 52; new wealth and innovation in, 280–83; oil consumption of, 48; pollution reduction in, 213–15; scarcity of resources in, 94–95; U.S. relations with, 93; working-age populations in, 287
Chinchias Islands, 131–32
chlorofluorocarbons (CFCs), 145, 202–5, 269–70, 276, 285, 295, 299
Chu, Steven, 241
Church, George, 171–72
Ciccone, Antonio, 291

Humboldt, Alexander von, 131
hunger, 23–25, *24*
hurricanes, 75, 85
Hyatt, Isaiah, 123
Hyatt, John Wesley, 123
hydro power, 159, 200, 224
Hyperion "Power Modules," 232

ideas: evolution of, 6–12, 27, 107, 142, 191, 197, 306–7; homogeneity of thought, 15; as knowledge commons, 285–86; as non-zero-sum resource, 97; power in copying, 9–10
idea sex, 7–8
incentives, 23, 184–85, 187, 190–95, 192, 212, 229, 235, 242, 270, 283
income inequality, 30, 183
Inconvenient Truth, An (Gore), 65, 218–21
India: barefoot solar engineers in, 173–74; carbon dioxide (CO_2) emissions, 213–14; economic reforms in, 189–90; efficient use of resources in, 272–73; new wealth and demand for commodities, 52; new wealth and innovation in, 280–83; scarcity of resources in, 94–95; working-age populations in, 287
indium, 176
Indus River Valley Aquifer, 55–56
infant mortality, 4, 21–22, 33, 271–72
information, access to, 26–27
information resources, 97, 107
infrared light, 63
innovation: in agriculture, 115–18; in auto efficiency, 146; in building efficiency, 147; in China, 5–6, 13–19; and Darwin, 6–9; and disease, 283, 288; divergence of, 4–6; and efficiency, 136–47; and evolution theory, 6–9; future vision of, 303–8; government investment in, 181–87; impact of capitalism on, 191–92; as infinite resource, 96–97; and

knowledge commons, 285–86; and market economics, 11–12; in nuclear power, 229–34; people as resource for, 280–83; in pollution reduction, 147; population growth and technology, 288–89; and population limits, 283–85; and printing press, 9–10; and scientific method, 11–13; as ultimate source of wealth, 293; and urban population growth, 289–92; and working-age populations, 286–88
insecticides, 116–17, 252–53, 256–58
insurance, 86
interconnectivity, 291, 296–97
Intergovernmental Panel on Climate Change (IPCC), 85–86
internal combustion engines, 146
International Energy Agency, 47–48, 87
Internet, 27, 32–33, 127, 135, 181, 192, 291, 307
Inuit, 263–64
IPAT equation, 89–90, 112, 266–67
iPhones, 120–21
irrigation, 38, 55–56, 94, 108–9, 114–15, 116–17, 245, 252, 272–73

Jacobson, Mark, 176
Japan: innovation in, 18; working-age populations in, 287
Jefferson, Thomas, 285
Jevons Paradox, 267

Kahan, Dan, 218–19
Katz, Lawrence, 183–84
Kelvin, Lord, 125
kerogen, 46
kerosene, 128
Khan, Genghis, 31
Kleiber, Max, 281
knowledge, accumulation of, 140–42
knowledge commons, 285–86, 308
knowledge resources, 96–97, 105–6, 122
Koch, Charles, 65

polystyrene, 123
polyvinyl chloride (PVC), 123
Population Bomb, The (Ehrlich), 27, 103,
    109–10
population growth, 103–5, 109–10, 266–
    67, 280–92, 303–4
"Population Growth and Technological
    Change: One Million B.C. to 1900"
    (Kremer), 288
Post, Mark, 250
poverty, 23–25, *23*
precipitation, 73–74
Price-Anderson Nuclear Industries
    Indemnity Act, 234–35
prices. *See* costs
printing press, 9–10, 14
private property, 194
productivity, worker, 191
Prudhoe Bay oil field, 43
public schools, elimination of, 185
pyrometallurgic recycling, 228

Quadrennial Defense Review 2010
    (Pentagon), 94

*Race Between Education and Technology,
    The* (Goldin and Katz), 184
radiation and radioactive waste, 202, 222,
    224–29, 231, 233, 243
Rahmstorf, Stefan, 75
rainstorms, 73–74
rare earth elements, 53, 152–54, 176, 277
Rau, Greg, 239
Reagan, Ronald, 145, 199, 202–4, 217,
    220, 297
recycling, 148–56, 306
Reese, Mike, 173
refrigerators and refrigeration
    equipment, 138, *139*, 145, 204
regenerative braking, 146
Remo Milieubeheer landfill, 151

renewable energy, 175–78, 212–13, 215.
    See also alternate energy sources
Renton, Alex, 173
rice, 117, 246, 248–50, 259, 265, 296
Ridley, Matt, 7–8
Rind, David, 67
rising poor, 91–93
rival goods, 106
Rogers, Jim, 162, 207–8, 214
Roman Empire, 13, 31, 88, 108–9, 301
Romer, Paul, 119–20, 122, 286, 288
Romney, Mitt, 218
Roundup Ready crops, 251
Rousseau, Jean-Jacques, 194
rubber, 123, 133
runoff, fertilizer and herbicide, 245, 251

saltpeter, 132
scarcity of resources, 94–95
schooling. *See* education
Schultz, George, 203, 218
Schwarzenegger, Arnold, 218
Schwarze Pumpe/Ketzin project, 237–38
scientific method, 11–13
seawater desalination, 148–50, *149*
self-interest, 8, 184, 192–95, 197, 285, 294,
    299
Selfish Game, The (Dawkins), 7
Semiletov, Igor, 83
semi-permeable membranes, 149
Semon, Waldo, 133
sequestration, carbon, 237–42, 296
Séralini, Gilles-Eric, 255
Severance, Craig, 230
shale gas, 162
shellfish, 79–80, 305
Shepard Glacier, 62
Sibudu Cave, 105–7
silicon photovoltaic cells, 176
Simon, Julian, 27, 52, 173
Singapore-Tuas seawater desalination
    plant, 150

wildfires, 75–76, 85
wind energy, 157–59, 161, 163, 174–76, 212–13, 215, 218, 304–5
woodblock printing, 10
worker productivity, 191
working-age populations, 286–88
Wright, T. P., 141

Younger Dryas event, 84–85

Zambia, GMO farming in, 254–55
Zentek, Jürgen, 255
zero-sum systems, 93–95, 106–7
Zheng He, 17
zinc-air batteries, 167